THEATRE IN SOUTHEAST ASIA

THEATRE IN

SOUTHEAST

ASIA

James R. Brandon

HARVARD UNIVERSITY PRESS

CAMBRIDGE, MASSACHUSETTS

FOR REIKO

P R E F A C E

My aim in writing this book is to present to the interested Western reader some of the basic facts about theatre in Southeast Asia as it exists and functions today. Important writings in European languages have been consulted for background and historical materials, but the largest part of the book is based on personal observations and interviews.

The book is organized on a topical rather than a country-to-country basis, so the reader will be able to see more clearly the interrelations among theatre forms. Its four parts correspond to the four perspectives considered: origins and background; theatre as art; theatre as a social institution; and theatre as communication. I have sketched in only the major outlines; hopefully others will be stimulated to conduct more extensive research which will fill in details not presently known.

Generally speaking, the amount of space devoted to a theatre genre reflects its importance today. In determining how important a genre is, I have taken into account its artistic value, its social and religious dimensions, and its popularity. About half of all the theatre activity in Southeast Asia takes place in Indonesia; the amount of material devoted to Indonesian theatre reflects this fact.

I have included several maps and charts in the hope that they would clarify some of the more complex relations among theatre forms. They are designed to simplify—and should be accepted in this light. The first time a non-English word or term is used it appears in italics; thereafter it does not. Words are spelled as they are in the various countries; therefore variant spellings may appear in different parts of the text. The material in this book describes theatre as it appeared to me in 1963–4. More recent information is presented in footnotes.

Preface

I would like to express my sincere gratitude to the many people who assisted in the preparation of this book. Particular thanks are due to Father Zoetmulder, Professor Ibrahim Alfian, and Mr. Hadian Soekarno in Indonesia and to Mr. Truong Cam Ninh and Mr. Nguyen Phouc Thien in Vietnam, all of whom offered unstinting personal help. Government officials in ministries of Information, Culture, and Education in every country I visited gave generously of their time and assistance. USIS officers and employees facilitated my field work.

For photographs I am greatly indebted to a number of persons and institutions including the Royal School of Fine Arts, Cambodia (figure 23); Embassy of Indonesia, Washington, D.C. (figures 20, 27, 35, 44, 45, 49, 57, 72); A. Rashid Ismail (figures 37, 38, 67, 68): Ministry of Education, Laos (figure 43); Malaysian Information Service (figures 36, 46, by Wong Swee Lin and Hong Weng Him); Information Services, Michigan State University (figures 16, 28, 29, 30, 31, 32, 33, 34, 52, 55); James L. Peacock (figures 10, 13, 41); Philippine Tourist and Travel Association, Inc. (figures 4, 5, 8, 12, 54, 62); Public Relations Department, Thailand (figures 7, 9, 25, 47, 50, 53); and Embassy of Viet Nam, Washington, D.C. (figures 11, 14). Maps and charts were drawn by Mr. Edward Andreasen. Mr. Joseph Withey and Mrs. Judith Becker kindly read parts of the manuscript. I am deeply grateful to Mrs. Bonnie R. Crown for her encouragement during the writing of the manuscript, to the Asian Literature Program of The Asia Society for its sponsorship and help in arranging the details of publication, and to Mrs. Philip C. McLaughlin for her understanding and sound editorial advice.

This book is the result of a year's research in Southeast Asia (1963–4) and a summer of writing (1966) on grants from Michigan State University–International Programs/Ford Foundation, for which support I am most appreciative. Finally, I wish to thank the artists of the more than two hundred theatre troupes I visited who answered my many questions with unfailing patience and good nature.

J.R.B.

September 20, 1966
East Lansing, Michigan

C O N T E N T S

[ix]

Contents

ILLUSTRATIONS

Folk Theatre　　　　　　　[following page 10

1　Villagers in trance in a barong performance in Bali.
2　The witch Rangda in a Balinese barong performance.
3　A monkey play for children in Thailand.
4　A Christian warrior vanquishes a Moslem opponent in a moro-moro play in the Philippines.
5　A ceremony in a Philippine village to placate local animistic spirits.
6　A legong dancer in a Balinese barong performance.
7　The lakon jatri folk-derived dance-play *Manora* performed in Thailand.
8　A local expert applying make-up to Philippine villagers acting in a lenten play.
9　Thailand's nang talung puppets.

Popular Theatre　　　　　　[following page 22

10　A female impersonator in Javanese ludruk.
11　Vietnamese hat boi performed before a painted backdrop.
12　A modern love story dramatized in the Philippine zarzuela play *Alamat Sa Nayon.*
13　Dagelan, or clown characters, in traditional Javanese dress in a ludruk performance.
14　A cai luong heroine in Vietnam.
15　A scene from the mohlam luong play *Saneh,* in Laos.
16　A *Mahabharata* play performed in Sunda by a sandiwara troupe.
17　Children view a likay performance in Thailand.
18　A Vietnamese costume based on Chinese models, worn by a Lao king in a mohlam luong version of the Western fairy tale *The Emperor's New Clothes.*

Court Theatre　　　　　　　[following page 34

19　Statue of Ravana in the Royal Palace, Bangkok, Thailand.
20　Rama and Sita from the *Ramayana* as danced in Javanese court wayang orang.
21　Hat boi performed in traditional Chinese-derived costumes and make-up in Vietnam.
22　Puppeteer in a Javanese *Mahabharata* play performed in wayang kulit.

Contents

[xi]

Contents

Contents

FIGURES

TABLES

CHAPTER 1

Introduction

From the Asian mainland there juts southward for 2000 miles a
peninsula of land, two-thirds the size of India. Burma forms its
western portion, Thailand (Siam) the center, and Laos, Cambodia, and Vietnam the eastern part. At the peninsula's southern tip, just above the equator, lies Malaya. Southward the con-
tinental land mass disintegrates into two great arcs of volcanic
islands. One arc made up of Java, Bali, Sumatra, Borneo, and
the other Indonesian islands sweeps southeast across the equator
3500 miles to Australia. The other, which includes the Philippines, runs northeast another 2500 miles as far as Taiwan. This
sprawling area of land and sea, twice the size of Europe, as
large as the United States and Canada combined, is Southeast
Asia. It is the home of an astounding amount of theatrical activity. No one knows how many theatre troupes are playing in
Rangoon, Phnom Penh, Saigon, Singapore, Djakarta, and the
other major cities or touring the "rice-paddy circuits" of the
countryside. There are so many troupes no one has even tried
to count them all, but my own estimate is that there are more
than a thousand professional troupes and double or triple that
number of amateur troupes operating today. Some 150,000,000
people see these troupes perform every year, or three out of four
of the 200,000,000 persons living in Burma, Cambodia, Indonesia, Laos, Malaysia, the Philippines, Thailand, and Vietnam.

The variety of theatre is almost staggering. There are shadow
plays in Java, dramatic folk rituals in Bali, masked pantomime
in Thailand, spirit dances in Burma, folk-song dramas in Laos,

classic Chinese-derived opera in Vietnam, puppet plays in Sunda, and the Royal Ballet of Cambodia, to name but eight of the twenty-five major theatre forms which are performed today. Performances are given in spacious palaces before royalty and on squares of packed earth before crowds of illiterate villagers, in new air-conditioned theatres built of concrete and steel and on small, temporary, and very rickety bamboo-frame stages floored with rough planking, at Buddhist fairs in Laos, at temple festivals in Bali, for Moslem circumcision ceremonies in Java, as Christian pageants in the Philippines, and as offerings to animistic spirits in Thailand. A performance may demonstrate a high level of artistry, or it may be inept, vulgar, and utterly worthless. One can see on stage Hindu gods, Islamic saints, Chinese generals from The Romance of the Three Kingdoms, European soldiers, and local Communist mass heroes. One can see plays based on Buddhist *Jataka* stories, on Shakespeare and Oscar Wilde, on movies in glorious color and in Cinemascope, and on the countless legends which are a part of the cultural heritage of Asia from the Mediterranean Sea on the west to the Sea of Japan on the east. You can hear the whine of a Chinese fiddle, the boom of a Javanese gong, and the thud of drums of every nationality and race.

The theatrical experience finds such a multiplicity of expression in Southeast Asia, one's initial impulse is to chalk it all up as a great disconnected jumble. Yet nothing would be more incorrect than to think of Southeast Asian theatre as a miscellaneous collection of unrelated forms and styles. Beneath their outward differences many genres are closely related. They have grown from similar cultural settings and they share common characteristics. In the first place, Southeast Asia is a distinct geographic entity. Straddling the equator, it is one of the world's true tropical regions. To describe the lush mosaic of the terraced rice fields, fish ponds, and coconut groves of the countryside is to describe equally well the broad river valleys of every country on the mainland and the fertile volcanic plains of the islands, where, as Le May so well says, "one has only to lie on one's back and wait for the bananas to fall into one's mouth."[1] On the most basic level, all of the theatre of Southeast Asia reflects the casual and easygoing tempo of tropical life. Although it is true that a dozen different races speaking a score of major languages and hundreds of dialects inhabit Southeast Asia, most of these peoples are closely related within either the Malay ethnic group or the Chinese-related mongoloid ethnic group. At different times, widespread and powerful waves of outside cultural influence have inundated all or large parts of the area: first Buddhism and Hinduism came from India, then Islam invaded from the Near East and Moslem India while Mongol armies introduced Chinese civilization from the north, and Western culture was brought by Spaniards, Portuguese, Dutch, French, British, and Americans. From each new overlay of foreign culture, common elements were introduced into the theatre. And a great deal of intermixing has occurred among neighboring cultures within Southeast Asia. Kingdoms have risen, have conquered their neighbors, and have imposed their culture—and theatre forms—on the conquered; they in turn have been conquered by *their* neighbors who have imposed on them *their* culture—and theatre forms. Some parts of Southeast Asia have changed hands eight or ten times during the period of recorded history. For all these reasons, theatre forms throughout Southeast Asia tend to share, to a greater or lesser degree, certain common characteristics.

A proper understanding of Southeast Asian theatre (whether as an art form, as an institution in society, or as a medium of communication) must proceed from a recognition of both the underlying common properties which link theatre forms together and the variety of differences which distinguish them from each other. In the following chapters I shall describe the theatre in terms of differences and similarities. My intent is not to prove a priori theories regarding the nature of Southeast Asian theatre, but rather to examine as rationally as possible the multitude of theatre forms we see today and to describe whatever relations between them come to light.

[3]

PART I

A Historical Background

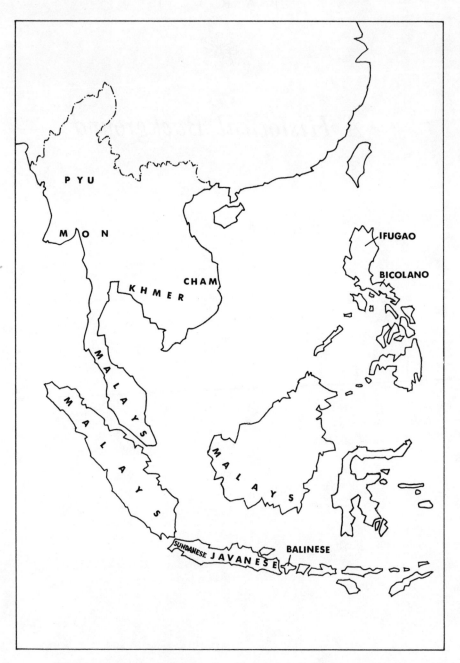

MAP 1. Prehistoric Peoples in Southeast Asia (ca. 2500 B.C.–A.D. 100)

CHAPTER 2

The Cultural Setting

Broadly speaking, there have been four major cultural periods in the history of Southeast Asia. Each has provided a distinctly different cultural setting for the development of theatre. The prehistoric period, from around 2500 B.C. to A.D. 100, saw the settling of Southeast Asia by peoples from the north who practiced animism and possessed a fairly high level of civilization. The beginnings of theatre can be traced from this period. From around A.D. 100 to 1000 Indian culture penetrated into Burma, Thailand, Cambodia, southern Vietnam, Malaya, and the islands of Sumatra, Borneo, Java, and Bali—that is, everywhere in Southeast Asia except into Laos, northern Vietnam, the Philippines, and the easternmost islands of Indonesia. During this period the foundations were laid for the later development of many classic theatre forms, especially dance-drama and the puppet theatre. The period from roughly 1300 to 1750 saw Malaya and Indonesia (except for Bali) converted to Islam and Chinese-related peoples replace the earlier Malay settlers as rulers of Burma, Thailand, Laos, and parts of Vietnam. This was a period of intense theatrical activity during which court theatre reached a high stage of development. From around 1750 until the end of World War II the United States and Europe gained political and economic control over all Southeast Asia except Thailand. Most present-day "popular" theatre forms evolved during this period.

THE PREHISTORIC PERIOD

Most authorities believe the years 2500 to 1500 B.C. saw mass migrations from southwestern China into countries to the south.* These peoples have been variously called Indonesian, Austronesian, and proto-Malay or deutero-Malay by anthropologists. I am calling them, for convenience sake, "prehistoric immigrants." For centuries these prehistoric immigrants moved south along the river valleys of the peninsula, and by ship along the coastline from island to island. They settled where they could fish or grow rice, particularly in the great river basins of the mainland and on the volcanic-rich plains of Java and Bali. They established communities and began the long process of developing their own civilizations, different yet related.

Who were these people? Or rather, who were the descendants of these people to become? Mon, Khmer, Cham, Malay, Javanese, Sundanese, and Balinese are the names of the most important groups. The immigrants who settled in the delta of the Irrawaddy River in Burma came to be known as the Mon. They ruled most of southern Burma and Thailand from capitals in Pegu and Thaton. At the height of their power they even attacked Assam in India. Later the Burmese with Chinese help put an end to Mon rule and almost exterminated the Mon people. The people who settled along the Mekong River and in the highlands of what is now Cambodia took the name Khmer. The Khmer carved out a great empire through conquest. From their capitals in and around Angkor, they ruled over an area including all of modern Cambodia, most of Laos and Thailand, and parts of Vietnam and Malaya. The magnificent temple ruins of Angkor Wat and the Royal Cambodian Ballet are legacies of this once great civilization which reached its zenith in the twelfth century. The immigrants in central and south Vietnam, who settled along the coastal plains and in the short river valleys, were the Chams. There they built their own brief

---

*The theory that Southeast Asia was populated by immigrants from central Asia, first made by Robert von Heine-Geldern, is generally accepted today. Other less popular theories are that: the original home of the races of Southeast Asia was India; in prehistoric times peoples from Southeast Asia migrated to India so that later Indian traders and missionaries merely brought back Southeast Asia's own culture with Indian overlays; and some of the peoples of the Pacific islands originally came from America.

civilization until the Viets, pressing down from the north, and the Khmers, invading from the west, destroyed their cities, killed their kings, and enslaved large numbers of the population until the Chams all but disappeared. In west Java, where the prehistoric immigrants came to be known as the Sundanese, and in central and east Java, where they came to be known as the Javanese, kingdom after kingdom rose and fell. Some of these kingdoms were petty; others, like Majapahit in the fourteenth century, exercised suzerainty over Sumatra, Malaya, Borneo, and parts of Thailand and Cambodia, as well as ruling Java. But through it all, for 1500 years, princely courts lavished patronage on the puppet theatre, music, dance, and literature. Meanwhile, just east of Java, on their own small island of Bali, another group of prehistoric immigrants developed a civilization in which the performing arts came to play as integral a role in the peoples' lives and religion as has ever been seen in the world.

This is what the descendants of the prehistoric immigrants from southwestern China were eventually to become; these are the kingdoms they were to build; these are the names they were to give themselves and their civilizations. In early megalithic times, however, while the migration was still going on, and immediately afterwards, when societies were first being established, there was little differentiation between them. The most salient fact about the migrants was that they shared a common origin and a common culture. This prehistoric culture was of considerable development and, as far as theatre is concerned, its most important elements were: the cultivation of rice, the practice of animism, possession of a common fund of myths, and bronze manufacture.

Even without written records of this time we can surmise the probable development of theatre within prehistoric culture. Because the immigrant peoples supported themselves mainly by growing rice, they established stable communities in which periods of leisure, following the harvest, occurred two or three times a year. Leisure time is an essential precondition for the creation of theatre of any degree of sophistication. A performer must have leisure time in which to develop his artistic skill and an audience must have leisure to attend a performance. Rice culture provided this precondition in Southeast Asia. Furthermore, the rice harvest was celebrated as a major community festival, stimulating the performance of dances, singing, and story-reciting. Throughout Southeast Asia special plays which honor the rice spirit are still performed at harvest time.

Animism was the common religion of all the immigrant peoples. One of its beliefs is that spirits reside in everything in the world—in a stone, in a grain of rice, in a tree, in a mountain, in a river. That the soul of the rice grain would be killed or frightened by using a large sickle to cut rice stalks is an animistic belief widely held in Southeast Asia; as a result rice is often cut, three stalks at a time, with a tiny knife held in the palm of the hand. An animist also believes in the existence of extraordinarily important "magic power" which a person can gain control over by his own acts, usually through some form of asceticism. When one person acts on behalf of another or for the community at large the act becomes a magic ritual. In prehistoric civilization animistic magic ritual must have been an important source of artistic inspiration. As Wagner says,

> . . . it is an indispensable prerequisite to gain control of *mana* [magic power] if one is to obtain those guarantees which, it is believed, will ensure the continued existence of the community. But control over *mana* and influence upon it require an external sign . . . "magic ritual" . . . one point stands out in relief: *those expressions of men who think and act magically and which can be termed "artistic expressions" were originally firmly rooted in magic ritual.*[1]

Many theatre performances seen today have their roots in just such ritual magic. One of the most common types of dance in Burma is a spirit dance specifically performed to placate the *nat,* or animistic spirit, of a particular locality. (Animistic spirits are called *nat* in Burma, *pi* in Laos, Cambodia, and parts of Thailand, *anito* in the Philippines, and by many names in Indonesia.) According to the Dutch scholar Rassers, Javanese *wayang kulit* shadow drama developed out of prehistoric, animistic rituals in which ancestors of the tribe were contacted through the medium of shadow figures.[2] Vulnerable children can be protected from death in Java by a wayang kulit performance of a special animistic play, *Murwakala.* A Thai can show his gratitude to the spirits for having received a favor from them by

1. Villagers in trance press daggers against their breasts as a Brahman priest enters from the temple to end a barong performance in Bali.

2. The witch Rangda gestures furiously as she discovers she is unable to kill Sadewa, bound to a tree, in a Balinese barong performance.

3. A monkey play for children in Thailand.

4. A Christian warrior vanquishes his Moslem opponent in a village production of a moro-moro play in the Philippines.

5. A ceremony in a Philippine village to placate local animistic spirits, incorporating music, singing, and prayers.

6. A legong dancer in a Balinese barong performance exhibits a high level of accomplishment.

7. The lakon jatri folk-derived dance-play *Manora* performed in Thailand with expensive costumes of female performers patterned after court models.

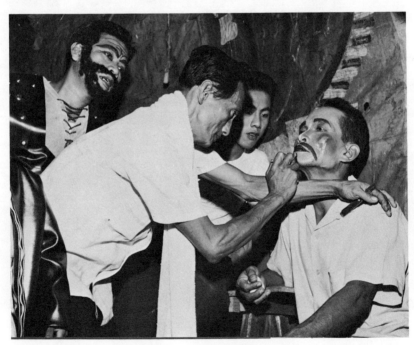

8. A local expert applying make-up to Philippine villagers acting in a lenten play.

9. Thailand's nang talung puppets are modeled after khon dance figures, but their translucency probably reflects the influence of Chinese shadow-drama.

paying for a theatrical performance in their honor; it is not even necessary for a human audience to attend.

It seems very likely that the prehistoric immigrants brought with them a common fund of oral myths and legends similar to Indian Sanskrit literature not so much because they were derived from Indian literature, but because both Southeast Asian and Indian stories came from the same prehistoric source in central Asia. It may be that, as Hall once theorized about Indonesia, "when later on, after the introduction of written literature from India, we meet them in literary form with an Indonesian setting, they are not necessarily foreign importations which have been given an Indonesian twist, but represent folk myths and legends, springing from the same remote origin as the Indian stories, which have maintained their original character in purer form."[3] These stories provide material for much Southeast Asian drama. The existence of ancient, pre-Hindu tribal legends among several isolated mountain tribes in the Philippines strongly points to this supposition.

The art of bronze-working was also part of prehistoric culture. Large bronze kettledrums, characteristic of southwest China of the pre-Christian era, have been found in Yunan, Vietnam, Laos, Sumatra, Java, Thailand, and Malaya. We have firm knowledge that these drums were made as early as 1135 B.C., so we know that the people who migrated from Yunan knew about bronze-working and how to make at least simple musical instruments of that metal.[4] It seems likely that by the end of the prehistoric period in Southeast Asia the technique of fashioning bronze instruments, in the form of tuned sets of bowls, bars, and gongs, was already well-established. From these early beginnings the complex percussion ensembles of Java, Bali, and Cambodia developed. There is carved on one of the reliefs of the ninth-century Buddhist monument in Java, the Borobudur, a bronze xylophone identical to an instrument used in the Indonesian *gamelan* ensemble today, the *saron*.

We need not imagine the music, the dance, or the drama of the prehistoric peoples of Southeast Asia were very complex. Some bronze instruments, probably drums, and the flute were used in performance, or bamboo lengths similar to the Thai *graw* or *grap* of today were beat together to mark time. Dance movements were probably rudimentary. It is unlikely that there was a specialized class of performers, doing no other work than performing. What we can imagine is the existence of a firmly established tradition of folk performances, closely tied to communal rites of animistic worship and propitiation and to cyclic festivals which served the dual purpose of religious worship and entertainment. And in the larger cities, where petty princes came to hold power, we can also imagine the beginnings of court-supported theatre. Therefore, when more sophisticated performing arts were introduced into Southeast Asia from the higher civilization of India around the first century of the Christian era (and again many centuries later from China), indigenous prehistoric forms of theatrical performance did not simply disappear. The new forms were in most cases warmly and immediately accepted, but in the process these new forms were adapted, altered, reworked, and fitted into older, already existing patterns of theatre activity.

THE PERIOD OF INDIAN CULTURAL INFLUENCE

The gradual expansion of Indian culture into Southeast Asia during the first millenium of the Christian era is one of the major events in the history of Asia. In the centuries immediately preceding the Christian era, trade was carried on between ports in India and in Southeast Asia, but it was not until around A.D. 100 that we hear of the first "Hindu" settlement in Southeast Asia. A Chinese source tells of the state of Funan, in the area that is now Cambodia, where an Indian script (resembling the Hon script of Central Asia) was used for writing and the king claimed to be a Brahman.* Fifth-century accounts relate how the rulers had "completely Indianized the customs of Funan."[5] Chinese records and Sanskrit inscriptions of the third century after Christ tell of the founding, a century earlier, of a

---

*D. G. E. Hall, *A History of South-East Asia,* 2nd ed. (New York, 1964), p. 25. The king may have been an Indian who gained access to the throne, either a Brahman or a pretender to this high caste, or he may have been a local man who, learning of the exalted status of Brahman priests in India, fabricated a Brahman genealogy in order to legitimatize his rule.

Hinduized kingdom called Champa in what is now central Vietnam (Annam). Between the second and the seventh centuries at
least three Indianized kingdoms are mentioned in Chinese accounts of Malaya. Rock inscriptions found in west Java, dating
from around A.D. 450, tell of the first kingdom on Java in which
Brahmanic rites were followed. Early evidence concerning the
dates of the establishment of Indian-influenced kingdoms in
Burma and Thailand is lacking, but by the sixth century at the
latest Mon and Pyu kingdoms were observing Brahmanic and
Buddhist religious practices.[6] Indian cultural influence grew
rapidly, and by the tenth century every kingdom in Southeast
Asia, outside of the Philippines and northern Vietnam (Tonkin),
had as its official religion Buddhism or Brahmanism, or a mixture of the two.

One of the most unusual things about this Indian cultural
invasion is the way in which it came about. No Indian armies
were dispatched to subdue the native kingdoms of Southeast
Asia. No fleets of warships from India tried to gain control of
the seas. We know of only one Indian military action against a
Southeast Asian kingdom during the whole thousand-year period
of Indian cultural expansion: in 1025 a Chola fleet from southern
India attacked and evidentally conquered the powerful kingdom
of Srivijaya in Sumatra. Even this, however, is not a case of an
Indian state introducing Indian culture by military means, for
in 1025 Srivijaya had been a thoroughly Indianized state for
500 years. There is no record of any Southeast Asian state ever
having been ruled by an Indian state. There may have been a
few Indians who came to rule as kings over Southeast Asian
states through their individual qualities of leadership, but, though
they certainly introduced Indian customs and religious practices
into their courts, they did not attempt to bring their states into
the orbit of Indian political control. Neither, apparently, did the
Indians come to Southeast Asia in large numbers. Nor did they
come as the Pilgrims came to America or the French to Canada
or the Dutch to South Africa, to establish communities that
would eventually grow into politically sovereign states.

All evidence points to the fact that Indian culture was brought
by traders, missionaries, and intelligentsia. In the early centuries
of the Christian era, before regular routes of trade were estab-

lished, voyages from India must have been a risky business. As Groslier says,

> The traders would land on an unknown and deserted, or almost deserted, shore . . . they could not carry food supplies over long distances in the stuffy holds of their slow-sailing ships. They therefore planted rice fields in the fruitful soil of the deltas where they landed, disposing the fields with all their skill and experience of drainage, just as the Greeks, when on long sea voyages, landed and sowed their corn, and did not sail again till the holds were full with the harvest. And just as at every anchorage the Greeks built an altar to their gods who alone could guard them on the hostile coast, so did the Indians erect dwellings for their gods in all their colonies.[7]

And so trading stations were established. The Indians were admired and respected, for they possessed such unheard-of knowledge as astronomy and mathematics, practiced higher and more complex religions, knew advanced forms of art, and were able to write (which must have seemed a tremendous achievement to peoples who did not know an alphabet). In the course of time, some traders married daughters of local rulers and established themselves in the local courts. But the Indianization of local courts was a gradual process that took centuries. In the last analysis it must have been Brahman priests and Buddhist scholars and Hindu artisans attached to local courts, rather than traders or merchants, who proselytized the complexities of the new Indian culture. And the proselytizers may well have included Southeast Asians who had been dispatched to Indian centers of learning by their rulers specifically to learn Indian knowledge.[8]

An important factor that facilitated the spread of Indian culture in Southeast Asia was the special nature of animistic kingship belief. The king was believed to represent the essence of the state; he personally symbolized the tribe; his palace was a model in microcosm of the macrocosm of the kingdom. Because the animist believed that spirit resided in everything and that man could accumulate the spiritual power of other things and people for his own use and protection, it followed that the king, as ruler of the state, was expected to amass more spiritual power than anyone else. It was believed the king's authority varied in direct proportion to the amount of magic power (*mana* in Polynesian, *semangat* in Javanese, *sakti* in Indonesian) he was able to create or appropriate. Of course the king could gain spiritual power by his own meditation and asceticism, and Southeast Asian drama is filled with stories of kings who fall on hard times, and who, by retiring to a hermitage in the forest, gather sufficient spiritual power to return and defeat their enemies; but in actual practice it was easier to appropriate for one's own use magic power already accumulated by others.

The local rulers of Southeast Asia immediately recognized in the more complex culture of India previously undreamed-of sources of spiritual power, in the worship of Vishnu and Shiva and Buddha, in the new system of communicating through written symbols, in Indian arts, and in Indian literature. Cambodian and Javanese kings came to deify themselves as the reincarnation of Shiva or Vishnu or Buddha and had statues of the god carved in their likeness. In Java weapons charged with great magic power were kept near the throne, and all dwarfs born in the realm were brought to live in the palace, for they too were believed to possess unusual amounts of magic power (this continued down until around 1950). In Java and Malaya, kings ordered poets to legitimatize their rule by creating imaginary ties to the great kingdoms of the past so they could share in the accumulation of their ancestors' spiritual power. We can see this same belief at work in the action of Kertanagara, King of Kediri, who, in 1275 had himself dedicated as a Bhairava-Buddha. He did this because in 1269 Kublai Khan had himself dedicated as a Jina-Buddha in preparation for his forthcoming expeditions of conquest. "By imitation of Kublai Khan's dedication he [Kertanagara] hoped to develop similar powers."[9]

In Java, Bali, Malaya, Burma, Thailand, Cambodia, and Laos, where Indian culture was most thoroughly assimilated, theatre was profoundly and for all time affected. Four aspects of Indian culture are most significant in this respect: Brahmanism, particularly the cult of Shiva worship, which provided a religious basis for theatrical performances; Indian epic literature, especially the *Ramayana* and the *Mahabharata,* which became a common source for dramatic material; Buddhist Birth Stories (the *Jataka* stories), which were introduced along with Hinayana Buddhism; and Indian-style dance, which spread over almost the entire area of Southeast Asia.

[15]

As Brahmanism came to be adopted as the official religion of ruling dynasties, it provided a new and powerful religious basis for performances of various kinds. Hindu religion and philosophy traditionally were communicated to the masses in India by organized recitations. There was a special class of reciters called *sutapauranikas,* who recited before "vast congregations of people gathered at sacrificial sessions," and this same practice was carried into Southeast Asia. "Hindu culture was carried to Cambodia and other lands by endowments made by rulers for the recital, in temples they built, of the Hindu epics," especially the *Ramayana.*[10]

A vital element of Brahmanism was belief in the institution of the god-king. The king was considered a living god, a human being in whom one of the Hindu gods, usually Shiva or Vishnu, was reincarnated. The god-king was divine protector of the community. He commanded total power, political, social, and religious, and toward him were directed all the aspirations of the community. The devotion of the people to their god-king was expressed periodically in ritual acts of worship carried out by special court officials, some of whom were musicians, dancers, and actors. In the cult of Shiva, the sacred personality of the king was enshrined in a phallus of stone, set at the highest point of the king's temple-mountain, which was at the exact center of the capital and was regarded as the center of the universe. Here the god-king, through his religious symbol, the enshrined phallus, was worshiped and sacrifices were made. That these ceremonies included theatrical performances of some kind, there is no doubt. As Ghosh says, Shiva is called "the great dancer actor . . . dance and drama propitiate Shiva more than any other form of worship."[11] It is no accident that the most striking developments in music, dance, and drama took place in this period in the courts of the Javanese and Cambodian kings, where the Brahmanic cult of Shiva worship was most strongly entrenched. Hall speaks of "hundreds of dancers" in the service of various temples during the reign of the Khmer king Jayavarman VII, who ruled from Angkor in the twelfth century.[12] On reliefs of the Borobudur, built in central Java in the ninth century, and on the various buildings at Angkor, scene after scene shows dancing girls and groups of musicians as a regular part of court life. Animis-

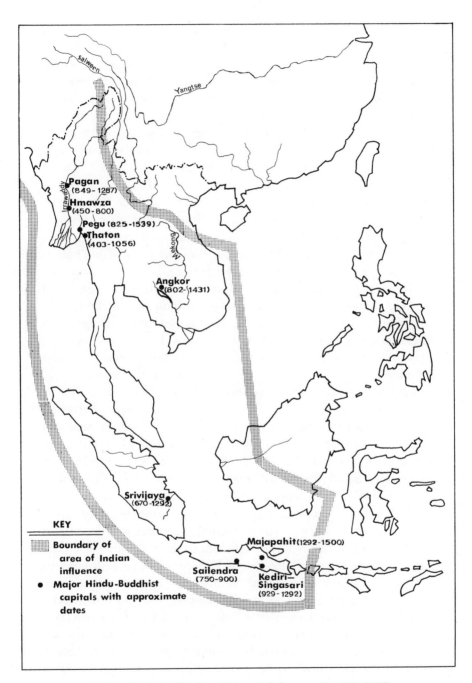

MAP 2. Period of Indian Cultural Influence (ca. 100–1000)

tic belief that the king ruled through accumulation of spiritual power easily fit in with the new Hindu belief in the god-king, especially since both tended to support ancestor worship which was "a special task laid upon a king. At certain set times he had to establish ritual contact with his ancestors in order to strengthen his position by the receipt of new magical powers from them."[13] When this ritual contact was accomplished as a theatrical performance, both animism and Hinduism combined to support the development of theatre art.

In calling attention to the support which Brahmanic courts lavished upon the performing arts from around the fifth to the twelfth centuries, I do not mean to imply that only religious motives were involved. The Khmer or Javanese ruler was both human and a god. In either guise, it was the duty of his harem of dancing girls to serve him. In the temple, before the symbolic phallus of the god-king, a girl's dance was a religious offering; in the king's chambers it was an erotic prelude to the offering of her body to a very human king. We cannot untangle religious from hedonistic motives very well from this distance in time, but regardless of motive the end result was generous court support not only for dancing girls but for other performers as well.

Dances, recitations, and dramatic performances given in the newly Indianized courts of Southeast Asia all drew on India's great epic tradition for their subject matter. The *Ramayana* and the *Mahabharata* are the two most important epics, though other epic cycles were also known, such as the Krishna Cycle. The *Ramayana* in Sanskrit runs to 24,000 verses, while the *Mahabharata* is over 100,000 verses long. Each has a cast of hundreds of characters. One of the characteristics of the versions of these epics brought from India was their Brahmanic content. Just as the mystery plays of the Middle Ages dramatized the life of Christ and so taught illiterate peoples of Europe to believe in Christianity, the Hindu epics showed the lives of the Indian gods and of their descendants and so taught the people of Southeast Asia to believe in Hinduism. Rama, the hero of the *Ramayana,* is a reincarnation of the god Vishnu. Here are the opening lines of a play based on the *Ramayana,* traditionally performed in Assam, and believed by Ghosh to be a relic of an extremely early form of theatre in India.

[1 8]

Benediction
I always adore with devotion Sri-Rama who can grant a boon even
to . . . Shiva, and whose name kills the sorrow of all the worlds,
inspires supreme love, serves as a broad boat for carrying people
across the limitless ocean of sin, and on reaching the ears of a Can-
dala makes him purified, giving him liberation even in this world.

Song
Victory to Rama, the life of the world, to him I bow down. By singing the merit of his name the sinner attains the highest region. By
remembering him one gets across the fire of worldly existence . . .

Stage Manager
Enough. Let me bow to Rama. (Turns to spectators.) Oh the learned
members of the assembly, observe carefully this play called *Rama's
Triumph* for it will bring liberation unto you.[14]

By merely singing the name of the hero of the drama, one was
supposed to achieve religious merit. In the *Mahabharata*, Krishna,
chief advisor to Arjuna, is likewise portrayed as a reincarnation
of Vishnu.

The epics extolled the virtues of the ruling class (*ksatriya*). In
the code of behavior they delineated, the king's power was absolute and a subject's duty was to serve and obey his king totally.
Naturally the rulers of Southeast Asia recognized the advantage
to themselves of having these sentiments given frequent public
expression. The following passage between a king and his son,
from an Indonesian wayang kulit shadow play, gives a good idea
of how strongly the idea of kingly supremacy came to be stated
in plays based on the epics.

Prince
My heart was shattered as though crushed against a rock; like grass
blown by the wind in the great square, my heart trembled with
surprise and anxiety when I heard I was to come before my King.

King
My Son, how is it you were afraid to come before me?

Prince
I trembled that were I guilty and condemned to death, it should be
your Majesty who condemns me to death. But, by day and by night,

[19]

I am ready to offer my life with both hands. To be pierced with a sharp arrow, to be beheaded, I am ready to do what your Majesty wishes.*

On the mainland of Southeast Asia the *Ramayana* provided material for dances and dance-plays that evolved in the royal courts. The *Ramayana* is long, but its story is direct and simple. The seven major episodes of the story comprise seven books in the famous Sanskrit version attributed to Valmiki (ca. 100–400 B.C.).

Briefly, the story goes like this. Book one: Rama competes in a great contest for the hand of Sita and, by bending the magic bow which no other person can bend, wins her for his bride. Book two: as Rama is about to be named heir to the throne of Ayodya, one of the king's wives asks that her son, Bharata, be made heir instead of Rama, and that Rama be sent into exile for fourteen years. Since the king had previously promised this wife two boons, he is forced to comply. Rama willingly departs. Book three: Rama lives in the forest with Sita and his brother Laksh-mana. Surpanakha, an ogress, falls in love with Rama and with Lakshmana, but both repulse her and Lakshmana cuts off her nose. Furious, the ogress begs her brother Ravana, King of Lanka (Ceylon), to avenge her insult. Ravana has long desired Sita so he agrees. While an ogre in the shape of a golden deer lures away Rama and Lakshmana into the forest, Ravana seizes Sita and flys off with her to his palace in Lanka. The Bird King Jatayu attempts to prevent the abduction, but is killed by Ravana. Book four: the brothers search for Sita. Rama helps the monkey Sugriva gain control of the kingdom of monkeys from his brother Bali (Subali) and in return Sugriva and his army of monkeys assist Rama and Lakshmana in their fight against Ravana. Book five: the white monkey Hanuman slips into Lanka, discovers where Sita is being held prisoner, and gives her a token of Rama's love. He is captured, but manages to set fire to the city and escape. Book six: in a great and prolonged battle, Rama, Lakshmana, and the monkey host slay the ogre army and finally Ravana himself. Sita's chastity is questioned by Rama, so she consents to undergo an ordeal of fire. She is unscathed by the

*Condensed from the opening section of "Irawan Rabi," found in M. Ng. Nojo-wirongko, *Serat Tuntunan Padalangan*, vol. II (Jogjakarta, 1960). See Chapter 15 for a more extended translation.

flames, proving her purity. She and Rama return in triumph to rule Ayodhya. Book seven: since rumors persist that Sita was unfaithful to Rama during her captivity, Sita is sent into exile where she gives birth to two children. The gods help demonstrate her purity once more, and she returns to Ayodhya as Rama's cherished consort. As Htin Aung points out, the epic actually consists of two separate stories: the first concerns Rama's marriage, the intrigues at the court of Ayodhya, and Rama's exile, while the second is about the abduction of Sita by Ravana and the resulting great war.[15]

The *Mahabharata* is a much more complicated epic than the *Ramayana*. This is partly because it is four times as long and therefore has a larger cast of characters and more episodes. It is also because, in addition to its basic story line, the *Mahabharata* accommodates numerous unrelated episodes which, over the centuries, fell into the epic's orbit and gradually became incorporated in the epic itself. The basic story of the *Mahabharata* concerns the struggle between two sets of cousins, the Pandavas and the Kauravas, to rule the kingdom of Astina. There are five Pandava brothers: Yudhisthira, the eldest, just and noble; Bhima, tremendously strong and impulsive; Arjuna, refined but possessing magic power that makes him invincible; and the twin brothers Nakula and Sahadeva. Against the five virtuous Pandavas are ranged the hundred Kaurava brothers, led by Duryodhana whose single aim is to gain and keep power, by no matter what unscrupulous means. Duryodhana cheats Yudhisthira of the Pandava's rightful share of the kingdom of Astina in a rigged dice game. He unlawfully exiles the Pandavas for twelve years, and then, when the Pandavas dutifully retire to live in the depths of the forest, attempts to kill them by burning their dwelling. Krishna, a reincarnation of Vishnu, is adviser to the Pandavas. He tries to negotiate a peaceful settlement with the Kauravas but they refuse to allow the Pandavas any share of their rightful inheritance. Then follow preparations for the *Bharatayuddha,* the Great War. Next, in the famous episode called the *Bhagavad-Gita* (commonly known as the *Gita*), Arjuna questions the propriety of killing the Kauravas, his cousins. In Krishna's famous reply, Arjuna is assured that he will only be carrying out the sacred duty of the ksatriya ruling class by destroying his enemies. The battle is joined and continues for twelve days and twelve nights. Multitudes of warriors are slain on both sides. One by one Duryodhana's bravest and most skilled generals are defeated and killed by the Pandavas. By the twelfth day, Duryodhana and his ninety-nine brothers are all dead. The Pandavas justly rule the kingdom of Astina for many years.

On Java and on Bali, the *Mahabharata* came to provide the major dramatic themes for early court dance and drama, just as on the mainland the *Ramayana* did. Literally hundreds of plays were derived from this one epic. In Java it was to subsidiary episodes more than the main story line that performers were attracted.

The two epics came to Southeast Asia from India via two separate channels. One channel was through writing. In Java, Bali, Cambodia, and Malaya, Sanskrit versions of the epics were known. In Java, the *Ramayana* was translated from Sanskrit into Old Javanese as early as A.D. 860, and during the next three centuries most of the *Mahabharata* and several shorter Sanskrit epic cycles were also translated. A second channel was through oral traditions of epic-reciting. The epics existed in India as oral literature long before they were written down. During this period they were known in dozens of vernacular versions in India (and are today as well). Apparently it was mainly from Indian vernacular versions of the epics, as recited in public, that Southeast Asians came to know the *Ramayana* and the *Mahabharata,* rather than through Sanskrit versions known at court. For example, comparison of Thai *Ramayana* play scripts with both Valmiki's Sanskrit version and with Tamil and Bengali vernacular versions show that the Thai play is much closer to the vernacular versions than to Valmiki's.[16]

It is extremely interesting to note that, while the Indian epics came to be known in Southeast Asia, the great Sanskrit plays of India and the well-known dramatic treatise, the *Natya Sastra,* apparently were not.* On Java or Bali, where scores of Sanskrit works were translated over a period of three hundred years, there

---

*Htin Aung refers several times to supposed Sanskrit play influence on Thai, Burmese, and Javanese drama (*Burmese Drama,* pp. 2–28), but gives no evidence to support his view. In any case, Burmese drama developed a full thousand years later than the period we are discussing, so evidence from Burmese drama is of little help.

10. A female impersonator in Javanese ludruk dances on a stage filled with children.

11. Vietnamese hat boi performed by a popular troupe before a painted backdrop instead of the traditional Chinese-derived curtain.

12. A modern love story dramatized in the Philippine zarzuela play *Alamat Sa Nayon*.

13. Dagelan, or clown characters, in traditional Javanese dress during a comic scene in a ludruk performance.

14. In Vietnam, this typical costume for a cai luong heroine in a Chinese play is a theatrical convention not historically accurate.

15. In Laos a scene from the mohlam luong play *Saneh*, with costumes similar to those of likay.

16. A *Mahabharata* play performed in Sunda by a popular sandiwara troupe.

17. Children gather at the footlights and sit on the stage to view a likay performance in Thailand.

18. A Vietnamese costume based on Chinese models, worn by a Lao king in a mohlam luong version of the Western fairy tale *The Emperor's New Clothes*.

is no hint of as much as a fragment of a Sanskrit play ever having been translated. In all the literature of Southeast Asia, there is no mention of the *Natya Sastra*. What this means is really quite remarkable. It means that, while Sanskrit drama was reaching the height of its development (between A.D. 400 and 1000) and the highly regarded *Natya Sastra,* among many other similar dramatic treatises, was part of the mainstream of Indian culture, neither of these intensely important *dramatic* forces had anything to do with the shaping of Southeast Asian drama. The amazing fact appears to be that it was the Indian epic which became the handmaiden of Southeast Asian drama.

Hinayana (or Theravada) Buddhism was also exported from India during this period. By at least A.D. 500, Hinayana Buddhism was firmly established in Burma. From Burma, from south India, and especially from Ceylon, Hinayana Buddhism spread eastward. The religion was proselytized directly to the people by traveling monks. This was quite unlike Brahmanism, which in its glorification of the god-king was essentially a religion of the ruling classes. Eventually Hinayana Buddhism replaced Brahmanism as the official religion in Burma, Thailand, Laos, and Cambodia (except that a few Brahman priests were retained at court). Buddhist missionaries brought with them the Pali script, *sutras* (prayers), and the Buddhist canon. The latter included *Jataka,* or Buddhist Birth Stories. These are 547 miscellaneous moral tales. Some are animal stories, like Aesop's *Fables.* Some are folktales of very ancient origin, dating from before the time of Buddha, which were only later incorporated into Buddhist literature in the form of *Jataka* stories. *Jatakas* became more widely known than the *Ramayana* among the peasantry in Hinayana Buddhist countries and eventually served as subject matter for court poets. So important were the *Jatakas* that, for example, they formed "the central core of all the Buddhist literature of Laos."[17] Many of these *Jatakas* came to be dramatized, especially as folk and popular drama. The story of *Sang Thong* is equally popular on Burmese, Thai, and Cambodian stages. *Rothasen* is a Thai play based on a *Jataka* in the famous collection known as the Fifty Jataka (*Pannasa Jataka*). *Sin Xai* is a Lao dramatization of a well-known birth story of the same name.

Perhaps the most widely dramatized of all *Jataka* is *Manora.*[18]

[23]

It is performed throughout Burma, Thailand, Laos, and Cambodia and is also known in Indonesia and Malaysia. It is a wistful tale. Manora is the youngest of seven lovely daughters of the king of the *kinnara,* a mythical race of bird people. One day when she and her sisters are bathing in a mountain lake, a hunter sees them. Struck by Manora's beauty, he steals her wings and tail. The sisters fly away when they see the hunter, but Manora cannot, and the hunter takes her to the palace of his king. There she meets the crown prince and in due time they fall in love and marry. Soon the prince is sent off to war. A minister, who hates Manora, advises the king that she must be burned in order to save the king's life. She is ordered burned and, as the flames rise around her, she asks to have her wings and tail returned. Receiving them, she miraculously ascends from the flames into the heavens. The prince eventually returns from the wars and, finding Manora gone, sets out to look for her. He struggles against all manner of obstacles for seven years, seven months, and seven days, until he achieves what no mortal ever has: he reaches the kinnara kingdom located on the summit of the Himalayas. Here he is reunited with Manora and they live happily ever after.[19] *Manora* is traditionally performed by *lakon jatri* folk-players in Thailand. The complete story cycle there requires twelve performances. In Burma the story is called *Dwemenaw* and court performances have been known to last three nights.[20] As with all *Jataka* stories, *Manora's* connection with Buddhism lies in a concluding verse which tells the audience that the hero, the prince in this case, is in reality the Buddha in one of his previous lives.

Mahayana Buddhism (or Great Vehicle) was brought to Southeast Asia from India at about the same time as Hindu Brahmanism and Hinayana Buddhism. It came to be the dominant religion in Java in the ninth century (the Borobudur is a Mahayana Buddhist monument) and in Cambodia in the twelfth century (the huge stone faces staring down from the towers of the Bayon represent Lokeshivara, the compassionate Future Buddha). Mahayana Buddhism is part of the living religion of Bali today, mixed, of course, with Hindu and Balinese elements. However, I cannot identify any specific influence which Mahayana Buddhism has had upon the theatre of Southeast Asia.

Possibly the most pervasive of all Indian influences on Southeast Asian theatre was dance. From one end of Southeast Asia to the other—everywhere except in northern Vietnam and in the Philippines—dance forms can be seen which, in all their variety, share a recognizable common basis in Indian dance. The essential "Indianness" of these dance forms is seen in the turned-out knees, the set finger positions, the angular break of the elbows, and the famous horizontal sliding movement of the head. One of the earliest records of Indian influence in Southeast Asia tells of a "present of musicians and products of his country" which the Brahmanic king of Funan sent to the Chinese emperor in the year A.D. 243.[21] There is every reason to believe there were dancers as well as musicians at the court of Funan in the third century. In Java on the reliefs of the Borobudur (ca. 800) and the Hindu Prambanan temples (ca. 915) are numerous scenes of dancing girls, musicians playing flutes, zithers, brass and bamboo xylophones, horns, conchs, and cymbals, and watching spectators. Indian-derived dance was undoubtedly known several centuries before this in the Javanese courts. Dances of this period, though created around characters taken from the Indian epics, were not yet extended dramatic dances. They mainly told a brief episode in dance form. It was not until perhaps the thirteenth century that full-fledged dance-dramas were created on Java and Bali, and it was even later that this occurred in Thailand and then in Cambodia.

From around 1000 onward, the performing arts fell into decline in India. Classical dance, as described in the *Natya Sastra,* virtually disappeared in its homeland, and it was not resurrected until the twentieth century. Sanskrit drama ceased to be performed and, like Greek tragedy, the original style of performance was irretrievably lost. Hereafter, India contributed nothing further to the development of theatre in Southeast Asia. But in the region during the next few centuries dance, music, and drama flourished at the courts of princes and kings and as folk art among the people. Indian influences were by now largely assimilated and incorporated into national, and in some cases regional, styles of performance. On the one hand, these styles of performance tended to develop in different directions because of differences in national culture. On the other hand, there was a

[25]

great deal of contact between the courts of this period so that the theatre of one country often influenced that of another. For example, when Jayavarman II, who was raised at the Javanese court and may even have been of Javanese blood, founded the Khmer empire in the first half of the ninth century, he brought with him to Cambodia Javanese artists as well as priests and court officials. Javanese influence is clearly seen in the temples Jayavarman had built in Cambodia[22] and even today the Cambodians say, "it was in fact Java that provided the great inspiration for Cambodian dancing and drama, in spite of themes borrowed from other sources."[23] Centuries later, from around the fourteenth century on, the Javanese story about Prince Panji became popular in almost all the royal courts of Southeast Asia. Numerous plays recounting the adventures of the prince (often called Inao, rather than Panji, outside of Java) found their way onto stages in Burma, Cambodia, Laos, Thailand, and Malaya.

One of the most far-reaching exchanges of theatre art between countries in Southeast Asia took place between the fourteenth and the eighteenth centuries during the bloody wars that raged back and forth across the central part of the mainland peninsula as the Thai, Khmer, and Burmese kingdoms alternately tried to annihilate each other. During the warfare, Khmer theatre forms were first exported to Laos, then expropriated by the Thai, and finally found their way to Burma. The carnage was appalling, but the theatrical story makes fascinating telling. For centuries Thai and Khmer had been struggling for supremacy. Gradually the Thai gained the upper hand. In 1353, a Lao prince named Fa Ngoun, who had been raised at the Khmer court at Angkor, was sent north into Laos to establish a loyal kingdom on the Khmer northern flank. Fa Ngoun married a Khmer princess and, taking a complete retinue from the court, he set up a Khmer-style kingdom at Luang Prabang. He introduced writing, he introduced Buddhism, and he introduced Khmer court music, dancing, and drama. In 1431 the long struggle between the Thai and Khmer ended when the Thai sacked the magnificent Khmer capital at Angkor. As was the custom, the Thai victors carried off into slavery much of the population. The entire court was carted off to the Thai capital at Ayudhya, including ministers, priests, the king's harem of mistresses and dancing girls, poets, musicians, and actors. The beginning of classical Thai dance-drama dates from this conquest.

For the next few hundred years Thai and Burmese armies periodically set out to destroy each other's capitals, and eventually the Burmese succeeded. The Thai capital fell to a victorious Burmese army in 1767. Again, as was the custom, thousands of people in the conquered city were carried off into slavery, including, again, the entire court. Htin Aung tells us that, though the Burmese were the victors, they had only admiration for the more advanced art of their Thai captives. Almost immediately, Thai nobles staged performances of the *Ramayana* at the Burmese court at Ava, where they were held captive, and soon they were training professional actors to perform in Thai style. Within a few years Thai versions of the *Ramayana* and Javanese *Panji* stories became the accepted standards for theatrical performance at the Burmese court. At first the Thai captives, who looked on the Burmese as barbarians, prevented any departure from Thai theatre traditions, but gradually the Burmese introduced their own ideas; in seventy to eighty years an independent Burmese court drama developed.[24]

As a postscript to this tale, in the eighteenth and nineteenth centuries Thai performers moved back to the Cambodian court where they revived the very Cambodian theatre arts their ancestors had sent to oblivion six centuries before when they sacked Angkor. The Royal Cambodian Ballet of today is actually a reimportation of ancient Khmer dance, as modified by some twenty generations of Thai court artists.

THE PERIOD OF CHINESE AND ISLAMIC INFLUENCE

From around 1300 to around 1750 Southeast Asian theatre was influenced by two new cultural invasions, one from China to the north and one from Islamic countries to the west. It was more or less coincidental that, at the same time Kublai Khan was conquering northern Vietnam (Tonkin) and the southern Chinese province of Nanchao, forcing Thai-speaking peoples to flee southward into Burma, Thailand, and Laos, Moslem Indians began the conversion to Islam of most of the peoples of Malaysia and Indonesia. Interestingly enough there is almost no overlap of these two cultural influences in Southeast Asia: Chinese influence remained restricted to the northern tier of countries, Islamic influence to the south.

Chinese annals dating back to the Han dynasty are filled with references to the exchange of missions with countries in Southeast Asia. The first such reference, dated around 100 B.C., tells of tribute sent to the emperor from "a number of large and populous islands" to the south.[25] Although China maintained regular contact with the countries to the south for the next thousand years, Chinese cultural influence in Southeast Asia was minuscule compared to that of India. But in the thirteenth century Mongol China began expanding southward by military conquest. In 1285 and 1287 the Mongols conquered Hanoi in northern Vietnam. In 1287 the grandson of Kublai Khan, Timur Khan, occupied Pagan, the capital of Burma. Kublai Khan himself, in 1253, had brought about the conquest of Nanchao with the result that by 1287 a Thai kingdom at Sukhotai had displaced the Khmer as rulers of central Thailand.

In one way or another Chinese performing arts entered Southeast Asia at this time. Throughout Burma, Thailand, Laos, and Cambodia one sees Chinese musical instruments, especially the two-stringed fiddle (*hu chin*), the moon lute, and the cymbal. Chinese stories are well-known and often staged. Court drama, in the Hindu-Javanese-Cambodian tradition, was largely unaffected, but popular theatre came to draw on both the Indian and the Chinese traditions from this period on. As far as we know Chinese drama per se was not introduced into Burma, Thailand, Laos, or Cambodia at this time.

In Vietnam the case was different. Northern Vietnam (Tonkin and part of Annam) had been ruled as an integral part of the Chinese empire for nine hundred years, from A.D. 40 to 939. During this long period of foreign rule the Vietnamese retained their essential national identity while they adopted from the Chinese Mahayana Buddhism, the ethical system of Confucianism, Chinese writing, and Chinese civil government with its elaborate mechanism of education in the classics, civil service examinations, and bureaucracy by the *mandarin*. Several times the Vietnamese gained their independence only to lose it again.

According to legend, Chinese theatre was introduced into Vietnam between 1010 and 1225 and again between 1225 and 1400. Spoken drama was introduced the first time and an early form of classic opera the second. Classic Vietnamese opera is supposed to have been copied directly from Chinese opera of the thirteenth century. In later centuries more developed forms of Chinese opera also found their way into Vietnam, and elements of these more sophisticated opera forms were incorporated into Vietnamese opera. The stylized makeup of present-day Vietnamese opera, for example, is based on Chinese models which did not evolve in China until around the eighteenth century. Once introduced, Chinese opera was adapted and modified to meet Vietnamese tastes: plays were translated into the Vietnamese language and Vietnamese melodies were added. Vietnamese emperors maintained large theatrical troupes at court. When the Vietnamese moved southward, driving first the Cham from central Vietnam (Annam) and the Khmer from southern Vietnam (Cochin China), they took their opera with them. By the eighteenth century, Chinese influence on theatre, via Vietnamese opera, was predominant throughout all of Vietnam.

The second major cultural influx during this period came from Islamic countries to the west. From time immemorial Arab traders had sailed the waters between the Red Sea and the coast of China and small colonies of Arabs had lived in coastal cities of Southeast Asia. Between the seventh and tenth centuries these Arab traders adopted the Islamic religion, but they in turn did not convert native communities around them. This was accomplished by Moslem Indians. As Harrison says:

> The acceptance of Islam among the islands and in the Malay Peninsula had . . . to await its acceptance by Indians who were prominently engaged in the overseas trade between India and Southeast Asia. It was not until the thirteenth century that this condition was fulfilled, when Islam began to entrench itself in north-west and north-east India under the rule of the Turkish sultanate of Delhi; and it was mainly from Gujerat (south of Sind), and by the Moslem mercantile community of its port of Cambay, that Islam was then transplanted.[26]

It is readily understandable that Indianized rulers of Southeast Asian states, who had looked to Indian civilization for so much in the past, would accept India's new religion as well. Marco Polo's description of the Islamic community of Perlak in northern Sumatra, written in 1292, is the first account we have of Islam in Southeast Asia. Within five years neighboring Samudra and Pasai had become Moslem, with their rulers styling themselves "sultans." In the early fifteenth century the important state of Malacca on the Malay Peninsula was converted to Islam. Tome Pires' account of this event, written 1512–1515, illustrates what was probably a typical pattern of conversion:

> And some rich Moorish merchants moved from Pasai [Sumatra] to Malacca, Parsis [from India] as well as Bengalis and Arabian Moors . . . and they were very rich, with large businesses and fortunes . . . and they brought with them mollahs and priests learned in the sect of Muhammad . . . Iskandar Shah was pleased with the said Moorish merchants and did them honour, giving them places to live in and a place for their mosques. . . . And there were many Moors and many mollahs who were trying hard to make the king turn Moor . . . At last when he was seventy-two years old, the said King Iskandar Shah turned Moor, with all his house and married the king of Pasai's daughter. And not only did he himself turn Moor, but also in the course of time he made all his people do the same.[27]

Within fifty years Malacca had become a center for Islamic studies, sending missionaries south along the trade routes to the islands of Indonesia. States around Malacca on the Malay Peninsula and even on Sumatra were forced to embrace Islam. On Java the first Islamic state was Demak, converted, it is believed, through the influence of Malacca around 1450. By the end of the fifteenth century the once powerful Hindu-Javanese kingdom of Majapahit was defeated by a coalition of four Moslem kingdoms from Java's north coast. Within another hundred years almost all the people of Malaya, Sumatra, Java, Borneo, the Celebes, the Moluccas (the Spice Islands), West New Guinea, and the southern islands of the Philippines had come to profess Islam as their religion.

It is extremely interesting to note that local populations converted en masse to Islam in pagan areas, such as the southern Philippines, where Islam was clearly a superior religion, and among the Indonesians, the Malays, and the scattered Cham

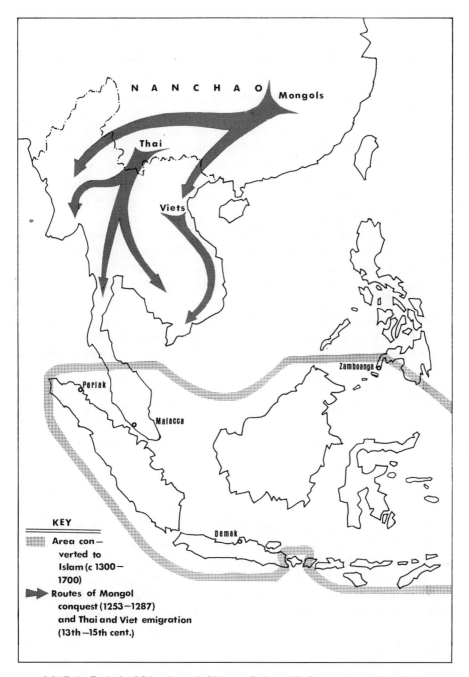

MAP 3. Period of Islamic and Chinese Cultural Influence (ca. 1300–1750)

communities in Vietnam and Cambodia, where ritual Brahmanism, the religion of the ruling classes, had failed to provide the masses with a religion of personal belief. But among the Thai, the Lao, the Cambodians, and Burmese, who were Hinayana Buddhists, Islam gained no more adherents than Christianity was to do in later centuries, because, though large foreign Moslem communities lived in the major cities, local populations saw nothing in Islam that they did not already have in Hinayana Buddhism. Hinayana Buddhism was a personal religion, like Islam, and it engendered in even the illiterate peasant a deep and abiding personal commitment that made the new religion of Islam superfluous.

Islam had two main effects on theatre in Southeast Asia. According to the Second Commandment of Islam, it is a sin to make an image of man, in stone or wood, with paint, or as portrayed in plays or dances. In countries of the Near East, where Islamic doctrine is maintained in its purest form, this prohibition has been strictly observed and from Egypt to Afghanistan the Moslem world knows little theatre. When Moslem conquerors subdued most of India, between the eleventh and fourteenth centuries, they destroyed thousands of Hindu temples and tens of thousands of statues of Hindu gods. Hindu dance and drama, already in a decadent state, were violently suppressed as blasphemous by India's new Moslem rulers.

Theatre activity in Malaya and Indonesia was curtailed to a degree under the restrictive influence of Islam. The new Moslem rulers and religious teachers of Java tried to lessen the popularity of such Hindu-imbued theatre forms as the wayang kulit shadow drama, and even today performances are still deeply resented and often forbidden in certain strongly orthodox Moslem areas. But all in all, Islam did not exert the same kind of totally stultifying influence on Southeast Asian theatre that it exerted in India, in Persia, and in its Arabic homeland. One reason for this was that the conversion of Malaya and Indonesia was accomplished by Indians, to whom dance and drama were normal forms of expression, whether in religion they were Buddhist, Hindu, or Moslem.

The second major effect of Islam on the theatre of Southeast Asia was that Arabic, Persian, Mesopotamian, and Egyptian stories were introduced into the region and these soon found their way onto the stage. Classic theatre forms, such as wayang kulit and court dance-dramas, were but little affected by these new stories, but folk and popular theatre troupes avidly dramatized Islamic stories, as much because they were exciting tales as because they were Islamic in content. Winstedt describes the situation in Malaya in the centuries immediately following the conversion of Malacca to Islam:

> The Malay world became flooded by romances from the Deccan that, still full of Hindu mythology and tags from the Panji tales, were compact of the Hinduized folk-lore of Muslim India, reminiscences from Persian tales like the story of Amir Hamza, allusions to the heroes of the Shah-Namah like Kobad, Jamshid and Bahram, incidents from the Alexander [the Great] legend, references to Baghdad, Madinah, Egypt and Byzantium, and even expositions of Sufi [Islamic] mysticism. . . . A romance like that of Alexander could hold Malays spell-bound. The valley of the ants, the giraffe-riders, the cave-dwellers with one foot and one eye . . . the great flies that stoned his troops and were only driven away when one of their number was caught saddled and mounted by a puppet rider; the angels, who pierced with lances the devils that dwelt in Coptic idols . . . Gog and Magog; the diamond mines of Ophir and the copper walls of Jabalqa; the riding on mares into the land of darkness and the visit to the spring of life—these and other episodes provided the Malay with what Europe found in the Odyssey, Marco Polo, Robinson Crusoe and Jules Verne.[28]

This "hotchpotch" of tales, as Winstedt calls it, provided new dramatic material not only for Javanese, Sundanese, and Malayan popular theatre troupes; as the tales became known in Thailand, Laos, and Cambodia, bits and pieces of this Islamic literature found their way onto the popular stage of the mainland as well, minus, of course, much of the religious content of the stories as done in Malaya and Indonesia.

One of the few peoples in Indonesia or Malaya who did not accept Islam were the Balinese. When Hindu Majapahit fell to Islamic conquerors in the fifteenth century, many Javanese courtiers moved to Bali, which nominally was under Majapahit suzerainty at that time. The Balinese withstood all later Islamic attempts to subdue or convert them, and Bali today remains the one area in the world outside India where Hinduism is a living religion.* It was not until 1906 that Bali was subdued by the Dutch and incorporated into the Netherlands East Indies. In the intervening five hundred years the Balinese developed sophisticated dance forms and drama in relative isolation from outside influences that are still, in the mid-twentieth century, a marvel to behold. Performing arts flowered on Bali under a unique set of social, religious, political, and economic conditions which are too complex to go into in detail here.† But it is important to note that both indigenous Balinese folk culture and imported Hindu-Javanese court culture contributed to the formation of the dance and drama forms known on Bali today. Until World War II every Balinese prince had his group of dancers. The dancers were peasants, chosen by the prince for their artistic abilities and trained by him at his palace. The performed not only for the prince's pleasure but for communal festivals and on religious occasions. All the people of the community attended these performances and therefore knew what "court style" dance was. Dance groups supported by villages performed at these same festivals and religious occasions, so that folk and court art forms were in close contact and constantly influenced each other. When Indonesia became a republic in 1945, the princes of Bali lost their political power and with it the economic capacity to support dance troupes. Today most performances are given by either "popular" commercial troupes, like *ardja*, or by folk performers, as with most *barong* or *wayang wong*.

THE PERIOD OF WESTERN INFLUENCE

After Marco Polo, who traveled through Southeast Asia in the thirteenth century on his way back to Venice from China, the next European visitors to this part of the world were the Portuguese. They entered the Indian Ocean by ship, forced open a trading settlement at Goa on the west Indian coast, and by the sixteenth century had captured Malacca on the Malay Peninsula. In the next three hundred years Spanish, Dutch, Eng-

---

*Balinese religion is very complex, being a syncretism of Hinduism, Buddhism, and local Balinese animism. The Hindu element is pronounced, however.

†Of the many books written on Bali, two are essential to anyone interested in Balinese performing arts: *The Island of Bali* by Miguel Covarrubias, for an account of the role of theatre in Balinese life, and *Dance and Drama in Bali* by Beryl de Zoete and Walter Spies, for an encyclopedic description of theatre forms.

19. Statue of Ravana in the Royal
Palace, Bangkok, Thailand, is a replica
of a dancer in khon mask and costume.

20. Rama and Sita from the *Ramayana* as danced in Javanese court wayang orang.

21. Hat boi performed in traditional Chinese-derived costumes and make-up in Vietnam.

22. Puppeteer in Java moving the hand of an ogre king in a *Mahabharata* play performed in wayang kulit.

23. H.R.H. Princess Buppha Dévi (in foreground) and other dancers of the
Royal Cambodian Ballet performing in Paris.

24. Ravana (center) attacks Prince Rama, standing on Hanoman's shoulders, in a Thai khon play.

25. An episode from the *Ramayana* in a lavish outdoor khon performance in Thailand.

26. Each week court artists air one of the many sets of wayang kulit puppets
owned by Sultan Hamengku Buwono of Jogjakarta, Java.

27. A battle pose of Gatutkatja and the ogre Sekipu in a Javanese wayang orang dance-play is similar to that of Rama and Ravana in khon.

lish, French, and Americans came in behalf of their own interests. Merchants came seeking fortunes in the spice or textile trade. Missionaries and priests (among them Francis Xavier) came to convert the "benighted heathen" to Christianity and to halt the spread of hated Islam. Politicians, bearing the "white man's burden," came to bring civilization and enlightened rule to peoples who for centuries had known only the despotic oppression of oriental potentates. The military came, to "pacify" the natives, to expand the overseas empires of their homelands, and, wherever possible, to make names and fortunes for themselves. However complex the reasons may have been for Western expansion into Southeast Asia, the end result was simple. By the close of the nineteenth century the region was a political colony of the West: the Dutch ruled Indonesia (the Netherlands East Indies); the British, Malaya and Burma; the French, Vietnam, Cambodia, and Laos (as French Indochina); and the United States replaced Spain as master of the Philippines. Only Thailand retained its political independence; it did not, however, escape Western cultural influence.

The impact of the West was felt on the theatre of every country of Southeast Asia, including Thailand. One of the most disastrous consequences was that court theatre declined everywhere. In part the decline was due to economic factors. Royal budgets were reduced drastically by the new colonial governments, and local kings and princes suddenly found they no longer possessed the financial resources to support lavish court entertainments. In part the decline reflected new cultural and political attitudes. As a ruler's power declined so did the prestige of his traditional court entertainments; as Western power increased so did the prestige of Western knowledge and Western forms of activity. Interest in traditional arts came to be viewed as old-fashioned. In former times accomplishment in the arts was one of the surest ways by which an aspiring courtier could win favor in the eyes of a sovereign. Now one had to learn to speak French, or Dutch, or English to rise in the new colonial governments, and the young man who could discourse knowingly with his new masters about Western political institutions or international trading policies or the wonders of the steam engine was marked as a man with a future.

In Burma traditional court drama declined and eventually ceased to be performed at all. Between 1826, when Rangoon was captured by the British, and 1885, when the last remnants of the Burmese court at Mandalay were wiped out, Burmese court drama simply passed into oblivion. At the end of the nineteenth century the Vietnamese emperor maintained at his palace in Hue a theatre troupe of three hundred actors and musicians; this dwindled in size during the years leading up to World War II until now, with the abolition of the monarchy, royal support for theatre is no more. Without court support performances of Vietnamese opera in its classic form have almost ceased. The Thai royal family managed to support four excellent dance-drama troupes down through the 1930's, but even in independent Thailand the monarchy found these troupes too expensive to maintain, and one by one they were disbanded in the years preceding World War II. The Dutch in Indonesia kept in power eight or nine Balinese princes and on Java the Sultan and Pakualam of Jogjakarta and the Sunan and Mangkunagara of Surakarta, rulers who extended court patronage to wayang puppeteers, musicians, and dancers through the depression years. But following the establishment of the Republic of Indonesia in 1945, these hereditary princes and sultans lost their political power (except for the Sultan of Jogjakarta) and, even more important, they became virtual paupers so that supporting artists was impossible. The last great court-sponsored dance-drama in Indonesia was performed in Jogjakarta in 1939, a generation ago; it is unlikely there will ever be another.

Southeast Asian rulers were mere figureheads for colonial administrations in the eighteenth and nineteenth centuries, and either purposely or unconsciously they looked to classic theatre for solace. On stage they could see their great ancestors consorting with the gods and wielding an absolute power which they themselves would never know but undoubtedly dreamed of one day recapturing from their foreign masters. Certainly most local rulers did their utmost to keep court theatre alive during the period of European colonial rule, though in every country except Cambodia and Laos their attempts eventually failed.

Further, most court theatre forms ceased to develop any further as art by the end of the colonial period. In Bali and in the courts of central Java, fresh artistic impulses continued to vitalize dance and dance-drama through the period of Dutch rule right down to the beginning of World War II, but this was an exception. With other court forms—wayang kulit shadow drama in Indonesia and Malaya, *hat boi* in Vietnam, Royal Ballet in Cambodia and Laos, *khon* masked-pantomime and *nang yai* shadow theatre in Thailand—Western economic pressures and native indifference spelled an end to further artistic growth. They fossilized as "classics" and, like the temples of Angkor in Cambodia, Pagan in Burma, and Borobudur and Prambanan in Java, they came to represent a glorious past, not the living present.

Perhaps the most significant new development took place in "popular" theatre during this period. Popular theatre troupes, troupes which performed commercially in public, had been known for a long time in Thailand, Vietnam, and Java. During the first half of the twentieth century, this type of theatre developed rapidly in every country in Southeast Asia, with the exception of the Philippines. New genres emerged and the number of troupes greatly increased. I do not think it mere coincidence that the growth of popular theatre occurred during the time of Western political control. I suggest that the impact of the West, as seen in the emergence of nationalist thought, belief in social reform and democracy, and the growth of urban centers, contributed to its rise. Nationalism is a common thread that runs through much popular drama. Popular plays were often banned by the authorities for expressing anti-colonial ideology (a charge not likely to have been made against a play of a court genre). Plays often openly advocated democratic sentiments or dramatized social problems, reflecting late nineteenth- and early twentieth-century Western political and social liberal philosophy. Due to a great expansion of trade brought about by Western rule, cities grew in size and in importance, the middle class expanded, and more money came into circulation, bringing into being for the first time in Southeast Asia a large and growing popular audience with cash to spend on the theatre.

Theatre in Southeast Asia is only slightly indebted to live theatre of the West, though this may seem strange in view of the enormous over-all impact of Western culture in the area. Third-rate English troupes often came to Singapore and Rangoon, after playing first in India. French troupes played in a few of the major cities of Indochina. Most of these troupes alternated a few tired classics with popular music-hall revues. The practice of playing in an enclosed theatre building, in order to control admission to a play to holders of tickets, first appears in Burma in 1870, where the idea was borrowed from the English.[29] Wing and drop scenery was first seen in Rangoon in 1899, copied from Chinese troupes, who in turn most likely picked up this nineteenth-century staging practice in Singapore or Hong Kong from English troupes. Popular Malayan troupes, working out of Singapore, brought drop-and-wing scenic techniques into Indonesia on their tours through Java and possibly into Thailand as well. One of the great "reforms" instituted in Vietnam by popular theatre troupes was the introduction of scenery. By the first quarter of this century canvas drops and wings had become standard in Southeast Asian popular theatre. However, Western drama per se had virtually no impact upon existing theatre forms, for those who performed professional theatre in Southeast Asia were not exposed in any systematic fashion to staged Western drama, though Western motion pictures have come to exert considerable influence on live theatre in recent years.

Western dramatic literature was avidly read by those in intellectual circles. Scholars became expert in the works of Shakespeare, Racine, and Sophocles. Little-theatre societies sprang up in almost every country, dedicated to introducing Western-style "spoken" drama. These groups were composed of intelligentsia and the audiences they reached were small. In general, in the years up to World War II they were not very successful, even within their own coteries, and they exerted only the most peripheral influence on the mainstream of theatrical activity. An important spurt of interest in Western-inspired spoken drama occurred immediately after the end of World War II. Professional troupes tried to establish themselves in Indonesia, Thailand, Vietnam, and the Philippines; but audiences still did not respond. Modern plays, which these troupes performed, were done better by the movies and, as national radio, motion picture, and television enterprises blossomed after the war, the artists working in the modern theatre movement suddenly found themselves highly sought after. Most good actors, writers, and directors deserted the young modern theatre movement, almost as quickly as they had flocked to it, to take relatively secure, high-paying jobs with the mass media. Today, a few professional *kich* troupes try to present straight spoken-drama in Vietnam, and in the Philippines there is quite a bit of amateur theatre based on Western models. All in all, however, Western drama still has found very little acceptance. Nothing describes it better than to call it the "non-popular" theatre of Southeast Asia.

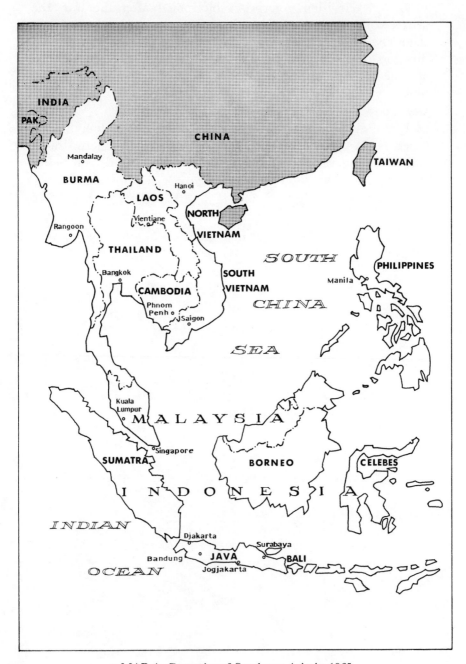

MAP 4. Countries of Southeast Asia in 1965

CHAPTER 3

The Development of Theatre Genres

It is true that widely diffused and powerful influences from outside the geographical area of Southeast Asia—from India, from
China, from Islamic countries, from the West—have left their
imprint on the theatre of Southeast Asia. And it is true that
within Southeast Asia, theatre of one country has often crossed
national boundaries to influence the theatre of neighboring
countries. But it is also true that in the various countries of
Southeast Asia theatre has evolved in different directions in response to local conditions and forces. In this evolutionary process
many separate genres of theatre have come into being. There are
over a dozen theatre forms in Indonesia and in Thailand, countries where the theatre arts are highly developed. Normally the
distinction between types of theatre is clear-cut and well understood by local audiences, and each is known by a specific, local
name. Except in rare cases, any one theatre troupe will perform
plays of a single type only, unlike Western troupes which often
pride themselves on being able to perform Shakespeare one night
and Sophocles the next. Therefore, a discussion of the development of theatre necessarily turns out to be a discussion of the
development of specific genres of theatre.

INDONESIA

Among the more than two thousand islands of Indonesia,
theatre has developed mainly in three places: in the "Javanese"
part of Java (Javanese-speaking central and east Java), in the

Sundanese part of Java (Sundanese-speaking west Java), and in
Bali. Theatre forms in each area are different enough to warrant
separate consideration.

JAVA

From this point on I shall use the term "Java" to mean the
Javanese-speaking cultural area of the island, rather than the
island itself. The earliest forms of Javanese theatre that we know
of are *wayang kulit* (shadow drama), *wayang beber* (paper-scroll
play), and *wayang topeng,* or just *topeng* (masked dance). They
crystallized into definite genres during the thousand years when
Indian cultural influence was strong in Java, but it is almost
certain the origins of all go back to animistic times.

The origin of wayang kulit has long been the subject of con-
troversy. Three main theories have been proposed. Hazeu argues
for Javanese origin, pointing out that, because all technical
terms used for wayang kulit are Old Javanese, because wayang
performances were common and highly developed perhaps many
centuries before A.D. 1000, and because wayang play structure is
unique among Asian drama, shadow theatre must be an indigenous Javanese art.[1] A second theory postulates Indian origin,
and is supported by some evidence that a shadow puppet theatre
was known in ancient India. If such a play form was known, it
seems reasonable to expect that it was introduced into Java
along with other elements of Indian culture. Similarities between
the misshapen clown (*vidusaka*) of Sanskirt drama and the dwarf-
clown Semar in wayang have also been noted. A third theory is
that China was the place of origin for all Asian shadow theatre.
This theory has been less popular than the other two and it has
not been formulated in much detail. Laufer, while not proposing
the Chinese origin of wayang, suggests that animism was the
basis for Chinese shadow theatre. He mentions the legend that
in 121 B.C. an image of the emperor's dead wife was cast on a
screen by means of a shadow puppet, concluding that, "shadow
figures, indeed, were the shadows or souls of the departed summoned back to the world. . . . this conception of ancestors as
shadow-souls is so characteristically Chinese, that it goes far to
prove the priority of this performance in China."[2] This is precisely what Rassers says about wayang in Java: the shadows

represent the spirits of tribal ancestors, and by producing the shadows on a screen the priest-puppeteer enables the living to communicate with their magically endowed ancestors.[3] If shadow drama in Asia did grow out of animistic rituals of ancestor worship, China, or at least central Asia, could well have been its original home.

However, regardless of whether the invention of shadow theatre is credited to the Chinese, the Indians, or the Javanese, wayang kulit developed in its maturity into a purely Javanese phenomenon which has no true counterpart in either India or China. Javanese court literature of the eleventh and twelfth centuries contains numerous accounts of performances of wayang kulit. Non-jointed puppets were manipulated by the chief performer, the *dalang,* who told a story to the accompaniment of several instruments, including some that are part of the present-day gamelan ensemble. Wayang was well-established and performances were evidentally common at court. Poets used wayang in poetic allusion, one writing, "though the shadows seem real, they are, like the sensuous pleasures people thirst for, only magic hallucinations."[4] Even at this early date shadow plays had reached a high degree of sophistication for it is recorded that audiences were moved to tears at the portrayal of sad scenes. The kings of this period patronized wayang kulit. They commissioned artists to cut new sets of puppets; they included dalang in their retinues; they commanded that performances be given in court; and some became dalang themselves. Wayang was also widely performed in public on religious occasions so that knowledge of wayang became widespread among all classes in Java.

Puppets evolved into their present form between the thirteenth and the seventeenth centuries. First, colored paint and gilt were added. Then costumes were delineated in detail, puppet figures were made larger, and the interior of the figures came to be incised with elaborate cutout designs. Animal figures were created, many new types of ogres (*rasaksa* or *buta*) were invented, and, according to tradition, movable arms were added in 1630 at the central Javanese court of Mataram.[5] A standard set of puppets consisted of about four hundred figures in the eighteenth century. By the nineteenth century the standard shape, size, design, and coloring of all important puppet figures had become fixed.

According to tradition, the unique, highly stylized shape of wayang puppets is due to Islamic influence. The Javanese say the Moslem Sultan of Demak, who passionately loved wayang kulit, ordered a puppet set cut in nonrealistic manner in order to evade the religious proscription forbidding the representation of the human form, thus setting the basic wayang shape as we know it. This is supposed to have occurred in the fifteenth century, shortly after the arrival of Islam in Java.

Some of the plays performed in wayang kulit relate pre-Hindu animistic stories. *Murwakala* is one of these. It tells how wayang kulit and the gamelan were created by the Great Teacher (Batara Guru), so that through the medium of ritual wayang performances certain evil occurrences could be prevented. The great majority of plays, however, concern gods, demigods, and mythological Javanese kings who appear in the *Mahabharata* and the *Ramayana*.

A number of other puppet forms grew out of wayang kulit. According to legend, the Sunan of Giri is supposed to have created *wayang gedog* in 1553 and the Sunan of Kudus *wayang golek* in 1584. In wayang gedog, shadow puppets tell the *Panji* cycle of stories; and in Javanese wayang golek, doll-figures (golek means doll) are manipulated to tell stories of the *Menak* cycle which center on the exploits of the Islamic hero Amir Hamzah.[6] Many other forms were made—*wayang madya* (leather puppets and stories about the kings of east Java), *wayang klitik* or *krutjil* (flat wooden puppets and stories about Damar Wulan of Majapahit), *wayang tengul* (leather puppets for Amir Hamzah stories), *wayang Djawa* (leather puppets for stories about Prince Diponegoro who rebelled against Dutch rule in the nineteenth century), and others. It was common practice for a Javanese ruler to order a puppet set made just to tell the story of the glorious reign of his ancestors. Among all these puppet forms only wayang kulit and wayang golek have ever been popular (in fact, most other forms have never been seen outside of court). Wayang kulit is the most widely performed theatre genre in all of Southeast Asia, while wayang golek is regularly performed in the south-central part of Java.

In our generation two new wayang puppet forms have been created. Like many other "spin-off" wayang forms before them, they were created to communicate a new message through new characters. *Wayang Pantja Sila* was created in the aftermath of President Soekarno's proclamation of the doctrine of Pantja Sila as the spiritual foundation of the new Indonesian Republic. The five major puppets in the drama symbolically represent the five principles of the Pantja Sila. In 1947, *wayang suluh* was created to tell stories about modern Indonesia. Shadow puppets represent Nasser, Tito, Nehru, Soekarno, and other contemporary figures in realistic fashion. Since wayang suluh's inception, performances have been encouraged and supported by the Indonesian government through its Ministry of Information.

The second early type of Javanese theatre, one of the simplest known anywhere in the world, is wayang beber. It is similar to wayang kulit in that a dalang tells a story to musical accompaniment; but, while the wayang kulit dalang manipulates leather puppets before a lamp so as to cast shadows on a screen, the wayang beber dalang illustrates his story by unrolling long paper picture scrolls.

Wayang beber is as old as wayang kulit, and may be older. There are many references to it in early Javanese writings. It may be that wayang beber originally was closely connected with animistic rites of ancestor worship, but that as wayang kulit became more sophisticated and highly developed as an art form and as it supplanted wayang beber as a court entertainment, it also took over many of the religious functions previously performed by wayang beber. In 1630 the ruler of Mataram in central Java forbade the use of wayang beber for performances at animistic *ruwatan* ceremonies, and ordered that only wayang kulit could be the medium of performance.[7] We know little of what happened to wayang beber since that time, but it is seldom performed today. Some scrolls exist, and one or two dalang are still alive, but the art is in such a degenerate state that on the extremely rare occasions when the dalang perform they are unable to match their garbled stories with the picture scrolls they own.[8]

The third type of theatre with probable roots in pre-Indian animistic culture is wayang topeng or masked-dance. Masks are among the common cultural properties of animistic societies in Southeast Asia. According to van Lelyveld, the early Javanese masked dances "laid stress upon magic performances where the spirits of the dead were honored; they were a part of the animistic ritual of the primitive Javanese and are therefore very ancient."[9] As wayang topeng is performed nowadays, two or three masked performers dance and speak episodes from the *Panji* cycle. This form crystallized when Indian-style dancing was incorporated into an existing masked dance and the resulting dance was used to tell *Panji* stories. This must have occurred after the fourteenth century when the *Panji* stories were composed. Topeng came to be known all over Java, in Sunda, and in Bali. It was danced at court and by villagers as a folk-dance. It was particularly popular in east Java, but when the center of Javanese court life shifted to central Java in the eighteenth century, different arts came to be favored. The influence of topeng on other forms of Indonesian theatre is slight, though wayang golek puppet faces may possibly have been modeled on topeng masks.

Wayang kulit, wayang beber, and wayang topeng were cultivated and developed in the courts of the kings and princes of Java, and at the same time were known and practiced by peasants in the countryside. Favored by sophisticates of the court, these forms still retained ties with village culture from which they originally sprang. *Wayang orang* or Javanese dance-drama, on the other hand, is purely a court creation. To many it is the most perfect form of Javanese court art. Wayang orang grew out of extended dance-dramas which were known in east Javanese courts at least as early as the fourteenth century and in which, it seems, the mythology of previous kingdoms was acted out. They were called *raket*. Even the King of Majapahit sang and danced in raket performances. He is said to have been particularly skillful at extemporizing poetic lyrics as he sang.[10] Schreike notes that raket and other unmasked dramatic dances were often performed in the early seventeenth century in the courts of west Java, Sumatra, and Borneo which, though hundreds and even thousands of miles from Java, were responsive to Javanese court art.[11]

In the eighteenth century, at the central Javanese courts of

28. Victorious in battle, the fearless Bima exultantly performs a victory dance at the conclusion of most plays.

29. Karna and Arjuna fighting with drawn daggers.

30. Irawan romantically carries Titisari off into the garden.

31. Gatutkatja cutting off the head of the ogre Mingkalpa.

32. The clown puppets Gareng and Petruk with Semar, their father, appear in every play.

33. Gatutkatja, Bima, Arjuna, Kresna, and Baladewa in a formal audience scene in wayang kulit.

Surakarta and Jogjakarta, *Ramayana* and *Mahabharata* stories were staged as dance-dramas. Thus wayang orang was born.[12] Wayang orang literally means "human puppet," and that is what the theatre form literally was: wayang kulit plays were set to dance and played on stage by human actors. At first ordinary court dress was worn by the actor-dancers, but in the nineteenth century costumes were made to conform to the style of wayang kulit figures. On special occasions sumptuous performances were given at court by carefully rehearsed troupes made up of male relatives of the ruler and of officials of the court. Court wayang orang reached a peak of sophisticated splendor at the turn of the century in Surakarta, under the lavish patronage of Mangkunagara V.[13] Until 1895, however, wayang orang was scarcely known outside of court circles. In that year a wealthy Chinese businessman, Gan Kam, established the first professional troupe in Surakarta. The troupe prospered, public interest was aroused, and more professional troupes formed. Today there are about twenty major commercial wayang orang troupes in Indonesia supporting themselves through box-office ticket sales. At the courts of Surakarta and Jogjakarta wayang orang fell on hard times during the depression years, and since the war it has ceased to be performed at either court because of lack of funds. In sum, wayang orang reached mature artistic growth as court-supported theatre, but today it exists solely as commercial theatre.

Ketoprak and *ludruk* are products of the twentieth century. In ketoprak we have an instance in which the genesis of a theatre form is known exactly and without qualification. In 1914, R. M. Wreksodiningrat, an official of the court of Pakubuwono IX of Surakarta, noted peasant women singing as they were stamping rice in traditional fashion in a hollow log (*lesung*). The sound and rhythm intrigued him. He brought this lesung to his residence and had it placed in the great hall. Every day he rehearsed with it, absorbing its rhythm. He added tambourine, drums, and flute and began composing music and dances based on the stamping rhythm of the lesung. He called his creation ketoprak, from the word *ketok*, meaning "to knock." He organized private performances in his pavilion; people came to watch and liked what they saw. Others began to perform the dances he had created and invented their own. By 1920 many groups both amateur and professional, had formed to perform ketoprak. It became usual to act and dance stories based on Javanese history and legend. There was a virtual ketoprak craze in the early 1920's. It is reported that there were four to five hundred troupes doing ketoprak in the immediate area of Surakarta and Jogjakarta around 1925. (It is not clear how many troupes were formed specifically to do ketoprak and how many were existing itinerant troupes which merely took over the ketoprak style of playing.) Spoken dialogue came to be emphasized rather than dance in Jogjakarta, while in Surakarta dance remained the predominant element of performance. The Jogjakarta style of performance, called *ketoprak Mataram* after the old Javanese kingdom of Mataram, was adopted by most professional troupes. Around 1927, gamelan instruments were added to the simple musical ensemble and, shortly afterward, Western instruments as well. By the 1930's ketoprak had jelled into a definite genre.[14] In the past decade ketoprak troupes have stopped using Western instruments and gamelan music is now the sole form of musical accompaniment.

Ludruk is an east Javanese creation, as wayang orang and ketoprak are central Javanese creations. Surabaya, the major port city in eastern Java, has always been the center for ludruk activity. The origin of present-day ludruk traditionally is traced back to a folk dance of invulnerability, called *ludruk lerog*. In the seventeenth century this evolved into a magical demonstration of invulnerability performed to the accompaniment of flute, drum, and a small bronze gong. This was called *ludruk bendang*. During the early twentieth century it in turn evolved into *ludruk besutan*. The chief performer, the *besut*, made numerous animistic offerings prior to dancing out the human life cycle, from birth through courtship, marriage, and the assumption of adult work to final self-knowledge.* Down through the 1920's ludruk besutan was a folk art, performed in Surabaya itself and in villages in the Surabaya-Modjokerto area. A performance lasted from ten in the evening until dawn. Since the roles were

---

*It may be that this is another version of what Rassers (*Panji*, p. 112) calls the "totemistic tribe myth" of Java, which he describes as relating "how they [the divine ancestors] are born and grow up, have to endure the pain of initiation, and finally, after much suffering and many vicissitudes marry, and found the great community which is the tribe."

so taxing, men were the only performers. In the 1930's some of these male ludruk besutan actor-dancers began performing adventure stories borrowed from visiting Malayan *bangsawan* troupes which, at that time, performed occasionally in the large cities of Java. During and after the Second World War they formed into professional troupes. They called themselves simply ludruk, and, perhaps because ketoprak troupes had already preempted the repertory of history and adventure plays, began to stage plays depicting modern Javanese life.[15]

Ludruk today is a realistic, spoken drama form. Every performance begins with a traditional dance (*ngremo*) and modern songs and dances may be inserted between scenes, but most plays are contemporary domestic comedies. Gamelan music may be used for background or mood effect. The major connection between today's ludruk and that of the past, is that men still perform all roles. The presence of female impersonators in an otherwise realistic theatre form is an artistic anomaly. Audiences in Java look on ludruk as something of a sexual curiosity for this reason.

One Chinese theatre form is regularly played in Java. This is *po the hi* hand-puppet theatre, known in China as *pu-tai-hi*.[16] It is unclear when po the hi was first performed in Java, but it was probably not before the twentieth century, when large numbers of Chinese immigrated to Java. In po the hi, Chinese stories are performed by Chinese-costumed puppets, but the language the puppets speak is Indonesian. Ironically enough, among Indonesia's many theatre forms, Indonesian, the national language, is spoken *only* in Chinese-derived po the hi.* Twenty to twenty-five po the hi puppet troupes operate in Java nowadays. They live in Surabaya and Semarang, the island's two largest cities, where there are large Chinese communities. These troupes primarily perform for Buddhist temple anniversary celebrations; they never perform in public theatres nor for private occasions.

---

*Young characters in ludruk plays may speak Indonesian rather than Javanese (or Madurese) as an indication of their modernity. Peacock observed certain types of ludruk plays in which Indonesian was spoken about 60 percent of the time and Javanese 40 percent of the time (Peacock, "Class, Clown, and Cosmology in Javanese Drama," p. 16). Over-all, however, Javanese is more commonly spoken in ludruk than Indonesian.

SUNDA

The most important theatre form in west Java, where Sundanese is spoken, is Sundanese wayang golek, in which *Mahabharata* and *Ramayana* stories are played by golek doll-puppets. The Sundanese speak of it as being an extension of wayang kulit, just changed in its outer form. It is said the Sundanese wanted to have daytime wayang performances and since this ruled out shadow plays they set the old stories to a new performance technique. Indonesian experts believe Sundanese wayang golek was created within the past two hundred years. In the early eighteenth century, wayang kulit was introduced into Sunda from Mataram, the most powerful and flourishing kingdom in central Java. In the mid-nineteenth century Sundanese court writers began translating wayang stories from Javanese. Shortly after this Sundanese wayang golek, as it is known today, was created.[17]

Wayang golek came to play much the same role in Sundanese society as wayang kulit did in Javanese society. It was patronized by local rulers, especially at the palace in Tjirebon and in Bandung. It was performed on religious and ceremonial occasions at court and in the smallest villages. The dalang, because he knew the ancient epic stories and because he was considered to have magic power, occupied a respected place in society. In otherwise strongly Islamic west Java, wayang golek has played a vital role in disseminating Brahmanic and animistic beliefs. In recent years, however, the more deeply religious and philosophic plays are performed less frequently. Audiences ask for, and get, plays of simple "entertainment." The female singer (*pesinden*), who often sings current popular songs, largely has supplanted the dalang as the key performer.

Sandiwara is the current name of the popular theatre genre which grew up in west Java during the twentieth century. It has had many names in the course of its brief history. In the 1890's, students at the Teacher's College and the School for Government Officials in Bandung organized amateur theatre troupes which they called *komedie*. They staged plays about contemporary life. Divorce rights, the value of monogamy (a man may have four legal wives in Moslem countries), and the faults of the colonial government were popular themes. In the 1920's some of these troupes became professional. They stopped calling themselves komedie and took, instead, the name *toneel,* meaning "drama" in Dutch. Probably to satisfy popular taste, problem plays dropped out of the repertory, and were replaced by exotic foreign stories called *roman,* borrowed from Malayan bangsawan troupes. Of course the name toneel was not tolerated by the Japanese when they occupied Indonesia during the Second World War. They ordered troupes to call themselves "opera," which is, after all, a good Japanese word. As part of their effort to build nationalist anti-Dutch sentiment among the people, the Japanese encouraged troupes to perform plays of Indonesian history. With the end of the war and the declaration of Indonesia's independence, troupes adopted their present designation as sandiwara, which means simply "play" or "drama" in Indonesian.

Current sandiwara troupes perform plays in several styles. They do *Mahabharata* and *Ramayana* stories in wayang orang style. Javanese wayang orang was introduced to west Java in the 1920's by Sultan Kasapuhan of Tjirebon. Sundanese language, music, and dance style replaced Javanese, but otherwise the theatre form was little changed. A few professional wayang orang troupes played in west Java for a few years, but by 1930 there were no more. Sandiwara troupes also put on Indonesian history plays, without dance, more or less in ketoprak style; and they stage plays based on contemporary life. Prior to the Second World War it was unusual for a sandiwara troupe to perform wayang orang plays. This was partly because, with their large casts and elaborate costumes, these plays were expensive to produce, and partly because audiences at that time did not appreciate this sophisticated form of theatre. Since Indonesian independence, audience interest has increased; most troupe managers try to stage wayang orang plays several times a week, even though it is often difficult to cover expenses.

In the 1920's and 1930's, Malay-speaking bangsawan troupes toured west Java regularly, playing especially in Djakarta (Batavia then), the capital of Indonesia, where Malay was widely spoken.* Most came from Sumatra or from Singapore, where Malay is the local language. These troupes lived a precarious

*Bangsawan is called *stambul* in Indonesia.

existence in Sunda, and many of them folded. Stranded bang-sawan actors joined Sudanese-speaking toneel troupes, thus adding a Malay influence which is still apparent in the sandi-wara of today. Bangsawan troupes do not come to Indonesia anymore, though some exist in Malaysia.

BALI

The theatre arts of Bali have received more attention than those of any other part of Southeast Asia and their fame is justly deserved. The performing arts flourish among the one million Balinese people as nowhere else in the world. You can see performances of all kinds continuously throughout the year, at one village or another, with the heaviest concentration of per-formances coming during the ten-day Balinese New Year. The Balinese perform over a score of different dance, dance-drama, and play forms. These have been written about extensively, and I shall discuss only those which most clearly fall within the defini-tion of drama: wayang kulit, wayang wong, topeng, ardja, and barong.

Although we have no records to tell us what the pre-Hindu Balinese performing arts were like, there must have been in prehistoric times strong local traditions of music, dance, and storytelling closely linked to Balinese animism. These traditions were fertilized by Indian-style dance and literature, introduced to Bali mainly through the intermediary of Javanese court culture. Most of the great works of Hindu-Javanese literature, composed between the eleventh and fifteenth centuries at east and central Javanese courts but long since lost on Java itself, are known to us only through Balinese manuscripts written on *lontar* palm leaves. Through the centuries these precious manuscripts have been preserved or recopied on Bali.

The slow infiltration of Hindu-Javanese artistic impulses into Bali took many centuries, but two peak periods of cultural inter-change occurred in the eleventh century, when Java was ruled by a Balinese prince, Airlangga, and in the sixteenth century, when the last Hindu-Javanese court on Java fled to Bali for refuge following the Islamic conquest of Hindu-Javanese Maja-pahit. Sometime between these two dates, Javanese wayang kulit, wayang orang (wayang wong), and topeng became known on Bali.

Balinese wayang kulit is like its Javanese model in most essentials, but it varies in details. Performances last about four rather than nine hours. The music is simpler. The puppet figures are less finely carved. In the only slightly stylized shape of the Balinese puppets we can see something of what Javanese wayang kulit puppets were probably like five or six centuries ago. A Balinese puppet set consists of sixty or seventy puppets, much fewer than a Javanese set. Most of the stories are from the *Mahabharata,* but the number of *Ramayana* stories performed is greater than on Java. A few of the most important and religiously connected Balinese legends are also performed. This is done by adding a few extra puppet figures. Chief of these purely Balinese stories is *Tjalonarang.* During the reign of King Airlangga, the fields of Bali are being laid waste and its people are being killed because of the evil forces being turned against the country by the witch Tjalonarang. King Airlangga calls on the most learned and magically powerful ascetic in the kingdom, Bharadah, to save the land. Bharadah discovers that Tjalonarang's power comes from secret knowledge gained from an ancient book. The knowledge is good, but Tjalonarang is turning it to evil purposes by doing everything backward. He confronts her, his magical power withstands all her attacks, and in the end he destroys her with a spell, giving her absolution as she dies. The story is animistic and performances are given particularly in times of illness or on magically important days.[18]

Balinese wayang wong is indebted to Javanese dance-drama, but it differs in several important ways from its Javanese namesake, wayang orang. It is essentially a folk art, whereas wayang orang evolved on Java as a court art. De Zoete and Spies say, "the two dance dramas are on an entirely different scale, the one being a court ceremony of the utmost splendour, perfect to the last detail in choreography and costume, rehearsed for years beforehand and involving the expenditure of vast sums of money; whereas . . . [wayang wong] . . . of Bali is a village production, performed in the dust instead of on marble floors, where cheap calicoes mix with splendid *prada* [gold] in the costumes, and a *rakshasa* [ogre] temporarily out of action will lift his mask and

chew tobacco."[19] Masks are used for all but *alus* or refined characters in Balinese wayang wong, whereas masks are seldom used
in wayang orang. Another major difference is that whereas dance
is the overriding element in wayang orang, in Balinese wayang
wong the emphasis is placed on the recitation of long poetic
passages "with practically no action."[20] And, finally, only *Ramayana* stories are performed in wayang wong.*

Topeng in Bali is rather like its Javanese counterpart. The
cast is small, usually two or three dancers, seldom more than
five. All characters are masked, and dance is the chief medium
of expression. But, whereas the Javanese topeng dancer also
speaks dialogue (or can when necessary), the main characters in
Balinese topeng never utter a word. Each has an attendant who
speaks for him. And whereas Javanese topeng draws primarily
on the *Panji* stories for subject matter, Balinese topeng dramatizes stories of Gadja Mada, Prime Minister of Majapahit, and
of King Hayam Wuruk of a later historical period.[21]

In Bali the *Panji* stories are dramatized in another form of
theatre—ardja. Ardja, the most "popular" of the genres, is something like operetta. The story is alternately sung and danced;
there is almost no dialogue, but a lot of clowning around. Pretty
girls play many important roles and in some cases all roles.
Stories are drawn from the *Panji* cycle,† from the *Ramayana* and
the *Mahabharata,* from Javanese romances, and even from Chinese love tales. Accent is on fast-moving action, on plot, and on
sentimentality. Ardja is performed by professional troupes. Ardja
is the only type of theatre in Bali in which a curtain is used to
conceal the performers and through which entrances are made.

The last Balinese dramatic form I will consider is perhaps
the most interesting of all, the barong dance-drama, nicknamed

---

Mahabharata stories are performed as dance-drama in a style similar to wayang
wong called *parwa,* according to De Zoete and Spies (p. 160). The account they give of
parwa does not make it clear whether parwa merely refers to a different type of story
which a wayang wong troupe might do or whether parwa and wayang wong are really
separate genres performed by different troupes.

† The *Panji* stories are also dramatized in the dance-drama form *gambuh,* which De
Zoete and Spies say, "mirrors the costumes, language, and gesture of the great courts
of east Java during the fourteenth century, when they were at the height of their
splendour and of their influence on Bali" (p. 135). Gambuh is practically never seen
nowadays. Its importance lies in the fact that topeng, ardja, and perhaps wayang
wong were influenced by it.

the "trance dance" because in its concluding scene villagers in trance turn their daggers against themselves. They press the sharp blades against their bare chests; with straining muscles, they shout and roll about in the dust in frenzied trance. But the barong is far more than exotic spectacle. Like *Tjalonarang*, the barong play represents in theatrical form the ritual conflict between the malevolent and ever-present forces of evil and the life-preserving forces of good which are believed by the Balinese to constitute the central element of their religious existence. If sickness or calamity occurs in life, it is the result of an imbalance between these two forces. Through performance of the barong dance-drama, a proper balance can be restored. Performance is a religious act itself. In simplest outline, the play shows the witch Rangda struggling to defeat the good Barong (a lion figure probably introduced from China in prehistoric times).* The essential point of the play is that neither good nor evil can destroy the other. This point is clearly illustrated by the villagers in trance: they attempt to kill Rangda, but she uses her magic power to make them turn their blades against themselves; yet she fails in this, for the Barong uses his power to prevent the blades from entering their flesh.

MALAYSIA

The Malay people of the peninsula have much in common with the Javanese, Sundanese, and Balinese. They are all of the same Malay racial stock, all hold similar animistic beliefs, they all spent centuries under Hindu cultural influence, and, except for the Balinese, later accepted Islam. But, where the Javanese, Sundanese, and Balinese have been intensely creative people in the arts, Malay culture has always been, as Winstedt says, "derivative." This is true of theatre. Of the three main Malaysian genres, wayang kulit was borrowed from Java, Chinese opera was transplanted from various regions of south China, and only bangsawan is a Malay creation.

During the thirteenth and fourteenth centuries the Javanese dominated politically and culturally much of what is now Ma-

*See Chapter 5 for a more complete story outline.

laysia. Parts of the peninsula were ruled directly by Majapahit kings of Java. In cities like Malacca, the army was Javanese and the lucrative spice trade was in Javanese hands. Wherever the Javanese went they tried to live as they were accustomed in their homeland. Wealthy merchant-princes brought to Malaya huge retinues of Javanese workers and servants. As late as 1511 a merchant-prince of Malacca kept six thousand Javanese slaves.[22] Among the retinues of the wealthy were gamelan musicians, dancers, and wayang kulit puppeteers. The Portuguese Tome Pires, writing of sixteenth-century Malacca, remarks that the Malays were "fond of mimes after the fashion of Java."[23] The wayang kulit shadow play became widely popular. The *Ramayana* in particular was performed in Malaya, and primarily through the medium of shadow-play performances this epic became as well-known on the Malay Peninsula as in Java or Bali.*

In Malaysia today three kinds of wayang shadow play are distinguished: *wayang djawa,*† *wayang melayu,* and *wayang siam.* The first two are direct adaptations of Javanese wayang kulit. Plays are performed in Malay, not in Javanese, and the form of musical accompaniment varies considerably from the Javanese gamelan ensemble (see Chapter 6), but the basic technique of performance follows Javanese wayang kulit closely and the puppet figures are Javanese in style. The major difference between wayang djawa and wayang melayu is that the puppets of the former have two movable arms and are more highly stylized, while the puppets of the latter normally have but one movable arm and are less stylized, possibly indicating that the figures of wayang djawa were introduced into the Malay Peninsula rather late (after the seventeenth century), and that wayang melayu figures represent an earlier style of Javanese puppet, perhaps of pre-Islamic times. In addition to *Mahabharata* and *Ramayana* plays from the wayang kulit repertory, *Panji* plays from the Javanese wayang gedog repertory and even Islamic plays about

*Winstedt says Javanese versions of both epics were translated into Malayan, the *Baratayuda* (the final section of the *Mahabharata*) in the twelfth or thirteenth century and the *Ramayana* somewhat later (p. 140). Apparently these written versions did not serve as the basis for Malayan wayang performances, however.

†In Java wayang Djawa means "wayang of Javanese history"; in Malaysia wayang djawa means "Javanese wayang." The names are the same but the puppet figures and plays are different.

Amir Hamzah are enacted by these Malayan shadow puppets. The third type of shadow play, wayang siam, appears to be the product of a historical process whereby the Javanese-derived shadow-play technique came to be used as a medium for telling Thai (Siamese) versions of the *Ramayana.* The puppet figures are arresting. They are carved and painted to represent dancing figures straight out of Thai khon masked-pantomime. The language of performance, however, is Malay.[24] Mixing of Thai and Malayan theatre forms is characteristic in the area along both sides of the Thai-Malaysian border, for in the border provinces Thai and Malay peoples have intermingled for many centuries. For example, before a Malay wayang performance begins, the dalang chants two invocations to the gods, one a Malayan prayer spoken in Malay, the other a Thai prayer spoken in Thai. Also Thai musical instruments such as the pear-drum and the bell-cymbals are more commonly used to accompany a Malay wayang performance than are gamelan instruments.[25]

Just as the Javanese brought wayang kulit to the Malay Peninsula five hundred or more years ago, immigrants from south China brought Chinese opera with them when they poured into the peninsula and the island of Singapore in the past century. Three main language groups of Chinese immigrated —Teochiu, Hokkien, and Cantonese—each addicted to its own variety of opera. Today there are Chinese opera troupes performing in each language, the number of troupes being roughly proportionate to the population of each language group. Troupes perform in Singapore where nine-tenths of the population are of Chinese descent and on the peninsula where one-third of the people are of Chinese descent. Older-generation Chinese—those who were born in China—are avid opera attenders, but their children and grandchildren are less interested. Young people are under pressure to learn English and Malayan. Many schoolchildren of Chinese descent do not even understand Chinese. As a result, audiences for Chinese opera are dwindling year by year and the number of troupes is decreasing.

Malay-speaking peoples reacted to the introduction of Javanese wayang kulit in a very different manner than they did to Chinese opera. They assimilated wayang kulit into their own culture, plays were translated into Malayan, and performances became part of Malay life. Chinese opera was not so assimilated. No Chinese operas have been translated into Malayan and performances are not given for Malay-speaking peoples. Chinese opera has been an entertainment directed almost exclusively at the Chinese-speaking community in Malaysia.

Bangsawan developed among Malay peoples in this century. It is a popular theatre form, with stories taken from Malay history, from Arab romances and Islamic literature, and from various contemporary sources including the movies. In the 1920's bangsawan troupes performed wherever Malay-speaking peoples lived, on the Malay Peninsula, in Singapore, in Sumatra, in Borneo, in Sunda, and in Java. In Indonesia it influenced Javanese ketoprak and Sundanese sandiwara. Bangsawan was extremely popular before the Second World War, but fewer than half a dozen troupes are now active.

CAMBODIA

A number of folk-dances seen in rural areas of Cambodia probably are descended from prehistoric times. The *trott*, a deer-hunting dance, is typical. Masked players represent hunter, demon, bull, girls, and deer. To the accompaniment of chanting and drum-playing they dance out the story of a deer hunt. It is believed this dance originally was performed prior to the hunt to invoke the blessing of animistic spirits.

The major tradition of Cambodian dance-drama dates from the early days of Indian influence. Cambodia was one of the first areas to be converted to Hindu Brahmanism, at least by the fourth century. Sanskrit writing was introduced at this time and numerous inscriptions covering the thousand years until the fall of Angkor in the fifteenth century are known. One inscription of the sixth century says explicitly "arrangements were made for the daily recitation of the *Ramayana, Mahabharata,* and the *Puranas,* and it was considered a pious act to present copies of these texts to temples."[26] The temples were connected with Brahmanism and the cult of Shiva was important in Cambodia since the fourth century. In 802, Jayavarman II came from Java to found the Khmer dynasty, and Javanese-style dance almost certainly was introduced by him. After the initial impact of Javanese influence, the Khmer went on to develop their own highly individual style of dance. For six hundred years, until Angkor fell to the invading Thai, Cambodian court dance flourished. Hundreds of carvings of *apsaras,* or heavenly dancing girls, on the ruins at Angkor attest to the important place which sensuous, albeit ritual, dances played in court life. A bas-relief on the Bayon (ca. 1200) represents scenes in the life of a dancing girl: bathing, combing and setting her hair, being massaged, and practicing dance positions. Other reliefs represent stories from the *Ramayana* and the Krishna Cycle, carved in exquisite detail. There is no evidence, however, that the lithesome apsaras performed dance-dramas based on these epics. As far as we know, extended dance-drama did not develop at all in the court at Angkor.

The year 1431 marks a violent end to the arts which were so lavishly patronized by Khmer kings, for in that year Angkor was sacked by the Thai and the court was carried off in captivity to Thailand. For the next several centuries the Khmer court was reduced to impotency and poverty, constantly moving from one insecure capital to another. We hear nothing more of the performing arts in Cambodia until vassal kings of Thailand reintroduced Thai dance much later. One group of Thai court dancers moved to the Cambodian court and settled there in the early nineteenth century, and another group did the same thing at the end of the nineteenth century.[27] It is popular to claim that the dance style of Angkor's apsaras of the twelfth century is perfectly preserved in the Royal Cambodian Ballet dance style. Unfortunately, this is romantic nonsense. A world of difference separates the elaborately costumed, chaste, and refined Cambodian dancers of today from the bare-breasted, hip-swinging beauties of Angkor. Between the thirteenth and the nineteenth centuries, the Thai developed Khmer dance and music in distinctive new directions. Present-day Cambodian dance-drama is virtually a copy of this Thai creation from earlier Khmer forms. Up until World War II, the Royal Cambodian Ballet performed its classic repertory in the Thai language; only since the war have the Thai play scripts been translated into Cambodian.

The single classical dance troupe in Cambodia is the Royal

Ballet, supported by the Royal Household at Phnom Penh. Until recently, the Royal Ballet contained a contingent of male dancers who could perform masked-pantomime (known as *lakon kawl*). But male dancers are no longer a regular part of the troupe and lakon kawl is seldom performed. The troupe does mainly all-female dances usually based on stories other than the Hindu epics.

Lakon kawl corresponds to Thai khon and, as far as we know, is a Thai creation which was brought to Cambodia at the same time lakon female dancing was reintroduced. A third form of Thai court theatre supported by the Cambodian court until recently was the shadow-puppet play, known in Thailand as nang yai. In a way, the shadow-play and the masked-pantomime were companion genres: *Ramayana* stories exclusively were performed in both, both were performed solely by men, both were highly ceremonial in nature (in contrast to sensual female-danced lakon), and usually the same artists could perform both forms of theatre. One shadow-play troupe still exists in Cambodia. It is a folk troupe in Battambang supported by a Buddhist *wat* (temple). Its members are old, when they die it is likely Cambodian shadow theatre will die with them.

Lakon bassac is the popular theatre of Cambodia. It takes its name from the district adjoining the Bassac River in southern Vietnam where it originated. Since the time of the Khmer empire, Cambodians have lived there. In the late nineteenth and early twentieth centuries, a distinctive play form was created by these people. They gave it the name lakon bassac or "theatre of the Bassac." Lakon bassac then spread to all parts of Cambodia. In the days of French rule before World War II, troupes freely moved between Cambodia and southern Vietnam, for both areas were part of French Indochina. Today there is bitter enmity between the two now independent countries. The border is closed, and most troupes have settled in Cambodia.

Since lakon bassac was created by Cambodians living surrounded by Vietnamese culture, it is not surprising to find the plays strongly influenced by Vietnamese theatre. In general, the Cambodian and the Vietnamese elements have not fused. A prince will wear a Vietnamese costume, but a princess will dress like a dancer from the Cambodian Royal Ballet. One dance gesture will be reminiscent of an Angkor carving, but another will recall Chinese opera. Cambodian classical xylophones will play in one scene, and Chinese two-stringed fiddles in the next. Lakon bassac is the only theatre form I am familiar with in which Indian-based theatrical elements and Chinese-based theatrical elements are mixed in almost equal amounts.

During a century of French rule, French culture penetrated deeply into the upper levels of Cambodian society. French language and literature became highly esteemed. French drama became the model for the small amount of work which was done in Western-style, spoken theatre. Cambodia's present ruler, Prince Sihanouk, is keenly interested in Western theatre, and has written several plays which he has directed in public performance.

THAILAND

Lakon jatri is the oldest form of Thai theatre. Its origins almost certainly lie in animistic rituals. Jatri means "sorcerer," and lakon jatri performers have always been thought to possess magic power. Dances are part of spirit offerings or serve as prologues to various animistic ceremonies in Thailand.* There are many such dances. Lakon jatri is one which evolved into dramatic form, after absorbing first Indian dance and later Buddhist subject matter. Indian dance was known in the Hinduized Mon kingdoms of central Thailand. In lakon jatri today we can see performed one of the oldest and most unusual of Indian dance movements. It is mentioned in the *Natya Sastra*. The dancer bends backward until his head appears between his legs. Acrobatic movements like this were eliminated from Thai classical dances as they became refined to suit aristocratic tastes. In lakon jatri we can see something of what the rougher, more primitive style of early Indian-influenced Thai dance was like. Up until recent years, the only play which lakon jatri troupes performed was the Buddhist *Jataka* tale *Manora*. In fact, troupes are commonly called *Nora*, a shortened form of the word *Manora*, for this

---

*For example, it is usual for a medium to perform "a ritual dance honouring the spirit" before becoming possessed by that spirit in trance. (Anuman Rajadhon, *Five Papers on Thai Custom*, p. 1.)

reason. The story of *Manora,* the lovely *kinnari* (half-bird, half-human) princess, was probably brought to Thailand by Buddhist monks entering Chiengmai in northwest Thailand from Burma.*

A typical early lakon jatri troupe consisted of three actors plus singers and musicians.[28] Only men were allowed to perform, probably for religious reasons. One actor played heroic male roles, one played female roles, and the third played alternately clown, ogre, and animal roles. The clown was often masked. Musical accompaniment was simple: flute, several drums (including the pear-shaped hand drum originally used only by lakon jatri troupes), and small bell-cymbals. The home of lakon jatri was the southern peninsula of Thailand, especially the area around Nakon Sri Tammarat. This is the only place where troupes exist today. One can see occasionally folk-troupes performing old style *Manora,* but most so-called lakon jatri troupes are that in name only. They either do not or cannot perform in the old style. They stage variety shows or plays in many styles and call them lakon jatri.

During the Ayudhya dynasty, probably in the fourteenth century, lakon jatri was brought to the Thai capital of Ayudhya. There the folk art underwent gradual development into a popular art form that came to be called *lakon nok.* Nok, which means "outside" or "southern," is the word Thai use to indicate the southern provinces of Thailand. Hence the name lakon nok means "drama from the southern provinces." In lakon nok, performance ceased to be a religious act, the number of actors increased, new stories were dramatized, and the orchestra was enlarged to include more melody-carrying instruments. Perhaps most important, dance was subordinated to the requirements of action. Popular audiences demanded fast action, colloquial language, lots of rough joking, and not too much boring dance. Many lakon nok troupes performed in Thailand up until the time of World War I. Theatres were run by wealthy merchants

---

*The story of the swan-maiden whose feathers are stolen, who marries a human being, and who eventually returns to her home in the mountains is known all over the world. Hatto mentions stories of this kind in China, Japan (the *noh* play *Hagoromo*), Korea, Persia, Scandinavia, Greenland, and among the Alaskan Eskimos and Indians of North and South America. The story, in one version or another, may have been known by the Mon in prehistoric times. The version performed in Thailand today, and in other countries of Southeast Asia, is the Buddhist *Jataka* version.

and occasionally by members of the royal family. That the genre was held in considerable esteem by the upper classes is shown by the fact that many lakon nok plays were written by royalty in the nineteenth and twentieth centuries. Among others, King Rama II in the early 1800's and Prince Naris, between 1899 and 1909, wrote many plays for public performance. After World War I lakon nok gradually died out; there are no troupes in existence today, although the style of performance is carried on by the Thai National Theatre.

The date traditionally given for the beginning of Thai classical dance is 1431, when the Thai captured Angkor and kidnaped the Khmer royal dance troupe. As a matter of fact, dance was known at the Thai court before this. There were local Thai dances like lakon jatri, and Khmer dance must have been introduced to central Thailand during the many centuries this area had been ruled as part of the Khmer empire prior to the establishment of the first Thai kingdom at Sukhotai in 1238. Thai classical dance as we know it today, however, is largely a Thai adaptation of Khmer court dance, and by and large that process of adaptation occurred between the fifteenth and the nineteenth centuries.

Many kinds of classical dance are distinguished by the Thai themselves, but female and male dance-drama are the two main theatrical forms. The custom of men and women dancing separately grew out of the circumstance that female dancers were part of the king's personal harem, segregated in a special women's quarter in the palace and forbidden to associate with men. They were the king's concubines; it was inconceivable that he should allow them to spend intimate hours in rehearsal with young and attractive male dancers. Social necessity and not artistic consideration dictated the development of separate female and male dance-drama forms. Only in recent years have men and women come to perform together on stage.

The major type of female classical dance in Thailand is *lakon nai,* generally believed to be a contraction of *lakon nang nai,* or "drama of women of the palace" (nang means "female" and nai means "inside," implying inside the palace). In the centuries-long and very complex development of lakon nai, three major steps are apparent. First, when the Thai took over Khmer-style dance they altered it. They reduced the number of figures used; they changed the meanings of dance figures; they created an "alphabet" of dance that, in modified form, is used in Thailand, Laos, and Cambodia today. Second, court writers turned to lakon nok for dramatic inspiration. Around 1750 they began borrowing the lakon nok technique of staging complex drama, which included dialogue, music, chanting, and dance. Full-length court dance-dramas were created for royal dancing girls to perform before the king and his guests (prior to this time it appears that female dancers were only called upon to do individual or group non-dramatic dances). Lakon nok stories were rewritten in elegant verse. The rough lakon nok style of movement was replaced by the languorous, studied, gently sweet style favored at court. This new dance-drama form was called lakon nai. Simon de la Loubere, ambassador from the court of Louis XIV, witnessed lavish performances of lakon nai, lasting from eight in the morning until seven in the evening, at the Thai court in the late seventeenth century.[29] And, third, lakon nai crystallized into its present form in the eighteenth century when Javanese *Panji* stories came to be staged as court dance-drama. During King Boromokot's reign (1733–1758), these stories became very popular at court. The king's two daughters each wrote a version for lakon nai. It is said that they learned the stories from a Malayan maid in their service. Rama I (1782–1809) ordered court poets to compose new versions for performance. And Rama II (1809–1824) personally composed a highly regarded version of the complete *Panji* story for lakon nai. It runs to 20,000 verses, almost as long as the *Ramayana*.[30] The Thai call the *Panji* cycle *Inao*. Since the eighteenth century, lakon nai has been inseparably linked with the *Inao* story. Many other plays have been written for lakon nai performance, but none has ever equaled its popularity. When one speaks of lakon nai today, one normally means *Inao* performed by female dancers.*

With lakon nai reserved for the royal harem, other forms of court theatre were performed by men only. Nang yai (shadow drama) and khon (masked-pantomime) are the most important.

---

*In the Thai court minor stylistic variations came to be identified, for example, *lakon pud* (much dialogue), *lakon dukdamban* (based on old themes), and *lakon phantang* (mixed themes, but similar to lakon nok), among others. (Yupho, *Khon and Lakon*, p. 75.)

Both dramatized episodes from the *Ramayana* and it is believed the latter developed from the former. The term nang yai means "large puppet," aptly describing a genre in which the puppets are approximately lifesized. Nang yai puppets are cut out of flat leather and incised with a pattern like all Southeast Asian shadow puppets, but they are also unique in several ways: they are not articulated (one person handles a single puppet by two fixed handles); an entire scene is carved onto a puppet often including several characters surrounded by trees and buildings; and the movements of the standing puppeteers are as clearly seen on the screen as the movements of the puppets themselves.* The origin of nang yai is obscure. Most Thai scholars believe that shadow drama came to Thailand from India, via Java and Malaya.[31] (Javanese wayang kulit puppets in the early days were not articulated.) It is very possible that an early form of shadow puppet was taken from Java to Cambodia by Jayavarman II in 802, and that the Thai subsequently learned of the puppets from the Khmer. The first reference to nang yai in Thai records occurs in 1458, or just twenty-seven years after the Thai sack of Angkor.[32]

That khon masked-pantomime evolved out of nang yai is fairly evident. Around 1515 King Rama Tibodi II organized large-scale performances of all kinds in celebration of his twenty-fifth birthday. It is reported that a performance of khon was given in which dancers copied the movements made by nang yai puppeteers while manipulating the great puppets over their heads. The dancers wore heavy make-up which later became formalized into the masks used in khon today.† The simple movements of the dancers were highlighted against the white screen. As further evidence that khon evolved from nang yai, khon plays are called *chud,* referring to a "set" of puppets, instead of being called *ton,* or "episode," as are most plays. The khon dancer also moves in a special sideways fashion, keeping in profile as much as possi-

---

*There is an intriguing picture of a performance in which the light was on one side of the screen and the puppets and the audience were on the other side. Instead of seeing a shadow play, therefore, the audience saw the puppets silhouetted against the screen. And, of course, the standing puppeteers were seen in silhouette also. (Bridhyakorn, *The Nang,* p. 2.)

†Some Thai scholars suggest that this make-up may have been modeled on highly stylized Indian *kathakali* dance make-up.

ble, like the puppets of nang yai.[33] The Thai distinguish five main types of khon that differ in details of performance.[34] Each form of khon consists of three elements: vigorous dancing, especially of battle scenes; narration, called *khamphak,* of the *Ramayana* text; and dialogue spoken by an offstage chorus. Although originally presented by an all-male cast, as female lakon nai became increasingly popular at court, many elements of female dance-drama were incorporated into khon. Lakon nai singing was added. Human figures and gods ceased to wear masks (now only ogres and monkeys wear masks). Perhaps most significant, female lakon nai dancers began taking roles alongside male dancers. At first only Sita and other female roles were danced by girls, but now it is not uncommon to see a girl dancing the part of Laksmana, Rama's brother, as well. Khon today is a blending of original rough, masculine khon with soft, feminine lakon nai. Both khon and nang yai were performed at court and among the people for weddings, funerals, births, and on other important occasions, and there used to be both folk troupes and court troupes. But today nang yai is virtually extinct (no one knows how to perform it), and khon is performed only by the Thai National Theatre.

The kings of Thailand were avid patrons of lakon nai, khon, and nang yai. Not only did they maintain troupes at royal expense and stage magnificent court performances, but they encouraged members of the court to write and wrote plays themselves. Dramatic versions of the *Ramayana* were written, or ordered written, by King Rama I, Rama II, Rama VI, Prince Damrong, and Prince Dhaninivat. Rama II wrote a new dramatic version of *Sang Thong,* a *Jataka* story. Rama VI wrote many plays, as did the Princes Naris and Narathip. When, in 1932, a constitutional monarchy was promulgated and the old system of lavish court patronage ceased, these magnificent court arts might have come to an end. To the great credit of the Thai government this did not happen. A Department of Fine Arts was created within the new government which took over the function of teaching khon and lakon nai. Somewhat later the Thai National Theatre was set up. It stages regular public performances of khon and lakon nai and, less often, of lakon jatri and lakon nok.

Unfortunately, the Thai are not interested in preserving nang yai; it is neither taught nor performed today.

At the turn of the century lakon nok began to be replaced by a new popular theatre genre, called *likay*. The word likay is a corruption of *digar*, the name of a religious chant of the Shiite sect of Islam. It is said that during King Chulalongkorn's reign (1868–1910) Malays of the Shiite sect living in Bangkok sang the chant to invoke the blessings of Allah on behalf of the king. The chant was lively and rhythmic and caught the fancy of the Thai. Popular troupes in Bangkok adopted the chant and its name, corrupting it to likay in the process, in an effort to capitalize on the current digar fad. Before performance the digar was chanted behind closed curtains (a custom maintained today), but likay plays themselves owe nothing to digar or to Islam. They have always been pure Thai in story, in music, and in dance.

In the 1920's and 1930's likay developed into a kind of vulgarized court drama under the influence and tutelage of ex-palace dancers who turned to the professional theatre to earn a living. Professional likay actors assiduously studied with court artists. For the first time actresses appeared with actors on the stage. Court plays like *Inao, Sang Thong,* and even parts of the *Ramayana* were staged as likay. This was likay's heyday. Hundreds of troupes played throughout Thailand. Audiences flocked to see this new drama, and competitions to select the best troupes aroused public excitement to fever pitch. Even princes wrote likay plays. Likay is still the most widely performed theatre genre in Thailand, but its popularity is not as great as it was a generation ago. After World War II several dozen troupes still played in Bangkok;[35] today one does. Likay no longer attracts important actors. Plays are no longer court dramas. Likay's once proud ties with court drama are evident mainly in likay music and dance, still largely traditional and court-derived.

In the five southern provinces of Thailand which border Malaysia, several types of shadow play are popular. Opaque puppet figures, in the style of Javanese wayang kulit and patterned after khon dancers, are used by wayang melayu and wayang siam troupes respectively. These troupes are often visitors from the Malaysian side of the border. They perform in the Malayan language, as the population of southern Thailand is composed of 80 percent Moslem Malays. A third type of shadow theatre is *nang talung*. Nang means "leather" ("leather puppet" in this case), and talung is an abbreviation of Pattalung, a southern city where the shadow play long has been popular. Nang talung puppets differ from every other type of shadow puppet in Southeast Asia in that they are translucent and rather small,[36] so similar to Chinese shadow puppets, in fact, that I am inclined to believe that in one way or another they were inspired by Chinese shadow theatre.

A doll-puppet theatre used to be fairly well-known in central Thailand. Troupes of twenty or more puppet manipulators, singers, and musicians were common. These were semi-folk troupes that performed at fairs, temple festivals, and for any occasion calling for entertainment. Dolls, painted and costumed like lakon nai and khon dancers, were used to enact a wide variety of plays, including episodes from the *Ramayana*. Thai kings of the eighteenth and nineteenth centuries had doll-puppet sets made, but evidentally performances at court occurred sporadically and were not very important. Today there is a single folk troupe in Thailand. It performs in Bangkok and nearby cities. Most of the troupe members are old, and Thai puppet theatre probably will not survive their death.

Thailand and Malaysia are the two countries in Southeast Asia where Chinese opera is important. Though the size of the Chinese-speaking population of Malaysia is roughly double that of Thailand (four million compared to two million), there are more Chinese opera troupes in Thailand than in Malaysia. As in Malaysia, the opera was brought into Thailand by immigrants coming from various parts of southern China, so that we find several forms of Chinese opera; and as in Malaysia, Teochiu-language opera is most common. It is fairly usual for troupes from Thailand to cross into Malaysia on tour. Bangkok actors are highly regarded in Malaysia and command high salaries there.

LAOS

In Laos, a small country with a total population of only two and a half million, the development of theatre forms can be described in fairly simple terms. Originally, there was *mohlam,*

[6 8]

the so-called "courts of love" folk-singing. Next, Cambodian court dance was introduced to the Lao court by the Khmer. And, finally, within the last decades likay from Thailand has been adapted to *khen* music to form a Lao popular theatre.

The khen reed-organ in Laos dates back to prehistoric times. The origin of reed-organs in Asia is not known with any certainty but they are found in China, where they are called *sheng,* in Japan, where they are known as *sho,* and in the interior of Borneo, where the Dayak tribes call them *kledi.*[37] We hear of a reed-organ existing in China as early as 500 B.C., when no less person than Confucius himself was "an accomplished performer on the *kin* (seven stringed zither), [and] the *sheng.*"[38] The khen is the Lao national instrument. Around it the art of mohlam singing developed. In old-style mohlam, one man sang while another accompanied him on the khen. The singer was a troubadour. He traveled about the countryside singing wherever he was invited. He sang bawdy, earthy accounts of sexual love, into which he wove bits of local gossip, news of the court, and fragments of the *Ramayana* and *Jataka* stories. In more recent times the singer has been joined by a female partner. News items and epic stories have dropped out of the repertory. Today mohlam is a highly erotic verse form, sung by a male and a female singer to the accompaniment of one khen. It is enormously popular wherever Lao is spoken.

Tradition says court dance, the *Jataka* stories, and the *Ramayana* were all introduced to Laos from the Khmer court by Prince Fa Nguan in 1353. Indian influences may have reached Laos before this, but Lao court theatre undoubtedly dates from the establishment at this time of the kingdom of Lang Xan with its capital at Luang Prabang. Cambodian dance, music, and possibly shadow theatre were transplanted intact to the new Lao capital. The king patronized the arts, a troupe of royal dancing girls was recruited and trained, and performances were given just as at the Khmer court. But the Lao court was small and lacked the resources of the great Khmer empire and new theatre forms did not evolve. After the Khmer empire was destroyed by the Thai, Laos split into three smaller kingdoms which during the eighteenth and nineteenth centuries alternately were under Burmese, Thai, Vietnamese, and Cambodian rule. Gradually the

Thai gained political and cultural dominance over the area and Thai dancing and music came to set the standard for Lao court theatre arts. The best Lao classical dancers of today go to Bangkok for advanced training, not to Phnom Penh. Because the small Lao court cannot afford the great cost of staging dance spectacles, the Thai repertory of full-length dance-dramas is not performed by the Lao Royal Ballet. Instead solo and small group dances are emphasized. The court troupe consists of many dancing girls but no male dancers. Khon dance, therefore, cannot be performed. Both nang talung and nang yai have been performed in Laos in the past, but they are rarely seen nowadays.

Likay was introduced into Laos early in the twentieth century. This is not as strange as it might at first seem. The Thai and Lao languages are closely related; to a large degree they are mutually understandable. Likay troupes, speaking standard Thai, played in northeast Thailand for the Lao-speaking Thai people of that region. From there it was but a short trip across the Mekong River to play for audiences in Laos. Around 1925, the khen was substituted for Thai musical instruments and mohlam singing replaced most of the Thai dialogue and dance while the stories, costumes, and staging practices of Thai likay were retained. This new theatre form came to be called by half a dozen names, but the most usual one is *mohlam luong,* or "story mohlam." * Mohlam luong has become extremely popular in Laos and northeast Thailand in recent years. Performers come from among the ranks of the thousands of mohlam singers born on the Thai side of the Mekong River. Thai likay actors are unable to play mohlam luong for the style of performance is totally different from that of Thai likay, though the stories are much the same.

BURMA

Burma has a long tradition of spirit dances, dances performed to propitiate one or more of the thirty-seven nats known in Burma. As the closest country to India in Southeast Asia, Burma learned of Indian dance early. In 802 a Burmese cultural mis-

---

*It is also called *mohlam mu* ("group mohlam"), *lam luong* ("sung story"), *lam mu* ("group singing"), and *likay Lao.*

sion to the Chinese emperor played music and sang songs which included Sanskrit words.[39] Dance and music developed in Burma for many centuries before any distinctive theatre genre evolved. In the sixteenth century Indian-influenced Burmese dances were being performed by professional entertainers. They called themselves "spirit dancers," and the type of performance they gave was called *nibhatkhin* or "spirit play." Actually, these performers were vagabond entertainers, who used religion as a convenient cover for their secular activities, much as the prostitute Okuni, who founded *kabuki* in Japan at almost the same time, posed as a "priestess" performing religious dances. A clown was the main character in most Burmese spirit plays. The present day *nat pwe* or "spirit show" is a direct descendant of these earlier spirit plays. Interestingly enough, the animistic element is more important in nat pwe than it was centuries ago. In contemporary nat pwe the main dance is performed by a *natkadaw* ("nat wife"), a professional dancer-medium who, through the dance, calls down into herself a nat spirit for the purpose of foreseeing the future. The dancer is esteemed more for her fortune-telling ability than for her skill as a dancer.

Burmese court drama dates from 1767, when captured Thai courtiers introduced their court drama. Burmese nobles, fascinated by the subtlety and refinement of this imported theatre, were quick to adopt it. At first Thai plays were reproduced as nearly as possible. Dramas based on the *Ramayana* and the adventures of Inao (Panji) were translated literally from Thai into Burmese. As in Thailand, the *Ramayana* was played as a birth story of Buddha with Rama portrayed as a Future Buddha.[40] Within a few years, however, Burmese court poets had begun to compose in elegant verse their own plays on both traditional and new themes and a distinctive Burmese court drama came into being. Court plays were performed mainly at the Burmese capital, first at Ava and later at Mandalay, but vulgarized versions found their way into the repertories of traveling professional troupes. Widespread knowledge of the Rama story in Burma dates from this relatively late period.

Court drama was already decadent when the British arrived in Burma in the middle of the nineteenth century; there were no new poets, and the art of performance was stagnating. Court drama had flourished for somewhat less than a hundred years when, a few years after the British conquered Burma, it ended almost as abruptly as it had begun. The last vestiges of Burmese court drama are seen in classical plays, called *zat,* in which dance and music and costume are reminiscent of Thai-Burmese classical dance-drama. They are performed by many *zat pwe* theatre troupes in central and southern Burma.

The Burmese also have had a marionette theatre. Originally only simple animal acts were performed, and animals danced and paraded for audiences of children. Under the influence of Burmese court drama, full-scale puppet plays came to be staged in the nineteenth century. Shortly after the conquest of Ayudhya, King Bodawpaya appointed a Minister of Theatre who was responsible for regulating and encouraging the drama. The minister tried unsuccessfully to recast existing theatre into a more suitable mold. He found live actors to be a recalcitrant lot, so he set about creating a puppet drama over which he could have complete control.[41] Puppeteers were recruited from among the best performers of the time, and troupes were sent around the countryside. Surviving marionette figures show ogres with red, green, and gold faces and conical headgear like the masks worn by Thai khon dancers. The technique of performance was quite advanced, as can be seen from the fact that up to sixty strings were used to manipulate the *apyodaw* votaress of the spirits, a figure which, though connected with animistic nat worship, appeared in every Buddhist *Jataka* puppet play.[42] Marionette plays became very popular in the early part of the nineteenth century, but since troupes were totally dependent upon court support, the annexation of Burma by the British in the middle of the century proved disastrous to the puppet theatre. In 1929 there was one puppet troupe in Burma; two are reported now.

Prior to the twentieth century it was unusual for zat pwe actors to perform *Jataka* plays, for it was considered contrary to the seventh law of Buddha for an actor to represent Buddha on stage. Hla Pe mentions *Mahazanaka,* by U Kho, as a "dramatization of the *jataka* [probably] prepared for some theatrical company and printed for sale" in 1875; even earlier, in 1872, the playwright U Pon Nya wrote *Wizaya,* based on a Ceylonese version of a *Jataka* story.[43] But by and large *Jataka* plays remained the province of the marionette theatre until, shortly before World War I, the great zat pwe actor U Po Sein introduced the custom of live actors performing *Jataka.*[44]

VIETNAM

Very likely the oldest form of play in Vietnam is *hat cheo.* One theory is that hat cheo developed out of folk songs, dances, and buffoonery which peasants of northern Vietnam performed at harvest time and for other festivals, and that gradually these folk plays came to emphasize social satire as they do today. According to another legend, the Vietnamese king, Le Ngoc Trieu, employed a Chinese actor to teach entertainers at his court the art of "Chinese satirical theatre."[45] This was supposed to have been about 1005. If the latter is true, satire trickled down from the court rather than springing spontaneously from peasant culture as the former theory would have it. In recent years stories from as far away as Korea and Europe have been incorporated into the hat cheo repertory. Hat cheo exists today as a semi-folk, semi-popular theatre genre, known only in northern Vietnam, in the Red River area.*

Hat boi, the classic opera genre known in all parts of Vietnam, was modeled directly after Chinese opera. Hat means "to sing" and boi means "gesture" or "pose"; together they describe hat boi very well—sung drama in which actors move in highly conventionalized patterns. Of the many legends purporting to explain its origin, the most commonly accepted says that in 1285 the soldiers of General Tran Hung Dao captured a Chinese opera troupe during a battle with an invading Mongol army. Ten actors and two actresses of the troupe were turned over to King Tran Nhan Ton. The troupe leader, one Ly Nguyen Cat, was ordered by the king to train suitable young Vietnamese in the art, which he did in exchange for his life.[46] Under the patronage of subsequent emperors, hat boi developed to suit Vietnamese taste. Libretti were translated from Chinese into Vietnamese; new melodies were composed; new plays were writ-

*It is in great favor with the Communist government of North Vietnam at the moment because of its presumed peasant origins and its suitability as a propaganda medium. (Song Ban, *The Vietnamese Theatre* [Hanoi, 1960], pp. 11–18.)

ten, some based on Vietnamese, rather than Chinese, history. Dao Duy Tu (1572–1634) and Dao Tan (1848–1908), both of the province of Binh Dinh, were two of the most famous hat boi playwrights. In its outer form, however, hat boi remained remarkably similar to Chinese opera. Costumes and make-up were closely patterned after Chinese models. Stage conventions and the symbolic use of scenery and properties, those unique features of Chinese opera, were taken over more or less intact in hat boi.

Down through the end of the nineteenth century, hat boi troupes performed for Vietnamese emperors and for high-ranking mandarins in their private chambers. Its first special theatre was built within the walls of the imperial palace in Hue by the emperor Gia Long (1802–1820). Between 1802 and 1945 all the emperors of Vietnam patronized hat boi. The emperor Tu Duc (1847–1883) encouraged court poets to write operas, he maintained a troupe of 150 female performers, and he brought into his court the Chinese actor Kang Koung Heou (though it was the same Tu Duc who uttered the famous dictum "actors do not belong to the human kind").[47] Within the last hundred years or so, hat boi has become known throughout Vietnam. In particular, it has been popular in the central Vietnamese provinces of Binh Dinh, Quang Ngai, and Tuy Hoa. The last traces of genuine hat boi—not the vulgarized kind staged in Saigon—are found in central Vietnam, where itinerant troupes still travel by foot from village to village performing classic plays in traditional fashion. During the twentieth century hat boi has declined rapidly. It lost court support; new, popular theatre genres began competing for audiences; and then the movies came along. It proved to be an inflexible art form which could not adapt to new conditions through further growth. Good troupes, no longer able to support themselves, disbanded. Marginal troupes continued to eke out an existence, but hat boi as an art form had reached a crisis. In better circumstances a revival of interest in hat boi might have occurred, as kabuki in Japan revived in the aftermath of the war. But the war never ended in Vietnam. After more than twenty years it still goes on, and it appears that neither the will nor the capacity to undertake a revival of classic hat boi is present in contemporary Vietnamese society. It can hardly be said that hat boi exists at all today.

Traveling troupes of actors, musicians, and singers have been part of Vietnamese life for many centuries. From the earliest period of Vietnamese history, emperors have kept singing and dancing girls as concubines and to provide royal entertainment. When these girls were released from their service to the emperor, many of them established troupes that performed in public.

> The dancers were young beauties from fifteen to seventeen, recruited among the people and trained to serve in the imperial ballet company, until the "flower of their youth began to wither" when they forfeited the privilege of appearing before the Dragon, that is, the Emperor. Discharged . . . they were returned to ordinary life. These young artists had to create jobs for themselves. They formed among themselves traveling companies to roam the country on foot, each individual carrying his equipment in bundles hung on either end of a long bamboo pole. They gave public performances for whoever would buy their services.[48]

It is from this ancient tradition that the most popular Vietnamese theatre genre, *cai luong,* has sprung.

In the early 1920's there were two main types of popular theatre troupes: *tuong tau* and cai luong. Tuong tau was a kind of popularized hat boi. Hat boi's stiff, difficult conventions of acting and raucous din of Chinese horns, cymbals, and drums were dropped, while its appealing costuming, make-up, and vigorous action were retained. Singers stopped singing in falsetto voices. Simple, modern Vietnamese was substituted for difficult Sino-Vietnamese words in dialogue and song lyrics. Esoteric melodies were replaced by more popular tunes. And, for the first time in Vietnam, elaborate stage scenery was introduced. For a time this exciting form of theatre, tuong tau, was immensely popular. Simultaneous with taung tau's development out of hat boi, a competing form of popular theatre, cai luong, grew out of southern singing traditions. At first cai luong singers simply sat on stage and crooned the touching melodies for which south Vietnam is so famous. Cai luong was often just an interlude at a private party, or one of a number of variety acts in a vaudeville theatre, or even part of a circus performance. Gradually singers began to rise from their chairs, to gesture while singing their songs, to sing duets and trios, and finally to act out short playlets as they sang. As dialogue, costumes, scenery, and extended plots came to be incorporated into cai luong, it took on its present form as a kind of light opera, or operetta.[49]

One particular melody is inseparably linked with cai luong. This is *Vong Co,* a ravishingly beautiful love lament written by the musician Cao Van Lau in 1920. When cai luong troupes began to sing Vong Co around 1927, both the song and cai luong became enormously popular. Vong Co is the most widely loved and often sung melody in Vietnam; although it is a southern melody it is equally liked in central and northern Vietnam. In every new cai luong play, it is sung at least a dozen times and no singer can establish a reputation unless he (or she) can thrill an audience with his (or her) rendition of this song.

In the 1930's cai luong was at its peak of popularity. Troupes were performing all types of plays: plays of Vietnamese history, European dramas, and contemporary stories. Audiences were enchanted with the musical style of cai luong, so when cai luong troupes began to add exciting Chinese tuong tau plays to their repertory this marked the end of tuong tau as a separate theatre form. Tuong tau gradually slid into oblivion, while hundreds of cai luong troupes sprang up all over the country.* Since World War II, competition from motion pictures has reduced the number of troupes somewhat; still, cai luong is far and away the most widespread and important theatre genre in Vietnam today.

Spoken drama in Vietnam is called kich.[50] Its origins lie in French drama. Performances of Western-inspired plays were alternately encouraged and forbidden by the French colonial government—encouraged when the plays favorably reflected the glory of France and of French culture, forbidden when nationalist, anti-French causes were espoused. Kich is the only professional, Western-inspired dramatic genre which has found any degree of audience acceptance in Southeast Asia. Today two or three professional troupes perform in Vietnam, but even these have found it impossible to draw audiences by staging only kich spoken drama. What goes under the name of a kich performance today is a variety show, in which an hour-long kich play is

*While the literal translation of cai luong is "reformed theatre," and this usually is interpreted as meaning "reformed from hat boi," it would be more accurate to call tuong tau "reformed hat boi."

preceded by two hours of musical entertainment—popular singers, dance teams, and jazz bands. These professional kich troupes perform mainly in Saigon and in a few of the larger cities.

THE PHILIPPINES

Some of the purest examples of prehistoric theatre known in Southeast Asia are found in the Philippines. Epic poems are recited at communal gatherings in many mountain tribes. Among the Ifugaos of central Luzon, tribal priests recite the *Hudhod* and the *Alim* epics; among the Bicolanos it is the elders of the tribe who recite their tribal epic, the *Ibalon*.[51] These epics and others have been handed down orally generation by generation. Early in the Christian era, Filipinos learned a rudimentary Indian-derived alphabet, probably through their contact with Java, but this alphabet was never used for writing anything as complex as literature. Westerners were the first people to record the epics in writing.

Some of the incidents in the epics are remarkably similar to myths of other races. Most tribes know a flood myth, like that of the Hebrews. In another, the hero causes water to spring from a rock by shooting the rock with an arrow, as does Arjuna in the *Mahabharata* and Moses in the Bible.[52] Does this mean that these myths came from India and from the Middle East? Probably not. Indian culture scarcely reached the Philippines, for these islands were on the furthermost western edge of Asia, thousands of miles from India. Islam did not arrive until the fifteenth century, long after the epics had become tradition. Even the Spaniards, in the four hundred years they ruled the islands, had practically no contact with tribes that knew the epics. These tribes were hostile to outsiders, vigorously repulsing every effort the Spanish made to penetrate the wild, isolated mountain regions where they lived.[53] It seems unlikely, then, that the mountain tribes learned the epics from these visitors. A few stories may have been brought by Indians or Javanese or Arabs, but there is every reason to believe the tradition of epic recitals and the vast bulk of epic stories are part of animistic, prehistoric Philippine culture.

In the seventeenth century Spanish Catholic priests in the

Philippines created a type of play which came to be called *moro-moro,* for it dramatized the victory of Christian Filipinos over the Moors. It is said the first moro-moro play was written by a Jesuit priest in honor of the conquest by a Christian army of the Moslem stronghold of Iligan in Mindanao, and that the play was staged in 1637. Because the play was so popular with the people and suited the purposes of Spanish religious and government authorities so well, hundreds of similar plays soon were written and produced by the Spanish. We do not know for certain what Filipino folk theatre was like before the Spanish came, for Catholic priests zealously stamped out or forced Filipinos to abandon whatever "heathen" performances they encountered, but the moro-moro play of the seventeenth century may represent a Christianization of some older, indigenous drama.[54] Moro-moro was staged as a folk-play. Villagers and peasants by the hundreds would take part, often rehearsing months for a single performance. Though many moro-moro plays have been written and produced during the past four hundred years, they all contain a similar obligatory scene in which an infidel Moslem army is slaughtered by a Christian Filipino army. Bloodshed and carnage alternate with scenes of extravagant romantic love. In this respect Christian moro-moro is no different from Greek or Hindu or Islamic epic literature. Moro-moro has never been popular in large cities, and today it has almost died out in the countryside as well.

Zarzuela is the one dramatic form in the Philippines that has been performed commercially. It came from Spain, where it was a type of light opera, a la Rossini. Zarzuela was brought to the Philippines by Spanish officials and merchants as popular entertainment for themselves and their women, but during the period of American rule it became popular among Filipinos as well. There were many professional troupes in the first two decades of this century. New plays were written, usually based on topical themes, many of them strongly anti-American and anti-colonial. After World War I professional zarzuela gradually died out; now it is performed in a few villages as folk drama.

Given the Philippines' long contact with Western culture and the dearth of indigenous theatre in the islands, it is not surprising to find Western spoken drama more widely and more deeply appreciated here than in any other Southeast Asian country. To the average Filipino "theatre" means "Western theatre." Virtually all drama to which he is exposed is based on Western models. There are no professional theatre troupes. In Manila there are about half a dozen long-established semi-professional community theatre organizations. These groups perform European and American plays for the most part, but they also produce some Philippine plays. One of the most unique is the Arena Theatre of the Philippines.* Since its founding twelve years ago it has been attached to Philippine Normal College in Manila. Though university-based, it is organized as a community theatre project with some sixty branches on the major islands of the Philippines. Each local group produces two or three plays a year. All the plays are written by Philippine authors, among them the best playwrights in the country, and all concern Philippine life. Through the Arena Theatre provincial folk-theatre producing groups are linked with sophisticated, big-city creative artists, to the benefit of both parties.

*The Rockefeller Foundation has given support to the Arena Theatre for the past several years.

C H A P T E R   4

Traditions of Theatre

Theatre is not the product of a single segment of society in Southeast Asia; it has been nourished in several social environments. The conditions under which theatre has developed within each have been sufficiently different and have left such a strong imprint that it is possible to identify four major "traditions of theatre" on the basis of social environment: the "folk theatre tradition," the "court theatre tradition," the "popular theatre tradition," and the "Western theatre tradition."

The Folk Theatre Tradition. Folk theatre is primarily connected with village life. It is linked with prehistoric animistic beliefs and ritual. Performances are given at irregular intervals and for special occasions. Performers are local villagers who act or dance as a hobby or to gain prestige; they are not professionals. Expenses attendant upon performance are provided by the community or a local sponsor; anyone may attend free of charge. Theatre forms tend to be relatively simple and the artistic level of performance may be low (though this is not always the case). Theatre buildings are seldom used.

There are several things which folk theatre is not. It is not performed by "everyone" in a village. As De Zoete and Spies say of Balinese theatre, even the simplest form of folk drama requires "special gifts and training" that are not everybody's business.[1] Only a very few people in any village are capable of performing folk drama. Neither is folk drama performed spontaneously, without preparation. Since performances occur in connection with some other event, they are carefully planned by the sponsor, often many months in advance. Finally, popular theatre troupes are often incorrectly identified as "folk theatre" (or "people's theatre") when they are found performing in villages. The mere fact that a troupe performs for villagers does not make the form folk theatre.

The Court Theatre Tradition. Many theatre forms evolved under court patronage reflecting the influence of outside cultures—Indian, Chinese, or other Southeast Asian cultures—presumed to be more advanced than the local culture. Performers of court theatre were court retainers; they lived at court, were supported by the sovereign, and were responsive to his desires. Performances were given in the precincts of the court. There was no admission fee, but, although sometimes the public was allowed to attend, attendance usually was limited to the ruler's invited guests. Performances were given irregularly on special occasions often connected with religious rites. The artistic level of performance was generally high. Theatre tended to develop into complex and subtle forms.

The Popular Theatre Tradition. Popular theatre is the least understood of the four traditions. But it has unique characteristics that set it apart from both folk and court theatre. Popular theatre belongs to the city and town, just as court theatre belongs to the palace and folk theatre to the village community. It is the theatre of the semi-literate urban middle-class. Popular theatre troupes are commercial enterprises. They try to make a profit, and support themselves by selling tickets to the public. Generally popular troupes perform every night the year round (the main exception being when it rains). Performances are given on the stage of a permanent or temporary theatre building, never in the open like the folk theatre performances nor in private residences as used to be the case with court theatre. Performers may be looked down on, ranked with beggars, prostitutes, and thieves. Eclecticism is the prevailing attitude toward art; performance styles and stories may be taken from various sources as long as the audience is satisfied. Some popular troupes are excellent, others are dreadful.

The Western Theatre Tradition. Western theatre is the product of the present-day, highly educated social elite in Southeast Asia. The form of drama was modeled on Western drama. Performers

[81]

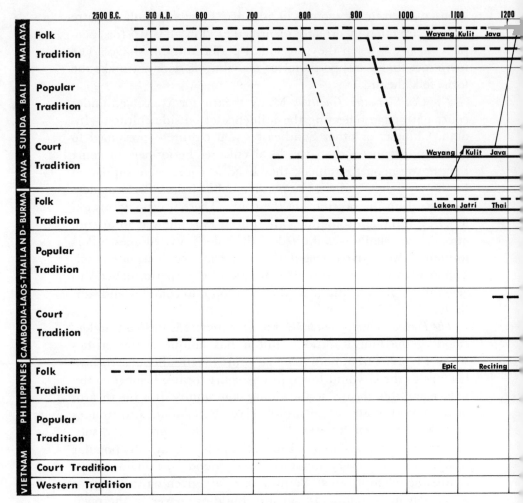

FIGURE 1. Chronological Development of Genres within Folk, Popular, Court, and Western Theatre Traditions ————————

tend to come from among university students and graduates, especially from among those who studied in Europe or America and are Western-oriented. Western theatre is mainly amateur theatre, but the aim of most troupes is to become commercially self-supporting (that is, become "popular" theatre troupes). The audience comes mainly from the same Western-oriented elite group as the performers. Performance standards tend to be fairly low (amateurish rather then vulgar).

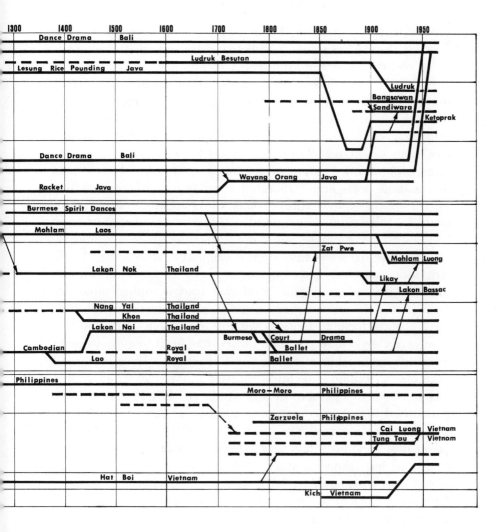

Social scientists who study peasant or traditional agrarian societies often describe them as containing a "Great Tradition," of sophisticated art and culture developed by the educated ruling elite of the court capital cities, and a "Little Tradition," which "works itself out and keeps itself going in the lives of the unlettered in their village communities."[2] Court theatre, as I have described it, fits within this larger concept of the "Great Tradition," as does folk theatre within the concept of the "Little Tradition." Such a view of culture, however, leaves "popular" culture untouched. Popular theatre lies somewhere between the extremes of sophisticated court theatre and village folk theatre.

A theatre form may move from one tradition to another or it may exist simultaneously in several traditions, as Figure 1 shows. Most movement occurs between the folk, popular, and court traditions. Geertz has described how, in Java, a theatre form may pass from the "Great Tradition" into the "Little Tradition," or vice versa, saying "fading urban forms 'coarsen' and 'sink' into the peasant mass and elaborated rural forms 'etherealize' and 'rise' into the urban elite."[3] This can happen. One example could be Indonesian wayang kulit. If it is assumed that wayang kulit began as a village ritual-drama connected with animism, as may have been the case, then it originated within the "Little Tradition" and only later became part of the "Great Tradition" when it was adapted and developed into a sophisticated art form in the Javanese courts. But the more common process is for a theatre form to move down into or up out of the middle ground of the popular tradition rather than for it to move directly from one to another of the extreme traditions. Here are a few examples. Mohlam folk music moved up into mohlam luong, which is in the popular theatre tradition, but it has scarcely penetrated into Lao court music traditions. Court lakon nai in Thailand grew out of lakon nok, a popular theatre form, and lakon nok previously had evolved out of lakon jatri in the folk tradition; but lakon nai did not evolve directly from folk lakon jatri. Court wayang orang on Java descended as far as the popular tradition when it lost court patronage, but it did not go all the way down into a folk theatre form.

I have been describing the characteristics which distinguish traditions partly in artistic terms. I was making an artistic distinction when I said, for example, that court theatre is "sophisticated" but folk theatre is "simple" or "crude." It is an artistic distinction to point out that a certain dance figure, which would be repeated loosely two or four times in a Thai folk dance, would be meticulously performed up to twenty times in succession at a Thai court performance.[4] The most usual explanation given to account for these differences is that a court audience was a discriminating audience which demanded refinement, while the uneducated village audience did not or could not. This is partly true, but other factors are equally important. A court had the financial means, political power, and prestige to command the finest poets, musicians, and performers in the realm. By virtue of their special position as court retainers, theatre artists were able to devote their full energies to perfecting their art. By contrast, village performers came from the small area around their village. They had little time to practice for they did other work for a living; they performed only a few times a year; and usually there was little financial incentive for them to perform well. Given social, political, and economic conditions as far different as we have here, it is not surprising that court and folk theatre are at opposite poles artistically.

When it comes to genre in the popular tradition it is impossible to make any such sweeping generalizations. The artistic characteristics of a genre in the popular tradition depend upon the specific circumstances under which it evolved. If a genre moved up into the popular tradition from the folk tradition, it will show for a time its folk origins, as Lao mohlam luong, which is just a dozen years old, retains a strong flavor of folk mohlam singing. After a period of years, however, folk elements tend to become assimilated or covered over with new elements as the genre develops within the popular tradition. For example, looking at them now, after fifty years in the popular tradition, one would never suspect that ludruk or ketoprak were ever related to folk performances. If a genre moves down into the popular tradition from the court tradition, court elements remain almost permanently identifiable. Though wayang orang is nowadays performed only within the popular tradition, its refined dance style, full gamelan orchestra, elegant costumes, and archaic language immediately indicate its court origin. One cannot mistake the evidences of Thai classic dance in popular likay, or of Cambodian court dance in popular lakon bassac. When one sees even the most degenerated example of hat boi, there can be no doubt of its former court ties. Musical patterns, dance figures, and poetic turns of phrase, once crystallized and then polished and burnished to perfection at court, do not easily disappear. You see them shining like diamonds, virtually indestructable, among the dross of popular plays all over Southeast Asia.

It is usual to think of popular theatre as vulgarized theatre, and this is often true. When audiences are small, income is low, and troupes must roam the back reaches of the countryside to eek out a paltry existence, talented performers stay away. Popular troupes of this kind are incapable of producing good art. But there is nothing inherent in the popular theatre tradition which says that all popular performances must be vulgar. Vietnamese cai luong is an outstanding example of a genre which has always been within the popular tradition and which has evolved into a superior art form. Cai luong is the national craze in Vietnam. A top cai luong singer earns double or triple the salary of a cabinet minister and is showered with fame and adulation that would make a Hollywood star of the 1930's envious. The double incentive of financial reward and prestige inspires thousands of young singers to train diligently and to sing in minor troupes in the hope of moving up into the half-dozen best troupes, and from there into the charmed circle of great cai luong singers. Because the singers are good and the plays excellently staged, audiences flock to the theatres. Large audiences generate enough income to pay high salaries to the good singers who draw the large audiences, creating a mutually reinforcing circular relation between solid financing, artistic excellence, and audience popularity.

If we apply the same analysis to the Western tradition of theatre, we see that Western theatre, like court theatre of the past, is the private accomplishment of an educated and sophisticated elite group in society. But this modern elite, unlike the old aristocratic court elite, has little political power and scant financial means with which to support its chosen theatre forms. Further, the gap between the artistic tastes of the modern elite and a popular audience is too great to expect much popular support for Western theatre forms. High artistic standards are striven for in the productions of Western-style plays, but excellence is seldom attained because of the lack of resources at the disposal of the elite and because of audience indifference. Western-style theatre is caught at the present in a vicious circle where lack of money, small audiences, and amateur art mutually reinforce the low position of this tradition.

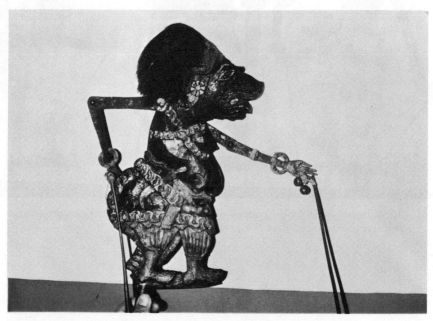

34. Real hair and bells adorn a wooden clown figure in Javanese wayang klitik.

35. Balinese wayang kulit puppets of Yudistira, Bima, and Arjuna are simpler and less sophisticated than the Javanese figures.

36. A giant kite of northeastern Malaysia, in the shape of a wayang siam puppet.

37. A Malaysian wayang kulit figure of Rama is almost pure Thai in the design of its headdress, costume, and dance position of the left hand.

38. The visual conception of this Malaysian wayang kulit puppet of the nine-headed Ravana (eight faces are carved in his crown) is also largely Thai.

39. Children's costumes in a Sundanese village, made of paper and cloth stretched over a bamboo frame, are designed to look like wayang golek doll puppets.

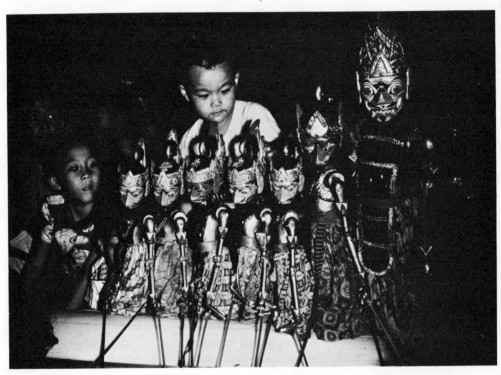

40. Children in Sunda admire wayang golek doll puppets ready for performance in the banana-log stage.

PART II

Theatre as Art

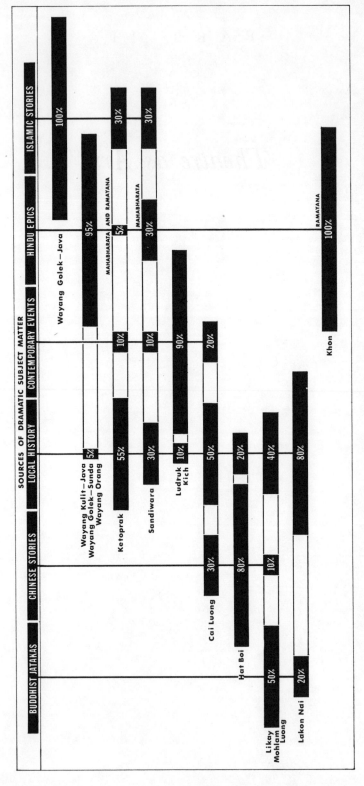

FIGURE 2. Approximate Percentage Distribution of Plays according to Source of Dramatic Subject Matter

CHAPTER 5

Drama

One of the most useful ways of looking at the plays of Southeast Asia is in terms of their origins. In spite of the tremendous bulk and variety of drama, most plays easily fall into one of six major categories of drama as far as the origin of subject matter is concerned.

SOURCES OF DRAMATIC MATERIAL

THE INDIAN EPICS

The first and perhaps most important source of dramatic material in all of Southeast Asia is the epic literature of India: the *Ramayana* and the *Mahabharata*. Most court dramas in Burma, Thailand, Laos, Cambodia, Malaysia, and Indonesia are based on one or the other of the epics, and popular and folk plays derive from them as well. On the mainland, the *Ramayana* is held in great esteem, but the *Mahabharata* is scarcely known. In Indonesia, both epics are known and performed but the *Mahabharata* is more commonly staged (I would estimate at a ratio of around ten to one). You will often hear Indonesians derisively refer to the *Ramayana* as "that monkey story."

It is instructive to note how differently the epics were treated as dramatic material in the Burma-Lao-Cambodia-Thailand cultural area and in the Java-Sunda-Bali-Malaya cultural area. In Cambodia, the first place on the mainland where the *Ramayana* was known, epic recitations were an integral part of the Hindu-Brahmanic religious political system. The story of Rama became widely known by all classes of society. But, the *Ramayana* was written in Sanskrit. It was not translated into the Khmer (Cambodian) language, hence no indigenous Khmer literature grew out of this great story. It remained for the Thai to take the elements of Cambodian dance, music, and, perhaps, simple dramatic dance segments, and create drama from them. The Thai were Hinayana Buddhists and felt no reverence for the Brahmanic content of the *Ramayana.* They translated the epic into their language, turning Rama into a Future Buddha. They made what alterations were necessary to make the story playable on the stage —something the Khmer could not do because to them the *Ramayana* in its Indian Sanskrit form was a sacred document. Through the centuries many Thai stage versions of the *Ramayana* were written.

Epic-based drama developed quite differently in Java. Here the *Ramayana* was translated into Javanese as early as A.D. 805. The Javanese translator did not slavishly reproduce the Indian text, but two-thirds of the way through began freely to compose his own version of the story.[1] In the *Mahabharata* the Javanese found unusual opportunites for developing a distinctive Javanese literature based on an Indian model. While retaining many of the original stories, Javanese poets and players created new plays using the *Mahabharata* cast of characters—the good Pandavas and the evil Kauravas. The great bulk of wayang stories performed in Java, in Sunda, in Bali, and to a lesser extent in Malaysia are these made-up stories.

In the wayang repertory today there are between two and three hundred such plays. On the mainland, perhaps ten or a dozen episodes from the *Ramayana* are staged as dramas, and these do not depart drastically from the Indian *Ramayana.* In brief, a copious and distinctive dramatic literature evolved out of epic materials in the islands, while on the mainland a limited number of dramas came to be written on the *Ramayana* theme.

Ramayana dramas of the mainland are often produced in a fragmented fashion. Sections of the story that might be considered important are left out while extraneous scenes are dragged in. This can be seen in the synopsis of the khon play given below. The play was staged in 1952 at the Silpakorn Theatre in Bangkok. The script is based on two of the most famous Thai language

texts of the *Ramayana* by King Rama I (1782–1809) and King
Rama II (1809–1824). The episode comes from Book Six of the
Ramayana.

Hanoman the Volunteer

Scene 1. Audience chamber, palace of Lanka: Ravana declares he
will take the field himself. Most of his many loyal brothers and
generals have been slain by Rama, Lakshmana, and the monkeys.
Ravana reviews the ogre army.

Scene 2. A pavilion in Rama's camp: Rama with Lakshmana; Hanoman, the white monkey; Ravana's brother Vibishana (who has left
Ravana); and others. Using magic powers that enable him to fore-
see the future, Vibishana warns Rama of Ravana's plan. Rama is
pleased that the war will end today and pledges the death of Ravana.
Rama reviews the army of monkeys. They march off to the battlefield.

Scene 3. The battlefield: The battle rages. Most of the ogre army is
killed. Though Rama severs Ravana's head from his body, he will
not die. Ravana uses magic power to heal his wounds and continues
fighting. At nightfall the battle is discontinued. Rama is discouraged
and asks Vibishana's advice. Vibishana reveals the secret of Ravana's
immortality: Ravana's soul has been extracted from his body and
the body cannot die unless the soul is simultaneously destroyed.
Hanoman volunteers to secure the soul from the hermit Gobut into
whose keeping Ravana has entrusted it.

Scene 4. At the hermitage (Goputra): Gobut receives Hanoman and
his companion Angada. Hanoman pretends to have been cruelly
treated by Rama, and asks Gobut to help him revenge himself. After
much entreaty, Gobut agrees to take Hanoman to Lanka; he asks
Angada to guard the soul of Ravana, for should the soul come near
Ravana's body it will immediately enter it. They depart.

Scene 5. The palace of Lanka: Ravana receives Gobut and Hanoman.
Ravana is furious when he sees his old enemy Hanoman, but Gobut
persuades him to take Hanoman into his service to fight Rama.
Ravana puts Hanoman in command of the ogre army, crowns him
as his son and heir apparent to the throne, and gives him his own
powerful sword. Hanoman reviews the ogre troops.

Scene 6. On the battlefield: Hanoman struts about, shouts taunts at
the monkey army, and challenges Lakshmana to fight. A mock
battle ensues in which Hanoman appears to slay thousands of monkey
soldiers.

Scene 7. The palace of Lanka: Hanoman returns victorious. Ravana
is delighted with Hanoman's supposed achievements; he presents to
the white monkey the palace of the heir apparent with all it contains, including the exceedingly beautiful widow of Ravana's slain
son. Hanoman is escorted to his palace.

Scene 8. In the palace of the heir apparent: Hanoman ardently courts Suvarn Kanyama, the widow. Hoping to divert his passion, she summons a troop of dancing girls to perform before him. He will not be distracted; he leads her to the bedchamber to make love.[2]

Unquestionably, the "obligatory scene" in this play is the scene in which Ravana's soul enters his body, thus making it possible for Rama to kill him. And up through the end of Scene 7 it appears as if this is the climax toward which the drama is building. But the climax and the obligatory scene are simply omitted. The action of the drama is left dangling in mid-air while a totally unrelated seduction episode is used to bring the play to a conclusion. We can imagine some of the reasons for this. The final scene includes a dance set-piece by a chorus of dancing girls (though this is a khon play), concluding an otherwise martial play on a romantic note. A Thai would likely point out that since the audience knows how the *Ramayana* comes out it is not necessary to show the end on stage. And to these reasons can be added one other: it is considered dangerous to portray the death of Ravana on a public stage. But whatever the reasons may have been, in this play the basic story line of the *Ramayana* is little changed, while minor rearrangements, deletions, and additions have been made for various reasons. In general, the core of the *Ramayana* story proved pretty much indigestible as dramatic material throughout Burma, Thailand, Cambodia, and Laos and from this epic no well-developed *dramatic* form emerged on the mainland (though many *theatre* forms did emerge).

To a Javanese, Allah created Adam and from Adam descended the Prophet Mohammed, Batara Guru (Shiva), and Vishnu. Vishnu was first incarnated as Rama in the *Ramayana* and later as Krishna—adviser to the Pandavas—in the *Mahabharata*. And from the Pandavas are descended, generation by generation, the kings and sultans who have ruled Java down into the twentieth century. Thus, the *Ramayana* and, more especially, the *Mahabharata* comprise a vital link connecting the Javanese present to the great mythological, religious past. One of the historic functions of wayang kulit drama has been to dramatize the spiritual succession of Javanese kingship. One of the most instructive of these plays is *Makutha Rama* (The Crown of Rama). It tells the purely Java-

nese story (there is no similar story in India) of the transfer of
kingship and royal legitimacy from the generation of the *Ramayana* to the generation of the *Mahabharata*. In its structure it is a
typical wayang play in most respects. Here is a rather complete
synopsis of the nine-hour play as performed in wayang kulit.

The Crown of Rama
Part I

Scene 1. In the kingdom of Astina: King Duryodana, eldest of the
Kaurava brothers, receives Prime Minister Sangkuni, Chief Adviser
Drona (Durna), Karna, and others. Duryodana recounts a dream
in which he has been assured of a long and successful reign, provided
he obtains a boon from the gods in the form of the "Crown of Rama."
He asks Karna to seek the crown for him. They all depart.

Scene 2. In the palace chambers: King Duryodana tells his wife
Banowati and his daughter Lesmanawati what has occurred.

Scene 3. In the palace courtyard: Many of King Duryodana's ninety-
eight brothers are noisily gathered awaiting the king's command.
They joke and roughhouse. Sangkuni enters, admonishes them to be
serious and to get their weapons, and orders the army to accompany
Karna. Karna and the army depart. During the march the soldiers
make crude jokes.

Scene 4. In the hermitage of Mount Kutharunggu: Hanoman (the
white monkey), Maenaka (a human), Jaksendra (a giant), and
Setubanda (an elephant) tell the hermit Kesawasidhi they are tired
of living; they wish him to intercede for their souls. Kesawasidhi
advises them not to seek happiness or magic powers, nor to seek
death, for this is to avoid being of service to the gods. They should
die only when the gods ordain it. Hanoman asks what their obligation to the gods is. Kesawasidhi replies they should wait for the gods'
will to be revealed. Karna and Sangkuni enter. Karna asks Kesawasidhi's help to obtain the Crown of Rama, but the hermit replies
that he does not know what it is. He asks why Karna leads an army
to obtain a boon from the gods. Karna, believing Kesawasidhi possesses the Crown, tries to drag the hermit off to Astina, but Hanoman comes to the hermit's defense. A battle (*perang gagal*) ensues.
Karna's magically endowed arrow is snatched from the air by Hanoman (who can fly). This so humiliates the proud Karna that he loses
all his magic power. Karna breaks off the fight and retires to the
forest to meditate. His leaderless army flees.

Part II

Scene 5. The village of Karangtumaritis: Semar, chief clown and
servant of Arjuna, enters with his two sons, Petruk and Gareng,
who are also clowns. They joke and sing humorous songs. Semar
advises his sons to seek Arjuna. They depart.

Scene 6. Hermit scene: Arjuna, the refined hero of the *Mahabharata*, meets Semar, Petruk, and Gareng. He tells them of a great boon which the gods are about to bestow on a man worthy of the honor. Arjuna vows he will obtain this boon—the Crown of Rama—for Yudistira, his older brother. He and the clowns depart for Mount Kutharunggu to seek the Crown.

Scene 7. A hermitage on Mount Deksana in the Kingdom of Singgela: Vibishana, who succeeded his ogre brother Ravana as king of Lanka, says he wishes to die since all his friends and his relatives, including Rama, are dead. He knows Vishnu is now reincarnated in the person of Krishna; his one wish is to meet Krishna to gain his advice on how to die. He orders his prime minister to proclaim his son, Bisawarna, the new king of Lanka. The prime minister goes. Four retainers of Vibishana reproach him, saying they are his spiritual brothers who serve his bodily and spiritual needs and whose only wish it is to live or die with him. Vibishana replies that if their feelings are genuine they should go to Mount Kutharunggu where a warrior will kill them. They all depart.

Scene 8. In the forest near Kutharunggu: The four retainers of Vibishana meet Arjuna and the clowns and ask to be killed. At first Arjuna refuses to kill them, for they are innocent of any crime; but soon a quarrel arises and in anger he slays them. Each time one is killed, however, one of the others leaps over the corpse, bringing it back to life through magic power. Arjuna creates a raging fire (with his greater magic power) which consumes his attackers and destroys them, thus ending the battle.

Part III

Scene 9. The hermitage on Mount Kutharunggu: Hanoman reports to the hermit Kesawasidhi that Karna has disappeared. Kesawasidhi reprimands Hanoman for four faults: intervening in a quarrel which was not his; doubting the hermit's ability to defend himself; humiliating a great warrior like Karna; and stealing another man's weapon. Hanoman laments that he is guilty whether he acts or not. Kesawasidhi advises him to become an ascetic, to go to Mount Kendhalisada and there stand guard at the cave where the soul of Ravana is kept prisoner. Hanoman and his three friends leave. Vibishana enters and demands to know why Kesawasidhi has not asked his permission to enter his kingdom. They fight. Each summons magic weapons to help him. Vibishana creates a serpent which is devoured by a garuda bird created by Kesawasidhi. Vibishana shoots an arrow into the breast of the hermit, who then turns into an enormous giant. Vibishana knows this must be Vishnu incarnated as Krishna for no one else has such great magic power. He has, therefore, found Krishna; he asks to be killed. Kesawasidhi burns Vibishana to ashes. As the king's soul rises to heaven it meets the soul of his brother,

Kumbakarna, in one of the lower levels of paradise. The two souls return to Kesawasidhi who advises Kumbakarna to seek one more reincarnation on earth to atone for his many sins in past lives. He is to find a great warrior with a talon on each hand, enter the body of the warrior, and ascend to heaven with the warrior's soul when the warrior dies. They exit.

Scene 10. The palace of the Pandava kingdom of Amarta: King Yudistira sends Bima's son Gatutkatja to find Krishna. They depart.

Scene 11. In the countryside: Gatutkatja flies on ahead, but Bima, not knowing which way to proceed, meditates until his alter ego, Dewa Rutchi, senses his need and sends a whirlwind to clear a path for him and to direct his way.

Scene 12. The garden of Arjuna's palace in Madukara: Four of Arjuna's wives discuss his long absence. Two of them, Srikandi and Sembadra, decide to set out to find him. While praying for heavenly assistance, the god Narada enters complaining that their prayers have caused a disturbance in heaven. In response to their requests for help he changes them into men and agrees to transport them to Arjuna.

Scene 13. In the forest: Srikandi, disguised as a man, meets and defeats Gatutkatja who promises to do anything the victor asks. Srikandi is incensed that Gatutkatja would so lightly set aside his duty to find Arjuna. "She" orders him to follow and be prepared to attack a great warrior when ordered to do so. They leave.

Scene 14. In the forest: The soul of Kumbakarna fights with Bima, who is the great warrior with talons on his hands. He enters Bima's body as Kesawasidhi had commanded.

Scene 15. The hermitage of Kesawasidhi on Mount Kutharunggu: Arjuna explains that he and the clowns have come to submit themselves as Kesawasidhi's pupils in order to gain from the hermit the secret of the Crown of Rama. The hermit replies that the Crown of Rama is not a crown of jewels but a crown of spiritual knowledge known as the *Hasta Brata*, or the Eight Precepts, meaning that every great ruler must possess the qualities of Earth, Sun, Moon, Ocean, Fire, Wind, Water, and the Stars. Accepting Arjuna as his pupil, Kesawasidhi orders Arjuna to find Karna and return to him his arrow. Arjuna exits.

Scene 16. In the forest: Arjuna meets Karna and returns the weapon. Karna demands that Arjuna give him the Crown of Rama. He does not believe Arjuna's explanation that the Crown is not a physical object that can be handed from one person to another. They fight with daggers (*kris*) until Karna is wounded and flees. Bima enters and Arjuna insists that both return to Kesawasidhi. They depart.

Scene 17. The hermitage of Kesawasidhi: Bima finds the clowns present; he chastises them for not having given their impetuous young master (Arjuna) better advice befitting their greater age and experience. Sembadra and Srikandi, still disguised as men, and Gatutkatja enter. They are furious with Arjuna for having been gone from home so long. They attack Arjuna and Kesawasidhi and order Gatutkatja to attack Bima (his own father). The sides are so evenly matched neither side can win. Kesawasidhi returns to his form as Krishna and the wives resume their normal shape. The wives nag Krishna for having put all of them to so much unnecessary trouble. He replies that as a god he had no power to choose the person who would receive the Crown of Rama; it was necessary for him to wait until Arjuna had revealed himself worthy of it.

Scene 18. The palace of Astina: King Duryodana becomes furious when Karna reports that Arjuna has received the Crown of Rama and that the Kaurava army has been defeated. Duryodana orders the army to prepare for war. They depart for Amarta.

Scene 19. The palace of Amarta: The prime minister reports that the palace is surrounded by the Kaurava army. King Yudistira orders Bima, Arjuna, and Gatutkatja to attack the Kauravas. They exit.

Scene 20. The battlefield: Bima attacks Duryodana; Arjuna attacks Karna; Gatutkatja fights all the others. The Pandavas are defeating the Kauravas when Krishna takes pity on the Kauravas. He creates a great wind which sweeps the entire Kaurava army back to Astina. Bima dances a traditional victory dance.

Scene 21. The palace of Amarta: Krishna with the Pandavas. King Yudistira orders a feast to celebrate their victory.[3]

Htin Aung's remark that Javanese wayang plays "have very little dramatic structure" and are "formless"[4] could not be more wrong. Wayang kulit plays follow a fixed dramatic structure. Every play is written in three parts. In Part I two (sometimes three) kingdoms attempt to achieve the same objective, thus precipitating the basic conflict of the drama. Part I ends with the armies of the kingdoms clashing and the "bad" side—either the Kauravas or a foreign (*sabrangan*) ogre kingdom—being temporarily bested. The clowns appear in the first scene of Part II and the hero of the play—usually a Pandava prince—is introduced. Plot complications follow, concluding in a battle scene in which the Pandava prince slays several minor antagonists. In Part III the Pandavas are about to accomplish their goal when they are attacked by either the Kauravas or the ogre kingdom. A general battle ensues. The Pandavas defeat their enemies and celebrate their victory.

Part I of every wayang play contains a major audience scene

(*djedjer*), a scene in the outer audience hall in which the army is dispatched (*paseban djawi*), a scene showing the army fighting its way through a forest (*perang ampjak*), an audience scene in a second kingdom (*djedjer sabrangan*), and a battle between the armies of the two kingdoms (*perang gagal*). The scenes always appear in this order. Other scenes may be included but they do not disturb the traditional pattern. The other two parts of a wayang play are somewhat less structured, yet certain scenes in each are obligatory.

Although the major conflict in the *Mahabharata* epic is between Pandavas and Kauravas, in many plays the introduction of a third side—a foreign kingdom—makes the conflict three-sided. In The Crown of Rama the role of the foreign kingdom is not particularly important. In the *Baratayuda,* after the Kauravas are killed, the foreign kingdom becomes the main antagonist of the Pandavas. This is a synopsis of the final play in the *Baratayuda.*

Parakesit Becomes King
Part I
In the Kingdom of the Gods: Batara Guru (Shiva), is discussing with the other Gods the outcome of the *Baratayuda.* The Pandavas have been victorious and all the Kauravas, including Duryodana, have been slain. But the Pandavas' ranks have been thinned by the conflict too. Only Parakesit, son of Abimanju and grandson of Arjuna, remains to carry on the line of Pandu. Batara Guru decides Parakesit should succeed Yudistira as king. Batara Narada is dispatched to earth to make arrangements. In the foreign kingdom of Imantaka, the ogre king Nirbita (or Niwatakawadja) is informed of the god's plan by one of his officers, Tjakil. The ogre army is dispatched. In the palace at Astina all the Pandavas are gathered to receive the god Narada. Parakesit is crowned king of Astina; Yudistira yields his throne to him. They all retire to face the attack of the ogre army from Imantaka. An inconclusive battle between secondary characters ensues.

Part II
The clowns Semar, Petruk, and Gareng enter. They joke and sing. Arjuna enters and is attacked by the ogre Tjakil. Arjuna cannot defeat Tjakil. He retires to the hermitage of Tjalandara, a powerful holy man. Bima arrives and requests the hermit's blessing. They are attacked by Kala, Batara Guru's bloodthirsty son, and by Kala's mistress, Durga. Initially Kala and Durga prevail, but Semar pelts them with a barrage of his feces until they flee in confusion. Arjuna meets Tjakil and kills him.

Part III

The Pandavas prepare to take their leave of the world. Accompanied by Krishna and Arjuna's wife Sembadra, they visit their mother, Kunti. Kunti enters the temple [supposedly a temple of the Dieng group in central Java], and as incense wafts around her, she flies up to heaven. Sembadra follows her. Yudistira, Bima, Arjuna, the twins Nakula and Sadewa, and finally Krishna enter the temple, die, and ascend to heaven. The ogre army attacks once more and it is defeated by Parakesit and the army of Astina. Narada, other gods, and the new King Parakesit celebrate their victory and discuss the future of the kingdom.

JATAKA BUDDHIST BIRTH STORIES

A second important source of dramatic material is the collection of Buddhist birth stories known as the *Jataka*. These stories are known mainly, but not exclusively, in the countries in which Hinayana Buddhism is embraced—Burma, Thailand, Cambodia, and Laos. Only a few of the 547 stories which comprise the official *Jataka* collection are performed on stage. *Manora*, the story of the lovely kinnari bird-maiden, is the best known of these. Many local myths and folk tales, converted into so-called *Jataka* stories by transforming the hero into a Future Buddha, are staged, especially in popular genre such as likay, lakon jatri, lakon bassac, mohlam luong, zat pwe, and nang talung. One of the latter type of *Jataka* stories is *Sin Xay* (also called *Sin Xai* and *Sininjaya*). It exists in both prose and poetic versions. Copies of the story are possessed by most Buddhist wats or temples in Cambodia and Laos. Here is a Cambodian version.

Sin Xay

The monarch of the kingdom has a beautiful sister who is carried off by the king of the Khaks, a race of ogres with supernatural power. The King abdicates the throne out of remorse. He becomes a monk and sets out in search of his sister. On his journey he meets and marries seven beautiful sisters. He hopes one will bear him a brave son who will defeat the Khak king and rescue his abducted sister. In time all his wives conceive. Nine sons are born. Six are normal, three are unnatural beings—Sihalat is an elephant, Sang Thong is a golden sea conch, and Sin Xay is a child carrying a bow and arrows. The King sends the three into exile, but Indra, taking pity on them, cares for them and builds them a magnificent palace in the midst of the forest. When the King's six normal sons reach the age of nine, they are sent forth to find their aunt. Meanwhile,

Sin Xay sends a magic arrow, speeding with the sound of thunder, to the king of the Khut (Garuda). The bird-king and all his subjects come to serve Sin Xay, recognizing he is King of the Worlds (Buddha).

Indra guides the six brothers to Sin Xay and, together with the bird army, the whole group sets out to search for the King's sister. At the first sign of danger the six brothers halt in fear; Sin Xay leaves Sihalat behind to protect them. With only San Thong as his companion, Sin Xay sets out on a series of adventures which eventually brings him to the kingdom of the ogres, but not before the nine-year-old boy slays a seven-headed, flame-breathing serpent, crosses the seven seas (Sang Thong transforms himself into a ship for the purpose), defeats four monstrous man-eating giants, climbs a precipitous mountain, evades a herd of elephants, avoids the seductions of an ogress transformed into an enchanting maiden, puts to flight an ogre hermit, and disports for a week with five hundred kinnari bird-maidens.

Sin Xay and Sang Thong rescue their aunt, then turn to face the attacks of the Khak army and many serpents (*naga*). With his magic bow, Sin Xay decimates the ranks of the Khak army. The Khak king turns for help to his brother, Vanula. But the gigantic Vanula is deep in sleep and cannot be roused. The Khak army is destroyed and the king of the Khak is killed. Vanula is proclaimed new king of the Khak. With his aunt and brothers Sin Xay returns to his homeland. He is acclaimed by the people and crowned their new king.

The similarity between this quest-epic and the *Ramayana* is evident. In both a disinherited son of the king redeems himself and returns to ascend the throne. In both the abduction of a woman of the royal family by an ogre antagonist precipitates the action of the story. In both the hero rescues the abducted woman (Sin Xay's motive is disinterested; Rama's is highly personal). In both an animal kingdom helps the hero (the apes because Rama first helps them; the birds because Sin Xay is a manifestation of Buddha). Vanula and Kumbakarna play almost identical roles as sleeping giants who might save the kingdom, but their fates differ: Vanula sleeps through it all and inherits the throne, while Kumbakarna is eventually roused, fights, and is killed for his trouble. Does this show that one epic influenced the other? Or that both derive from a common source? I don't know, but the similarities are remarkable.

A common attribute of *Jataka* stories, in addition to the fact that the hero is Buddha in a former life, is the great magic power which the hero comes to possess through knowledge of Buddhism. We can see this in the brief synopsis which follows of the first part of *Sang Thong* or The Golden Prince of the Sea Conch. A companion story to *Sin Xay*, it relates the adventures of Sang Thong, the sea conch, who is Sin Xay's brother. This is a condensation of a Thai version.

Sang Thong

There once lived a king named Yosavimol, whose principal wife gave birth to a sea conch. A jealous minor wife of the King bribed a soothsayer to warn him the conch would bring him evil. The wife was banished. From the conch there came forth a beautiful boy, who was called Sang Thong. When the minor wife heard of this she had the King order the boy thrown into the ocean. A naga saved the boy and gave him to an ogress, Panturat, who raised him as her own child. So that Sang Thong would not know her real identity, she assumed human form and hid from him her magic pools of gold and silver (in which a person could dip himself), her disguise as a negrito (Ngo) which could make its wearer invulnerable, and her crystal shoes and golden staff with which one could fly through the air.

When fifteen years old, Sang Thong discovers his mother is in fact an ogress. He steps into the golden pool, to become the "Golden Prince"; he steals the magic clothes and flies off to a mountain top. Panturat pleads with him, but he will not return. She then passes on to him a secret formula known as the Great Jewel, which, when scratched on a stone, will deliver up to the owner all the fish of the sea and the deer of the forest.* Having done this out of love for him, she dies of a broken heart.

CHINESE NOVELS AND PLAYS

Chinese novels and plays constitute a third source of dramatic material. Two important novels are *San Kuo Chih Yen I* (The Romance of the Three Kingdoms) and *Shui Hu Chuan* (By the Water's Edge). Both are long, rambling, and filled with exciting incidents suitable for dramatization. The former chronicles the struggle among the kingdoms of Wei, Shu, and Wu for control of China during the years A.D. 220–265. A whole series of Chinese *wu*, or military, plays were written based on the wars and

---

*In later sections of the story, Sang Thong uses these magic powers to defeat his enemies, win a bride, and obtain the throne of his father's kingdom.

intrigues delineated in the novel. The latter deals with events of the Sung dynasty (A.D. 960–1279) set against a backdrop of the social unrest that prevailed at the time. Major characters portrayed are commoners: corrupt officials, landlords, comic servants, aspiring scholars, thieves, and spirited young girls. Many Chinese *wen,* or domestic, plays were adapted from this novel. *Hung Lou Meng* (The Dream of the Red Chamber), *Hsi Yu Chi* (Trip to the Western Regions), and other novels also were dramatized in China. These novels and plays based on the novels were introduced into Vietnam and also into Cambodia and Thailand over a period of several hundred years. In Thailand *San Kuo* (The Romance of the Three Kingdoms) was translated under the Thai title *Sam Kok,* in the eighteenth century.[5] Plays based on Chinese stories are staged by popular troupes in Cambodia, Laos, and Burma, but it is only in Vietnam that Chinese literature constitutes the largest single source of dramatic material. All but a few plays in the hat boi repertory are of Chinese origin and a large number of cai luong plays are as well.

Here are brief synopses of two cai luong plays, originally adapted from Chinese for hat boi and then borrowed from hat boi by cai luong. I cannot say how much they have been altered in the borrowing, but presumably they differ in many respects from the originals. The first appears to be based on a Chinese wu or military play, but with a love story added. The second is primarily a love story, typical of many cai luong plays being performed today. It is based on a Chinese tale, but in its sentimental romantic atmosphere it is characteristic of cai luong. Note that the characters in both plays have Vietnamese names.

The End of Love's Raging War

A traitorous mandarin, Ho Phuoc, has poisoned Emperor Anh Vuong and usurped the throne. When two loyal generals protest, they are executed summarily. The late emperor's wife begs for mercy for the young crown prince and princess. Ho Phuoc has her blinded and drives her from the city with the princess. He orders the prince buried alive. The prince, however, is rescued by a holy seer, Truong Khong, who raises the prince along with another young pupil, Cam Son, at a hermitage deep in the mountains. From the seer the prince learns military arts and the law. Years pass. One day when the usurper Ho Phuoc is hunting in the forest, he is attacked by an enemy general, Ky Chau. The prince happens to be passing by. He intervenes and saves Ho Phuoc's life. The prince does not know who Ho Phuoc is, so he accepts from him many honors, including marriage to his daughter. The prince enjoys his new life at the imperial court. Soon Cam Son joins him there.

Several years pass. Ho Phuoc orders the prince to lead a punitive expedition against General Ky Chau. En route, the prince encounters and kills Kuong Liem Tran, only to discover he has killed the father of Cam Son. Cam Son retires to the forest in anger. He finds shelter in a woodcutter's hut, in which the former empress and princess have taken refuge. Cam Son and the princess fall in love. The prince seeks out Cam Son to ask his forgiveness. He does not recognize his mother and sister until they produce a brooch with the emperor's insignia on it. The prince's mother tells him he is living at the court of his father's murderer. She urges him to revenge their wrongs. The prince and Cam Son vow to kill Ho Phuoc. They set off for the capital. After fierce fighting Ho Phuoc is killed and the prince ascends the throne.

A Hero of Humble Origin

Han Vu Lang is a simple peasant who tends his fields in a remote and quiet spot along the river. One day Yen Ly, a prince of the kingdom of Yen, is set upon by a band of robbers. Han Vu Lang rescues the prince. In gratitude, the prince brings Han Vu Lang to the capital of Yen where he installs him in the court as his sworn spiritual brother. Dressed in his simple black country clothes, Han Vu Lang feels ashamed among the splendidly dressed mandarins and warriors of the court. He meets and falls in love with a young lady of high rank, but, since he believes she could not love him, he remains silent. To his grief he finds that she is the Princess Phuong Anh, engaged to marry Prince Yen Ly. His grief turns to distraction when she reveals she loves him, not the prince. She implores her father (the king) to release her from her marriage pledge to the prince. The king refuses.

At this moment a loathsome courtier, Trieu Dat, asserts his claim to the princess' hand. The king acquiesces. But Han Vu Lang fights Trieu Dat to protect the honor of both his country and his spiritual brother the prince. He kills Trieu Dat. Princess Phuong Anh is restored to the prince.

Accompanied by his clown-servant, Han Vu Lang goes deep into the forest, where he tries to ameliorate his sorrow through fasting and meditation. He is visited by a court lady who has fallen in love with him. He rejects her advances. Princess Phuong Anh appears. She has fled from court and from her new husband to be with Han Vu Lang. He implores her to return to the prince, but she will not leave. Prince Yen Ly finds them together and, furious with jealousy and outrage, he orders Han Vu Lang beheaded. Han Vu Lang accepts the sentence without protest. He is about to be executed. The clown-servant reminds the prince that he owes his life to Han Vu Lang and that Han Vu Lang is not at fault for what has happened. The prince is chastened. He relinquishes Princess Phuong Anh to Han Vu Lang, and they are all united in friendship once more.

LOCAL LEGEND AND HISTORY

Innumerable plays are based on local legends and local history. Just as the stories are various, so are the plays, but perhaps the single most common type of plot concerns local wars of rebellion against foreign domination. Almost every country in Southeast Asia has known periods of foreign domination, by both Asian neighbors and European powers. Plays depicting the evils of the enemy and the virtues of the local hero appeal to nationalistic sentiments and are particularly popular in theatre in the popular tradition—ketoprak, sandiwara, bangsawan, cai luong, mohlam luong, likay, lakon bassac, and zat pwe. Here is a ketoprak play, produced in central Java in 1964. In Indonesia, the Dutch are the chief "foreign enemy," as in this play.

Untung Suropati

Scene 1. Susana, daughter of Edleer Moor, a high Dutch colonial official, and Untung, a young Javanese of good social position, are in love with each other. When Untung, in a polite and dignified manner, asks Moor for Susana's hand the father furiously forbids the marriage. It is unthinkable that a Dutch girl would marry a Javanese. He has Untung and his clown-companion, Saridjan, clapped into jail. Susana tearfully promises to wait.

Scene 2. In prison: Untung is a model prisoner. Others in the common cell react violently to the arrogant bullying of their Dutch guards; they plan to kill the guards and escape. The guards, however, suspect the plan. They choose the smallest prisoner in the cell and beat him severely. Untung becomes incensed. He speaks passionately to the other prisoners about the equal rights of all men. He rouses them to rebellion; they overpower the guards and make their escape.

Scene 3. In the countryside: Dutch troops under Captain Rois pursue Untung and the prisoners. Using superior strategy, Untung traps the Dutch and forces them to surrender. Captain Rois praises Untung. He offers him a commission in the Dutch army. Untung accepts. Saridjan calls Untung a traitor to his people. He stands on a stump and delivers a tirade against disloyalty to the people, cowardice, and self-seeking opportunism. Untung quietly explains that he wants to gain time to get badly needed weapons in order to fight the Dutch more effectively. He asks the prisoners to have faith in his leadership. They give him their support.

Scene 4. On Mount Tjikendul: Untung and his troops have been dispatched by the Dutch to capture Prince Purbaya, a rebel against the Dutch colonial government. Untung joins forces with the prince. The prince is in dispair, for many farmers and villagers in his band have been killed. He feels he cannot ask them to sacrifice themselves for the rebellion any longer. A young girl, Ratu Gisik Kesuma, urges the prince to fight and never cease fighting for the sake of the ordinary people already slain by the Dutch. Saridjan brings a letter from Susana. She is going to marry a Dutch merchant who can offer her a settled life, and asks Untung's forgiveness. Untung is not bitter, but he is deeply hurt. A Dutch force approaches. Untung courageously leads his rebels against them, but they are forced to flee before the superior Dutch army. Untung decides to seek the protection of the Sultan of Tjirebon.

Scene 5. The palace of the Sultan of Tjirebon: Prince Purbaja admonishes the district ruler, Prince Suropati, about his arrogant conduct toward the common people. He should respect the will of the people, not the will of Dutch officials. Suropati replies that as he is the sultan's son he needs neither the people's advice nor their help. Untung and his friends enter. Suropati instantly takes a liking to Ratu Gisik Kesuma and announces she will be his mistress. Untung denounces Suropati as a tyrant. They fight; Suropati is killed. The rejoicing people give Untung the nickname "Untung Suropati" in honor of his brave deed. The Sultan of Tjirebon enters. He suggests they seek protection of the Prime Minister of Kartasura (Surakarta) in central Java. They all depart.

Scene 6. In Kartasura: Untung and his group are received by the Prime Minister. He tells them the Dutch have troops on the way. He cannot possibly shelter them. Untung has recently married Ratu Gisik Kesuma. Partly out of consideration for her, he orders the rebels to retire to a secret cottage in the mountains.

Scene 7. A mountain cottage in east Java: Dutch troops attack Untung and his band. Their commander is killed by Untung. The rest of the Dutch troops flee. However, Untung knows another unit of troops will soon be after them. He and his band leave for yet another hiding place, at Pasaruhan a short distance away.

The structure of this play is extremely loose. Episodes are simply strung together and halfway along the plot ceases to develop any further. The last two scenes add nothing new to the story. However, the story of a historical Suropati serves as an excellent peg on which to hang contemporary pronationalist, anticolonial sentiments. The troupe which produces this play is affiliated with the Indonesian Communist Party.

In Thailand the chief foreign enemy has always been Burma. Likay troupes do many plays which chronicle Burma's invasions of Thai soil. The following play was produced by high school students in Bangkok in 1963. It is adapted from a well-known Thai historical work written in the 1940's.

Mahadevi

The Thai armies have been defeated by a vicious Burmese king, San Daw. He is greatly hated for his overbearing attitude toward the Thai. He has killed the deposed Thai king and insists that the late king's daughter become his wife. She refuses. San Daw is about to take her by force, when a young Thai commoner from the north comes to her aid. He fights a host of Burmese soldiers, kills the Burmese king, and reinstates Thai rule.

The historic invader of Vietnam is China. A common plot in cai luong shows a Vietnamese hero rising against Chinese overlords. This is a cai luong play performed in Saigon in 1963.

Falling Petals in the Garden

In the fourteenth century Vietnam was repeatedly invaded by armies of the Ching emperors. Chief among the generals of the Tran dynasty who fought against the invaders was Kha Quyen, who is presently living in solitude in a ruined temple in the forest. He is disguised as a demon. He is visited by Lady Diep Anh. Seeing her he says: I know who you are and why you have come. You are Diep Anh, mistress to the hated Chinese general, Moc Thanh. You once loved Kha Quyen, when he was young and an unimportant scholar. But later you found that your sister, Co Le, also loved Kha Quyen and, burning with jealousy, when the Chinese came you took the opportunity to marry the lecherous Moc Thanh. Now he uses you for his own purposes and under his order you come to lure Kha Quyen to captivity and death.

With that, Kha Quyen drops his disguise and reveals himself. Diep Anh explains she has come to find him, but only to redeem her father who is suspected of treachery by the Chinese. They confess their love. They prepare to leave their homeland and build a new life far away. At this point Co Le appears. She reminds her sister of her sacred mission to save their father. The women persuade Kha Quyen to surrender himself, for Moc Thanh has promised to treat him well. Kha Quyen cannot resist their appeals; they leave for Moc Thanh's mansion.

Kha Quyen is seized, tortured, and blinded by a gleeful Moc

Thanh. He is not killed outright in order to prolong his torment. To make the sisters suffer as much as possible (Moc Thanh knows both are in love with Kha Quyen), Kha Quyen is driven from the city destitute. Blind and forsaken, he wanders through the countryside.

This play combines a love story with an antiforeign theme. So does *Untung Suropati*. It is interesting to note how the love story is used differently in the two plays. Love is the key motivating force in Falling Petals in the Garden and the romantic atmosphere of the play is strong. In *Untung Suropati*, on the other hand, the hero's love affairs are mainly plot devices to precipitate further action in the play, and the ideological theme soon overshadows the love theme.

Past wars with neighboring states provide ready-made foreign enemies for popular history plays in many countries. In Laos the foreign enemy is usually Vietnam or China; in Cambodia, Vietnam or Thailand; in Burma, Thailand; and in Thailand, Burma or Cambodia.

One of the most famous local history legends in Southeast Asia is the story of the Javanese prince Panji. *Panji* plays are produced in ketoprak, sandiwara, and ardja in Indonesia. In Java, Raden Panji is considered to be a descendent of the Pandavas, heroes of the *Mahabharata*. On the mainland, where Panji generally is called Inao, the hero Inao is thought of as a Future Buddha, hence the plays are considered *Jatakas*. In Thailand the *Jataka* version of *Inao* that is most commonly staged is that written by King Rama II (1809–1824). Here is a synopsis of the over-all story line; many plays are drawn from this material.

Inao (or Panji)

Prince Inao has been betrothed since childhood to the Princess Busba, daughter of his uncle, King of Daha. Inao, however, has fallen in love with another princess and refuses to carry out his obligation to Busba. He goes to live with his new bride at the court of her father, who is King of Manya.

The King of Daha is deeply incensed. He offers Busba's hand in marriage to the first person who requests it. Immediately Choraka, a crude and repulsive warrior, asks to marry her. It is too late for the king to withdraw his rash offer. He is about to order Busba to marry Choraka when the King of Kamankunin appears to press his suit. When told she is already promised to Choraka, the king gathers his army and attacks Daha.

[106]

Inao, being a nephew of the King of Daha, is obliged to come to Daha's defense. He does so, but with great reluctance. He is made commander-in-chief of Daha's armies, and leads the armies to victory. When the king invites him to visit the palace to be honored, Inao cannot refuse. During his visit he sees Busba for the first time. She is ravishingly beautiful. His passion is aroused. He curses himself for having rejected her. He finds every reason he can to remain at the palace. As the day for Busba's marriage to Choraka approaches, Inao falls into deep melancholy. Finally he retires to the forest to compose himself and to gain peace of mind.

In time, Inao emerges from the forest strengthened with magic powers. He overcomes innumerable obstacles, finally defeats all his enemies, and makes Busba his bride.[6]

The early romantic episodes of the story are most commonly performed in Thai and Cambodian lakon nai. In Indonesia and Malaysia both the early episodes and those recounting the hero's adventures following his meditation in the forest are popular on the stage.

The following synopsis is of a local Cambodian legend which is performed in lakon bassac and a *Jataka*. The magical powers so important in the plot of the play are probably related to a fairly primitive level of Buddhism.

Lien Ton

In order to escape from an ogre king, Prince Lien Ton turns himself into a horse. The ogre king sees through the ruse, however. He catches and devours the horse except for a scrap of flesh which becomes a fish. A beautiful princess bathes in the river with her handmaidens. She notices the fish swimming near her. It nuzzles her. She catches the fish and takes it back to the palace with her.

In her chambers the prince reveals his true identity. He flirts with her. They fall in love. When the king enters, the prince turns back into a fish. The prince alternates between his handsome human form and being a fish in a series of rapidly moving farce scenes. Finally the prince reveals himself long enough to make love to the princess and marry her.

Years pass and the prince takes as a second wife the beautiful younger sister of his first wife. The prince is now middle-aged. With his grown son, he goes to fight the ogre king. The ogre king and his warriors are slain with the help of magic weapons. The prince now meets a third princess and falls in love with her. His first two wives object. After several scenes of flirting with his new love and fleeing from his wives, the prince marries for a third time.

ISLAMIC STORIES

Islamic tales, brought to Southeast Asia from Arab countries of the Near East, make up the fifth major source of dramatic material. Apparently many reached Southeast Asia by way of India.[7] Some have only the loosest connection with Islam, such as popular romances about Alexander and other Near Eastern adventurers that become swashbuckling action dramas in likay, bangsawan, sandiwara, and ketoprak. Others are famous tales known throughout the Islamic world that tell of the might and the glory of Islam. One series of the latter type concerns Amir Hamzah, who, according to the story, converted most of the Arab world to Islam by warfare and example. They are usually called *Menak* plays. They comprise almost the entire Javanese wayang golek repertory and are also performed in ketoprak, sandiwara, Malayan wayang kulit, and bangsawan. Here is a *Menak* play as seen in Jogjakarta, Java, in a nine-hour wayang golek performance in 1964. The synopsis is greatly condensed and gives only the major outlines of the plot.

Audience in the palace of a powerful king of Arabia: The king receives the ambassador representing Amir Hamzah's brother who is ruler of a neighboring kingdom. Amir is hated by his brother for having embraced the Islamic faith. The ambassador asks the king's help to kill Amir. The king advises the ambassador to have Amir's brother send Amir an invitation to a wedding. When Amir arrives he will be unarmed; the powerful king will strike him down. The ambassador agrees and departs.

In Amir's palace: Amir and one of his brothers, Maktal, discuss the invitation which has just arrived. Maktal warns it is a trick, but Amir declines to follow his brother's advice. Maktal departs with Amir's two clown-servants and a small group of warriors. In the countryside they meet and are attacked by a small army of the powerful king. Maktal's forces are driven off.

Meanwhile, Amir has decided to send his son to the wedding as his representative. The son departs. Maktal reports the previous fighting to Amir. Amir sends off his prime minister at the head of a large army. They encounter the army of a vassal of Amir's wicked brother. The vassal is killed by the prime minister, who discusses the death of the pagan prince in Islamic religious terms.

In Amir's kingdom: The prime minister returns to report the death of the vassal prince. Amir's son arrives at the wedding; he presents himself respectfully to his uncle. His uncle is enraged at Amir's "deceit" in not coming and orders his son to kill Amir's son.

The two cousins fight. The battle rages through the fields and into the forest. At last Amir's son defeats his opponent, but spares his life according to Islamic teaching. The defeated son reports his failure to his father. His father berates him for weakness and cowardice. The king orders his son to dwell in the forest as an ascetic in order to develop strength of mind and soul.

The structure of this play is similar to the structure of the wayang kulit play given a few pages earlier. Characters and religious content are different, but they have been poured into the basic pattern long set by Hindu-Javanese wayang kulit. This particular play ends on an inconclusive note because it was performed as one part in a series. In the next play, the story would be picked up where this one leaves off. Were a dalang to perform this play by itself, he would most likely end the play with a celebration in the palace of Amir Hamzah after the son returned to report his victory.

CONTEMPORARY STORIES

Contemporary stories are the sixth major source of dramatic material. Plays based on contemporary life make up the great bulk of the repertory of kich and ludruk troupes and are sometimes performed in ketoprak, bangsawan, sandiwara, and cai luong. Plays deal with such issues of modern life as equality of social status, free choice of marriage partners, crime, the roles of women in society, economic inequality, and the conflict between the older and the younger generations. In general there is little true discussion of the issues presented. Right and wrong are boldly stereotyped. The good and the bad may be different from the good and the bad of traditional drama, but the distinction is just as clear.

At the risk of oversimplification, I suggest that contemporary plays tend to fall into two types: those which offer new solutions to the issues raised, and those which do not. The former are usually strongly ideological. The following ludruk play, performed in 1964 by a well-known professional troupe affiliated with the Indonesian Communist Party, is a good example.*

*The inclusion of two Communist-oriented scenarios from Indonesia and none from other countries reflects the actual state of affairs among professional troupes in Southeast Asia as of this writing. The Communist Party has been the main political party active in theatre and it has been active mainly in Indonesia. See Part IV.

A Happy Wedding

Scene 1. Living room of an upper middle-class home in a large east Javanese city: The heroine, daughter of a government official, is flirting with the houseboy. He is played as a comic character. They are in love, but in traditional Javanese fashion, he will not rise from his knees in her presence since he is a servant. She tries to kiss him. He scurries away from her on his knees. The boy's father enters. He is a poor laborer, the chief comic character—*dagelan*—in the play. He tells his son to abandon his feudal attitudes. There is much comic horseplay as the father urges the son to stand straight and to propose to the heroine. The bashful son skulks behind the chairs; the heroine tries to pull him out; the dagelan berates his son. The heroine's family-approved suitor enters. He is a swaggering young hoodulm, dressed in black shirt, yellow necktie, and black fedora hat a la American gangster movies. He forces the girl to kiss him. The boy tries to interfere; the suitor kicks him out of the room. The dagelan takes a yardstick and drives the suitor away. The son returns and the heroine showers him with kisses, as if he had been the one who saved her. The dagelan proudly pantomimes how he beat the suitor. At that moment the suitor returns with the police, charging the dagelan with assault and battery. The police take the stick from the dagelan's hand and march him off to the police station.

Scene 2. The police station: Brought before the police officer, the dagelan assumes the pose of the wronged "little man." He is all wide-eyed innocence, and pretends to be cowed by the majesty of officialdom. "Me? Beat that man? With a stick? What stick? Oh, *that* stick. I never saw it in my life. My stick, you say? Is that my stick? How could that be? I'm just a poor man. How could I ever afford to buy a stick like that? (He sniffles.) Holding it you say? Me? The policeman saw *me* holding it? (He laughs deprecatingly.) Well, it's such a *small* stick, isn't it? (He breaks it in half.) Such a *small* stick!" The police officer pretends to accept this explanation. The charges are dropped. The suitor protests. He shows his black-and-blue marks. He is waved aside. The police officer and the dagelan light up cigarettes and discuss mutual friends as the suitor, furious, storms out of the police station.

Scene 3. A dark alley that night: The suitor and some gangster cronies are on their way to rob the heroine's home as a way to gain revenge. The dagelan and his son pass by. The gang taunt and bully them, but, by tricking the gang, the dagelan and his son manage to escape without being harmed. More angry than ever, the gang pull out their guns and knives and slip off.

Scene 4. Living room of the heroine's home (same as Scene 1) a few minutes later: The gang steal on, bumping into chairs in the dark. They begin to get frightened. They bump into each other in comic fashion. They go off into other rooms, then return with boxes of jewels, money, and silver. Tipped off by the dagelan, the police arrive. The suitor is captured, but the rest of the gang escape with most of the valuables. The dagelan struts about triumphant.

Scene 5. The living room, several weeks later: It is the wedding day of the heroine and the houseboy. The heroine's mother and father are complaining to their friends about their bad luck: not only have they been robbed, but their foolish daughter has married a common servant. They are distraught and humiliated. The newly married couple enter in their wedding clothes, she very happy, he apprehensive about suddenly finding himself in such a high social position. The dagelan enters. He revels in his new position. To the extreme annoyance of the others, he greets each one formally but as an equal: he shakes hands, chats casually about the weather, offers the men cigars. When the bride's father complains about his financial troubles, the dagelan launches into a long speech extolling the virtues of poverty. Money is evil, the root of materialism. People sweat for money, steal for it, kill for it, hurt their own friends for it. True happiness in life comes not from having money but from simple friendship between people, all people, rich or poor, farmer or townsman, laborer or government official. The others are impressed by the dagelan's speech. They agree. The bride's father rises and officially welcomes the dagelan and his son into their family. Henceforth, they all will strive to improve themselves, to bring unity to the people of Indonesia, and to promote world peace. The father raises his clenched fist in the air, "Crush Malaysia! Crush Malaysia! (*Ganjang Malaysia! Ganjang Malaysia!*)."

The ideological content of the play is clear enough, even in a brief synopsis. The over-all theme—that the poor are equal to the rich—is organic to the play's dramatic structure. In dramatic terms, then, it is a good propaganda play, marred only by the gratuitous political slogans inserted at the end.

Perhaps the majority of plays which raise contemporary problems do not offer new ideological solutions. Most cai luong plays set in the present are of this type. Right and wrong are presented in black and white terms, as in ideological plays, but in a more romantic, sentimental context. The following cai luong play was performed in Saigon in 1963.

Mother Love

A middle-class home in Saigon: On stage is the mother, a flighty, ineffectual woman dressed in slacks, sweater, and high heels. She is eating chocolates when her daughter enters. She complains about the high cost of permanents, the scarcity of good fingernail polish, etc. The daughter, who is coldly beautiful, pays no attention, but summons the maid to bring them tea. The daughter's boy friend arrives to take her out on a date. He is tall, handsome, well-dressed. The daughter quarrels with the young man until he becomes angry and leaves. The mother protests, "Why do you do that when you know he wants to marry you? His father is rich. He's important. You're foolish to chase him away." The daughter says she wants to discuss an important matter. She summons the maid and the maid's mother who has worked for many years as the family's cook. The daughter scornfully accuses the maid of having an affair with her younger brother. The maid admits she is in love with him. The daughter turns to the mother and demands that she order them from the house. The mother falls weeping into a chair; she does not know what to do. The old cook approaches the mistress of the house and on her knees asks forgiveness. She is mortified that after all these years in which the family has treated them so well her daughter has sullied the family's reputation in this shameful way. The daughter demands that the maid give up the affair. At this point the son enters. When he discovers what is going on, he declares that he wishes to marry the maid. The mother is distraught; the daughter rages at her brother; the cook, with tears in her eyes, says she and her daughter will leave. The maid looks beseechingly at the son; she is carrying his child. The son kneels before his mother to ask her help. The father, master of the house, returns home from work; he is tired, unhappy, and irritable, with no time for such foolish goings-on. He summarily dismisses the cook and the maid. He upbraids his son for demonstrating such lack of discretion, and asks for his slippers and a clean shirt. The daughter is pleased. The rest of the characters weep profusely as the cook and the maid leave the house, presumably forever.

MODERN FOREIGN INFLUENCES

In addition to these six major sources of dramatic material, some mention must be made of modern foreign influences that more and more are reaching the drama. Foreign movies and modern foreign literature translated into local languages inspire a certain number of plays every year. Genres in the popular tradition are most susceptible of modern outside influence; genres of the court tradition not at all. For example, you will see from time to time plays like Peasant Lands, a story of land redistribution in Communist China, adapted to ketoprak from a modern Chinese play, or Oscar Wilde's *Lady Windermere's Fan* performed in cai luong, or *Tarzan* transferred from the silver screen to sandiwara, but you will never see these plays in wayang kulit, in khon, or in wayang golek.

LOCALIZING FOREIGN DRAMATIC MATERIALS

From these plot synopses it is clear that Southeast Asian drama is deeply indebted to outside literary sources. It is at this point that we find a most fascinating characteristic of the drama: time and time again foreign dramatic materials are "localized." There are exceptions—mainly Arabic and Chinese stories—but as a rule foreign stories are presented to an audience as if they were local stories. For example, nowhere is the *Ramayana* presented as an Indian story. In Thailand, Rama is a Thai prince. He wears Thai dress, follows Thai court etiquette, listens to Thai *pi phat* music, and watches Thai dancing. Since Thailand is a Buddhist country, Rama is Buddha in a previous life. In Java, Rama is a Javanese prince. He wears Javanese dress, follows Javanese court etiquette, listens to Javanese gamelan music, and watches Javanese dancing. Java was Hindu-Brahmanic and now is Moslem, so Rama is a reincarnation of Vishnu, a descendant of Adam, and a child of Allah. Localizing foreign stories is by no means restricted to court genre, but is found in virtually every form of theatre. Hamlet becomes a Sundanese prince in a sandiwara production; when *Panji* stories are done in zat pwe, Panji is played as a Burmese prince; a Chinese story is played in a Thai setting in likay; Lady Windermere is transformed into a Saigon *grande dame* in a cai luong performance; and the enemy king, who is Thai in a Burmese version of a story, will become metamorphosed into a Vietnamese enemy king if the play is done in Cambodia as lakon bassac.

Of course the educated in the audience know the story of Rama originally came from India, for example, but for the vast majority of people history and legend and even religion are learned from what they see played upon the stage. And what do these people see? They see a view of life which is ethnocentric to a remarkable degree. One's own culture is the center and focus of all valued activity. The existence of other countries and cultures is acknowledged to be sure, but the chief dramatic function of the "foreigner" in a play is to be the ritual antagonist which the local culture-hero kills. I do not think I am exaggerating this point, as comparison with Western drama will show. We do not turn Oedipus into an American or a Frenchman when we produce *Oedipus Rex* in the United States or in France. We know Chekhov's characters are Russians. Even chauvinistic, super-patriot Shakespeare set plays in Rome, Denmark, France, Athens, Egypt, and once even used a barbarous Scotsman for a hero.

A consequence of this process of localizing can be seen in the way people think of foreign legendary events as having happened just over the mountain, or across the rice fields. For example, the people of Uttradit in central Thailand will show you the place where Sang Thong, of the foreign *Jataka* story, lived.[8] So will people in southern Thailand. The highest mountain in Java is called Semeru, after Mount Meru in the Indian epics, and it is the abode of Batara Guru, or Shiva. Raffles reported in 1817 that the Javanese believe the Great War of the Indian *Mahabharata* occurred on Java and that the site of the Kingdom of Astina, of the same epic, was near Pekalongan on Java's north coast.[9] Many similar examples could be given.

One final example will illustrate both how many different foreign influences can be absorbed into a single play and how they can be thoroughly localized. The brief outline that follows is of the barong dance-drama as it is usually performed at Singapadu, Bali.

> *Scene 1.* The Barong (a mythological animal wearing a Chinese lion mask and representing the forces of good) enters. He is followed by his friend the monkey. They fight three men in the forest.
> *Scene 2.* Two young *legong* dancers enter. They are servants of the evil witch Rangda, on their way to find the prime minister of Dewi Kunti, who is the mother of the Pandavas.
> *Scene 3.* Servants of Dewi Kunti meet the servants of Rangda. One of Rangda's servants changes herself into a witch, similar to Rangda. She enters the bodies of the two servants of Dewi Kunti. The prime minister is met; they all go off to see Dewi Kunti.
> *Scene 4.* Dewi Kunti and her son Sadewa enter. Dewi Kunti has promised to sacrifice her son to appease Rangda, but she is loath to do so. A witch now enters Dewi Kunti, causing her to become angry with Sadewa. Dewi Kunti orders the prime minister to take Sadewa to the forest for the sacrifice. He is sympathetic, until a

witch enters him also. Roughly the prime minister ties Sadewa to a tree in the forest.

Scene 5. Unknown to Rangda, the god Shiva appears and gives Sadewa immortality. Rangda enters, raging and implacable; she tries to kill and eat Sadewa, but when she finds she is unable to, she surrenders herself to Sadewa in order to be redeemed. Sadewa kills her and her soul goes to heaven.

Scene 6. A servant of Rangda, named Kelika, enters and asks Sadewa to redeem her also, but he refuses. They fight. She changes herself into the form of Rangda, with such magic power that Sadewa cannot kill her. He meditates and changes himself into a Barong. Still, neither can kill the other. Human followers of the Barong enter the fight. They try to kill Rangda with their swords, but her magic power is so great she causes the men to stab themselves with their daggers. [Villagers playing these roles are supposed to be in trance so that while they actually force the daggers against their chests, no blood is shed.] Priests enter from the temple compound. They sprinkle the men with holy water to bring them out of trance. The fight ends in a stalemate.

Here is a remarkable cast of characters. Kunti and Sadewa are from the *Mahabharata*. The monkey figure is probably from the *Ramayana*. The outer form of the Barong lion figure, especially the great mask, seems certainly to have come from China. Shiva is a Hindu God. The character of Rangda, with her grotesque face, pendulous breasts, and eighteen-inch nails, is either pure Balinese or an elaboration on the figure of Durga.[10] However, irrespective of their actual origins, all of the characters are thought of as "Balinese" by the audience.

CHARACTERISTICS OF THE DRAMA

A complete analysis of the dramatic elements of all the types of plays we have been discussing cannot be carried out here. Both space and data are lacking. This is an area where research is badly needed. Apart from translations of five Burmese language plays, we have no English translations at all of Southeast Asian plays and there are only a few collections of English language synopses of plays available.* I shall limit myself, therefore,

*The five Burmese translations are *Daywagonban, Parahein, Paduma,* and *The Water-Seller,* by Htin Aung in *Burmese Drama,* and Hla Pe's translation of U Pok Ni's *Konmara.* Dhanit Yupho's *The Khon and Lakon* contains detailed synopses of thirty-two classic Thai dance-dramas.

to mentioning only those major characteristics of the drama which seem, even in this early stage of investigation, to be beyond serious dispute.

First, plays tend to be discursive and episodic in structure. A play may have fifty scenes, as in lakon bassac, or it may have only seven or eight, as in cai luong, but the basic structural pattern is one of "extension"—many scenes, many characters, action spread over months and even years—as opposed to a drama of "compression" which we value so highly in the West. Events are portrayed larger than life size: the fall of great kingdoms, meetings with the gods, royal abductions, and complex battles are dramatized in all but contemporary plays. (In contemporary plays the events are more realistic, but dramatic structure remains episodic.) Originally derived to a large degree from oral and written epic sources, the drama of Southeast Asia retains much of the aim of the epic, which is to present a panoramic view of the unfolding of great events (rather than psychological introspection or discussion of social, political, or ethical issues as in post-Ibsen modern drama of "compression" in the West). It does not seem surprising that the drama retains much of the form of the epic as well. Only in Vietnamese kich and in the Philippines are nonepisodic plays at all common. It should be noted that tightly constructed, short, unified dramas are not unknown in other parts of Asia. One-act drama was a recognized form in Sanskrit drama and Japanese noh dramas are famous for their brevity and compression.

Second, most Southeast Asian drama fits none of the West's usual drama types: it is not pure tragedy, comedy, farce, or melodrama. Tragedy has never been known in Southeast Asia. The harshness of tragedy, its implacable view of man failing in spite of his best efforts coupled with the death of the tragic hero, are concepts alien to Southeast Asian culture. No right-thinking Hindu, or Moslem, or Buddhist, or animist would consider as a "hero" a man like Oedipus, who rashly challenges the gods that rule man's destiny or whose character is so flawed as to bring on his destruction. Such a person would be considered a fool or an immoral person, or both; he could not be the hero of a Southeast Asian play. By and large, a single play will be made up of a mixture of comic, farcical, melodramatic, and genuinely serious elements. Audiences respond with a laugh, a tear, or a thrill of excitement, and are deeply stirred by serious religious or philosophic moments. All in a single play. It is rare to find a play in which any one of these elements is not present. The most important exceptions I know of are some cai luong plays—of which A Hero of Humble Origin is an example—that emphasize pathos and sentimental romance to the exclusion of comic elements.

Third, drama tends to be didactic. Good and evil are sharply defined and good must triumph over evil. The major instrument of didactic instruction is the hero. Through his actions he sets an example of right conduct. He personifies the virtues of society and, in one of the final scenes of the play, he destroys the personification of evil, the villain. There are different kinds of heroes. Arjuna in The Crown of Rama is refined, passionless, cooly indifferent to danger to an almost superhuman degree; Kha Quyen in Falling Petals in the Garden is stalwart, self-effacing, and rather dull; Prince Lien Ton, though handsome and appealing, tends toward fickleness and irresolution and, after marriage, becomes woefully henpecked. The hero may have minor faults, but nothing is allowed to detract seriously from his essential "goodness" nor to obscure the fundamental difference between him and the coarse, noisy, ruthless, and usually stupid "bad" villain. Even the irresolute and sometimes effeminate prince-hero popular with Lao, Cambodian, and some Thai audiences is always able to dispatch the villain when the proper time comes.* Because a didactic aim requires that virtue triumph over vice, virtually all plays have happy endings. The main exceptions are a small number of popular plays in which good does not necessarily win over bad (though the distinction between good and bad is as clearly drawn as ever).

What are the values which the hero upholds in the drama? Generally they are the traditional values of society. I asked one young writer-director in Saigon about this. He said: "Vice-punished and virtue-rewarded is what the audience wants to see.

---

*Anderson, in *Mythology and the Tolerance of the Javanese*, discusses what he calls traditional Javanese "tolerance" for heroic characters of widely divergent personal characteristics, mentioning the refined hero, typified by Arjuna, as uniquely Javanese. This type of hero is popular all over Southeast Asia, and even in Japan, the soft, erotic, irresponsible hero of *kabuki* and the puppet theatre is one of the standard hero types, called in Japanese the *nimaime*.

The common man tries to live by traditional values—filial piety, honesty, marital fidelity, kindness—but in real life all around him he sees vice, cruelty, murder, corruption go unpunished every day. The theatre helps him retain his beliefs." I could give scores of examples of poetic justice in Southeast Asian plays, but let me quote just one passage by the heroine of the Burmese play *Konmara,* concerning the disaster which befalls one who disregards the requirements of filial piety: "Whoever disregards the words of his mother and the words of his father will suffer relentless calamities to the end of his life. Such is the saying. Bear it in mind. I, Me Kun, a girl of golden graces . . . am truly an example of this truth. My parents did admonish and advise me; yet, I disobeyed . . . how violent, therefore, are the buffets of calamity I have suffered! Who can outdo me in misery? Endless was the succession of my woes."[11]

Two interesting areas of morality are warfare and sex. Both have their codes of traditionally sanctioned conduct. It is clear from the synopses given that in most plays warfare is the accepted means of settling disputes. The hero gains his victory, not through debate nor through appeal to reason, not through diplomacy nor by having his enemy deposed, but by physically defeating, and usually killing, his opponent. It is easy to understand why this was so. Most heroes were princes and kings, rulers whose primary duty was to protect the state. They were warriors. The code they followed glorified the duty to kill. This code applies now to most plays, except some contemporary ones. Audiences today respond with a roar of approval when the hero attacks the villain. When it comes to showing the hero destroying his enemy with kicks, blows, sword thrusts, arrows, lance, or club, no gangster or cowboy movie is more explicit or brutal. Marquis of Queensbury rules do not apply. The hero kicks the villain when he is down and strikes him when his back is turned. I say this not to criticize but to indicate that underneath the surface elegance and beauty of most Southeast Asian theatre beats the pulse of war. Until a hundred years ago, Western drama was no different; serious disputes were settled by murder. In line with democratic belief in discussion as a means of solving conflicts, however, modern drama in the West—from Ibsen through Shaw to Arthur Miller—has developed in a new direction, away from using death as an arbiter. A similar tradition has only scarcely begun in Southeast Asian drama (mainly in kich, and ludruk, and in some contemporary cai luong and ketoprak plays).

We will understand almost all the plays of Southeast Asia better if we recognize how their codes of sexual morality differ from our own. It has always been common practice to have multiple consorts in Southeast Asia, provided only that one could afford the expense. Kings, who occupied a position at the apex of the social and political pyramid, had more wives than anyone else. Harems containing hundreds of concubines were usual. It is common knowledge that most rulers in Southeast Asia today—be they president, prime minister, prince, or king—maintain many mistresses in addition to their legal wife (or wives in Moslem Indonesia and Malaysia). It is a normal reflection of society, then, for the hero of a play to have several wives: Arjuna of the *Mahabharata* marries uncounted times; Prince Lien Ton marries three times in the one synopsis I gave earlier. As for the wives in the plays, they are supposed to live together amicably, the younger ones respecting their elders. Initially, a wife may show her jealousy toward a younger rival, but in the end she is expected to accept her husband's decision with good grace.

It is considered bad taste in Southeast Asia to demonstrate sexual familiarity publicly through kissing, stroking, or other physical contact. On-stage, romantic scenes seldom involve any direct physical contact. Sein and Withey describe the courting dance of the prince in a Burmese performance of *Manora* in which the dancers portraying the prince and Manora circle ever closer to each other, but never so much as brush a feather of Manora's costume.[12] Because the usual physical caressing of Western drama is absent in Southeast Asian plays, to Western eyes most performances seem peculiarly sexless, even during courting and love-making scenes. Actually, sexual intercourse may be enacted on stage, in Bali and Java, for example, but in decorous, stylized dance movements that give little external clue to the surging passions being portrayed. Not knowing the dance code, even the fairly knowledgeable foreigner does not suspect how emotionally exciting these scenes are to local audiences.

On the other hand, references to physical organs and bodily functions are not considered offensive on the stage as they are in the West. The major element of old-style mohlam was banter between male and female singers about physical organs and sexual intercourse. On Bali, the witch Rangda often is seen in performance devouring the testicles of the clowns. Colin McPhee has described a Balinese wayang kulit performance he saw in which the chief clown unfastened his erect penis and clubbed to death hundreds of ogres with it.[13] I have already mentioned the scene in the Javanese wayang kulit play Parakesit Becomes King where the clown Semar pelts Durga and Kala with large balls of his feces until these most ferocious of the gods turn tail and flee. Normally, such scenes are presented as farce or burlesque and are received with hilarious laughter by audiences. The latter incident was broadcast over the government radio network, presumably without objection. In the West, we would cringe with embarrassment if we saw physical activities of this kind portrayed on stage, though we would not mind watching a man and woman kiss on stage. In short, sexual conduct as shown in the drama of Southeast Asia is neither stricter nor looser than in the West, it is just different in certain ways.

Fourth, a constantly recurring plot tells of the hero, temporarily defeated by the enemy, who retires to the forest to meditate, and who, after receiving magic powers, returns to wage a victorious war against the enemy. This story is so common, and found in so many variations in different theatre genres, that it almost constitutes a "master plot" of Southeast Asian drama. On the constant repetition of this plot in Javanese wayang drama, Geertz says: "For the Javanese, mystical experience is not a rejection of the world but a temporary retirement from it for purposes of increasing spiritual strength in order to operate more effectively in the mundane sphere, a refinement of the inner life in order to purify the outer. There is a time for the mountain-top (where most really advanced mythical mystics do their meditations) and a time for the city."[14] The whole action of The Crown of Rama revolves around a quest to accumulate the greatest possible amount of spiritual, magic power from the gods, in order to ensure continuity of kingship. Similar plots are found in mainland *Ramayana* plays, in Buddhist *Jataka* plays, in

Arabic plays (note the end of the Amir Hamzah play scenario mentioned before), and in many traditional Chinese plays. We find it in brief but classic form in a Balinese wayang play preserved on a lontar manuscript.

> A demon king, desiring the beautiful young daughter of the neighboring King of Tasikmandhu, dispatches his prime minister, Pragalba, with a letter demanding the daughter in marriage. The King of Tasikmandhu receives Pragalba with courtesy, but when he reads the ultimatum from the demon king, he orders Pragalba out of the kingdom. The army of the demon king attacks Tasikmandhu. The King of Tasikmandhu sends his brother to seek help from Arjuna, who is meditating at a hermitage in the forest of Gondhamahi. Arjuna agrees to help. He enters the battle, but is unable to defeat the demon army. The god Indra appears before Arjuna. He gives Arjuna a magic arrow, and with it Arjuna succeeds in killing Pragalba, after which it is an easy matter to rout the rest of the demons.[15]

In this script Arjuna receives the magic arrow from Indra, not as a gift, but as a natural consequence of having meditated. In The Crown of Rama, Krishna explicitly says he does not have the power to choose the recipient of the Crown of Rama—through his own acts, the most worthy human will reveal himself and to this man will be given the gods' gift. Man, in other words, gains supernatural powers by his own efforts. Accumulating this power can be accomplished through fortitude and willpower, much as a man can save and put money in a bank. The money is his, not the banker's, and the spiritual power is his, not the gods' (though the gods may be the intermediaries through which specific powers are received). It follows that an evil person can build up spiritual power just as well as a good person. This is the source of power of the ascetic Gobut, who helps Ravana in *Hanoman the Volunteer*.

The connection between meditation and the receipt of magic powers is not always specifically shown in the plot of a play. Dramatic shorthand may be used. The audience may only see the action of receiving the power, and be left to imagine that it follows as a consequence of an earlier act of religious meditation by the hero. This is true in plays of popular genres as well as court drama. The most influential manager of likay troupes in

Thailand told me there always used to be an "obligatory scene" in every likay play, a scene in which "a youth meets a hermit-sage in the forest and learns from him magic powers," but, in recent years, to speed up the action of the play, "this scene generally has been abolished and the information is given to the audience in a few lines of exposition instead." In the scenarios mentioned earlier, there are several examples of dramatic shorthand of this kind. In The Golden Prince of the Sea Conch the ogress Panturat is encountered at the beginning of the play already possessing her magic staff and shoes. Bima is shown receiving the gods' blessing in Parakesit Becomes King without meditating. The hero-prince is able, in the first scene of the play *Lien Ton,* to turn himself into a horse, and so on. Since most of these plays are based on episodes taken from well-known stories, the majority of the audience can be expected to know the necessary antecedent action.

Fifth, characters are strongly typed and tend to be used in certain regular patterns. Very broadly speaking, I suggest there are six main types of characters that appear in Southeast Asian drama: gods; nobility; religious ascetics; clown-servants; middle-class urbanites; peasants or laborers. Also, there are "good" and "bad" characters of each type: "good" and "bad" gods; "good" and "bad" nobility; "good" and "bad" clown-servants, and so on.

We can tell much about the world-view of different plays by noting the types of characters that appear in them. Typically, plays from the court tradition that draw heavily on Indian dramatic sources and plays in the popular tradition derived from similar sources—that is, most wayang forms, ardja, barong, lakon nai, nang yai, khon, and some likay, lakon bassac, sandi-wara, and mohlam luong—use just the first four character types: gods, nobility, religious ascetics, and clown-servants. In subject matter these plays are the most ancient. They concern the mythological ancestors of the race. The world-view they present is that of a legendary but human aristocracy in close communion with the gods. Mythical kings and princes are the heroes of these plays; their human needs are tended to by their clown-servants, and religious ascetics minister to their spiritual needs. They speak to and can visit the gods. It is noteworthy that in Indian Sanskrit drama of around the fifth century, townsmen were often portrayed, and in several types of plays commoners were the heroes and heroines, as in *The Little Clay Cart*. Nothing similar is found in early Southeast Asian drama. It is true that clown-servants make fun of their noble masters and in wayang a clown can even become a king, but nothing in these plays indicates that life outside an aristocratic framework was given any value, except as it served the needs of the mythical aristocracy.

Moving forward in time, we come to the pure history plays of lakon nai, ketoprak, sandiwara, likay, bangsawan, cai luong, and lakon bassac, and the Chinese-derived plays of hat boi and cai luong. Now we are among known historical figures. Great monarchs remain, but the gods and most religious ascetics drop out of the cast of characters. A rich merchant may appear in a Chinese play and a few peasants as extras may appear in a local history play, but essentially these plays are about nobles and their clown-servants. The world-view presented in these plays is that of a more recent, earth-bound aristocracy: kings and princes no longer have contact with the ancient gods and they are only just beginning to recognize the existence of the world of the commoner.

Moving still closer to the present, to a time just a hundred or more years ago, we have portrayed in other sandiwara, bangsawan, ketoprak, and cai luong plays a world in which the aristocracy still rules, but no longer absolutely. These are plays in which nobility, clown-servants, and peasant and laborers mix, often uneasily. Modern nationalistic and democratic ideas conflict with the old aristocratic order. In *Untung Suropati* the whole aristocratic system is under attack by the people; in A Hero of Humble Origin the real hero is not the prince but the peasant who saves the throne for the prince. There seems little doubt that this kind of play takes the best of both worlds, appealing both to the popular audience's romantic interest in a distant world of kingship, splendor, power, and warfare, and to their natural desire to see themselves and their humble lives portrayed on stage. In this type of play, the clown-servant may become the chief character. Being a commoner who serves the king or prince, the clown-servant occupies a strategic position. It is easy for his role at the center of the play to expand as the role of the aristocratic hero loses importance.

[1 2 3]

And finally we have the contemporary plays of kich, ludruk, cai luong, and ketoprak in which characters are of the last two types only: middle-class urbanites and peasants and laborers. The world-view of these plays is that of present-day society. There are no gods (or if there are, they do not appear). Any religious ascetic who appears is a crackpot dragged in for a laugh.* The world of kings and princes, though still existing in some parts of Southeast Asia, is ignored.

*Hla Pe notes that as early as the latter part of the nineteenth century, "hermits, brahmans, and spirits are often comic characters, and are made to speak in the vulgar idiom" in the Burmese popular theatre (*Konmara,* p. 11).

CHAPTER 6

Music and Dance

Music and dance are inseparable companions of most drama in Southeast Asia. In all probability, drama is the youngest of the three performing arts and grew out of earlier music and dance forms. In some cases, music is so important we must liken a dramatic form to opera and in others dance is so important we must properly speak of a form as dance-drama. Although Aristotle mentioned music and spectacle as parts of Greek tragedy and we have opera and ballet in the West, we are, nevertheless, largely conditioned to think of drama in terms of the spoken word. To get a proper feeling for Southeast Asian theatre, we must abandon this preconception. Music sets a tone and an atmosphere within which a performance is created. It offers possibilities unrivaled by the spoken word for conveying and amplifying emotional states. The movement patterns of dance provide a visual structure on which the action of a play can be hung. Both music and dance appeal to our sense of the beautiful in a way no spoken drama can. I cannot convey through printed words the affect of a lyrical song or a courtship dance on a Southeast Asian theatre audience. I will, however, try to show that music and dance *are* important, that they perform specific functions within the dramatic structure of a play, and that they are used in the theatre in complex yet highly systematized ways.

MUSIC

MUSICAL INSTRUMENTS

Percussion, stringed, and wind instruments are known in all parts of Southeast Asia. There are many kinds of percussion instruments: drums of a dozen shapes and sizes, cymbals, woodblocks, and a wide variety of tuned sets of bronze bars, bowls, and gongs. Among stringed instruments, zithers are known everywhere, Chinese-derived two-stringed fiddles are played on the mainland, and in Indonesia-Malaysia they play a two-stringed fiddle which probably came from the Middle East. Wind instruments include the flute, which is played in every country, a double-reed instrument similar to an oboe played on the mainland, and the khen reed-organ, popular in Laos and Thailand. Brass wind instruments are not used anywhere in Southeast Asia.

The origin of all instruments found in Southeast Asia is not known and perhaps never will be known. We can make two general statements about the historical development of theatre music in Southeast Asia which relates to instruments used, however. First, though certain Indian instruments, such as drums, harp, and possibly the flute, may have been brought to Southeast Asia in the early part of the Christian era, and possibly earlier, Indian music per se apparently has had virtually no effect upon Southeast Asian music. The Hindu *raga* melodic system is totally unrelated to Indonesian-Malaysian gamelan music and musical scales[1] and to traditional Cambodian, Thai, and Lao music. The conclusion seems unescapable, that the bronze xylophone carved in the Borobudur relief in the ninth century and the semicircle of tuned bronze bowls pictured in thirteenth-century reliefs at Angkor[2] are examples of musical instruments indigenous to Southeast Asia, around which developed theatrical musical ensembles unique in the world. And second, through the borrowing of Chinese instruments, Chinese music has influenced some forms of Southeast Asian theatre.

Broadly speaking, I would identify three major kinds of musical ensembles used in the theatre: the pi phat ensemble of Thailand, Cambodia, Laos, and Burma (normally referred to as *saing* in Burma); the gamelan ensemble of Java, Sunda, Bali, and Malaysia; and the string and percussion ensembles used in

Vietnam and, in some cases, in neighboring mainland countries. The pi phat and gamelan ensembles are, by and large, indigenous, while the ensembles used in Vietnam are Chinese-derived.

The pi phat ensemble is a percussion ensemble plus one woodwind. In its basic form it consists of six instruments: a set of tuned bronze bowls arranged in a semicircle (*kong wong* in Thai, *khong vong* in Lao, *kong thom* in Cambodian, *kyi waing* in Burmese); wooden xylophone (*ranat* in Thai, *raneat* in Cambodian, *rangnat* in Lao, *pattala* in Burmese); large tripod drum struck with a padded stick (*glong* in Thai, *skor thom* in Cambodian and Lao, *patma* in Burmese); horizontal drum tapped on both ends with the fingers (*taphon* or *saphon* in Thai, *sampho* in Cambodian); small bell-cymbals (*ching* in Thai, *than lwin* in Burmese, *nao bat* in Vietnamese); and double-reed oboe (*pi* in Thai and Lao, *hne* in Burmese, *sralay* in Cambodian). These instruments may be doubled to make a larger ensemble, but the character of the music is not changed. Pi phat music can be described as sounding "hollow," an impression created partly by the disimilarity of timbre of the soft thunking of the wooden xylophone and the sharp penetrating sounds of the bell-cymbal and the oboe.

The gamelan ensemble is composed mainly of bronze percussion instruments, augmented by other percussion instruments, strings, and a flute. A full Javanese gamelan ensemble consists of: xylophone of heavy bronze bars (*saron*); bronze xylophone with resonance chambers beneath (*gender*); set of bronze bowls (*bonang*); hanging gongs (*gong* and *kempul*); single inverted bronze bowl (*kenong* and *ketuk*); wooden xylophone (*gambang*); two-stringed fiddle (*rebab*); flute (*suling*); horizontal drum beat with the fingers on both ends (*kendang*); and a zither of thirteen double strings (*tjelempung*). In large ensembles there will be several gender and saron arranged in octaves, and often there will be several instruments of each octave. In smaller ensembles some instruments are eliminated. The preponderance of bronze instruments gives gamelan music a bright, lingering sound, ranging from the slow, majestic melodies of the Javanese gamelan to the clangorous vibrancy of Balinese gamelan. Fiddle and flute add delicate counterpoint to a four-square pattern of percussive melody.

Chinese-derived ensembles vary in size and composition, but major instruments are: two-stringed fiddle with small cylindrical sounding box (*dan co* or *dan nhi* in Vietnamese, *saw duang* in Thai, *yi i* in Cambodian, *so i* in Lao, *hu chin* in Chinese); two-stringed fiddle with large coconut-shell sounding box (*dan gao* in Vietnamese, *saw u* in Thai, *tro u* in Cambodian, *so u* in Lao, and *hu hu* in Chinese); moon-shaped lute (*dan kim* or *dan nguyet* in Vietnamese); raucous reed horn (*ken tau* in Vietnamese); wooden clackers (*song lang* in Vietnamese); cymbals (*chap choa* in Vietnamese), small stick drum (*trong* in Vietnamese); flute (*sao* or *ong dich* in Vietnamese); and the sixteen-stringed zither (*dan tranh* in Vietnamese). Two sound patterns are characteristic of these instruments: an ear-splitting cacaphony of cymbals, drums, raucous horn, and wooden clackers played simultaneously, and quiet melodies played on the fiddles, lute, flute, and zither.

THEATRE ENSEMBLES

Typical musical ensembles used for theatre performances today are shown in Figure 7. From it we can see that gamelan is the sole musical form used in Indonesia-Malaysia. In Java, a full gamelan ensemble accompanies wayang kulit, wayang orang, and ketoprak (though small, poor troupes often lack certain of the large expensive instruments). In Sunda, the gamelan is smaller: instruments are seldom doubled, there are fewer gongs, and the bronze bowl set and xylophone with resonators are not used. In Bali, the fiddle (rebab) is almost never used (which is logical, for it probably came from Arab culture). Some Balinese ensembles are small: four gender only accompany wayang kulit, and ardja requires just three or four instruments. Most dances and dance-dramas, including the barong, however, employ the largest Balinese gamelan ensemble, the *gong ageng* ("great gong gamelan"). Wayang kulit in Malaya is accompanied by a rudimentary gamelan grouping typically composed of one or more large gongs, several small gongs, as many as six drums, and a version of the Thai reed-oboe (*serunai* in Malay),[3] plus sometimes a rebab.

The basic pi phat ensemble is used for Thai khon, nang yai, and lakon nai, and for Cambodian and Lao Royal Ballet, that is, for all court theatre of these countries. When *Ramayana* plays are performed in khon or nang yai (or their Cambodian equivalents), a gong and special drums are added to the standard pi phat ensemble, as is a three-stringed fiddle when *Inao* is staged.[4] Popular theatre forms employ altered and usually smaller versions of the pi phat ensemble. In likay the expensive semicircular set of tuned bronze bowls and the difficult-to-play oboe are seldom seen, but otherwise the musical ensemble is the same as court pi phat. Popular Burmese dance-drama troupes add flute, cymbals, and a unique Burmese instrument—a set of twenty-one tuned drums (*saing waing*). A typical Cambodian lakon bassac troupe will perform with an ensemble composed of most pi phat percussion instruments, plus fiddles, cymbals, wooden clackers, and zither from the Chinese group of instruments.

Lakon jatri and nang talung are rather special cases. Originally lakon jatri music was nonmelodic; just a bell-cymbal, double-gong, and two pear-shaped drums accompanied performance. Later, apparently, nang talung troupes took over this same simple musical ensemble (it will be recalled both types are performed only in southern Thailand). Old-style lakon jatri troupes still use only these instruments, as Figure 7 indicates. But most nang talung troupes and modernized lakon jatri troupes now use a mixed ensemble of lakon jatri instruments plus pi phat melody and percussion instruments adapted from the court (wooden xylophone, oboe, and several kinds of drums) as well as plucked and bowed string instruments from the Chinese group (usually coconut-shell fiddle and zither). The only instrument used in Lao and Thai mohlam luong is the reed-organ, khen, which, as I said, probably originated aeons ago in China. The khen is not used in any other type of theatre in Southeast Asia.

All Vietnamese musical ensembles are composed of instruments of the Chinese-derived group. Six musicians typically comprise a classic hat boi music group: one musician each plays the cylindrical and coconut-shell fiddles, one the lute, one the flute, one the raucous horn, and one plays all the other percussion instruments (wooden clackers, gong, and cymbals). These instruments can produce an absolutely deafening din when required by the action of the play. In contrast, the largest cai luong musical ensemble would consist of flute, moon-lute, zither, cylindrical and coconut-shell fiddles, and wooden clackers.[5] More usually cai luong troupes get along with a combination of only

FIGURE 3. Typical Musical Ensembles Used in Major Theatre Genres

Ensembles	JAVA	SUNDA	BALI			MALAYA	BURMA
Musical Instruments	Wayang Kulit Wayang Orang Ketoprak	Wayang Golek Sandiwara	Wayang Kulit	Ardja	Barong	Wayang Kulit	Zat Pwe
GAMELAN — Two-string Fiddle	■	■				■	
Bronze Xylophone	■			■	■		
Bronze Xylophone with Resonators	■		■	■			
Single or Double Bronze Bowls	■	■	■	■			
Gong Set	■				■		
Plucked Zither	■						
Wooden Xylophone	■				■		■
Bronze Bowl Set	■				■	■	
Horizontal Finger-Drum		■		■	■		
PIPHAT — Vertical Stick-Drum							
Bell-Cymbals							■
Oboe							■
CHINESE — Two-string Fiddle Cylinder Resonator							
Two-string Fiddle Coconut Shell Resonator							
Moon-Guitar							
Cymbals							■
Raucous Horn							
Mallet-struck Zither							
Single Gong							
Wood Block							
Small Drum							
SPECIAL — Flute	■	■			■		■
Lao Reed-Organ							
Burmese Tuned Drum Set							■
Thai Pear-shaped Drum							

three or four of these instruments. Cai luong music, regardless of the number of instruments used, is the most romantic and, to Western ears, melodic of all Southeast Asian theatre music, I believe. The emphasis is upon quiet but emotion-laden songs.

The most degenerate popular troupes also add Western musical instruments—piano, saxophone, trumpet, snare drum—to these traditional ensembles. The worst offenders are desperately poor, small, urban-centered hat boi, cai luong, lakon bassac, and bangsawan troupes. Only in some cases with cai luong have

CAMBODIA	LAOS		Lakon Khon Nang Yai	Lakon Jatri	Nang Talung	Likay	Hat Boi	Cai Luong
ikon Bassac	Royal Ballet	Mohlam Luong						

Western instruments been reasonably accommodated into the over-all framework of the theatre form; otherwise, they are simply added for their curiosity value and no attempt is made to integrate them artistically into the performance.

DRAMATIC FUNCTIONS OF MUSIC

In addition to setting the mood or atmosphere of a play, music has two major dramatic functions in the theatre. It accompanies singing or chanting and it accompanies stage action, including dance. The importance of each function varies from area to area and from theatre form to theatre form.

In Java, Sunda, Bali, and Malaysia singing is not a major element in theatre performances. There are opera forms—*langendrian* and *langenmandra wanara* in Java and *gending karasmen* in Sunda—but these are rare types, seldom performed. Only in Balinese ardja is singing important. In wayang kulit and in wayang orang the dalang sings mood songs (*suluk*) at regular intervals during performance; in a nine-hour wayang kulit, he may sing fifty or sixty. Nevertheless, they are considered relatively unimportant except as mood pieces. The same generalized lyrics may be used in play after play. Suluk are never accompanied by the full gamelan ensemble. Often a single instrument accompanies the singer, never more than three or four. The major dramatic function of gamelan music is to accompany stage action. In wayang kulit, wayang golek, wayang orang, ketoprak, sandiwara, and in all Balinese drama entrances, exits, and fight scenes are executed in time to gamelan music.

In Vietnam, on the other hand, singing is extremely important. It is usually considered the single most important dramatic element in both hat boi and cai luong. As much as 70 or 80 percent of performance time may be devoted to singing. Melody-carrying instruments support the singer either by playing in unison with the vocal line or in counterpoint to it. In hat boi two fiddles and the moon-shaped lute are the chief instruments used for this purpose, in cai luong the zither, moon-shaped lute, and one fiddle. Also all entrances, exits, pantomime movement, and fight scenes are set to the tock-tock-tock of wooden clappers in cai luong and in hat boi to the crashing of cymbals, the wail of the raucous horn, and the beating of the small drums.

In Thailand, Cambodia, Laos, and Burma dances typically are performed to music of the full pi phat ensemble, while songs, of which there are many, are not. In Thailand the most common style of singing is one that evolved in lakon jatri known as *rai*. In rai verses are sung (or chanted) alternately by an actor on stage and an off-stage chorus. In lakon jatri there were no melodic instruments, so originally rai was accompanied by a bell-cymbal and drum only. Largely this tradition was maintained when rai was adopted successively by lakon nok, lakon nai, nang yai, khon, Cambodian and Lao ballet, and likay. In some instances the wooden xylophone or the oboe will be used to play simple melodies behind rai singing, but this is not usual. Songs are extremely important in both modern and classical Burmese plays. The translation of the Burmese play *Konmara* that I have mentioned contains one hundred twelve songs, with eight to ten often strung together one after the other![6] The function of music in lakon bassac is quite unique. Pi phat instruments accompany classical Cambodian dance scenes; Chinese cymbals and drum punctuate dialogue, as in Vietnam, and underscore fight scenes; Chinese stringed instruments accompany singing; and between scenes, Western drums, piano, trumpet, or saxophone play current European and American pop music.

MUSICAL FORM

One of the most interesting characteristics of Southeast Asian theatre music is that certain traditional melodies are used over and over again, and that often specific meanings are attached to them. This is true of theatre in the popular tradition as well as theatre in the court or folk tradition. Let me give a few illustrations.

There are around one hundred traditional cai luong melodies, some adapted from hat boi and tung tau, some based on folk songs, and some specifically written for cai luong. They are classified according to type, so that a certain number are considered love laments, a certain number battle tunes, a certain number for court scenes, and so on. When a playwright composes a new cai luong play he selects appropriate melodies from each type and writes new lyrics to fit the traditional tunes. The playwright has considerable latitude in his selection, but a few traditional tunes are used in every play. *Xuan Xe* is used when the hero flees from the enemy, and *Tau Ma* accompanies a scene in which a running horse is supposed to appear. I have mentioned that Vong Co is sung upwards of a dozen times in a play, each time with new lyrics. It is the most popular love lament in cai luong. Audiences demand to hear Vong Co, and singers demand to be heard singing it, since their reputations rest on their ability to sail faultlessly through its intricate vocal arabesques.

Books on the technique of wayang kulit list upwards of one hundred fifty gamelan melodies that may be used in performance.[7] Theoretically at least, meaning is attached to each, though some melodies have only generalized meanings. Thus, *Sampak* indicates a fight scene and *Ajak-ajak* accompanies a character when he leaves a scene. These two melodies are used many times in a nine-hour wayang kulit performance, and are so familiar that even young children recognize what is coming next when they hear the first phrases of the gamelan. A large number of gamelan melodies convey precise meanings in relation to the action of a wayang kulit play. For example, if the character in the first scene of the play is the god Shiva (Batara Guru), then the gamelan melody *Kawit* must be played, but if the chief character is Krishna, then *Krawitan* must be played, or if Duryodana, *Kabor*. *Mangu* must be played if Yudistira is arriving as a guest, but *Moncher* if the guest is Baladewa, *Lerelere* if the guest is Sangkuni, *Sabah* if the guest is Karna, *Srikaton* if the guest is Arjuna, and so on. In some situations the dalang may choose among several sanctioned melodies. The idea, of course, is that certain melodies should go with certain characters or situations or actions. The system as it exists in wayang today is very complex. Considering the hundreds of possible melodies, and the extreme length of the plays, it is not strange to find that in practice only a few of the most experienced dalang perform in line with these complicated theories. The average dalang uses only a few dozen of the most important, popular melodies.

It is said there are two hundred to three hundred traditional likay tunes of which around fifty are used regularly. According to one manager I talked to, a likay troupe can get along using just a dozen of the best-known tunes, however. These are of different types and are well-known to the audience. What Htin Aung says of Burmese popular theatre holds true for popular theatre almost everywhere. He says when the orchestra plays a "royal procession tune," a "battle tune," or a "woodland melody," the "audience recognized it . . . at once."[8] In lakon bassac, just four types of stage music are distinguished: sad

41. Gongs of a Javanese gamelan ensemble used in ludruk.

42. Isolated Vietnamese mountaineers play bamboo xylophone, stringed instruments, and a wind instrument related to the Lao khen.

43. Traditional mohlam sung by one male, accompanied by a single khen; the performers wear traditional but informal costume.

44. A Sundanese wayang topeng dancer illustrates the typical narrow stance and restrained gestures of female dance in Indonesia.

45. A Javanese wayang topeng dancer showing the broad stance and expansive gestures typical of male dance in Indonesia.

46. The "Tarian Ashek," a Malay folk dance popular in ancient times, shows the immobile face and hand gestures typical of Indian-style dance in Southeast Asia.

47. Female dancers in Thailand dancing male and female roles in a greeting dance and dressed in typical costume for lakon dance-drama.

48. A carving from the fourteenth-century Panataran temple in eastern Java
with profile position of monkey's body and curled hair typical of wayang
kulit puppets.

49. Wayang orang dancers showing profile body position and arm position borrowed from wayang kulit puppets; here the ogre Tjakil challenges Arjuna (played by a female).

50. Thai performers dress and move like puppets in a special performance combining traditional and contemporary forms.

music, gay music, "walking music" for entrances and exits, and fighting music. Although Chinese opera knows sixty-five different melodies for entrances and exits (each of which identifies place or situation or character),[9] the musical system for Vietnamese hat boi is simpler. Most music is divided into imported Chinese melodies (*hat khach*) and native Vietnamese melodies (*hat nam*). Within each division half a dozen melodies refer to generalized emotions (such as *Khach Tu* as a funeral dirge, *Nam Xuan* or gay Vietnamese song, and *Nam Di*, an expression of anxiety). Other melodies refer to specific people, such as the fool's song (*Bai Dien*), the song of the poor (*Bai Phuong*), the chant of a barrier guard (*Bai Tuong Tran Ai*), the chant of the doctor (*Bai Thuy Thuoc*), and others. They are used less often than the generalized melodies and are not well-known by the audience.[10]

DANCE

Dance experts identify a bewildering number of dances and dance styles in Southeast Asia. Broadly speaking, however, theatrical dance can be broken down into Indian-influenced dance and Chinese-influenced dance. The former is found in those countries which adopted many aspects of Indian culture during the first millenium of the Christian era—Burma, Thailand, Cambodia, Malaysia, and Indonesia (Indian-style dance was introduced somewhat later into Laos). The latter is found in Vietnam and to a lesser extent in popular Cambodian theatre.

There has been a long tradition of dance as an art form independent of drama in India, while in China an independent dance tradition has been weak. In India there were a multitude of dance forms performed in public or at court or for religious occasions, quite apart from dramatic performances. Organizations of dancers have existed independent of theatre troupes for centuries. As far as we can tell, both traditions of Indian dance— the dramatic and the nondramatic—were brought to Southeast Asia. In Southeast Asia, religious dances, which were at least partially dramatic in concept, flourished side-by-side with nondramatic dances, such as the *srimpi* and the *bedaya* court dances in Java. Later, when extended and more complex dance-dramas evolved at court (in Java, Cambodia, and Thailand in particular), whole dances from the nondramatic repertory were simply inserted into the plays, as, for example, srimpi and bedaya dances were grafted onto wayang orang dance-drama. These nondramatic dances were popular at court and had a long and honorable history, but they seldom had anything to do with the play into which they were put. One reason they were smuggled into dance-dramas was that they showed off harem favorites to good advantage. But nondramatic dances never really could be absorbed into the new dance-dramas; they still maintain their separate identity.

In China dance has been associated with music since the beginning of the recorded history of the Celestial Empire. During the Tang dynasty (A.D. 618–906) court dances were greatly in favor. Some of these dances were later brought to Korea and from there to Japan where they became the basis of Japanese *bugaku* court dance. In subsequent centuries the Chinese did not build on this early dance tradition, however. On the contrary, dance as a separate performing art was little patronized, and early forms of court dance died out (though they are still preserved and performed in Japan). The major impetus for dance development in China came from the theatre, especially opera. Chinese opera dance became very elaborate over the years and was ordered into a meticulously detailed system: Scott lists and describes 299 separate movements of the hands, arms, and legs that are used in classical Chinese opera (*ching hsi*) today.[11] When Vietnamese hat boi troupes and later cai luong and Cambodian lakon bassac troupes borrowed from Chinese opera, they borrowed the basic pattern of Chinese opera dance movement as well as the dramatic literature, music, and costuming. In the Chinese models movement was always designed to support the action of a play; there were no dance set-pieces which were superfluous to the play's structure. This same use of movement as subsidiary to the dramatic needs of a play is reflected in hat boi, cai luong, and, to some extent, lakon bassac. In the genres most affected by Chinese opera models, hat boi and cai luong, and audience might demand that a singer encore a popular aria, but it would never demand that a dance section be encored (as might a Thai or a Javanese king). In short, Chinese-derived dance movement exists solely for the sake of the drama while, in some cases, drama may exist for the sake of Indian-derived dances in Southeast Asia.

INDIAN STYLE DANCE

The best known canon of Indian dance is the *Natya Sastra,* ascribed to one Bharata Muni. It may be as old as Aristotle's *Poetics;* in laying down rules for every aspect of theatrical art, including dance, gesture, music, vocal representation, preperformance ceremonies, stage construction, costume, make-up, dramatic construction, and aesthetics, it is far more inclusive than the *Poetics.* Eight chapters are devoted to stage movement. Hand, foot, torso, and facial movements are catalogued in minute detail. One part of the *Natya Sastra,* for example, lists 32 foot movements, 36 glances, 9 movements of the eyeballs, 9 of the eyelids, 7 of the eybrows, 9 of the neck, 7 of the chin, 5 of the breast, and 67 hand gestures.[12] Out of the these basic movements, hundreds of more complex patterns of movement are built; all are listed in the *Natya Sastra.*

According to the *Natya Sastra,* a movement has a meaning, or several meanings, attached to it. This can be seen most clearly with the hand gestures, known as *mudra* (or *hasta*). As I have said, there are 67 hand gestures or mudra. As an illustration of how meaning is derived from hand gestures, let me take just one of these gestures, the simple, "open-palm" mudra called *pataka.* This is, by the way, the first mudra listed in the *Natya Sastra.* Of itself, the pataka mudra has no meaning. In combination with other movements, however, it can convey up to thirty different meanings. First, it can be used as a single-handed gesture. The single hand may be positioned in seven ways: level with the forehead; with fingers separated; with hands separated; pointing down; pointing up; moving up and down; or rubbing on the second hand. Used in any one of these ways, the mudra may have several meanings. For example, if level with the forehead, it can indicate urging, happiness, heat, conceit, or a beating; or, if pointing down, it can mean privacy, denseness, an open or closed place, or a protected thing. Second, the pataka may be used as a two-handed gesture. There are several kinds of two-handed gestures, each with different meanings. Placed palms together, the pataka hands form a new mudra called *anjali,* which is the famous Indian and Southeast Asian gesture of respect or obeisance. Both pataka hands hanging limply at the sides of the body may indicate sadness, or intoxication, or being wounded, or hurriedness. One open palm placed over the other, may indicate a tiger, a lion, an elephant, a shark, or any of a number of other animals or fish. And, third, meaning may be created by a larger pattern of movement in which the hands in the pataka position combine with other gestures of the eyes, feet, arms, neck, shoulders, or torso. Here the whole process of conveying meaning becomes enormously complex, for many different movements contribute to building a series of related meanings. This is with one mudra. If we were to analyse the other 66 mudra, as well as all the other possible movements of the feet, arms, torso, face, and so on, .we can appreciate what a remarkably expressive system of symbolic movement was created within Indian dance.

It is said that the meanings found in Indian dance originally derived from natural gestures or pantomime. As two examples, the thumb-up gesture, signifying a man, is said to have come from the idea of man standing upright (or it may be considered a phallic symbol), and the fingers pointing to the forehead indicate Shiva for in Shiva's forehead is his distinguishing mark, a third eye. But, as centuries passed, people forgot why most gestures meant what they did. By the time Indian dance was exported to Southeast Asia, whatever naturalness or logic this code of meaning may have had in the past was largely lost in India itself. This helps explain the two major changes which Southeast Asians wrought in imported Indian dance: they modified the movements themselves, and they altered, and sometimes completely eliminated, whatever vestigial meanings still clung to certain dance movements.

Facial expression is described in the *Natya Sastra* as a vital part of the Indian dance system. Eye movements were considered particularly expressive. But in Southeast Asia, facial expression was almost completely eliminated from the dance. The face is held totally immobile in Thai, Lao, Cambodian, Malaysian, Sundanese, and Javanese classical dance. Only Balinese dancers use eye movements, and these are striking indeed. Apparently facial expression was considered a vulgar emotional display and its use was rejected in order to heighten the elegance and dignity of the dance.

The anjali gesture of respect is described in the *Natya Sastra* as being done in three ways: for gods the hands are lifted above the head, for honored ascetics the hands are held before the face, and for friends the hands are held at chest level. These distinctions fell into disuse in Cambodia, Laos, Thailand and Indonesia; only one form of anjali gesture—the hands held before the face—is known in Cambodian, Lao, Thai, and Indonesian dance.

In Thailand, dancers learn an "alphabet" of dance patterns which evolved from Indian dance. Many of the basic movements are similar to movements described in the *Natya Sastra*. But whereas the *Natya Sastra* mentions 108 movements of this type, in Thailand this has been reduced to alphabets of 64 or 19 movements. For example, in India "the stag walking in the forest" was performed simply by clenching the first, second, and third fingers while stretching out the thumb and little finger. Many years ago it was danced in Thailand by spreading out the fingers of both hands and bringing the hands in front of the body; today in Thailand the dancer will "stretch the forefingers and middle fingers out, clench the others, stretch the arms down till the palms are level with the seats, invert the hands so as to bring the palms below, raise the first and second fingers up till they are level with the waists and move them from side to side and up and down alternately."[13] Here Thai dancers have kept the Indian meaning, but have reversed the action of the fingers, and, as is quite apparent, have completely altered the over-all movement pattern. We can also see that while a single hand *sign* told the Indian audience what was intended, in Thailand, where mudra pretty much ceased to have symbolic meanings, the idea to be conveyed had to be acted out in pantomime to be understood. The fact that traditional dance movement patterns are carefully preserved nowadays in most countries in Southeast Asia should not obscure the fact that down until this century dance innovations were being made constantly. According to the Director General of the Fine Arts Department of Thailand, "the greater part of the 'Alphabet of Dancing' has been adopted from the evolutions which . . . the students learn to dance at the beginning. But while interpreting words histrionically some more postures and gestures were found necessary to make the spectators understand the words better. So they were either invented outright or adapted from those already executed."[14]

In Java and Bali Indian dance was greatly simplified. Only 4 hand positions, or mudra, 6 foot positions, and 4 arm positions make up the entire repertory of basic positions in Javanese dance. All dance patterns are built up from combinations of these few basic positions, and movement based on them functions to distinquish between different types of characters (*alus* or refined, *gagah* or muscular, and *kasar* or coarse masculine characters and feminine characters). Movement does not, as in Indian dance, convey emotional or symbolic significance. The Balinese vocabulary of dance positions is equally restricted, and, as in Java, there is no specific meaning connected with any mudra or arm or leg position.[15]

In Cambodia, Laos, Thailand, and Burma, dance developed into an identifiable regional style. Typical movements of this style are: one foot lifted behind the body; the tips of the thumb and index finger touching, with the other fingers curling back (like the finger positions of the apsaras carved on the pillars of the Bayon at Angkor); one leg crossed sharply in front of the other with the weight of the body on the forward leg. Dance steps for male and female follow the same general patterns, though the former will be executed more vigorously. The overall effect of this type of dance is one of exquisite delicacy of movement, of highly abstract and convoluted gesture. The dance-dramas themselves have a precious, fragile quality.

Typical movements of Indian-style dance which developed on Java and Bali are the half-crouch position of female characters and the outthrust clenched fist or the raised and fully extended leg of male characters. In Javanese dance both male and female performers wear sashes at the waist which they flick, grab, swirl, twist, drop, or merely hold.[16] Sashes are not worn by Balinese dancers. Balinese dance is easily identified by the unusual asymmetrical torso position—hip thrust to one side, shoulders to the other—and the flashing eye gestures used by preadolescent girl dancers. In Java, in Sunda, and in Bali, one feels a strong contrast between the gracefully smooth, sinuous, ever-moving dance patterns of women dancers and the abrupt thrusts, lunges, and powerful movements of male dancers. If the dance-drama of Thailand, Cambodia, and Laos is all brittle and glitter, like the gold, jewels, and brilliants the dancers wear on their costumes, then Indonesian dance-drama can be thought of as warmly elegant, like the powdered skin of the dancers' bodies and the black velvet and deep browns of their costumes.

CHINESE DANCE STYLE

From earliest times, Chinese opera has developed as a conventionalized, as opposed to realistic, art. A highly codified system of dance, in which gestures and movement patterns are executed in rhythmic cadence to the accompaniment of music, is one of its salient characteristics. Scott describes 54 hand movements, all conventionalized but in general based on identifiable natural movements. Only a very few could be called symbolic in the manner of Indian mudra. Sleeve movements are extremely important (Scott mentions 107 different kinds). In addition, arm movements, foot movements, and leg movements are divided into 138 types.[17]

Not all of these movements are used in Vietnamese theatre. Some had not yet evolved in China at the time Chinese opera was introduced to Vietnam, and others that were introduced later fell into disuse. But by and large the basic system of Chinese stage movement was adopted in Vietnam. Over the centuries the Vietnamese have somewhat modified these Chinese movements; however, there has been no significant development of an independent Vietnamese dance style as a departure from Chinese models, in the way Cambodians, Thai, Javanese, and Balinese developed their own stage dances based on, but departing from, Indian models.

A few of the most easily identifiable Chinese dance movements seen in Vietnamese theatre and in lakon bassac are: the stiff-legged strut of a high court official; the upright index finger moved forcibly for emphasis; the intricately choreographed battle scenes (including Chinese tumbling in hat boi); the suddenly clenched fist of the warrior; and the staff held horizontally behind the back during the exit of a rough masculine character.

DRAMATIC FUNCTIONS OF DANCE

Dance is used in Southeast Asian theatre in three important ways: battle scenes may be staged as choreographed dances; dance movements may be used by actors during dialogue or song passages as a kind of conventionalized gesture language; or segments of the story may be told through dance scenes, as is done in the West in ballet. These three uses can indicate an ascending order of dance complexity within the drama. In a theatre form where dance is unimportant, it will be found only in battle scenes. Moving on up the scale, if a genre has closer connections with dance, actors will use dance gestures while speaking or singing. At the top of the scale are genres which are truly "dance-drama," those which contain large sections of pure dance as well as dance gestures during speaking or singing and danced battle scenes.

If we apply this scale to some of the major genres we find kich and ludruk at the very bottom. There is no dance at all within the drama proper, though before every ludruk play the ngremo dance is performed and modern dances and songs normally precede a kich play. Moving up one notch we find that, in ketoprak and mohlam luong, battles are fought in conventional dance style (Javanese dance style in the former and Thai in the latter). However, actors almost never use dance gestures while speaking; they act in a more or less realistic style. In these four cases, then, we have theatre genres which are either completely or very largely outside the great dance traditions of Southeast Asia.

Midway on the dance scale are likay, cai luong, hat boi, and lakon bassac, which contain a considerable amount of dance but not as much as dance-dramas proper. Likay actors use Thai classical dance gestures while speaking; all of their movements across stage and battles are performed as dance movements to the accompaniment of music. In most cai luong plays, actors use at least some Chinese gestures, taken over from hat boi, and battle scenes are danced in the same style. The amount of dance gesture a cai luong actor uses depends upon the play being performed—much if the play is traditional, little or none if it is contemporary. Every gesture or movement the hat boi actor makes on stage is a dance gesture or a dance movement based

yai puppet movements, for the puppets cannot move in the sense wayang puppets do. They have no movable parts. They cannot gesture. All they can do is be moved on and off stage, and jiggled up and down a bit. What the khon dancers did was copy the body and foot movements of the puppeteers, creating a formal dance out of their incipient and incidental movements.

Burmese classical dance plays have been greatly influenced by marionette performances. Marionette theatre in Burma is very old, but until the eighteenth century it was largely a children's show in which animals paraded and danced about. After the Burmese captured the Thai capital in 1767 the marionettes came to perform *Ramayana* and *Jataka* stories newly introduced from Thailand, and for about a hundred years thereafter, human actors in Burma seldom performed *Jataka* stories. The marionette theatre held the monopoly. When popular troupes of actor-dancers (zat pwe) began to perform *Jataka* stories in the late nineteenth and the twentieth centuries, they not unnaturally adopted many of the movements the marionettes used in telling the stories. Among Burmese dancers it is said that, "puppets set the standard a good dancer must abide by."[18] In all probability present-day Burmese theatrical dance is a blend of native pre-Hindu dance, dance which came directly from India, Thai classical dance of the eighteenth century, and the movements of Burmese marionettes, which were themselves influenced by classical Thai dance, Thai marionette theatre, and possibly Thai shadow theatre (nang yai).

CHAPTER 7

Production

Drama, music, and dance are three elements of the art of theatre. Production is a fourth. Certain over-all artistic patterns in the theatre of Southeast Asia have been noted: patterns of musical instrumentation and the use of music related to cultural areas, dance patterns related to either Chinese or Indian influences, and dramatic patterns reflecting sources of dramatic material. But the single most pervasive and widespread artistic pattern in Southeast Asian theatre is the pattern of production. With but two exceptions, all plays of all genres of all countries are "put together" in the same general way.

THE PRODUCTION SYSTEM

Plays are produced in Southeast Asia in a manner which differs fundamentally from any production system we know in the West. The difference reflects in a most revealing way fundamentally different artistic aims for the theatre. In the West, the play is the measure of all things. Each play is thought of as a unique creation, an artistic entity complete unto itself. It is especially created by a writer—the playwright—and it may be totally unlike any other play ever written. In both of the main systems of production in use in the West—repertory and the producer system—the play is the unit of production. In the producer system, the system we have on Broadway, theatre artists are brought together to produce a single play; after that play is finished the group disbands, perhaps never to work together again. In repertory, though actors work together on a series of plays and a play may be revived, still each play is prepared and mounted as a separate work of art. The focus of Western dramatic art, that is, is on the uniqueness of each play. Above all we prize individual creativity, newness in theatre. And our production systems are geared to provide just that: they are systems for "hand-crafting" each production.

In Southeast Asia the aim of production is not to produce one play, or even ten or a hundred separate plays, but to stage examples of a specific genre. The genre, not the play, is the unit of production. Production is organized around permanent troupes of from ten to a hundred and fifty actors, writers, producers, musicians, singers, technicians, and administrative staff. It is not at all unusual for actors to have performed together in the same troupe several thousand times. Since a troupe performs in a single genre (with few and minor exceptions), dancers are expert in the dance patterns of the genre, musicians and singers know its traditional melodies and songs, actors know the stories on which plays are based, the standard dialogue patterns, and the style of performance. As a rule a troupe performs a different play every night. Actors play the same type of role night after night, and in some cases they play the same character all their lives (for example, the clowns). A few standard types of scenery, costumes, and make-up satisfy the production needs of any play that might be given. If theatre productions are "hand-crafted" in the West, they are "prefabricated" in Southeast Asia. In successive performances the standard parts of the genre are shifted, rearranged, put into different combinations. Each of these particular combinations is, of course, a "play." Like the patterns of a kaleidoscope, all the combinations or plays are regroupings of the same basic elements. No two patterns are exactly alike; none are totally different.

In this kind of production system the actor is top man. Directors as such scarcely exist. Actors know what to do without being told. The highest managerial position in most troupes is the stage manager, the actor-manager, or the so-called playwright, who selects and rearranges scripts. The playwright does not as a rule write dialogue for the actors. Actors improvise dialogue around the story line, using certain set patterns of dialogue and in some cases set speeches.

In Djakarta I visited the best-known sandiwara troupe in the city, Miss Tjitjih, and found the playwright-manager looking through his books of scenarios of *Mahabharata* stories. They had just decided to change the play scheduled for that evening. In a few minutes he had decided what to do: he took fragments from three well-known episodes, added some ideas of his own, and came up with a "new" play of thirteen scenes. Later that afternoon he talked the idea over with the manager and the chief actor, then posted a two-page scenario and a casting list backstage. Around seven, the performers began to come into the theatre to don make-up and get into costume. Prior to that time, at least half the cast did not know what parts they would be performing; the others did, for they play the same roles each night. There was no rehearsal. Actors glanced at the scenario from time to time during the performance. The play lasted three and a half hours; court scenes, pitched battles, farce scenes by the clowns, and dance sequences went off without a flaw. The effect was the same as though the troupe had rehearsed this one play for weeks.

Another time, in southern Thailand, I stopped in at a little closed-in nang talung stage on a hill in the middle of a fairground. The stage was perched on stilts to raise it above the heads of the crowd. It was about 11:30 at night, thirty minutes before performance time. The chief puppeteer was pouring over four thick books of handwritten manuscript. I asked what he was doing. "Making up the story," he replied. He was putting together a plot, using elements from several stories in the books before him. After about twenty-five minutes of intense and silent reading, the puppeteer closed his books. Without a word he moved up to the banana log at the front of the stage and began to stick puppets into it. He began the performance about five minutes later, without, as far as I could tell, telling the musicians what the play was to be about.

In a village in south Bali, I went to see a wayang kulit performance. I arrived around 9 P.M. While the dalang's musicians and local villagers set up the banana-log stage and stretched the cloth screen across the front of the temporary stage, the dalang went off with the village head to find out what the villagers wanted performed that night. He came back about an hour and a half later, told the musicians the name of the play, fiddled a bit with the puppets and the screen, then began the play.

One reason it is possible to choose a play a few minutes before performance is that actors are skilled ad-libbers. Some ad-libbing occurs in 99 percent of the plays produced in Southeast Asia. Likay performers are incredible; they not only ad-lib dialogue and song lyrics, but they regularly improvise the plots of plays as well. Often when a performance begins, no one in the troupe knows how it will end! Actors may spin out the plot of a play, in nightly installments, for a week or more. It depends upon their inspiration of the moment and upon audience reaction.

More typically, actors know a basic repertory of plays within which they ad-lib variations. Large troupes, such as the major wayang orang troupes in Java, will have upward of a hundred standard plays in their repertory. Partly for advertising purposes they schedule plays several weeks to a month in advance. A troupe will try not to repeat a play more often than once every few months, though a few of the most popular plays may be staged more often. Smaller troupes cannot keep so many plays in their repertory; twenty to thirty standard plays is about maximum for these troupes. Of course any troupe can add to this number by inventing new plays or making major alterations in the basic repertory. One small ketoprak troupe I visited displayed large signs advertising:

> Damar Wulan and the Sword
> Damar Wulan and the Jewels
> Damar Wulan and the Ghost.

I thought these were three different plays until I talked to the troupe manager and he told me they were the same play except for one scene in which the sword, or the jewels, or the ghost exerted magic power on Damar Wulan's behalf. In most theatre forms there seems to be a fluctuating balance between sticking to a set pattern and trying new variations.

The two major exceptions to this general production system are court productions in Cambodia and Laos, where traditional dialogue and lyrics are completely memorized, and productions of cai luong and the Thai National Theatre, where new plays (or at least new versions of old plays) are written out in complete dialogue form and memorized. The first exception need not concern us much here, for court performances are rare these days and of minor importance in the over-all theatre picture. The operation of the Thai National Theatre will be described later. Here it is enough to say that modern stage adaptations of khon and lakon are produced by the Thai National Theatre, each production being given fifty to a hundred times. Old scripts are edited or adapted by staff members of the theatre, and these scripts are memorized. The production process can be likened to that of a Western opera troupe reviving a seldom-produced work. Each play is conceived of and mounted as a separate work, but within the context of the genre.

Cai luong is unique in that it is the only genre in which new plays are constantly being written, and in which a play may have a long run. The only full-fledged professional playwrights in Southeast Asia are cai luong playwrights. There are perhaps a hundred people writing new plays, or new versions of old plays, for the dozen or so major cai luong troupes that work out of Saigon. A playwright usually directs his own work. A play is carefully rehearsed for several weeks. The full dialogue text is memorized by the actors (except that the clowns are allowed to ad-lib). An average production will run nightly for two to six weeks in Saigon, then tour for about the same length of time in the provinces. A hit play will run two to three months.

STAGING

Outdoor staging is the simplest kind of staging used in Southeast Asia. Actor-dancers perform on the bare earth of a village square or a temple courtyard. The audience sits or stands on all sides. There is no stage, no scenery. All that is required for performance are costumes, make-up, musical instruments, and light of some kind (sunlight in the daytime or coconut-oil lamps, torches, or gas pressure-lamps at night). This is how barong and wayang wong are performed in Bali today and how Burmese zat and Thai lakon jatri were staged until not too long ago.

The staging of court dramas in the past was scarcely more elaborate. Performances were moved indoors, usually into an

Production

51. Western proscenium staging as seen in a ketoprak performance.

52. An example of pure central staging is this outdoor wayang wong performance in Bali in which the audience surrounds the four open sides of the earthen playing area.

53. In this example of modified central staging in Thailand, the audience in a semi-circle watches outdoor khon performance.

54. A Western-influenced performance of *Becket* presented by the Dramatic Guild of the University of the East in the Philippines.

open-sided hall (like the Javanese *pendapa*). The only essential was that the building be large enough to accommodate many people and that the floor be smooth for dancing. There was no raised stage, no scenery, no curtains, no stage machinery. Performers and audience merely occupied different parts of the same hall. Honored guests and the ruler sat on raised seats; less important spectators watched from the courtyard outside. In time, costumes became more elaborate and props, like chariots, sometimes were used, but the basic concept of staging indoor court drama did not depart from that of outdoor folk performances.

What was this concept? In the West we would call it "staging in the round," "arena staging," or "central staging." Central staging, as I shall call it here, has two distinguishing characteristics: there is no curtain or other architectural feature which physically divides the theatre into separate acting and audience areas; and the audience surrounds the acting area on all sides (as in Balinese wayang wong) or on three sides in a semicircle (as in Balinese barong). The great virtue of central staging is its simplicity, its directness. The audience learns the location of a scene by a character introducing himself, "I am King X, of Kingdom Y . . ." Or the chorus sings, "Hermit A journeys to the neighboring land of B . . ." Or a clown yells, "Look at those forest ghosts! Let's get out of this lonely place!" And if a battle takes place, well, the scene is a battlefield. Scenery is quite unnecessary in this staging concept, and without scenery there is no practical limit to the number of scenes a play may contain (as there is in modern Western theatre, where the high cost of scenery sets a premium on the one-set play). It isn't necessary to argue whether multiple-scene dramatic structure or central staging came first. What is important is the realization that, prior to the middle of the nineteenth century, the normal dramatic form throughout Southeast Asia was episodic and multi-scene, and the normal method of staging was central staging. This was true of khon, lakon nai, Lao and Cambodian Royal Ballet, lakon jatri, zat, raket, wayang orang, Balinese dance-dramas of all types, and, if we accept Rassers' theory that originally dalang and audience sat on the same side of the shadow screen,[1] wayang kulit as well. (Nowadays the wayang kulit audience sits on both sides of the screen, so, for those on the shadow side, the screen hides the technical workings of the theatre, and the staging technique can no longer be called central staging).

Sometime in the nineteenth century many types of plays came to be staged with scenery of one kind or another. Exactly when and how this came about we don't know, but certainly touring companies from Europe using drop-and-wing scenery exerted some influence. At the Thai court, lakon plays were staged with elaborate scenery; this was such a special thing that the productions were given a new name—*lakon dukdamban* or "lakon with scenery." In general, however, scenery was not commonly adopted for court performances (partly it would seem because existing pavilions were not equipped with raised stages on which to place scenery). And folk theatre troupes could not afford the expense of buying or making scenery. It was mainly within the newly developing popular theatre tradition that built stages and canvas scenery came to be widely employed. Theatre buildings for popular plays were usually ramshackle affairs, with stages made of bamboo and rough planking and roofed over with palm thatch. Today most popular theatre is presented in theatre buildings, permanent or temporary, equipped with raised stages, proscenium arch, front act curtain, and drop-and-wing canvas scenery painted to represent palace interiors, forest glades, rice fields, temples, roads, prisons, and so forth.

This "proscenium staging" does not differ in any important respect from standard proscenium staging in the West. The audience sits on one side of the stage, separated from the acting area by the raised stage, proscenium wall, and curtain, and it peeks through an opening in the proscenium wall to watch the action of a play unfold. When parts of court plays were taken over by popular theatre troupes, as frequently happened after the turn of the century, the change from central staging to proscenium staging was hardly noticed. However, when entire wayang orang dance plays, which had been performed for more than a century in central staging, were transferred bodily to the proscenium stage, a fundamental change in dance aesthetic occurred. In court wayang orang, the dancer was oriented toward the four points of the compass: a dance figure was performed first for honored guests sitting at one end of the hall, and then it was danced in the other three directions, because the audience sat on all sides of an open-sided hall. On the proscenium stage, however, it made no sense to repeat a dance figure in four directions, for all the audience was on one side. "The result was tragic," a respected dance teacher in Jogjakarta said to me, "professional troupes ripped the heart out of Javanese dance when they stopped repeating dance figures. They destroyed the dance's essential symmetry, and they arbitrarily speeded up the tempo of performance to four times what it used to be." The popular Javanese audience largely is unaware of what Javanese court dance was like and so cannot make comparisons. But even if they could they still might prefer their newer, speeded-up version of wayang orang. Certainly commercial wayang orang is very popular today.

The nature of the proscenium stage also requires the use of scenery. This is the source of endless artistic difficulties for most popular theatre troupes. The episodic plays of most Southeast Asian theatre genres are simply incompatible with the scenic demands of the proscenium stage. Even with a handsome budget it would be difficult to create artistically satisfying sets for a play set in fifteen or twenty locations, and to do this for a different play every night, week after week, is impossible. Consequently, most troupes compromise on the quality of their settings. The best are fair, the average pretty bad, and the worst atrocious. Mythological plays inevitably lose some of their appeal when staged in front of obvious canvas pieces. It would be far better to abandon the attempt to depict scenes on stage realistically, and to perform before a neutral background. Only the Thai National Theatre and half a dozen large cai luong troupes operate within a production system which makes possible the building of believable, artistically acceptable scenery, including large, three-dimensional set-pieces. It is economically feasible for these troupes to construct scenery specifically for each production (as we do in the West) because the initial high cost of construction can be recovered during the long run of the play.

C H A P T E R   8

Transmission of Theatre Art

Change occurs in any art form with the passage of time. Chapter 3 has shown how major theatre forms in Southeast Asia developed and, in some cases, expired. At the same time, general patterns of music, of dance, and of drama have tended to persist down to the present day. For example, over the years new gamelan melodies have been composed, first for wayang kulit, then for wayang orang, and finally for ketoprak and ludruk; but the essential nature of gamelan music—as compared to other forms of music—has not changed. In spite of numerous alterations which have occurred in Indian dance since it was taken up in Southeast Asia a thousand years ago, the characteristic pattern of Indian dance is still clearly discernable in, say, Javanese or Thai dance style.* The clown-servant, who speaks words of wisdom to the hero (and to the audience), takes the stage in 1964 just as he has for more than ten centuries; that is, the pattern of the clown-servant remains, though the content of his jokes may be different. In speaking of Javanese theatre, Rassers makes the comment that its historical development "could be described as a constant, unconscious attempt to find a new content which more or less fitted into the old forms and satisfied

---

*Here I am speaking in very general terms. Dance style can be divided and subdivided almost without end. For example, within Indian style dance one subpattern is Indonesian-Malaysian dance, and within it Javanese dance is a sub-subpattern. Beyond this, a Javanese dancer would distinguish between regional styles practiced in Jogjakarta and Surakarta (sub-sub-subpatterns) and if from Jogjakarta would further distinguish stylistic differences as taught at the two main classical dance schools in the city (sub-sub-sub-subpatterns). It serves no purpose to make this kind of minute distinction here, however.

the changed needs."[1] This may be an extreme statement, but there is much truth in it. Until the middle of the nineteenth century Burmese court regulations "forbade a new song to be sung before the king. Disobeying this rule was treason, punishable by death."[2]

TRADITIONAL TEACHING METHODS

The forms and formulas of Southeast Asian theatre are preserved and transmitted to succeeding generations through traditional teaching methods conspicuously different from those used in the West. The simplest of these is perhaps the most common: a youngster sits backstage; he watches and listens to performances; he learns. As time goes by this young apprentice is given minor tasks. He becomes a spear-carrier or plays one of the easier instruments. How high he rises in a troupe depends largely on talent and on luck. The learning situation is unstructured and informal. The "student" learns by rote and is expected to reproduce exactly what he sees and hears his elders doing. This is the way most popular theatre performers learn their art (or skill, if you prefer). Master-disciple teaching is a similar but more formalized teaching method widely practiced in most countries. A master of an artistic discipline—*guru* in Sanskrit and Indonesian, *gru* in Thai—is a revered person. He possesses "secrets" of his art, and may possess religious powers as well. Almost without exception the best performers are considered the best teachers. (It would be considered absurd in Southeast Asia for a teacher to say to a student, "I can't do it but I can teach you how to do it," as we often do in the West.) Famous performers are besieged by eager youngsters who wish to learn from them. A pupil is expected to study with but one master-teacher, though a teacher may have many pupils. A pupil has no inherent "right" to learn; it is only through the kindness of the master that he is allowed to gain access to some of the teacher's profound and very personal knowledge of the art. Until the day he dies, a pupil will feel obligated to his master for the favor of his instruction.

The performer-teacher may give favored pupils individual instruction, but more commonly pupils learn in somewhat formal class situations. Near Songkhla, in southern Thailand, I visited a well-known lakon jatri troupe manager-teacher at his school, set in the midst of rice fields half a mile from the nearest road. Every year six to eight farm boys come to his house, which has a small stage attached to it, for instruction in lakon jatri. They stay during the rainy season and pay him 300 bhat ($15) a month for instruction, plus another 200 bhat ($10) a month if they board there. Instruction in acting, dance, and music is given every day. After six months a pupil is considered sufficiently trained to perform lakon jatri in public. As a kind of certificate of graduation, each student is allowed to copy out of the master's dog-eared manuscripts the twelve episodes of the *Manora* before leaving. The master is proud of the fact that he still teaches the traditional folk-version of the *Manora* play, and that none of his pupils learn from him the debased lakon jatri.

A master performer rarely passes on everything he knows to all his pupils. He is more apt to single out one or two favorites on whom he will bestow the "secrets" of his knowledge. The best known wayang golek dalang in central Java is typical in this respect. He lives in a village about thirty miles from Jogjakarta and is so famous that twenty to thirty adult dalang study under him constantly, as well as youngsters. He spoke of the strong family system that supported the art of dalangship: there are only five names a dalang may take (Djermo, Gondo, Terti, Kuno, or Widi, his name). Although he teaches many people, he declared "a good dalang is the son of a good dalang." His son is being prepared to take his place when he becomes too old to perform. None of his other pupils receives training as thorough as that given his son.

Master-disciple teaching has two sides to it, as these illustrations show: it tends to preserve traditions and hand them on to the next generation quite exactly; but, because the master teaches all he knows to only one or two pupils, the diffusion of knowledge of the art form tends to be limited.

In the examples just given, pupils visited their master for instruction. In some interesting cases a master teacher may be engaged to come to a village to instruct local performers. This is a common way for folk troupes to learn sophisticated theatre forms. In Bali, it is common for a village to hire a renowned teacher from some neighboring village to teach its preadolescent girls the legong dance, for example. The teaching process is simple, direct, and very efficient: the teacher stands behind the young pupil and guides her arms and legs through the proper movements until the pupil has mastered the fundamental elements of the dance. Training may continue daily for several months. The teacher returns to her village when her instruction is finished. Or, a well-known performer may be brought into a village as a kind of resident teacher. I visited one village in Cambodia just south of Phnom Penh where the village elders had decided, some seventeen years ago, that they wanted to produce dance-dramas once or twice yearly for important festivals at their large Buddhist temple, in which they take great pride. A former dancer of the Royal Cambodian Ballet was engaged, and brought to live in the village. The richest merchant in the village became her sponsor, and has assumed the costs of her support for the past seventeen years. For several months prior to each performance, the teacher trains the village girls in dancing, singing, and acting on a rigorous schedule: four hours each morning, two hours each afternoon, and several hours each evening.

Characteristically, youngsters who learn to perform through a master-disciple relationship are loath to change anything they have learned from their master. They revere and honor their teacher, and to alter his teaching would indicate disrespect. Learning by rote also reinforces the tendency to preserve precisely what one has learned. Even the highly creative pupil hesitates to carry out his own ideas. Since few people were literate in earlier times, the teacher was in a very powerful position because he and he alone possessed the vital written play scenarios. Until a pupil had obtained copies of his master's scripts, he was quite literally bound to servitude to his master, for he could not perform without them. I found it difficult to imagine the true importance of a literate person in a largely illiterate society until I attended a folk-song performance in Bandung, west Java, one evening in which illiterate old women had to wait for a male villager to read off verses from a textbook before they sang them. The performance illustrated the traditional way in which these villagers sang epics in verse form in their isolated mountain community. The male villager sat apart from the women. He held a small book containing the verses of the epic. First he would rattle off a verse in an undertone, then the women would repeat it, singing in unison. In this fashion the group sang through an episode of a Sundanese legend. Because the legend is sung only once or twice a year, the illiterate singers are unable to remember the lyrics from performance to performance. They rely upon someone else in the village, who can read and write, to copy down the song lyrics and preserve them for them.

In past centuries, artists working in one genre often have learned performance techniques or have taken stories from other genres. The *Panji* stories spread from Java throughout Southeast Asia; khon dancers learned dance steps from nang yai puppeteers; wayang orang dancers adapted wayang kulit puppet movements to the live stage; and so on. Within this century, likay and lakon bassac performers have adapted Thai and Lao court dance to popular theatre. Likay actors studied lakon and khon dance techniques from former palace dancers during the 1920's and 1930's. In Cambodian lakon bassac, the borrowing process is still going on. Several large lakon bassac troupes have as their leading ladies former Cambodian palace dancers. They dance leading roles in performance and teach young actresses the rudiments of classical dance style. It seems likely that the influence of these few dancers will gradually spread (for their dances are extremely popular with audiences) and more court-derived dance will find its way into lakon bassac in the future.

Music, dance, and drama do not necessarily preserve or transmit in similar ways. In one sense, patterns of music are the easiest to maintain over a long span of time. Musical instruments are physical objects which may last hundreds of years and can be reproduced when worn out. On the other hand, prior to recent times, music scales and melodies have never been written down. There has been no "bureau of standards" for music is any Southeast Asian country as there was in ancient China nor a treatise codifying musical custom as did the *Natya Sastra* in India.[3] Music was preserved and transmitted orally. Consequently, many traditional melodies have been forgotten and irretrievably lost. Within the last fifty years, however, most of the classical music of Thailand, Vietnam, and Java has been transcribed. The preservation and transmission of dance traditions is somewhat more complex. Music is built on notes, discrete, measurable, fixed. But dance works with bodily movements which are infinitely variable, at least in theory. Dance, by its very nature, is amorphous; it is harder to set down than music. Still, dance patterns are learned; and the more codified a dance style is, the more likely it is to be preserved and transmitted intact through the years. I have mentioned that Thai lakon and khon dance use an "alphabet" of gestures and movement phrases. Thai dancers are highly conscious of this alphabet, and try to reproduce it exactly. There is every reason to believe the alphabet is being preserved accurately at present. In Bali, to go to the other extreme, new things are highly prized. If a traditional dance becomes boring, it is dropped for something more interesting. Both the *baris* war dance, highly regarded as recently as twenty years ago, and the *djanger,* a dance popular with rambunctious adolescents several decades back, are scarcely known on Bali today. This is not to say that fundamental Balinese dance patterns have been discarded outright. Rather, it means that, as new dance compositions are created and old ones fall into disuse, gradual changes in style are bound to occur. And they will occur more often and more rapidly than in Thailand, for example, where change in the dance is not consciously sought.

Dramatic texts are still another matter. Written texts of epics have been known in Java since the early ninth century and on the mainland from around the eleventh century. Theoretically, written dramatic sources have been available since then. In fact, however, we don't know just when written sources came to be used by theatrical performers. By at least the fifteenth century, many palace and temple libraries in Indian-influenced countries, contained various versions of the Indian epics, *Jataka,* and local stories, and, in Vietnam and parts of Cambodia and Laos, written versions of Chinese and local stories. Palace and temple texts were considered sacred, and not everyone was allowed to copy them. But some performers had access to them and did copy them for theatrical use. The folk troupe in Cambodia I just mentioned uses scripts kept by elders of the temple. The scripts I was shown were full of worm holes and literally falling to pieces. The old villager to whose care the scripts were entrusted explained that these were copies received by his father from his father's father, each of whom had lived to be older than he was, making the probable age of the scripts more than 150 years. These copies, in turn, had been made from much older manuscripts in the possession of a famous wat some miles to the north of the village.

Most of the manuscripts I have been talking about are epics or stories written in narrative form; they are not plays written in dialogue form, nor even plays written in scenario form. Performers had to fashion play scenarios from them by extracting a series of scenes that would tell a story in dramatic form. Performers and troupe managers put these scenarios together into "handbooks." And it is from such dog-eared, handwritten, passed-on-from-father-to-son "handbooks" (consisting of scenarios, bits of key dialogue, songs, famous poems, and scraps of story material) that most troupes have produced plays. There are only a few exceptions. From the time of Rama I (1782–1809), Thai court drama has been partly written in dialogue form. Complete texts for many hat boi operas exist and are used, to some extent at least, by hat boi troupes today. Dialogue used to be written out for some wayang orang plays when produced in the Javanese courts, but popular troupes today do not use these scripts. Most cai luong plays are newly written in complete dialogue form, as are kich and modern Philippine plays. With these very few exceptions, plays have never been written in dialogue form in Southeast Asia. This is in striking contrast to our Western practice of making the playwright's script the basis of a dramatic production. The best teachers and performers in Southeast Asia possess handbooks that contain excellent versions of scenarios; poorer troupes and less talented teachers operate with ill-organized and often garbled materials. How much of these story materials that are now written down for theatrical use originally came out of the oral tradition? To this tantalizing question I have no satisfactory answer except to suggest that a good deal of what is now transmitted via the written word very likely was transmitted orally in the dim past. I would describe the system of preserving and transmitting dramatic materials which prevailed until very recent times as a mixture of both written and oral methods: play scenarios were written, but patterns of dialogue were handed down orally.

MODERN MEANS OF TRANSMISSION

Today artistic traditions are passed on pretty much as in the past—through informal learning situations and master-disciple relationships—as well as through typically modern means. The printing press was the first major modern innovation. In the nineteenth century, when printing was introduced into Southeast Asia, theatre was not greatly affected. In 1872, U Pon Nya's play *Wizaya* was published in Rangoon, the first of hundreds of popular plays, one hundred to one hundred and fifty pages in length, which poured from Burmese printing presses.[4] But, otherwise, prior to World War II few plays were published for commercial distribution. Occasionally plays appeared in European-sponsored scholarly publications, as, for example, the series of wayang kulit plays published in a Dutch journal in the 1930's.[5] These publications reached scholars but were rarely seen by performers, and at most they only indirectly affected the living theatre of the time.

Following World War II, every new independent government committed itself to achieving mass literacy in the shortest possible time. The amount and variety of printed literature available to the public increased rapidly. Not unnaturally national literature was given priority in most countries, and, as a result, traditional stories such as the *Ramayana*, Chinese novels, *Jataka* stories, and local histories are now sold in cheap printed editions almost everywhere. For the first time in Lao history, traditional stories in Lao are published for use by mohlam performers. The *Ramayana* is published in Cambodian. Cai luong sheet music is sold at every Saigon newsstand. In Indonesia *Mahabharata* stories are published in the Javanese, Sundanese, and Indonesian languages. Many wayang play scenarios and even some complete dialogue scripts are now published commercially in Java. On Bali, texts of the *Ramayana*, the *Mahabharata*, and *Sutasoma* (which concerns the supposed introduction of Buddhism to the Javanese court of Astina, thus connecting the *Mahabharata* with Buddhism in the Balinese mind) have existed for centuries, handwritten on lontar palm leaves. But the ordinary Balinese did not have access to these precious texts, and, even if he had, he could not have understood the ancient mixture of Sanskrit, Javanese, and Balinese in which they were written. Today the texts are published in a form any Balinese with a grade-school education can understand. On each printed page there appear four columns: the first for the original text written in Javanese characters; the second for a transliteration of the text into Roman letters; the third for a Balinese language translation written in Balinese script; and the fourth for an Indonesian language translation written in Roman letters.

Other books explain the art of classic theatre. A series of short pamphlets on Thai dance-drama are published by the government's National Culture Institute in Bangkok. A book on Cambodian dance-drama is published and sold by the Institut Bouddhique in Phnom Penh. In Java and in Sunda handbooks of wayang kulit and wayang golek puppet performance techniques have been printed, whose importance can scarcely be overestimated. They describe speaking, singing, and movement techniques and include such detailed information as lists of "desirable words" to use in various scenes.

A second modern innovation has been the establishment of government schools for the performing arts in every country in Southeast Asia. The oldest and most successful of these is the Thai School of Dramatic Art in Bangkok, established in 1934. It is operated by the Department of Fine Arts of the central government. There are other theatre schools in Thailand, but none as important. Three levels of instruction are offered: the Preliminary course (six years at primary school level); the Intermediate course (three years at high school level); and the Advanced course (two years at university level). The bulk of instruction in theatre is devoted to khon and lakon drama, including theatre music and dance. A total of 825 students were enrolled for full-time instruction in 1963. In the thirty years the school has been operating it has trained a large number of teachers and professional performers; were it not for its pioneering work it is unlikely that khon and lakon would be living art forms today. Since World War II schools similar to this have been established in most other countries in the region.

55. Cover illustration of the play script Petruk Becomes King in Indonesia showing a human Petruk whose facial features and pointing finger are taken from wayang kulit.

56. A puppeteer of the court of Sultan Hamengku Buwono of Jogjakarta, demonstrates how two Javanese wayang kulit puppets (the monkey Hanoman and an unusual nine-armed Ravana) can be held and manipulated simultaneously, a technique mastered only after long instruction.

57. Mario, the greatest Balinese dancer of the last generation, teaches a young pupil in the 1930's in the traditional manner—by moving the boy's arms and body.

58. A Thai likay actor costumed and dancing in the style of court lakon dance-drama, techniques introduced into likay from the Thai court several generations ago.

The Indonesian Ministry of Education operates schools of music and dance (*Konservatori Karawitan*) in Bandung, Surakarta, and Surabaya on Java, and in Den Pasar in Bali. In 1962 the Vietnamese government established schools of music and drama in Saigon and Hue. Hat boi and cai luong are the chief theatre subjects taught, some instruction also being given in Western drama at the Saigon school. In 1960 the Cambodian Ministry of Education, through its Division of Fine Arts, set up National Schools of Theatre, of Music, and of Fine Arts. Instruction at the School of Theatre is primarily in folk-theatre and modern, Western-style theatre (classical dance-drama remains a royal monopoly). About eighty students are currently enrolled in the four-year course. There are two government theatre schools in Laos: one is attached to the royal court at Luang Prabang and is directed by the king's advisers, the other (the Natasin School of Music and Drama), was established in Vientiane in 1959 and is run directly by the Department of Fine Arts of the Ministry of Education. Both specialize in instruction in classical Lao dance, in the style of Thai khon and lakon. About eighty students are enrolled in the Vientiane school. In the Philippines, theatre instruction is offered as part of the regular academic program in most large colleges and universities, following the American practice. The Arena Theatre of the Philippines attached to Philippine Normal College has trained over fifteen hundred students in the theatre arts since its establishment in 1953. The Burmese government operates schools for the performing arts in Rangoon and Mandalay.

Government schools make unique contributions toward preserving and transmitting traditional theatre art. They offer high-caliber instruction to young people who otherwise might not have an opportunity to study under traditional theatre training systems: tuition is low or nonexistent; admission is by open examination; schools are located in major population centers. As in academies throughout the world, the classic traditions are treated with reverence, and students are taught to reproduce exact patterns. There is some experimenting with new forms and ideas, but the main emphasis is on preserving and passing on traditional theatre patterns. To date, considerable numbers of students have graduated from government schools of theatre

[163]

only in Thailand and the Philippines. (None have yet graduated from the new schools in Laos, Vietnam, and Cambodia, and just a few have in Indonesia.) Apparently many of the Thai and Philippine graduates are going into public schools in the provinces as teachers of the performing arts. If this pattern is repeated in other countries, and instruction in the performing arts begins to reach down into the public schools, the result will be a wider dissemination of knowledge of theatrical art than has ever been known before.

At the same time, there are practical limits to the influence which these schools may be expected to exert on professional theatre. At best, most schools can turn out only a few graduates each year and this number is small indeed compared to the great number of people in professional theatre. A good example is the Habirando school for wayang kulit dalang in Jogjakarta, one of the two best dalang schools in Java. It is affiliated with the court of the Sultan of Jogjakarta and has been open to the public since 1925. The course of instruction lasts three years. Although around 200 new students enroll each year, less than 10 percent complete the course and receive diplomas. Of the 27 students who took their final examinations in 1963, just 15 were passed, and 15 new dalang per year, for a population of 60,000,000 Javanese, is not a sizable number. Liaison between government schools and professional theatre is poor in most cases. School graduates are not sought by professional hat boi, cai luong, lakon bassac, likay, wayang orang, ketoprak, or ludruk troupes. I met several cai luong troupe managers who laughed at the "artificially trained" students, saying that they wanted actors and actresses who had come up through the professional ranks. In Indonesia, students of government schools are being trained in wayang orang dance style, but it is unlikely that any will join professional wayang orang troupes on graduation. Students of the school in Cambodia are aiming for jobs in radio and television; none indicate interest in lakon bassac. Only in Thailand are there close relations between the school teaching khon and lakon and the professional troupe performing khon and lakon. The reason for this is that the government operates both school and troupe through its Department of Fine

Arts, and the school is both training ground and feeder system for the troupe.

Government schools do not train students in all forms of national theatre. Popular theatre forms are not taught at all (with the exception of cai luong in Vietnam). Some folk theatre is taught, like lakon jatri and topeng. Most instruction is in classic theatre, that is, court or former court genres—khon, lakon, Lao and Cambodian Royal Ballet, hat boi, wayang orang, wayang kulit, and wayang golek. But not all former court forms are taught. Nang yai is ignored by the School of Dramatic Art in Thailand; as a result it is virtually extinct. Hat boi is close to extinction in Vietnam, and it seems unlikely that the amount of training in hat boi now being given at the two government schools in Vietnam will halt, or even slow, its slide to oblivion.

In Sunda active steps are being taken to preserve wayang golek in its traditional form. In recent years dalang have tended to cater to popular taste by dropping out serious passages and substituting comic scenes. The personality and skill of the female singer (pesinden) has come to have more appeal than the story itself. In a 1964 survey of 178 professional dalang, 63 percent said the art of wayang golek was deteriorating and attributed this chiefly to "lack of adequate training" for the dalang.* The local government and the dalang's association have since acted together to set minimum standards for licensing future dalang. The aim is to restore wayang golek to its traditional form through better training. It is possible the experiment may work.

Amateur dramatic organizations, dance clubs, and music societies are a third modern means of disseminating theatre. Amateur organizations existed in the past, but since the Second World War their number has increased spectacularly. Middleclass families place a high value on accomplishment in the performing arts, for both children and adults. The true extent of amateur theatre activity in Southeast Asia has hardly even been guessed at. Statistics are hard to obtain. Let me, therefore, give two sets of figures I was able to obtain. As shown in Table 1,

---

*Conducted by me, February 1964, at the first convention of the Foundation for the Art of the Dalang (*Jajasan Padalangan*) held in Bandung, west Java. Approximately two hundred professional wayang golek dalang attended the convention.

Table 1. Number of amateur theatre troupes registered in East Java, 1963.

Troupe type	Number
Wayang kulit	1258
Ludruk	594
Wayang orang	286
Ketoprak	120
Seni-drama (modern drama)	112
Total	2370

Table 2. Number of amateur theatre troupes registered in the District of Purwokerto, 1962.

Troupe type	Number
Wayang orang	3
Seni-drama (modern drama)	6
Ketoprak	1
Dagelan	1
Total	11

in the Province of East Java, population approximately 22,000,000, there were registered with the Provincial Office of Culture in the year 1963, around 2370 amateur theatre groups.[6] Of approximately one hundred amateur music, dance, and drama groups registered with the Cultural Office, District of Purwokerto, Central Java in 1962, eleven were drama groups, as shown in Table 2. (The population of Purwokerto is approximately 500,000. The registration of troupes is voluntary, so there are undoubtedly more troupes than these figures show.)

The fourth new factor influencing the dissemination of theatre is mass communication: radio, television, and pulp publications. Performances of almost all types of theatre are broadcast over local or national radio networks at regular intervals.

Comic books are big business. Many tell simplified versions of traditional dramas. In others, well-known and traditional characters from the drama are used to tell modern stories. In Java, for example, a child can read a comic book in which a *Mahabharata* story is drawn in wayang kulit puppet style, or he can read a comic book in which Semar, Petruk, and Gareng, the traditional wayang clowns, cavort through twentieth-century adventures. The cultural level of comics may be questioned but through them millions of youngsters are exposed to traditional plays and characters. Television as yet is not a major force in popularizing theatre. There are few television sets, few stations, and few telecasts of stage drama (it is expensive to telecast plays with large casts and many sets). In all, the mass media are bringing elements of theatre to a vast number of people in Southeast Asia, either introducing them to theatre forms for the first time, or reinforcing, and in some cases capitalizing upon, already established knowledge of the drama.

Theatre as an Institution

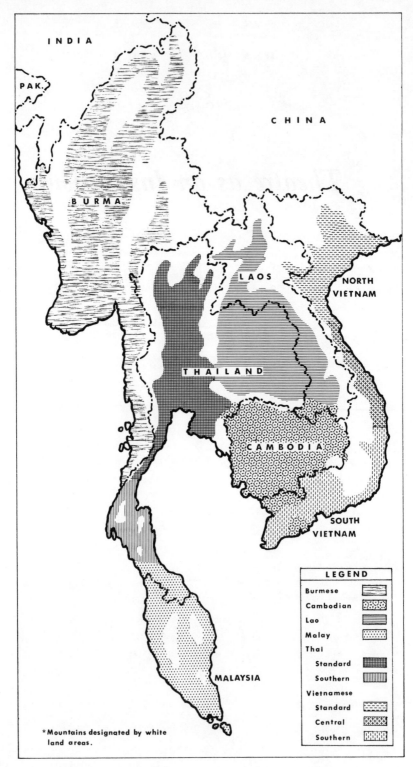

LEGEND

Burmese
Cambodian
Lao
Malay
Thai
   Standard
   Southern
Vietnamese
   Standard
   Central
   Southern

*Mountains designated by white
land areas.

MAP 5. Major Languages of the Southeast Asia Mainland

CHAPTER 9

Extent and Distribution

If genre defines the artistic dimensions of theatre in Southeast Asia, the troupe defines its social dimensions. Up until now I have been writing of theatre forms as if they were tangible things. For example, earlier I wrote that "nang yai is virtually extinct," as if something called nang yai physically existed in this world, but, like the ancient auk, was failing to reproduce itself and was in danger of dying off. Actually, a genre has no concrete existence at all. The term is only a convenient abstraction which serves to identify particular constellations of artistic patterns in the theatre—music, dance, drama, costume, make-up, setting. What exists are the performers. A genre exists when there are performers performing it; it is dead or extinct when performers cease to perform it. The most famous example of an extinct Asian theatre form is Indian Sanskrit drama. Sanskrit play scripts have been preserved; we even know something about the music and dance which was used in performance. But, from seven hundred to one thousand years ago performers stopped performing Sanskrit plays, and the form became extinct. It is as if the genre were the soul of theatre and the performing troupe its corporal body. Just as the soul needs a body through which it can manifest itself, the finest, most subtle art of the theatre needs the physical body of the troupe in order to reveal and to perpetuate itself. The theatre troupe is a social organization. It is subject to political pressure, responds to economic forces, and exists in relation to other social organizations. How many troupes are there operating in Southeast Asia today? Where are they? How do they support themselves? How are they organized? Who are the members comprising them? Who are their audiences? These are some of the questions I would like to consider, if not answer.

THE NUMBER OF PROFESSIONAL TROUPES

In attempting to estimate the number of theatre troupes active in Southeast Asia today, I must limit myself to professional troupes. It is impossible at this stage to make any kind of reasonable estimate of the number of amateur troupes. There are too many. No government knows how many troupes are active within its own boundaries. In all, counting amateur and professional troupes, there may be as many as 10,000 troupes in Southeast Asia. Table 3 contains my personal estimates of the number of professional troupes active in 1964. In every case I have deliberately made conservative estimates, based on my own observations, compiled data, and the estimates of troupe managers and theatre experts in each country. It is likely that there are more professional troupes than my figures show, and it is almost certain that there are not less. I define a troupe as "professional" if it performs in some public capacity more or less regularly, and if its members consider theatre their major occupation[1] and earn all of their income or a large portion of it from performing. Hence the purely amateur troupe, which earns no money performing, is excluded; the commercial troupe, which performs nightly and only when paid, is included. Other troupes, which perform for pay but whose members have other sources of income—landlord, farmer, teacher, and so on—may or may not be included depending upon how nearly they meet the criteria of professionalism.

There is an estimated total of 1,168 professional troupes in all of Southeast Asia except Burma and North Vietnam (excluded because data is lacking). By any reckoning this is a very large number. Since Southeast Asia has a population of 200,000,000, the average is about one professional troupe for every 200,000 people. By way of comparison, in the United States we have no more than 50 professional theatre troupes for a nearly comparable population, or about one troupe for every 4,000,000 people. In other words, Southeast Asia supports twenty times as many

[172]

Table 3. Estimated number of professional theatre troupes in Southeast Asia.

Area	Population	Theatre genre	Number of troupes	Language spoken in performance
Cambodia	6,000,000	Royal Cambodian Ballet	1 [a]	Cambodian
		Lakon bassac	25	Cambodian
Indonesia	100,000,000			
Java		Wayang kulit Java	400	Javanese
		Wayang golek Java	10	Javanese
		Wayang orang	30	Javanese
		Ketoprak	120	Javanese
		Ludruk	30	Eastern Javanese dialect
Sunda		Wayang golek Sunda	150	Sundanese
		Sandiwara	40	Sundanese
Bali		Wayang kulit Bali	10	Balinese
		Ardja	12	Balinese
Laos	2,000,000	Royal Lao Ballet	1 [a]	Lao
Laos-Thailand	10,000,000	Mohlam luong	40	Lao
Thailand	29,000,000	Lakon nai/khon	1 [a]	Thai
		Likay	100	Thai
		Nang talung	55	Southern Thai dialect
		Lakon jatri	20	Southern Thai dialect
		Chinese opera	20	Teochiu Chinese dialect
Malaysia	11,000,000	Wayang kulit Malaya	6	Malayan
		Bangsawan	4	Malayan
		Chinese opera	5	Teochiu Chinese dialect
South Vietnam	15,000,000	Hat boi	10	Central Vietnamese dialect
		Cai luong	75	Southern Vietnamese dialect
		Kich	3 [a]	Vietnamese
		Total	1168	

[a] Figure exact

professional theatre troupes on a per capita basis as does the United States.

From the estimates in Table 3, it is clear that, while on the mainland only a dozen troupes today perform traditional, highly sophisticated court, or former court, genres (one each in Cambodia, Thailand, and Laos, and about ten in Vietnam), in Indonesia a truly amazing number of troupes—an estimated five hundred and ninety—perform former court genres (wayang kulit, wayang golek Sunda, and wayang orang). The latter account for half of all the professional theatre troupes in Southeast Asia. Troupes performing popular theatre forms (likay, mohlam luong, lakon bassac, cai luong, ketoprak, sandiwara, ludruk, and bangsawan) are very numerous—an estimated four hundred and

[173]

thirty-four. On the mainland—in Thailand, Laos, Cambodia, and Vietnam—these troupes far outnumber any others. The only folk-connected theatre performed by professional troupes is nang talung, lakon jatri, and ardja. There are an estimated eighty-seven of these troupes. And, finally, three professional troupes perform kich, a genre which evolved largely out of the Western tradition of theatre.

There is every reason to believe that far more professional troupes are active today than in the past. It is true that there are fewer troupes performing lakon nai in Thailand (one in 1964, compared to four in 1935), the number of professional hat boi troupes continues to decline, most theatre experts in Thailand and Vietnam say 1930–1940 was the heyday for likay and for cai luong and that since then the number of professional troupes has declined somewhat, and that there are fewer bangsawan troupes now than previously. These relatively minor decreases, however, are outweighed by other spectacular increases. A generation ago mohlam luong did not exist; today there are at least forty professional troupes. Ketoprak, ludruk, and lakon bassac were performed by a handful of professional troupes before World War II; now an estimated one hundred and sixty-five perform them. The number of wayang kulit and wayang golek dalang has doubled and may have tripled or even quadrupled within this century.[2] However, the population of Southeast Asia has increased markedly within the past hundred years, so the ratio of professional troupes per capita may not have increased. Just to keep up with the rate of population growth would require an absolute increase in the number of theatre troupes of a very large order. In Thailand, for example, the population jumped from an estimated 6,000,000 in 1854 to 29,000,000 in 1963, for a fivefold increase in a hundred years. The population of Java has doubled in the last half-century. In Malaysia the population increase is 4 percent per year, well over a fourfold increase over a hundred-year period.

DISTRIBUTION OF TROUPES

The most important factors affecting the location of troupes are language, population, economic conditions, religion, and cultural traditions. Not all troupes are equally responsive to these factors though. Some troupes have a permanent home. The Thai National Theatre (which performs lakon nai and khon), the Cambodian Royal Ballet, the Lao Royal Ballet, and the half-dozen largest wayang orang troupes in Java have permanent homes and never travel. Other troupes perform for as many years as possible in a single location, and move only when forced to do so. Most sandiwara and lakon bassac troupes and some ketoprak troupes stay in one location for one or more years: I visited five sandiwara troupes, two lakon bassac troupes, and three ketoprak troupes that had been in their present locations more than five years. Some local troupes—usually folk-connected—work out of a home base, traveling to an engagement and returning within a few days. Most nang talung and lakon jatri troupes in Thailand and wayang kulit, wayang golek, and ardja troupes in Indonesia operate this way. They do not perform every night and they retain close ties with their home communities. Still other troupes, itinerant, are constantly on the road. Most cai luong, kich, ludruk, bangsawan, and Malayan wayang kulit troupes and many mohlam luong, likay, wayang orang, ketoprak, and hat boi troupes are on permanent tour. Troupes which tour regions or provinces are perhaps most common. Typical is the medium-sized Budi Wanita ketoprak troupe I came across in central Java: between 1960 and 1963 it had performed in eighteen locations in the two adjoining districts of Purwokerto and Kedu, each engagement lasting from one to four months.* A likay entrepreneur in Thailand owns six troupes: one plays in Bangkok, one tours the "northern circuit" (northeast Thailand), one tours the "southern circuit" (the southern provinces of Thailand), and the other three move from one area to another on an irregular basis. Large troupes sometimes tour from one end of a country to the other. When the important cai luong troupe Kim Chung is on tour, it performs in the capital cities of most of the provinces of southern Vietnam for a week or more each. Troupes of these different kinds quite naturally respond differently to the forces which tend to determine their location.

*In chronological order, it performed in the towns and villages of Gombang, Prembun, Putoh, Kemiri, Petanahan, Sampang, Banjumas, Sukaradja, Wangon, Tjilongok, Binangun, Kotawinang, Nambal, Kemiri, Djatiroto, Adjibarang, Tjilongok, and Purowokerto.

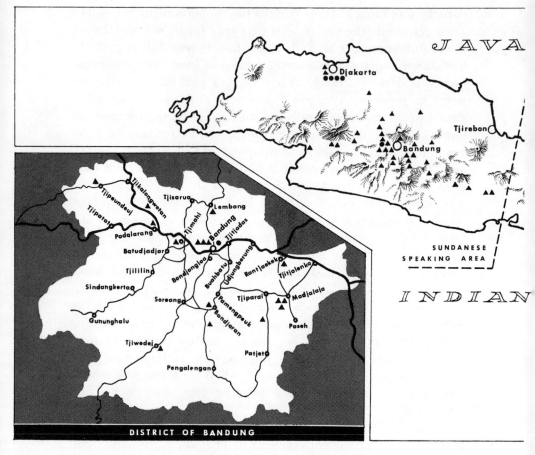

MAP 6. Location of 159 Professional Theatre Troupes in Java, March–May 1964

LANGUAGE

Most troupes perform in areas where the language spoken by the audience is the same as that spoken in performance. Thus, zat pwe troupes perform in the central river valley of Burma where Burmese is spoken, likay troupes congregate in central Thailand where standard Thai is spoken, sandiwara troupes are found in Sundanese-speaking west Java, ardja troupes perform only on Bali, and so on. The language spoken in performance in Table 3 can be matched with the language distribution map (5) and the map of Java (6) to find the geographical areas in

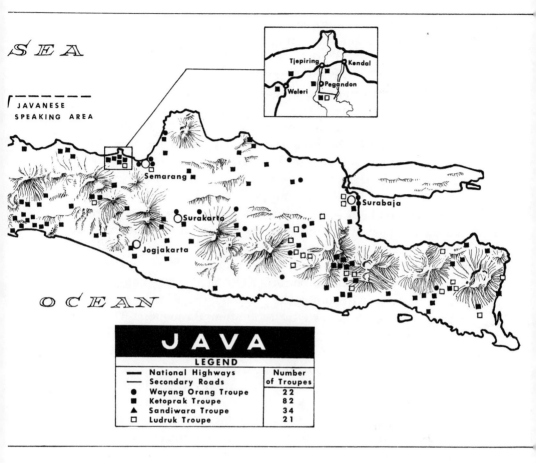

SEA

JAVANESE
SPEAKING AREA

Tjepiring   Kendal

Pegandon
Weleri

Semarang

Surabaja

Surakarta

Jogjakarta

OCEAN

JAVA

LEGEND	
National Highways	Number
Secondary Roads	of Troupes
● Wayang Orang Troupe	22
■ Ketoprak Troupe	82
▲ Sandiwara Troupe	34
□ Ludruk Troupe	21

which troupes of different genres are generally found. In most cases language areas closely correspond to political units, but there are some important exceptions. Lao is spoken both in Thailand and in Laos, hence Lao-speaking mohlam luong troupes are found in both countries. Cambodian is spoken by 400,000 people living in the three Vietnamese provinces near the Bassac River, which explains the fact that Cambodian-speaking lakon bassac troupes perform there as well as in Cambodia. Malay is spoken by some 80 percent of the population in the southern tip of Thailand, and so Malay-speaking bangsawan and wayang kulit troupes are able to perform in Thailand as well as in Malaysia. Large Javanese-speaking communities living in Djakarta and in Bandung—in otherwise Sundanese west Java—support Javanese-speaking wayang orang troupes in these two cities.

Where both a standard language and a regional dialect exist in a country, theatre troupes using the standard language can perform in the dialectal area more easily than troupes using the dialect can perform in the standard-speaking area. Likay troupes, employing standard Thai, are most commonly found in central Thailand in the area around Bangkok where standard Thai is spoken. But likay troupes also perform in Lao-speaking northeast Thailand and in southern Thailand, where a southern dialect of Thai is spoken. On the other hand, neither lakon jatri nor nang talung troupes, which use southern Thai dialect in performance, nor mohlam luong troupes, which use Lao, ever venture into Bangkok to perform. This is so even though Bangkok is bursting with prosperity these days and these three folk-derived forms are known by reputation throughout Thailand. In Indonesia, wayang orang and ketoprak troupes, speaking standard Javanese, commonly play in east Java where a dialect of Javanese is spoken, but ludruk troupes, working out of Surabaya in east Java and speaking the east Javanese dialect, almost never perform in central Java where standard Javanese is spoken (note the distribution of wayang orang, ketoprak, and ludruk troupes in Map 6). In both cases the difference between the regional language of the audience and the language of the performance is slight. The southern Thai dialect differs only slightly from standard Thai and the dialect of east Java varies from standard Javanese only in pronunciation and some vocabulary. Though different languages, Lao and Thai belong to the same family and are mutually intelligible to a great extent. Audiences, then, normally attend plays performed in a language they can understand.

There is one extremely interesting exception. The twenty or so Teochiu language Chinese opera troupes in Thailand do not as a rule perform for audiences who understand Chinese. The reason is not that the Thai are a perverse people who enjoy watching what they cannot understand, nor that Chinese opera has such incredible audience appeal that it smashes the language barrier. The reason lies in the economics of performance: most Chinese opera troupes are engaged by Chinese merchant organizations to perform at fairs, festivals, and other local celebrations as a civic contribution. Performances are given in the open. Anyone may wander up to the stage to watch for a time free of charge. The vast majority of people attending events of this kind are Thai who do not speak Chinese, so the audience for Chinese opera is mainly non-Chinese speaking.

The area around Tjirebon on the north coast of Java has a large population but no professional theatre. The city lies on the boundary between Sunda and Java, and, consequently, both Javanese and Sundanese are spoken as well as a local Tjirebon dialect. Apparently the language confusion is so great that troupes cannot operate effectively in the area.

Although plays are usually performed in the national language (or its regional dialects), Indonesian is not the language of performance of any of the professional troupes discussed.* Indonesian became the national language only after World War II and it has not yet replaced local languages as the primary medium of cultural expression in Indonesia. Troupes continue to perform in Javanese, Sundanese, and Balinese—not in Indonesian.

POPULATION

Population is a second factor which affects the distribution of troupes. Obviously there are no troupes where there are no people to make up an audience—in the mountain ranges of the Philippines, Burma, Thailand, Laos, Cambodia, and Vietnam or in the jungles, swamps, and vast interior forests of Sumatra or Borneo. On the other hand, the mere existence of a large population does not necessarily mean a correspondingly large number of theatre troupes in any given area. The number of troupes per million population varies widely from area to area, from four per million in Cambodia to eight per million in Indonesia, as Table 3 indicates. Even more striking is the difference in the number of troupes per million population in major cities, which ranges from one per million in Bangkok to eight per mil-

---

*Indonesian language is used by a few musical and variety show troupes and in some ludruk plays, as has been mentioned earlier.

Table 4. Number of theatre troupes related to
population in selected cities.

City	Population	Number of troupes
Phnom Penh, Cambodia	500,000	4
Saigon, Vietnam	1,000,000	8
Bangkok, Thailand	2,000,000	2
Djakarta, Indonesia	3,000,000	6

lion in Saigon and Phnom Penh (Table 4). Large cities do not
have proportionally more theatre troupes than small cities.
Phnom Penh is one-quarter the size of Bangkok, yet in absolute
numbers it hosts twice as many troupes, and on a per capita
basis has eight times as many professional theatre troupes.

If we compare the number of troupes in major cities with
the number in the country as a whole we see some interesting
contrasts. Cambodian lakon bassac is apparently big-city-
oriented: in Phnom Penh the ratio of troupes to population—
eight per million—is double that of Cambodia as a whole—
four per million. On the other hand, Thai likay, nang talung,
lakon jatri, and Chinese opera are far, far more popular in the
countryside than in the capital city: in Thailand as a whole the
ratio of troupes to population—seven per million—is fully seven
times that in Bangkok—one per million. In Vietnam, theatre is
slightly more popular in Saigon than in the countryside: the
ratio of troupes to population is eight per million in Saigon
and six per million in the country as a whole.

Most troupes seem to operate in small and medium-sized
communities which have large surrounding rural populations.
One ketoprak manager put the minimum population that could
support his troupe at 5000. This may seem an extremely small
number of people to support a professional troupe, but two
points should be kept in mind: first, these 5000 people would
live very close to the settlement where the troupe was performing, no more than two or three miles away; and, second, the
troupe would be small and would require an audience of only a
hundred or so people a night to survive.

Troupes in the countryside draw their audiences from the

immediate vicinity. Most people I spoke to indicated that they would ride a bicycle a mile or two or take a horse cart perhaps another mile to attend an evening performance, but no further. Some say they "don't travel at all" after dark (outside their immediate neighborhood). Convincing evidence of this is shown in the insert in Map 6. In the spring of 1964, six theatre troupes were operating within a radius of two-and-a-half miles on the northern coast of Java, each in a country hamlet. The total population of the immediate area is around 100,000. I visited all six, and discovered that none of the managers evidenced the slightest concern that the other troupes were performing just a few miles away.

In Vietnam, professional cai luong, hat boi, and kich troupes perform in theatres in about two hundred provincial towns, villages, plantations, and rural settlements. In Saigon and vicinity there are 27 legitimate theatre houses.* On a per capita basis, then, there are almost as many theatres in the countryside as there are in Saigon.

ECONOMIC CONDITIONS

A third factor which affects the distribution of troupes is the condition of the local economy. A professional troupe is in business, if not merely to make money, at least to make whatever money is possible within a given circumstance. One might expect to find more troupes where the money is and less troupes where the money is not. In Saigon and in Phnom Penh, where the economy is booming, there are many troupes, presumably, at least in part, because of favorable economic conditions. On the other hand, Bangkok, which has an equally booming economy and is a big city to boot, has the fewest troupes of any major city in Southeast Asia, while Djakarta with a fair-to-poor economy has relatively many. There is a basic fallacy in assuming that troupes will be found where economic conditions are good: it presupposes that troupes are free to move in unqualified response to economic factors. But some troupes are located per-

*By actual count there are 143 major theatre buildings in Vietnam: 27 in Saigon and vicinity, and 116 in the provinces. I am estimating that an additional 80 temporary theatres, public halls, and *dinh* (Taoist temples often used for hat boi performances) are also regularly in use. I would not be surprised if the actual number were double this.

manently and cannot so respond. Troupes which travel from one area to another as a matter of course try, whenever possible, to play in areas where they are likely to make a good profit. But theatre is a risky business and managers make mistakes. One of the large, established wayang orang troupes quit its theatre in central Java three years ago and moved to Djakarta because its provincial audience was dwindling. The manager was certain that things would be better in the capital city. But he was wrong. Business became even worse, and in 1964 the troupe was on the verge of bankruptcy. Conversely, troupes try to avoid, if they can, desperately poor regions where people have little money to spend on theatre. Yet even this is not always true. I ran across a troupe which was doing the opposite: the manager was purposely moving the troupe to progressively poorer and poorer areas where he hoped they could live for less. There may be more troupes like it. It was a pathetic little ten-man ketoprak troupe, so destitute it could hardly afford to pay 100 rupiah—about 15 cents—nightly theatre rental. Often actors take part-time jobs when times are bad, but there were no day-labor jobs to be had in the godforsaken fishing settlement of a dozen houses where they had set up their theatre. The situation seemed utterly impossible, but there they were. In any case, even mobile troupes may be unable to respond to economic condition for any one of a variety of reasons. The troupe manager may not know a better place to go. Even if he does, it may be too far away, in another language area, already crowded to capacity with troupes, or lacking an adequate theatre building. Or, indeed, there may be no better place to go at all.

RELIGION

Through its encouragement or disapproval of theatre, religion can affect the distribution of theatre troupes within a country. In southern Bali, where folk performances are an integral part of religious ceremonies, there are folk troupes in scores of villages; but in eastern Bali, where religious rites are less strictly observed, religiously motivated theatre performances are not common and there are almost no troupes. In a few areas of west Java, central Java, and Malaysia, where orthodox Islamic beliefs are strongly entrenched, the Islamic ban on representing the human figure in art is applied to theatre, with the result that in these areas one will find almost no professional live theatre companies and few wayang dalang. On the other hand, in other places the Islamic fasting month of Ramadan is traditionally the month of greatest theatre activity. In 1963, eight troupes performed during Ramadan in the district of Purworedjo, in central Java—double the number which played there the preceding and following months.

CULTURAL TRADITIONS

Past cultural traditions may play an important part in determining where troupes locate. The lakon nai/khon troupe of the Thai National Theatre is in Bangkok because Bangkok was the last royal capital—the place where troupes had performed these two forms of theatre for the past two hundred years—and because Bangkok is today the largest city in Thailand and the seat of the Thai government. The Royal Ballet of Cambodia and of Laos perform in Phnom Penh and in Luang Prabang, respectively, because that is where the royal courts are. Hat boi evolved principally in central Vietnam, and that is where most hat boi troupes are today. Lakon jatri and nang talung have always been part of the culture of southern Thailand, and that is where we find most troupes of these two genres today.

Between one-quarter and one-third of the Javanese wayang kulit dalang live in the Jogjakarta-Surakarta area, where about one-tenth of the Javanese population lives. Why? It is not because of favorable economic conditions (the area is one of the most destitute in Indonesia). Nor is it a question of language, for standard Javanese is spoken over a much wider area. It may be that religion has something to do with it, for wayang performances are given on religious occasions. But the main reason is simply an accident of history. Several centuries ago Surakarta and Jogjakarta became the most powerful capitals on the island of Java. Wayang was assiduously cultivated at both courts, and the tradition spread to surrounding areas. Dalang congregated at the palaces and nearby; some performed for court celebrations and others were influenced by court performances. Today court wayang performances scarcely ever take place, but the influence of their traditions can be felt everywhere. Dalang live here because they have always lived here; they perform because audiences are used to wayang and want to see it; and because audiences demand wayang, the dalang continue to perform and to live in large numbers in the Jogjakarta-Surakarta area. And so the self-perpetuating circle of cultural tradition goes on, with existence creating consciousness, consciousness creating demand, and demand creating and regenerating existence.

Finally, troupes sometimes are where they are for quite accidental reasons. There is an empty theatre in the town of Meret but not in the town of Klah, so a troupe locates in Meret rather than in Klah. A jewelry store manager considers theatre a good investment and sets up a troupe across from his store. The village head inherits a gamelan ensemble from his deceased grandfather; he hates to let it stand idle, so he rents it to a local troupe which is just turning professional. A troupe manager, returning to his home town for a vacation, decides he doesn't want to travel any more; he forms a local troupe. A local rice-mill owner supports a troupe as a favor for his actress wife. Or a wealthy widow, with a penchant for amour, discovers that a good way to keep a bountiful supply of acquiescent young males on hand is to manage a troupe. The reasons governing a troupe's location may be of considerable import, or they may be as inconsequential as these.

As a summary illustration, let me describe the distribution of theatre troupes in one area of Southeast Asia for which I have complete data, the District of Bandung, Province of West Java (Sunda). The insert in Map 6 shows the location of all the professional live theatre troupes there during the first week of March 1964. The district (*kabupaten* or *daswati II*) of Bandung lies at the center of the rich Preanger plateau, and the city of Bandung is capital of the Province of West Java. Rice, tea, coffee, rubber, pineapple, and cinchona (quinine), as well as considerable light industry, make the district one of the most prosperous in Indonesia. Seventeen professional live theatre troupes perform for the 2,500,000 people living in the district. Four of these troupes are located permanently in the city of Bandung, which has a population of 1,000,000, and the other thirteen are scattered among the twenty-seven rural sub-districts (*ketjamatan*) of the district, which have a combined population of 1,500,000. Proportionally the rural population of the district of Bandung is served by twice as many theatre troupes as is the urban population of Bandung city.

Three troupes in Bandung city are sandiwara troupes: one in Kosami market is noted for history (*babad*) and wayang stories and has been in that location for fifteen years; one in Tegalga market is noted for its productions of modern plays—unusual for a sandiwara troupe—and has been there for eleven years; and a new troupe moved into the southern outskirts of town about a year ago. The fourth troupe in the city is extremely unusual: it is a Javanese wayang orang troupe which has been performing for Javanese audiences in this otherwise Sundanese city for fourteen years.

The thirteen troupes outside Bandung city are all sandiwara troupes and they are all in small towns or villages. Four are located alongside the national highway which connects Bandung with Djakarta to the west and Surabaya to the east: two are in the sub-district of Bandjar and are owned by the same person (one is in the town seat and has been there for eight years; the other is in a small village ten miles away and has been in existence only a year; the former is parent troupe to the latter), one has been in the army garrison town of Tjimahi for three years, and one fly-by-night troupe is temporarily playing in a police hall out in the countryside of the sub-district of Udjungbrung. There are no troupes in the other five sub-districts along the highway: Tjipatat, a wild and lightly populated area of lime hills and precipitous valleys; Tjikalong Wetan, a high-plateau area also lightly populated except by rubber trees and pine-apples; Tjitjadas, just outside Bandung city where a former theatre is now headquarters for a vegetable market cooperative; Rantjaekek, a rail junction but otherwise unimportant; and Tjitjalenka, where a once-flourishing theatre is now a rice mill. On the mountain slope to the north of Bandung city, a troupe is playing for a few weeks in the resort sub-district of Lembang.

In the sub-districts of Batudjadjar, Tjililin, Bondjongloa, Soreang, Buahbatu, Pameungpeuk, and Tjiparai, which make up the rich flat rice plain to the south of Bandung city, there are no troupes and have not been any for many years. This entire, heavily populated area boasts a single movie house. (A second is closed.) Apparently the good network of roads leading into Bandung city and a regular commuter-rail service (one of the few in Southeast Asia) to Bandung make it easy for people living in these nearby sub-districts to see their plays and movies in the city; as a result, local troupes find it impossible to compete with the city troupes. Going a little further south we find three sandiwara troupes (and two movie houses) operating in the single town of Madjalaja. The town is only medium-sized (perhaps 100,000), but it is the center of a fast-growing spinning and weaving industrial complex. People have money to spend ("farmers have money twice a year at harvest time; factory workers get a paycheck every week," was one troupe manager's comment), and in Madjalaja they spend a lot on theatre. One of the three troupes in town has been there for five years; the other two moved in from nearby towns within the last two years, attracted by Madjalaja's economic boom. To the west, Bandjaran, a town with light industry but less of it than Madjalaja, has had a troupe for three years. Another two troupes are at Tjiwedej and Tjipeundeu. The former town is situated high and deep in the mountains that stretch from the southern border of the district of Bandung to the Indian Ocean on Java's south coast, while the latter is in an isolated tea estate. Each is reached by a single rough road.

The final two troupes are small (ten members in one), poorly equipped wandering troupes that perform for a week or so here and a week or so there. One is located in the low foothills below Patjet, in a crossroad village. It plays in a dirt-floored garage two blocks down a footpath leading from a cart trail that connects up with the secondary road that runs to Bandung. The other is high in the hills between Bandjaran and Pengalengan. The village school—temporarily out of session—is the theatre. A nod and a perfunctory "from over the hills" was their reply when I asked where they had come from. In Paseh, perched high on a ridge and almost inaccessible, no troupe has ever performed as far as anyone in the sub-district town can remember. And in the southwest, along the whole grinding, twisting, lonely road from Tjililin through Sindangkerta to the tea estate town of Gununghalu, there has never been a professional theatre troupe, though the tea estate owns gamelan instruments and golek puppets and encourages employees to perform wayang golek from time to time. In sum, there are four large permanent troupes (three Sundanese-language sandiwara and one Javanese-language wayang orang) in the city of Bandung and in the outer rural areas seven medium-sized permanent troupes, two small semi-permanent troupes, and four marginal wandering troupes (all sandiwara).

CHAPTER 10

Theatre and the Social Contract

Professional theatre troupes support themselves in a variety of ways. Underlying each means of support is the concept of a social contract which regulates the relation between a troupe and its supporters. The contract may be expressly stated or implied. It may be for a period of several years or for a single performance. It may involve a large sum of money or a trifle. But always the basis of the contract is an agreement to render service for payment received. The service rendered by the troupe is a performance or performances; the payment received may be hard cash, housing, clothes, or a lifetime post. By the term "social contract," I mean to convey the idea that the contract is often more than a simple monetary agreement. It can encompass complex social obligations and privileges on both sides.

TYPES OF SUPPORT

There are three main ways in which professional theatre troupes are supported nowadays in Southeast Asia: government support; commercial support; and communal support. Each is based on a different concept of the social contract.

GOVERNMENT SUPPORT

The oldest form of government support is that traditionally extended to court artists by kings and princes. At one time or another theatre troupes have been supported at royal courts in

Burma, Thailand, Laos, Cambodia, Vietnam, Malaya, and Indonesia (Java, Sunda, Bali, Sumatra, and Borneo). But after Southeast Asia came under European and American domination in the nineteenth century, rulers lost much of their wealth and power, and, as a consequence, court support for theatre has gradually dwindled until today it lingers on only in Laos and Cambodia. To get an idea of how it functioned, Cambodia can be studied. Today the Cambodian royal family maintains a complete troupe of dancers, musicians, and singers at the royal palace in Phnom Penh, continuing a tradition that Khmer rulers began a thousand years ago. In times past minor nobles and court officials found it politically expedient to present to the king an especially talented or lovely daughter. She would be trained as a dancer, live in the king's harem under close supervision, dance at state functions and for the king's private enjoyment, and, at the king's pleasure, serve as his concubine. In exchange, the girl's father received two, three, or four bars of silver (depending on the girl's beauty and her father's importance), and the girl was supported in a relatively privileged position.[1] A king could marry a dancer formally but apparently few were so honored. She could never become the king's first or chief wife, only a lesser wife. On reaching maturity the dancer was released from service to return home where she might easily make a suitable match. Or she might remain on at the court as a dance instructor. Male musicians and poets were attached to the court and supported by the court treasury in a similar manner. Members of the royal family often performed as skilled amateurs alongside these professionals. Details of court support varied from Cambodia to Laos to Thailand to Java to Vietnam, but essentials were the same. Highly skilled court performers practiced long hours under demanding instructors. In addition to being performers, however, they were also minor court officials subject to the will of the king and totally subservient to him. Through court support came security, preservation of artistic traditions, permanence for the troupe, and a general atmosphere of sophisticated appreciation of the arts (except when the ruler was a boor as did happen from time to time). Today, the Royal Cambodian Ballet and the Royal Lao Ballet are still supported in this traditional fashion.

The modern equivalent of court-supported theatre is subsidized state or municipal theatre. One might expect to find many troupes subsidized by national, provincial, or city governments in Southeast Asia in view of the centuries-old tradition of court support. However, this is not the case. In all of Southeast Asia there are but two government-subsidized troupes—the Thai National Theatre and the Javanese wayang orang troupe Sri Wedari. The Thai National Theatre is the producing wing of the Department of Fine Arts of the Thai central government in Bangkok. It works hand-in-hand with the School for Dramatic Art. Pupils enrolled at the school act minor parts in productions of the Thai National Theatre, its graduates play leading roles. The management, directors, designers, musicians, choreographers, and technical staff are permanent civil servants of the central government assigned to the Thai National Theatre. Performers are paid a nightly wage (not a large sum except for performers of star caliber). Since World War II the troupe has produced for the Bangkok public two or three classic dance-dramas every year—lakon nai, khon, and modernized versions of lakon jatri and lakon nok—for a combined total of 100 to 150 performances per year. Tickets are sold to the public on a regular commercial basis. The Thai National Theatre is therefore partially government supported, through tax funds, and partially commercially supported, through ticket sales. Though many of the performers are amateurs and semiprofessionals, the theatre organization—the troupe—is professional.

Sri Wedari, a wayang orang troupe, is partially subsidized by the city of Surakarta. Its members are all city employees. Irrespective of the amount of income the troupe earns at the box office, members receive standard civil-servant salaries. Considered one of the two best wayang orang troupes in Indonesia, the troupe plays to standing-room audiences virtually every night of the year. Consequently it earns a very handsome profit, all of which reverts to the city treasury. Under different circumstances, Surakarta might find itself subsidizing the troupe; at present, however, Sri Wedari is subsidizing the city. Troupe members' salaries are less than they would be were they performing on their own. In sum, the list of government-supported theatre troupes is a short one indeed: the Royal Cambodian Ballet, the Royal Lao Ballet, the Thai National Theatre, and Sri Wedari.

Let us look at some of the characteristics of the social contract that regulates relations between a troupe and a government which supports it. The contract is usually long-term: the staff at the Thai National Theatre are engaged virtually for life; the royal dancing girl in Laos or Cambodia expects to have her position for at least twenty years, possibly more; the Sri Wedari actor is a permanent civil servant. A general interest in encouraging the arts for their intrinsic value—rather than as a commercial commodity—is implied as being one of the major reasons government supports a troupe. A government is not interested in a single performance or a single play, but in maintaining the continuity of a prized theatrical heritage. There are differences between court support and modern subsidy. The contract between a king and a dancing girl is between unequal partners, and a whole series of subtle social conditions are implied in the contract that have nothing, really, to do with the art of theatre. Terms of the contract often are not spelled out in detail; it is more a gentlemen's agreement than a cut and dried contract. A member of a subsidized troupe, on the other hand, knows precisely the terms of his contract. His salary is fixed, just as is the postman's and the secondary school teacher's. Also, while a court-supported troupe performs at the whim of the sovereign, a subsidized troupe performs on a fixed schedule for public audiences. If a court troupe sometimes is a private plaything, a subsidized troupe is a public utility.

COMMERCIAL SUPPORT

There are just two essentials of commercial support: tickets are sold to the general public, and the troupe receives as income at least part of the proceeds of the sale of tickets. A troupe may function as a free and independent unit, assuming full financial responsibility—selling tickets, paying ticket taxes, assuming the risk of financial loss if audiences are small and, conversely, keeping profits if audiences are large. The troupe acts on its own initiative. In this circumstance the social contract is between the troupe and a multitude of ticket buyers. The duration of the contract is brief—a single performance—and its terms are businesslike and simple—admission to one performance upon the payment of a fixed admission fee. Additional implied conditions are few. This kind of contract gives a troupe no security at all. A troupe is under pressure to please a new audience every night. This form of support can be called "direct" commercial support and is so common throughout the world there is no need to describe it in detail.

There is a second form of commercial support, which I am going to call "indirect" commercial support. While not unknown in Western theatre, it is of great importance to theatre in Southeast Asia. In indirect commercial support a troupe is invited to perform in a town for a specified period of time—usually several weeks or several months—by some local sponsoring organization which assumes direct financial responsibility for its engagement. Tickets are sold and from the proceeds the sponsoring organization pays the taxes, takes care of theatre rent, and pays the troupe a fixed fee for each performance, keeping for itself whatever profit is realized. Sponsoring organizations are local charities, veterans' groups, religious groups, and, in some cases, local governments. The aim of the sponsoring organization is to earn profits, and since it has excellent local connections it is virtually certain to do so. Indirect commercial support involves two social contracts: one between the ticket purchaser and the sponsoring organization, and one between the sponsoring organization and the theatre troupe. The first seems to take precedence over the second, or at least it establishes the conditions for the second. Because the sponsoring organization relieves the troupe (at least in theory) of the responsibility for entering into thousands of one-night contracts with the audience, it assumes the right to retain all profits, which the troupe, in accepting the security of a guaranteed income, relinquishes.

Here are four examples of how indirect commercial support works in different parts of Southeast Asia. In the summer of 1964 a local sponsoring committee brought the famous wayang orang troupe Ngesti Pandawa to play for a two-month run in Jogjakarta, central Java. Every night a huge, 1,400-seat, bamboo-and-thatch theatre building, erected in the town square especially for the engagement, was packed to capacity. According to the troupe manager, a local committee, representing five organizations, paid the troupe 37,500 rupiah (about $60) per performance, plus furnishing lodging for the troupe and transportation to and from its home theatre in Semarang, eighty miles away. The average nightly gross income was in the neighborhood of 150,000 rupiah. Even after paying a small tax, the sponsoring committee realized an enormous profit from this engagement.

I visited the yearly *boun,* or fair, held at the famous Dong Mien Buddhist temple in Vientiane, Laos, in November 1963. After paying a token contribution of 10 kip (about 10¢) for flowers and incense, I was free to enter the grounds and see anything of interest at the fair, including a *lamlung* taxi-dance show from across the Mekong River in Thailand, a United States Information Service (USIS) movie, a Thai boxing match, and a mohlam luong play. Hundreds of people were standing around watching the mohlam luong performance. For 60 kip (about 50¢) more, however, you could buy a first-class ticket and sit on a metal chair set on the grass facing the small raised platform where the play was being performed. I watched the play—about a son of Indra who, through Buddhist magic powers, was able to change himself into a snake—for about two hours, and then went backstage with my interpreter to talk to the troupe manager. Between stints joking and singing onstage as the chief clown, he told me that this was their second of three nights at the fair, and that the boun committee of elders of the Dong Mien temple handled ticket sales, paid the troupe a flat fee of 6,000 kip (about $50) per night, and had a sizable surplus remaining. Since I estimated that there were some four hundred chairs set up, most of which were occupied, the temple was making a profit of from 50 to 75 percent of the gross income. When I asked the manager why they did not ask for a higher fee, his reply was that when the profit goes to help support a famous wat they are happy to play for a nominal fee. It is a religious duty. This troupe performs in their own theatre in Vientiane most of the year. It performs outside on invitation, like this, only about thirty times a year.

One day in March 1964, I was driving along a back road in

the Sundanese district of Sukabumi. Leaning against a tree in a small country village was a blackboard, with a notice written on it:

Tonight
Wayang Golek
Village Hall
8 P.M.
Tickets – 30 rupiah

I had never heard of tickets being sold for either wayang kulit or wayang golek before, so we stopped to investigate. We located the village chief and spoke to him. He said the village had a special Entertainment Committee which sponsored some type of performance—a puppet play or a movie—ten days each month during the three-month harvest period (*pannen*). A performance was arranged partly for entertainment, for there was no formal entertainment available in this remote area, and partly to raise money for village improvements. Then they needed to construct a new canal for rice irrigation. To pay the performers and to make money they sold tickets. The preceding night, although it had rained, about 240 people from the village had come to see the puppet drama, and they expected more that night. About that time the chief puppeteer, either a woman or a transvestite dressed as a woman, entered the room. She said she and the four other members of the troupe were from the north coast town of Krawang, a considerable distance away. As part of their contract they were living in the village head's house and had their meals there during their three-day stay. At six o'clock the dalang excused herself, saying it was time to meet with the Entertainment Committee to decide what play they would perform that evening.

In October 1963, while looking for hat boi troupes in Vietnam, a friend and I came across a Taoist temple (*dinh*) in the southwestern part of Saigon. We asked the chief priest of the dinh if any troupes played there. He said in the past the priests arranged performances six or eight times a year. Now a troupe is invited to perform at the temple only for the lunar New Year or other important religious occasions. They prefer to bring a hat boi troupe in from the country, he said, because the few troupes in Saigon perform a modernized kind of hat boi in which cai luong songs and Western tunes are incorporated. The priests do not actually sell tickets at the temple, but everyone who enters is asked to give a contribution. People in the neighborhood are sent "invitations," and, even if they don't come to see the play, they are expected to make a contribution. I asked if cai luong troupes ever performed at the dinh, but he said that was impossible. This dinh is dedicated to Kwan Kong, one of the three brothers in The Romance of the Three Kingdoms, the Chinese novel on which so many hat boi plays are based. Only hat boi would be appropriate. He said that, though the priests counted on the income from performances to help support the dinh through the year, performance is also considered a form of worship to the guardian spirit of the community who is enshrined in the dinh.

COMMUNAL SUPPORT

The third form of troupe support—communal support—is extremely important in Southeast Asia. In communal support a troupe is hired by an individual or an organization to perform for a stipulated fee with the performance being offered by the sponsor as service to the community. Tickets are not sold and anyone may see the play without charge. As no one can offer their community continuous free entertainment, some special occasion is required to justify the expense of hiring a troupe. Religious occasions are perhaps the most important times at which performances of plays have become sanctioned as appropriate means of communal celebration. Professional troupes are invited to perform for temple anniversaries, birthdays of local guardian spirits, the end of the Islamic fasting period, and on religious holidays like the lunar New Year in Burma, Thailand, Laos, Vietnam, Malaysia, Java, Sunda, and Bali today just as they have for centuries in the past.

Sometimes the performing of a play is an obligatory part of a religious act. In Thailand it is common for people to pray for help (to cure an illness, to get a son through his school examinations, or for prosperity) and to promise a play performance should their wish be granted. Every day of the year lakon jatri (and sometimes a form of old-fashioned lakon nok) can be seen staged at the Lok Muang temple in Bangkok, paid for by people whose prayers have been answered. These *ram tawai* or "gift dance-play" performances have been given at the Lok Muang temple since the city of Bangkok was founded and the temple built by King Rama I in 1782. The scheduling of performances is handled in an efficient, businesslike manner by the Veteran's Welfare Organization (why this organization instead of a religious one, I cannot say). Two troupes hold exclusive performing rights and perform during alternate weeks. In the fall of 1963 over a hundred people were on the waiting list to have their ram tawai performed. The average performance cost 436 bhat (about $22) and, though many donors wanted to hire performances for a week or even ten days, they were usually limited to a single day or two at the most. Most plays performed by the two all-female troupes are Buddhist *Jataka* stories, like The Golden Prince of the Sea Conch. All the performances I saw at the temple were executed in a desultory fashion. One very old woman sat on the side of the stage following a printed text. Whenever an actress forgot her lines, which was often, she prompted her. The dancing was downright inept. Other than half a dozen elderly women who planted themselves in front of the stage and watched for hours on end, the only people who saw these performances were visitors to the temple who watched casually for a few minutes before going on about their business. Performances are not intended for human spectators and presumably the gods, to whom the plays are dedicated, have no artistic taste.

Plays are an obligatory part of religious celebrations in many Balinese villages. Folk troupes, rather than professional ones, are the usual performing groups. The Cambodian folk troupe mentioned earlier performs classical dance-dramas just two or three times a year, always in connection with either Buddhist or animistic religious occasions. Performances are dedicated to Buddha or to Lok Ta Kon Heng, the animistic guardian spirit of the village, or to both. Though the performers in this village are amateurs, they are not asked to perform solely as a religious offering or as a service to the community, for before each performance the village head visits each household collecting gifts of food and clothing for the actors.

While it is sometimes obligatory for performances to be given on some religious occasions, in most countries of Southeast Asia it is more customary for performances to be traditional and desirable though not absolutely necessary. On Java it is every parent's wish to sponsor a wayang kulit performance on the occasion of a son's circumcision ceremony, one of the crisis events in a boy's life. But it costs a great deal of money to hire a troupe—usually too much for an ordinary person to pay. In Sunda, wayang golek is considered the "best" performance to give for a circumcision, but if the cost is too much to bear a few dances or some gamelan music will do as a substitute. The lunar New Year is the occasion for many kinds of theatre performances in Bali, Vietnam, Malaysia, and Thailand. It is not that every community must sponsor a performance every year, but if a performance is going to be given, the New Year festival is a highly suitable occasion. As another example, Chinese po the hi puppet troupes in Java perform only at Chinese temple festivals.

In addition to religious occasions, communal-supported performances often are arranged in connection with secular celebrations—county or district fairs, national holidays, the dedication of a new school, and the like. The sponsoring organization is likely to be a government agency. At a county fair in Lampoon, northern Thailand, the fair committee, established by the county government and headed by a local official, hired and brought in for the fair a likay troupe from a neighboring county, a group of *rambong*[2] taxi-dancers from Bangkok, an American movie, and, also from Bangkok, a modern dance band. A small fee (3 bhat or 15¢) was charged to enter the fairground. Once inside everything was free including the likay performance. In Bangkok, for the King's birthday each December, the national government hires half a dozen troupes of different types to perform at public fairs. Again, the only cost to the spectator is a small charge to enter the fairground. Local government units in Indonesia arrange the year's most elaborate festivities to celebrate Independence Day, August 17th. In addition to encouraging amateur groups to stage plays, it is common in Java and in Sunda for local government committees to hire professional ketoprak, ludruk, sandiwara, wayang kulit, or wayang golek troupes to perform for the public. The troupes are paid from regular government funds.

Finally, some communal-supported performances are tied

neither to religious nor to secular events but to personal events in the lives of individuals. In Thailand a man who wins a lottery may wish to share his good fortune with his neighbors; one way of doing this is to hire a likay troupe for a night. In Laos a man may bring in a mohlam luong troupe to celebrate a promotion. In Sunda a man who is opening a new business may sponsor an all-night wayang golek performance at the site of the new building, partly as a religious measure to assure the success of the business and partly as social aggrandizement. In each case a personal and private event is broadened into a public, communal event through the medium of a theatre performance.

The differences between communal-supported theatre performances for religious, secular, or personal events are relatively minor and should not obscure the essential similarity of the social contract for all varieties. The basic distinguishing features of communal support are three: funds to pay the troupe for its performance are not raised by selling tickets to the performance; the formal contract between sponsor and troupe is usually for a single night only; and implied in the social contract is the thought that the performance is being offered by the sponsor for the benefit of the community.

SUPPORT OF TROUPES IN EACH COUNTRY

In Thailand the only troupe which regularly performs khon and lakon nai—the Thai National Theatre—is supported jointly by national tax funds and by commercial ticket sales. All likay troupes perform at least part of the time in commercial theatres where they are supported through ticket sales. Communal support for likay is also common. Most troupes rely on both commercial and communal support. A small troupe I visited at a village fair in northern Thailand is perhaps typical. According to its manager, the troupe performs most often for temple festivals (*wat boun*) and somewhat less often for private boun and at local fairs. Their usual run is from one to three nights for temple festivals and fairs and one night for private boun. Though they do not make much more than expenses through these performances, he said, at least there is no risk involved. When they have

59. A lakon dance-drama given in a Bangkok alleyway as a token of thanksgiving to the gods.

60. A female dancer (playing Gatutkatja), a singer, and a gamelan ensemble perform in the backyard of a private home in Djakarta to celebrate an Islamic circumcision.

61. Villagers in Sunda celebrate Indonesia's Independence Day (August 17) with gamelan music and dance performances on a temporary outdoor stage.

62. Judas Escariot repents in a lenten play produced by the village of Pilar, in Rizal, the Philippines.

63. A Buddhist holiday being celebrated with a Chinese opera performance
in a temple courtyard in Vietnam.

no invitation to perform they set up a temporary stage in some hamlet and play for as long as the audience keeps coming, normally one to two weeks. Generally speaking, the larger the likay troupe is, the more it relies on commercial support, and the smaller it is, the more it relies on communal support.

Nang talung troupes never perform in commercial theatres; they rely completely on communal support. Traditional lakon jatri troupes are also communal-supported. Because lakon jatri has the deepest religious connections of any Thai theatre form, it is the genre most often performed in southern Thailand on occasions for religious, secular, and personal celebration. According to the lakon jatri teacher mentioned before, his troupe performs only on invitation and only for funerals, weddings, national holidays, and, most frequent of all, for ordination ceremonies of new Buddhist monks. The other type of so-called lakon jatri troupe, which performs in a mixture of styles, may perform at fairs—communal support—or in public theatres—commercial support. The twenty or so Chinese opera troupes in Thailand now rely almost exclusively upon communal support. Until recently, commercial performances used to be fairly common in Bangkok; now they are rare. The manager of a Teochiu-language opera troupe, which was performing at the yearly provincial fair at Sukothai, central Thailand, in 1963, described the operation of his troupe in some detail. It works out of Bangkok, as do all Chinese opera troupes in Thailand. An agent there makes bookings, and the troupe goes wherever the bookings take them. Most engagements, like this one, are for about seven days. Their sponsor here is not the fair committee but the Sukothai Chinese Chamber of Commerce, which contracted directly with the booking agent in Bangkok to bring the troupe to the fair. This is the normal procedure, the manager said. A local Chinese chamber of commerce assesses its members, collects the assessment, contracts with a troupe, and pays the troupe. Were a chamber of commerce to give its contribution to a fair committee, made up mainly of Thai, the money might be used to hire a likay or a dance troupe. This way the Chinese community has full control over the use of its contribution. The manager said his troupe performs most frequently at temple festivals and less frequently at fairs, traveling from one end of Thailand to the other. In previous years it used to play commercially in Bangkok theatres, but this is no longer profitable, for the present generation of Thai-born Chinese is not much interested in Chinese opera.

Several times I heard the remark from indigenous Thai that Chinese "got along well" with the Thai in spite of the deeply resented Chinese monopoly of rural trade. More than in any other country in Southeast Asia, the Chinese in Thailand have attempted to integrate themselves into local society. The firmly established custom of the Chinese business community's contributing theatre performances to local fairs and to wat boun is one manifestation of the generally good relations between Chinese and native Thai.* It is notable that only in Thailand do Chinese merchants sponsor Chinese theatre performances as a contribution to community affairs.

The Royal Lao Ballet is a court-supported troupe. Mohlam luong troupes on both the Lao and Thai sides of the Mekong River are mainly commercial-supported, with some support also coming from invitations to perform for wat boun, private boun, and fairs (communal support). The Royal Cambodian Ballet is the other court-supported troupe in Southeast Asia. Cambodian lakon bassac troupes tend to be almost completely commercially supported. They not only sell tickets themselves and take the risk of earning or losing money, but often the person who owns the troupe owns the theatre building in which it performs. Troupes rarely perform outside of public theatres. Burmese zat pwe troupes perform in theatre buildings and are commercially supported most of the time. Sometimes a zat pwe troupe is invited to perform when a boy enters the monkhood for a brief period, or for a funeral, a birth, or a marriage, but more frequently an *anyein* variety troupe is hired on these occasions.[3]

Hat boi troupes in Vietnam rely on both commercial and communal support. A troupe may perform in a public theatre on its own initiative, it may perform at a dinh on a contract

---

*The large and wealthy Indian minority group does not make a similar contribution to community affairs. One Thai expressed his feelings about the matter this way, "A Chinese takes with one hand and gives with the other; an Indian just takes, with both hands." Part of the Thai's difference in attitude may be explained by the fact that most Chinese make Thailand their permanent home and become Thai citizens, while many Indian merchants zealously retain their own citizenship and in time plan to return home, taking with them whatever fortune they have been able to accumulate.

basis, or it may perform in a village where it is paid a flat fee by a local sponsor. Conditions are so unsettled in the rural areas of Vietnam that it is difficult to say with certainty how most hat boi troupes operate at present. Almost all cai luong troupes work solely in public theatres where they play on their own initiative (direct commercial support). The same is true of kich professional troupes.

Only rarely is wayang kulit in Java, Bali, and Malaysia, or wayang golek in Java and in Sunda performed in public theatres or are tickets sold to support a performance. These forms depend almost solely upon communal support. Figures taken from the 1964 survey of some two hundred Sundanese wayang golek dalang show occasions on which performances are most often given in Sunda.

Performance occasion	*Number of dalang who said they "often" performed*
RELIGIOUS OCCASIONS	
Marriages	32
Circumcisions	26
"Gift performances" as thanksgiving offerings	15
Religious feasts (*slametan*) of various kinds	65
	138
SECULAR OCCASIONS	
National holidays	45
Army events	21
Propaganda performances	11
Local government events	11
Police events	6
	94
PERSONAL OCCASIONS	
Birthdays and anniversaries	18
Entering school	6
New business enterprises	2
	26

More than half the occasions are religious, an indication of the strongly religious content of the dramas themselves as well as the persistence of a long-established tradition of celebrating religious events with theatre performances. I have no similar statistics for wayang kulit, but believe Javanese wayang kulit is performed somewhat less often for personal events and more often on secular occasions (nationalistic sentiments are particularly strong in Java and this is expressed partly through large-scale patriotic celebrations that normally include some theatre performance). Wayang kulit is more intimately bound up with religious beliefs than is wayang golek so there is every reason to think considerably more than half of all wayang kulit performances are hired to celebrate religious occasions.

Wayang orang, ketoprak, ludruk, sandiwara, and bangsawan troupes are for the most part commercially supported. Sandiwara troupes generally perform on their own initiative (direct commercial support). Wayang orang, ketoprak, and ludruk troupes often perform on invitation at "night fairs" (*pasar malam*) and for charity benefits. This is indirect commercial support: tickets are sold and profit motivates both troupes and sponsors. Small ketoprak or ludruk troupes may also be invited to perform at a private home for a personal or religious event. The manager of a small ketoprak troupe in central Java described how they received about thirty invitations per year to perform for feasts (slametan) in people's homes and less often to perform for organizations. On such occasions half the troupe goes out to perform and half stays behind to give the regular performance in their more-or-less permanent theatre. It is also the custom in Java to invite one or two well-known performers from a wayang orang troupe to give a concert of dance excerpts at one's home. Compared to hiring a whole troupe of lesser performers the cost is about the same while the prestige is greater.

Professional Balinese ardja and wayang kulit troupes are communal-supported. Usually a village hires a troupe to perform for a religious festival. The specific hiring arrangements vary from village to village and from occasion to occasion. Folk and professional theatre are closely integrated into the social and religious life of the Balinese community, as I discovered. In May 1964, I was looking for a particularly well-known wayang kulit puppeteer who lived, I was told, in Sukawati, south Bali. When I inquired at the village market in Sukawati for *pak dalang,* "grandfather dalang," several people immediately knew who I meant and one showed me his home. I talked to him for about an hour and a half about his sixty-year career as a puppeteer. For four generations there has been a dalang in his family. He is training his third son to take his place when, in a few years, he gets too old to perform (his first son is a bus driver and his second son is in Djakarta studying law). This was the Balinese New Year, the ten-day period between Galunggan and Kuning-gan, when performances of all kinds are given throughout the island. He was scheduled to perform that night (as well as six-teen other nights during May). Later that evening we drove together to the village, a few miles east of Klungkung, where he was to perform. He said he was being paid 4000 rupiah (about $6) plus transportation for himself, his four accompanying musicians, and his equipment. We turned off the main road and drove slowly over a grass-covered path leading into the countryside. Parking the truck, we walked to a slightly elevated area surrounded by rice terraces and groves of coconut trees. At the end of the clearing was a village temple where the shadow play was to be given, its towers and archways bathed in the cool light of the newly risen full moon. As we approached the temple the dalang excused himself and went off to have a meal, part of his contract.

At this point the director of the local Village Cooperative Association introduced himself, and began a long exposition of how they happened to invite this particular dalang to perform. The village is one of fifty-five in the district of Gianjar, one of Bali's eight districts. It has four temples, all supported by men's associations (*bandjar*). Each bandjar represents a ward within the village, and, since the village has nine wards, each with a band-jar, and four temples, each temple has two or three bandjar sup-porting it. Members have great pride and spirit and compete for the privilege of helping their temple. One of the finest things a bandjar can do is to own its own gamelan, a very expensive undertaking, and maintain its own dance group. In this village two bandjar have gamelan ensembles; a barong dance-drama group is attached to one, an ardja group to the other. Each gamelan ensemble plays many times a year at the four temples in the village and outside the village as well. The barong and ardja groups perform once or twice a year for festivals at one or another of the temples. They are small, however, and not good enough to be invited to other villages. But the favorite theatre form in the village is wayang kulit, he said. At least every New Year they have a performance at this head temple of the village, the *pura desa*. Usually a nearby professional dalang performs, but this year one of the bandjar decided to hire the best dalang in Bali. Everybody agrees that pak dalang is the best for "he is the oldest active dalang, his voice is the best, and he knows the old stories better than any other dalang on Bali." The people of this village make a sharp distinction between the imported professional dalang and the local amateur barong and ardja folk-troupes.

Not all cases on Bali are as clear-cut as this. As amateur troupes gain in skill and become better known—and hence come to be invited more frequently to perform at neighboring villages—they can, and do, charge higher and higher fees. The very best dance and drama troupes on Bali are singled out to perform for the tourist trade. These troupes earn very large sums of money. The world-famous (as of this writing) legong dance troupe from the village of Pliatan is hired to perform at festivals all over the island, for tourists several times a week, and for visiting state dignitaries. The barong troupe at Singapadu existed for many years as a folk troupe, performing on religious occasions in Singapadu and neighboring villages. Today it performs its barong "trance dance" for tourists four or five times a week. With the money the troupe has earned over the last few years the village has built a magnificent new temple, in which the central entrance arch has been altered to make a massive and dramatic stage setting, and it has purchased superb new costumes that cannot be matched on the island. But most extreme of all are the three *ketchak,* or monkey-dance troupes in south Bali whose performances for tourists three or four times a week are the *only* performances these troupes ever give! What can we call these unusual troupes? They are not professional in the sense that I have been using the word. Performers do not earn a living performing (though most do receive something as a gratuity). The large sums of money earned by the troupes go to improve the artistic quality of performance, to buy new costumes or new musical instruments, to hire good dance teachers, and the like. But neither are they what we usually think of as "folk" troupes. Their very existence depends upon the sale of luxury-priced tickets to Indonesian and foreign visitors to Bali— 500 to 2000 rupiah per ticket compared with 20 to 200 rupiah for most commercially supported troupes in Java or Sunda. Though I cannot call these troupes professional, nor perhaps even semiprofessional, we must at least note how in the middle of the twentieth century they have adopted commercial theatre practices to support their performances.

To summarize the way professional troupes in Southeast Asia support themselves:

The Royal Cambodian Ballet and the Royal Lao Ballet are completely court-supported (government support).

The Thai National Theatre and the Sri Wedari wayang orang troupe are supported by both tax funds (government support) and public ticket sales (direct commercial support).

Cai luong, lakon bassac, and sandiwara troupes are supported by ticket sales and their engagements are self-initiated (direct commercial support).

Ketoprak, ludruk, wayang orang, and bangsawan troupes are supported mainly by ticket sales (commercial support), either through self-initiated engagements (direct commercial support) or under contract to a sponsor (indirect commercial support).

Likay, mohlam luong, hat boi, and lakon jatri troupes are supported partly through ticket sales, with engagements either self-initiated (direct commercial support) or initiated by a sponsor (indirect commercial support), and partly by performing for a fixed fee on occasions where tickets are not sold (communal support).

All puppet theatre troupes—wayang kulit in Java, Bali, and Malaysia, wayang golek in Java and Sunda, and nang talung in Thailand—as well as ardja troupes in Bali receive a fixed fee for performing on occasions when tickets are not sold (communal support).

CHAPTER 11

The Troupe

The troupe system so completely dominates theatre production I can think of no more than two or three minor exceptions to it in all of Southeast Asia. It is the logical way for a group of performers to stage plays of a particular theatre genre. Individuals may move from troupe to troupe. Troupes may form or disband. Nevertheless the troupe is the semipermanent unit around which theatre organizes itself. While it is usual to view it primarily as a producing group and to be concerned with its artistic function, the troupe is also a social institution. Every troupe has an identity within society. It has an internal structure and it has relations with other social organizations.

INTERNAL ORGANIZATION

To begin with, troupes can be described in terms of their membership. Every troupe has an owner or manager, one or more artistic directors, many performers, and backstage workers. A wealthy person may own stage equipment, costumes, musical instruments, and props of a troupe giving him either outright or tacit control of its affairs. If he wishes, the owner may hire, pay, and fire actors and other staff and decide when, where, and under what conditions the troupe shall perform. He absorbs the troupe's financial losses or disposes of its profits as he sees fit. Typical of this kind of owner is a hat boi theatre and troupe owner whom I visited in Saigon. His father had founded the troupe thirty years ago and built the theatre in which it still plays. He lives in a tiny home attached to the theatre and from there supervises every aspect of the troupe's work. Owning and managing the troupe and the theatre is his full-time occupation. In other cases financial ownership of a troupe is distinct from its management. It is common for a cai luong troupe to be backed by a group of very rich investors. They either lend money to the troupe manager—in which case their risk is great and they charge a high interest rate—or they take out shares of stock in the company, assuming some of the risk of the venture themselves. Cai luong backers do not exercise direct control over their troupes; this is the responsibility of managers. One of the large lakon bassac troupes in Phnom Penh is owned by a member of the Cambodian royal family. Day-to-day management is handled by a troupe manager in the employ of the owner. The giggling manager of a medium-sized likay troupe in southern Thailand told me that he had always wanted to act but hadn't the talent; so, to keep him happy, his wealthy mother in Bangkok puts up enough money for him to run "his own" troupe.

The artistic director selects or writes play scenarios, casts plays, and directs performances. Usually the artistic director is, or was, an actor. He is seldom a young man for the job requires long experience. In small troupes, he and an actor-manager may share the leadership of a troupe. In a large troupe there may be several artistic directors. It seems to be unusual for an artistic director to become the owner of a troupe although actors often become troupe owners and managers. One such actor-manager-owner is the leader of a small likay troupe in northern Thailand. For years he traveled all over Thailand as a young actor. He played leading roles, saved his money, and seven years ago formed his own troupe which now plays in the provinces around Chiengmai. He is starring player, manager, and owner all rolled into one. Once an actor is established, if he wishes he can save from his fairly large salary and can capitalize on his popularity with audiences to form his own troupe. But the artistic director is unknown to the audience and he usually earns less than the leading actor. His function is that of middleman between management and the performing artists. He seldom strikes out on his own in the theatre world.

Performers are the third type of troupe member. Singers, musicians, and dancers are performers as well as actors and actresses. In most troupes performers make up the majority of members. They are the troupe's lifeblood, and a single virtuoso actor can make its reputation. Stars are sought after in every country and in every genre. Most performers, however, are not stars, but run-of-the-mill theatre practitioners, highly interchangeable quantities. A ketoprak gamelan player is able to play with any ketoprak troupe for the same melodies are used everywhere. The average hat boi singer knows hundreds of roles, which makes it easy for him to fit into almost any conceivable performance situation. I met one ludruk actor who had performed with four different troupes between January and May 1964. A likay actor in Bangkok told me he was a "pick-up" actor, by which he meant he filled in, often for just a few days, with any troupe that needed him. A sandiwara manager, in bewailing the sad state of Sundanese theatre, mentioned that it was not unusual for half his troupe to leave during the year. The smaller the troupe, the more rapid the turnover seems to be. Yet, even in these extreme cases, the troupe remains the nuclear unit of organization. In large troupes turnover is slight, for there are fewer large troupes and hence fewer places to which discontented or foot-loose actors can move.

The fourth category is composed of the backstage workers, the troupe's least important members. Traveling troupes simply pick up day-laborers in each new town to perform the fairly simple backstage chores. Or, youngsters aspiring to become actors hire on to do rope-pulling, prop-moving, or scene-shifting as a way of breaking into a troupe. Large troupes may have several permanent backstage staff members; small troupes almost never do.

The composition of troupes does not vary particularly from country to country; the major differences are between large and small troupes. As one would expect, there is far greater specialization of function in large troupes. In medium-sized and small troupes many members carry on simultaneously several of the four functions just mentioned. Some actors are owner-managers. In other troupes the owner-manager may act as the artistic director, or an actor may be the troupe's artistic director. In the very smallest troupes, you can even find the owner-manager-actor

Table 5. Membership composition of four different types of troupes.

Small likay troupe		Medium-sized cai luong troupe	
Position	Number	Position	Number
Owner-manager-artistic director	1	Owner-star actress	1
		Manager	1
Actors	7	Artistic director-teacher	2
Actresses	3	Playwrights	2
Pi phat musicians	5	Actors	15
Total	16	Actresses	13
		Musicians	6
		Backstage workers	5
		Total	45

Royal Cambodian Ballet		Large wayang orang troupe	
Position	Number	Position	Number
Patron (Queen Mother)	1	Owner (absentee)	1
Ballet masters	2	Manager (owner's deputy)	1
Ballet mistresses	3	Manager's assistants	9
Dance instructors	8	Artistic director	1
Female dancers	55	Actors	36
Musicians	15	Actresses	12
Total	84	Narrator (dalang)	1
		Gamelan musicians	17
		Female singers	2
		Backstage workers	15
		Total	95

who is his own artistic director and moves scenery as well. Membership composition of four troupes of different sizes are given in Table 5. The largest professional troupe in Southeast Asia I am aware of was the 180-member zat pwe troupe once assembled by the famous Burmese actor of the last generation, Po Sein.[1] There are perhaps a dozen troupes of around 100 members—cai luong, wayang orang, and the Thai National Theatre. The smallest troupes may have 10 or even fewer members. In most troupes actors outnumber actresses about two to one. The major exception is cai luong—where the sexes divide about evenly on stage—and all-female Thai, Cambodian, and Lao dance-drama. The 13 instructors in the Royal Cambodian Ballet are an indication of the importance attached to high artistic standards in that troupe, and the 10 managerial positions in the wayang orang troupe reflect its highly commercial orientation.

Puppet troupes are organized somewhat differently. The chief puppeteer is the most important person. He is almost always owner, manager, artistic director, and star performer. He can perform with the help of one or two stage assistants, who hand him puppets, and several musicians and singers—three or four in wayang kulit Bali or nang talung, six to eight in wayang golek, and twelve to twenty-five in wayang kulit Java. It is possible for a puppeteer to perform with a strange orchestra, but normally he works with his assistants, musicians, and singers in a fairly permanent troupe. The major exception to this is among the best-known wayang kulit dalang in Java. When asked to perform in cities hundreds of miles from their homes, it is too expensive to transport a whole gamelan orchestra. In such a case it is customary for the dalang to be accompanied only by his lead gender player and possibly by a puppet assistant. The gender player is often the dalang's wife. Knowing the idiosyncrasies of the puppeteer's style of performing, the lead gender player guides the strange gamelan ensemble much as a conductor would.

Since most puppet troupes work out of a home base, troupes are often made up of relatives and neighbors. Typical is the nang talung puppeteer in southern Thailand whose youngest son is his regular puppet assistant, whose eleven-year-old nephew occasionally serves as the son's substitute, and whose relatives and neighbors make up his orchestra. Smaller troupes of other kinds that remain in one locality for a long period of time also tend to draw their personnel from that area. Sandiwara, lakon bassac, and ketoprak troupes are the chief among these. I visited a medium-sized sandiwara troupe that has been playing for the past eight years in a small town on the south coast of Sunda. The manager told me the troupe originally came from Krawang on the north coast and that at that time most of the troupe members were natives of Krawang. Gradually these people left the troupe. They were replaced by local fishermen, day-laborers, tricycle-cab drivers, and peddlers, so that today the troupe is made up largely of local people. The personnel of large troupes, on the other hand,

tend to come from over a wide area. This is true of every country. It is natural that the best performers of the whole country—or area of a country where a genre is performed—are attracted to the biggest troupes, for this is where they can earn the
most money, have the most security, and win the greatest renown.

Contractual arrangements between management and troupe
members vary widely. Some are formal, written agreements whose
conditions are spelled out in detail. Others are the vaguest of
oral agreements. Whether oral or written, agreements cover such
provisions as salary, lodging, and fringe benefits. Here are some
examples. An actor entering a large Saigon cai luong troupe is
signed to a preliminary six-months written contract after which,
if he does well, he is signed to a three-year written contract. His
nightly salary is specified, but he has no guarantee he will act
every night and when he does not work he is not paid. Members
of a large wayang orang troupe in Djakarta receive three-month
written contracts, the terms of which include free medical care,
free rice ration, and two weeks paid vacation per year. An actor
is paid a fixed monthly salary plus a bonus if he performs ten
consecutive nights. Actors of a medium-sized likay troupe in
Bangkok do not sign written contracts with the management but
each knows what percentage of the night's income is his share.
Actors are paid nightly if they work and receive free lodging in
the theatre building.

One reason written contracts are as common as they are, even
among small troupes, is that often actors are in debt to troupe
owners. The written document is an IOU as well as a contract.
In Vietnam indebtedness to the troupe owner is a way of life. I
spoke to no actor who was not in debt. A money lender may
even travel with a cai luong troupe when it is on tour just to
keep the actors' money needs supplied. Most cai luong actors
are "paid" nightly. Actually the actor signs a receipt and the
night's salary is applied to his debt. Often actors in Indonesia,
Cambodia, Laos, and Thailand are also deeply in debt to the
troupe owner. If an actor wishes to move to a new troupe, the
new troupe owner is expected to assume his debts. If the new
owner will not do this the actor cannot move. A ketoprak troupe
manager told me that defaulting on debts is no problem. Actors
know they have to repay the money they borrow. Owners in an

area know each other, and so can check up on an actor's story easily. If an actor leaves without paying his debt, "he is just a criminal and we call the police," this manager said. In extreme cases an actor can become a virtual slave of the troupe owner. Like a geisha girl in feudal Japan, his debts can become so great that all the earnings of his lifetime are insufficient to repay them.

Two major factors seem to contribute to the actor's being in debt. To begin with, indebtedness seems to be an inherent occupational hazard of acting. Actors tend to live beyond their means, partly perhaps because adventuresome, extroverted people go into acting, partly because they are imprudent, and partly because actors often feel they must cut an impressive figure in public. To catch the audience's attention may be half the battle of achieving success. To do this an actor needs money. Second, usurious interest rates make it difficult to repay money that has been borrowed. A legal investment in Indonesia can earn 12 percent interest per month! Interest rates in other countries are even higher. When I asked the manager of a large cai luong troupe to explain how the borrowing–lending system worked, he said, "If, for example, an actor borrows 5000 piaster, he will pay back 100 piaster a day from his salary for three months." In other words, the actor repays 9000 piaster for a three-month loan of 5000 piaster. This is an interest rate of 27 percent per month!

Troupe owners generally are more than happy to lend money to their actors: they earn a tidy profit in interest, and it keeps the actors content. And one way of holding onto a top actor is by lending him so much money no other owner can afford to hire him away. Being hopelessly in debt is not unattractive for star performers. Because the star can borrow large sums of money, he can live far better than his salary alone would permit. Perhaps he will never completely pay off his debts. It need not matter as long as he is successful. For the ordinary actor, however, being deeply in debt can be a nightmare.

In a very few troupes, mainly ketoprak and ludruk troupes affiliated with Communist art organizations, a contractual agreement between owner and member is replaced by an agreement between all members to share jointly in the troupe's management and finances. Normally members of such a troupe elect a manager, who is responsible to them rather than to a financial backer or an owner. This kind of organization follows Communist share-and-share-alike principles and is at least partially a reflection of a troupe's ideological committment.

OUTSIDE RELATIONSHIPS

The functioning of a theatre troupe is affected at every turn by the nature of the outside social institutions and social forces with which it has contact. In Southeast Asia a troupe's most important external relationships are with other troupes, with religion, and with government agencies.

VOLUNTARY ASSOCIATIONS

The great majority of professional theatre troupes in Southeast Asia act independently of each other. Most do not belong to associations or to larger "umbrella" organizations. The half-dozen associations of theatre troupes which do exist, however, are extremely interesting and some are quite important. Each is made up of troupes of a single genre, and membership by troupes is voluntary.

The one important association of theatre troupes in Thailand is the Society of Northeast Thailand Folksong Singers, founded in 1955, with headquarters at Khon Kaen in the heart of the Lao-speaking area. Membership consists of both individuals and troupes, and the majority of mohlam performers and mohlam luong troupes belong. Estimated membership in 1963 was 5700 performers—1200 straight mohlam performers (400 male singers, 400 female singers, 400 male khen players) and 4500 mohlam luong performers (300 amateur and professional troupes with an average membership of 15 performers per troupe). The Society serves its members in several ways. It publishes in a series of small books traditional stories in the Lao language that are used by performers. It acts as an extremely effective booking agent for members; it demands and gets for its best performers as much as 1500 bhat ($75) per performance. A member pays a 10 bhat (50¢) membership fee on joining, and thereafter a commission of 5 to 10 percent of each booking made through the Society. This provides the Society with a regular and sizable revenue which makes its operations self-supporting. The strong leadship exerted by this association on behalf of mohlam has contributed to mohlam luong's rapid rise in popularity in recent years.

The other associations of professional theatre troupes are in Indonesia. There are many regional and local associations of wayang kulit puppeteers in central and east Java, and perhaps several thousand dalang and musicians are affiliated with them. However, these organizations are of no practical consequence as they do not play an active role in Indonesian theatre life. They exist mainly on paper. They meet seldom, collect no dues, and do not act as booking agents. The Foundation for the Art of the Dalang (*Jajasan Padalangan*) in west Java, however, is an extremely active association, to which about 650 of the estimated 1500 amateur and professional wayang golek dalang in Sunda belong. The Foundation has its permanent headquarters in the city of Bandung. Its officers largely control who is invited to perform wayang golek on broadcasts of the Bandung regional station of Radio Republic Indonesia, the national radio network. Since radio broadcasts set the seal of success to a dalang's career and help establish his reputation with millions of listeners, the Foundation wields very considerable power. The first convention of the Foundation was held in Bandung in February 1964, with some 200 wayang golek performers attending. At the convention it was voted to establish minimum training standards for dalang in the future. Female singers (pesinden) of wayang golek were vigorously condemned, and the major stated aim for instituting a strict licensing system was to shore up the dalang's position vis-à-vis the singer. It is extremely unusual for a voluntary artistic group to attempt to police itself in this way. Enforcement of the new licensing system will rest, not with the Foundation, but with the National Front, a semiofficial government agency which sees to it that private organizations support government policy. The National Front's interest in wayang golek is essentially political: it wants to prevent politically undesirable dalang from performing, and a licensing system would represent an important step in that direction.

Indonesian society today is intensely political. Political parties have sections devoted to youth, women's, student, labor, agricultural, and cultural activities. Until a few years ago political parties even sponsored their own Boy Scout troops, but recently the government has banned scouting as being tainted with foreign ideas and has set up its own Youth Pioneer groups. Even sports events are charged with politics. A stated objective of holding the Games of the New Emerging Forces (GANEFO) in Djakarta was to rally political support for President Soekarno's foreign and domestic policies. It is perhaps unavoidable that theatre troupes should be mobilized for political purposes along with most other segments of society.*

The largest politically oriented theatre grouping in Indonesia is BAKOKSI (*Badan Kontak Ketoprak Seluruh Indonesia* or the All-Indonesian Ketoprak Organization). Founded in 1957, with headquarters in Jogjakarta, BAKOKSI is aligned with the Indonesian Communist Party (PKI) though not as one of the party's formally affiliated organizations. As the name suggests, it claims to speak for "all" ketoprak troupes in Indonesia. BAKOKSI claims a membership of 801 troupes—about 40 professional and the rest amateur—and I see no reason to doubt that this number of troupes has had some form of contact with BAKOKSI during its seven-year existence. However, only a fraction of its so-called member troupes are in active contact with the parent organization. One ketoprak troupe manager, who vehemently insisted his troupe was a member in good standing, had had no communication—either in person or by letter—with BAKOKSI headquarters for the past seven years. Another manager said he agreed with the principles behind BAKOKSI and that his troupe had joined four years ago, but, since they were so far from BAKOKSI headquarters in Jogjakarta, the organization meant nothing to them in practical terms. "Two years ago I wrote asking them to send me a script with a modern theme," he sighed, "but they didn't even answer my letter." Among the 82 ketoprak troupes I visited in Java, for every one that appeared to be an active member, there was another which was not, by any stretch of the imagination, active but which, presumably, was still carried on BAKOKSI's rolls. Although smaller than its membership roll would suggest, BAKOKSI is a potent organization whose influence stems less

---

*The alignment of political forces in Indonesia has undergone a radical change since the field work for this book was completed in 1964. Some of the theatre groups described—such as BAKOKSI and the Ludruk Association—probably no longer exist. However, it seems likely that theatre continues to be mobilized toward political ends in Indonesia, though by different groups and toward different ends than in 1963–1964.

from its size than from its activist tactics. BAKOKSI is particularly strong among amateur troupes in the Jogjakarta–Surakarta area and in eastern Java. A roving representative from BAKOKSI regional headquarters in Djember visits troupes throughout eastern Java encouraging them to join the association. The headquarters directly manages one of the largest and best-known ketoprak troupes in Java—Krido Mardi. It sponsors an "All-Indonesia Ketoprak Congress" every few years. And it encourages troupes of all persuasions to produce plays with themes which support government policy and Communist ideology (a major policy line of the PKI is that the two are identical).

The Ludruk Association (*Lembaga Ludruk*) is a sister organization, and, like BAKOKSI, it is aligned with the PKI and supports its policies. If anything, it is even more activist and its member troupes more dedicated to Communist ideology than BAKOKSI. There may be around 30 ludruk troupes, amateur and professional, which are members of the Ludruk Association. Headquarters for the association are in Surabaya, east Java.

The Nationalist Party of Indonesia (PNI) is the largest political party in Indonesia. One of its many organizational affiliates is the Nationalist Cultural Association (*Lembaga Kebudajaan Nasional*) which contains departments for painting, music, dance, modern drama, and a special subsidiary organization for ketoprak called the Association of Nationalist Ketoprak (*Lembaga Ketoprak Nasional*) or LKN. The LKN has perhaps one-fourth the number of BAKOKSI's member troupes. Its main troupe, Ketoprak Mataram, is considered the best in Indonesia. This troupe has an unusual status. It is the mainstay of LKN, and its plays tend to support PNI political policies (the troupe recently performed for the party's thirty-seventh anniversary celebration). It is also the official ketoprak troupe of Radio Republic Indonesia's Jogjakarta station. Troupe members are, therefore, PNI party functionaries and government civil servants at the same time. Inasmuch as the PNI is the government's staunchest supporter, the troupe's dual ideological committments are not too dissimilar. The Nationalist Cultural Association at present is increasing its activities in the area of theatre. It has established a dalang school enrolling 785 students (half from the military forces). The school's aim is twofold: to teach the art of wayang kulit to interested young people and to teach student dalang PNI ideology. Students attend both traditional wayang kulit training sessions and classes in political indoctrination. Dramatic plots, dialogue, and song lyrics are selected or composed to reflect PNI policies and beliefs. The association is also actively recruiting ludruk troupes in eastern Java.

Since the third major political party, the NU or Orthodox Moslem Party, does not interest itself in theatre, and since the seven other legal political parties are too small to be effective in this area, ideological struggle in Indonesian theatre centers around the conflict between the PKI and the PNI.*

The foremost aim of politically oriented "umbrella groups" like BAKOKSI, LKN, and the Ludruk Association is to advance their party's cause. The most direct way of proceeding is for an umbrella group to recruit troupes which share its ideology. Among genuinely dedicated troupes commitment is not easily shaken, even in adverse circumstances. I visited a large BAKOKSI-affiliated ketoprak troupe in east Java which was in dire economic straits. The troupe had built its own theatre building during more prosperous times, several years earlier, but then they were taking in barely enough to keep troupe members alive. "I don't earn enough money to buy a bottle of soda-pop each week," the manager said. The building was beginning to fall apart. Troupe members' clothes were in tatters. Yet the troupe continued to levy an additional "one-rupiah contribution to BAKOKSI" on every ticket sold. Audience members complained, and even refused to buy tickets because of the extra charge. But, in spite of the hardship, the troupe, as the manager explained, had "its duty as artists to support government policy and to lead the Indonesian revolution." The troupe got no help from BAKOKSI; in fact for several years its only contact with headquarters has been sending in its meager financial contributions.

But the majority of troupes which belong to one or another of the three political umbrella organizations in Java have only vague political leanings or none at all. Knowing this, inducements other

---

*Modernist Moslem student groups, as well as the PKI and the PNI, are active in amateur seni-drama (modern drama). Some of these Moslem student theatre groups were formerly affiliated with the Masjumi, a reformist Moslem political party generally opposed to President Soekarno's policies. The Masjumi was an illegal party in 1963–1964 when this data was collected.

than political argument are a normal part of recruitment programs. These inducements are usually indirect: free acting lessons, an invitation to join a local theatre festival, assistance to an amateur group trying to set up its own theatre program, and the like. Friendly relations are cultivated with nonpolitical troupes in the hope that eventually they will become disposed to accept the political views of their benefactor. Some troupes are quite aware of the umbrella groups' political motives. Not concerned with politics themselves, they cheerfully take advantage of all offers of help, whatever their source. One of the most amusing comments I heard was from a ketoprak manager in central Java who described how his troupe, chameleonlike, switches affiliation from LKN to LEKRA—the over-all PKI cultural organization—and back again. As they move from town to town, they join the cultural group of whichever party—PNI or PKI—is in power locally.

In recruiting new member troupes PNI and PKI follow somewhat different tactics. LKN is officially affiliated with the PNI; its political connection is a matter of public record, and LKN and PNI signs are posted side by side at party headquarters. But both BAKOKSI and the Ludruk Association claim they are not officially a part of the PKI political apparatus. In theory, both groups are politically unaffiliated. One never sees a BAKOKSI sign at PKI headquarters. As a result some troupes join BAKOKSI and the Ludruk Association completely unaware of the fact that they are joining Communist-run organizations. The manager of a small ketoprak troupe told me his troupe was planning to join BAKOKSI, "because it is good for all ketoprak troupes to join 'The All-Indonesia Ketoprak Association,' " When asked if he agreed with BAKOKSI's political views, he replied that he wasn't aware the organization had political ties. Actually, neither BAKOKSI nor the Ludruk Association are an organizational part of PKI or the PKI cultural arm, LEKRA (*Lembaga Kebudajaan Rakjat* or People's Art Association). There is no doubt, however, that both are ideologically committed to PKI aims. When I spoke to the chairman of BAKOKSI at their headquarters, he carefully pointed out that the organization was not affiliated with the PKI and that they fully supported the government of President Soekarno. However, he added that most actors in

BAKOKSI belong to LEKRA as individuals, and that a major aim of BAKOKSI is to arouse the people's patriotism against neo-colonialism and imperialism. Peasants in the countryside especially must be indoctrinated in USDEK and Manipol (abbreviations of two major state policies enunciated by President Soekarno in recent years). When asked if BAKOKSI supported the policies of the PNI and NU parties, he laughed and said, "No, we support the government and the PKI."

The public stance of the Indonesian Communist Party in 1964 was almost unassailable for it claimed that its policies were identical with the government's: to attack the PKI directly was to attack the government, something which at that time was out of the question. From this tactical position the PKI was able to advance its cause. We can see this process in action in the final communique issued at the Third BAKOKSI Congress, held in Surakarta, August 1964. It contains a dutiful call to all members to be "true Manipolists," but the rest of the pronouncement is straight PKI cultural line: announce support for the government; don't mention the PKI directly but urge "cooperation" with PKI goals such as "revolutionary" activities; work toward building an all-inclusive organization; strengthen ties with peasant and worker groups. The complex and abstract language of the communique is typical of public statements in Indonesia irrespective of their ideological message, as is its mild tone of exhortation.

This Congress of All-Indonesian Ketoprak recognizes that the cultural art of ketoprak has reached its present limit, and that no further development can take place until ketoprak becomes part of a renewed movement for broadening and strengthening the people's culture of the times. Our goal is more than ever to broaden our political efforts toward mobilization of the masses. The Congress wills: every ketoprak artist, every member of BAKOKSI, must stand as a true Manipolist, for Manipol must be the basis for cultural work of every movement which is progressive and revolutionary. For ketoprak to become a renewed movement, it is first essential that each ketoprak artist educate and toughen himself, by accepting instruction in revolutionary theory, especially that concerning revolutionary philosophy and the history of national movements, and by accepting instruction in the art of drama from expanded and new directives manifesting revolutionary techniques and based on the integration of the artist with the people, most especially the peasant group. In the future we shall broaden and strengthen cultural-political cooperation, especially between literature and art, and most particularly drama, and Revolutionary Cultural Institutes [*read* LEKRA], mass revolutionary organizations [*read* PKI and its affiliates], and progressive cultural groups from outside the nation [*read* Communist countries], and most particularly those from the New Emerging Forces. It is most necessary to broaden the repertory of ketoprak, especially in relation to present-day themes of the masses, which they need and urge on us. The will of this Congress is that all ketoprak artists should unite with their fellow artists. For this it is necessary that we cooperate with workers' art and revolutionary artistic organizations.[2]

BAKOKSI and the Ludruk Association constantly recruit troupes as members, in part out of ideological fervor (PKI party stalwarts are tireless in their devotion to their cause) and in part because mass organizations form the basis of PKI political power. The LKN, on the other hand, is less concerned with membership size. PNI strength lies in its extensive control of the bureaucratic structure of the Indonesian government, particularly in Java. PNI officials, appointed by the central government in Djakarta, occupy a majority of the key positions in provincial, district, sub-district, and city governments. Almost without exception, PNI party members run the offices of the Ministry of Information and the Ministry of Education in Java. This is not to say the PNI, through the LKN, does not recruit ketoprak troupes as members, but only that the party's first priority is maintaining its bureaucratic network in government (including its Ketoprak Mataram troupe). Only secondarily, does the party recruit mass support.

BAKOKSI, the Ludruk Association, and LKN are always short of funds. Although BAKOKSI is perhaps the best organized of these groups, it apparently receives almost no income at the present time. According to BAKOKSI regulations, each professional troupe is assessed a "contribution" of one percent of the troupe's yearly income, but no more than one or two troupes of the more than forty supposedly enrolled as members of BAKOKSI send such contributions. Each amateur troupe is supposed to contribute $2\frac{1}{2}$ rupiah per troupe member per year. Although for the average-sized troupe this would amount to no more than the cost of a single pack of cigarettes per troupe per year, by the last quarter of the year BAKOKSI headquarters had not received a single rupiah contribution from this source in 1963. A magazine for member troupes, started in 1957, folded with the second issue from lack of funds. BAKOKSI's Krido Mardi troupe used to run an acting and indoctrination course for young ketoprak actors, but that had to be abandoned because it cost too much. The last BAKOKSI congress scheduled for mid-1963 was postponed once until April 1964, and again until August 1964, because there was not enough money in the organization treasury to finance it. The Ludruk Association and LKN are probably in worse financial straits. There is strong enthusiasm among many Indonesian theatre artists to use the theatre for political propaganda but little money is available to support their ends.

THEATRE AND RELIGION

Theatre and religion have always been closely bound up together in Southeast Asia and they remain so today. I have discussed how deeply religion has influenced the subject matter of drama. The social function of a theatre troupe is also affected by a troupe's relation to organized religion and to religious practices.

In troupes of many genres performers say prayers prior to performance. The saying of prayers may be a purely private matter, the performer reciting a prayer backstage out of view of the audience. Or it may be recited in front of the audience and partially for the audience. The performer in this case is carrying out a public religious ritual.

The wayang kulit dalang in Java is required by custom to say six prayers: at home, on arrival at the place of performance, during the introductory music, while bringing the oil lamp up to full brightness, before first speaking, and as he places the first shadow figure—the *kayon* "tree of life"—in the center of the screen to start the play. The prayers are ostensibly to Allah, but they contain animistic, Brahmanic, and Buddhist sentiments as well. Five of the six prayers are spoken in the presence of the audience.

Malaysian wayang kulit puppeteers present offerings as well as prayers to the gods prior to performance. Winstedt calls the ceremony one of the "two most elaborate Hindu rituals" which survive in that country today.[3]

[2 2 1]

Wearing the yellow scarf appropriate to gods and kings about his shoulders, the . . . reciter . . . claims to be the incarnation or representative of Vishnu. . . . There is a special plate of uncooked rice, and there are a raw egg, raw thread and money for Batara Guru, that is, Siva the supreme teacher and, as Nataraja, lord of dancers and king of actors. . . . Then censing the leather puppets that represent Siva and Vishnu, he begs them to drive away all spirits of evil.[4]

The dalang concludes his performance with the following prayer:

Om! I salute you. . . . Open the big gates! For Siva the destroyer is descending from the summit of heaven to expel all evil powers, all spirits of disease. Before earth was the size of a foot or the vault of heaven was framed, when only the throne of Allah and the tablet of fate and the Kuran [Koran] existed, I was the original magician, uttering the original incantation to disperse spirits of evil. It bid them disperse to their masters, King Solomon, Siva, the Spectre Huntsman, Vishnu, and the great Dragon at the navel of the sea. It is not I who bid them go but the original primal salutation that bids them; not I but Siva the first of actors, not I but Siva, the first of teachers. And my magic has the power of that teacher's magic. One! Three! Five! Seven! Avaunt! Avaunt.[5]

In lakon bassac, in likay, in mohlam luong, in cai luong, and in hat boi, actors say a prayer before a portable shrine backstage before making their first entrance.

Like all the arts, the hat boi has a patron god who necessarily accompanies theatrical troupes in their peregrinations. He is represented by a doll or an earthen statue painted or brocaded, and placed in a wooden niche behind a vase filled with incense sticks. Before appearing on the stage, each actor must prostrate himself four times before the god, named Ong Lang. If he fails to do so, he will lose his memory or his voice before the spectators. The legend says that Ong Lang was originally a prince, whose favorite diversion was the theatre. In fear of his royal father's punishment he secretly assisted actors performing in honor of the monarch. One night, the actors played so well that the enthusiastic crowd swarmed onto the stage to hail the players. The stage, being a frail structure of wood and bamboo, yielded and fell upon the head of the prince, who was killed at a stroke. His insatiable soul continued, however, to give protection to the actors. He would give them inspiration or a good voice or facilitate their improvisation. The actors made him a divinity and honored him in a cult after several such miracles had been accomplished to their benefit.[6]

Once a year performers of khon and lakon in Thailand, Cambodia, and Laos pay obeisance to the gods who preside over theatre.
They drink holy water and also have it sprinkled on their hair.
They present offerings of food and drink to khon masks of Rama
and Ravana of the *Ramayana* (often in Cambodia, offerings are
made to the mask of Ravana only). Candles and incense are
burned on the horizontal drums in which it is believed the soul
of the orchestra resides. Similar offerings are made by students to
their teachers.

One reason a performer says prayers is simple self-protection.
He prays to the gods to bless his performance, to make the audience like him. But the performer may also become, at least
partly, a medium through which the gods can speak to the
audience. In the Malay prayer just quoted, the performer is
taking on the attributes of a priest when he says it is not himself,
the dalang, who is speaking, but Siva. And the dalang claims for
himself the same religious power as Siva when he says, "and my
magic has the power of that teacher's magic." When the puppeteer of Balinese wayang kulit or Javanese wayang beber performs with torso bare, we see the outer sign that he is both priest
and performer (the Brahman priest traditionally wore no clothes
above the waist). On special occasions in Bali—cremations, birthdays, temple anniversaries—an afternoon *wayang lemah* performance may be given in which no screen is used and no audience
attends. The performance is a religious ritual. Only dalang well-
versed in Brahmanic ritual are allowed to perform. The dalang
is, in fact, a priest who performs. On Java, only the oldest, wisest,
most magically endowed wayang kulit dalang may perform the
special ruwatan play, for in performance the dalang is a priest.
He calls on the gods to bless the young child. He sprinkles the
child with holy water to symbolize its protection from evil. In
each professional zat pwe troupe in Burma there is an apyodaw
dancer, a young girl dedicated to the service of the nat, who
dances an invocation to the spirits as the first part of every performance. When she offers to the nat platters of coconut and
banana and does obeisance to the nat in four directions, she is
acting as intermediary between the gods and the people gathered
in the theatre. She is priestess as well as performer.

Religious ties may determine in part when, where, and under

what conditions a troupe may perform. The viability of the troupe as a social unit may be affected. (If a local nat in Burma objects to pig, only a foolhardy performer will dare eat pork while in the area.) Because the religious implications of wayang kulit performances are highly appreciated by audiences in Java, many hundreds of troupes find regular employment today. On the other hand, because nang yai was so closely connected with Brahmanic rites (especially funeral rites), when these rites gradually lost their importance troupes found themselves out of work and were forced to disband. On Bali *"Tjalonarang* is often given in times of illness, and on certain magically important days. But its performance is not without danger, for its magical content may be a source of peril as well as of protection. . . . Very special and costly offerings have to be made."[7] Wayang wong troupes which perform *Tjalonarang* are assured of a certain number of performances each year because of the play's religious importance. At the same time the religious danger which attends performance tends to limit the number of times a troupe might be able to perform it. The most famous of all Javanese wayang kulit dramas are the twelve plays of the *Baratayuda* in which dozens of mythical heroes and demigods are slaughtered. The Javanese have long held that terrible disaster would result should any troupe perform these plays. Only since 1957 have *Baratayuda* plays begun to be fairly regularly staged. Performances are now exceptionally popular, though still fraught with religious danger.[8] Similarly, in Burma live actors were thought to be too impure to act the sacred *Jataka* stories down until the late nineteenth century. Puppets, being made of wood, however, "cannot act unwisely," and hence held a monopoly on performance of *Jataka* plays.[9] Once zat pwe troupes broke the monopoly and began to do the always popular *Jataka* stories, puppet troupes lost their special niche in Burmese culture. Live troupes soon drove puppet troupes out of existence.

Islamic teaching if strictly followed can make it difficult or impossible for a troupe to perform in a particular area in Indonesia and Malaysia. Geertz mentions a village in east Java so strongly Islamic that gamelan playing is considered an evil, and "even today a man who holds a wayang is likely to fall sick or grow poor as a result."[10] Some Philippine Catholic priests tried, unsuccessfully, to prevent performances of two plays by the well-known contemporary playwright Severino Montano: one because it dealt with suicide, which is contrary to Catholic belief, and the other because it depicted Rizal, the Philippine national hero, being persecuted by the Franciscans. In other parts of Southeast Asia the Christian attitude toward theatre is generally repressive; if a theatre troupe had to depend upon a Christian audience it would not last long. An American missionary in Thailand told me, "Any young person who shows an interest in the theatre is branded as immoral or perverted. Thai Christians are more puritanical about this than Western missionaries."

Troupes are often hired to perform for religious ceremonies; in this sense religious ties can help a troupe maintain itself economically. Especially in Thailand, Laos, and Burma local wat or temple fairs give employment to hundreds of likay, lakon jatri, nang talung, mohlam luong, and zat pwe troupes. However, troupes rarely have other than temporary connection with temple organizations. Even the two lakon jatri troupes which have the exclusive rights to perform at the Lok Muang temple in Bangkok are not part of the temple organization. They are only hired to perform there. In Thailand, Cambodia, and Laos, lay organizations of elders of Buddhist temples may support local folk troupes. Costumes, masks, and musical instruments may be kept in the main temple and performances may be given primarily for temple celebrations and in the temple grounds. The troupe may even rehearse in the temple precincts. But technically speaking the temple is not party to this. Religious orders are forbidden by canon law to actively support theatre. Priests and monks are forbidden to witness performances. I know of no professional troupe which is directly affiliated with or managed by a religious organization. The least affected by religion are ketoprak, ludruk, kich, and cai luong troupes. They seldom perform religiously oriented plays; they seldom perform on religious occasions; and performers (except cai luong performers) seldom follow religious customs or ritual of any kind.

THEATRE AND GOVERNMENT

Government ministries of information, education, or culture and the police exert a pervasive and continuing influence on the

activities of theatre troupes. With few exceptions present governments in Southeast Asia try to control the flow of information
within their boundaries, and this control extends to theatre. Ten
years ago there were democratic governments in most countries
of Southeast Asia generally sympathetic toward freedom of expression. Today Thailand, Burma, and Vietnam are under absolute
rule of military juntas; Laos is under partial military rule; Cambodia and Indonesia are under one-man authoritarian civilian
rule—Prince Sihanouk in Cambodia, "Lifetime President" Soekarno in Indonesia.* None of these governments will tolerate
direct criticism of government policy. Some form of censorship,
overt or covert, is applied to every means of public expression
including theatre, motion pictures, radio, television, newspapers,
magazines, and public speaking. Few governments like to admit
to censorship, so double-talk—to say nothing of double-think—
often surrounds the subject. Here is a quote from the Djakarta
Daily Mail of May 19, 1964:

> Djakarta. The Chairman of the West Sumatra branch of the
> National Front declared here that it was entirely untrue to say that
> the Indonesian press is government-controlled. People who assert this
> are great liars, he said. In fact the Indonesian press is quite [cap]
> able of picturing conditions in Indonesia as they really are without
> any pressures. On the other hand, however, the Indonesian press
> *will not contradict the people's aspirations and the government's policy* . . . The
> press constitutes an important and vital instrument in the people's
> and state's affairs and therefore the function of the press is closely
> related to the basic principles, and goals and ideology of the state.
> (Italics mine.)

The particular ideological slant of this statement marks it as
Indonesian, but the general thought which it expresses, that dis-
sent is not allowed, could as well apply to Burma, Laos, Cambodia, Vietnam, or Thailand.

Theatre censorship ranges from subtle, indirect government
pressure to codified systems of legal censorship. In the Philippines
there is no formal censorship law for theatre, motion pictures, or
the press reflecting the fact that a multiplicity of opinion is regarded as the normal, and in fact the desirable, condition of

---

*Between 1965 and 1966 political control in Indonesia has passed very largely from
President Soekarno to a group of military and civilian leaders.

society. Nevertheless, while it may be legal for a producer to stage almost any play he wishes, unofficial government pressure may be expected if a play goes too far in criticism or in advocacy of unpopular causes. One modern playwright was under great pressure from officials of the presidential palace to withdraw a play which gently satirized Philippine diplomats and nouveau-riche socialites overseas. Had the President himself not cleared the play (the playwright was a schoolmate of his), it could not have been presented.

In Thailand, although there is no censorship law, unofficial government control constantly is in evidence. As one likay manager put it: "Criticize the government? You're joking! We can't show a bad Thai king or a corrupt Thai official. We can't mention high taxes or the high cost of rice." Through long experience with officialdom, theatre managers and artistic directors know what is allowed and what is frowned upon without there being any formal system of censorship to ensure compliance.

Laos and Cambodia both have censorship laws which are enforced. Each professional troupe is required to submit a scenario for approval before performance, or a full script if it is a modern play. In Laos the police are the censors. In Cambodia there is a censorship division within the Ministry of Information that contains separate sections for radio, motion picture, press, and theatre. Theatre censorship in Cambodia is extremely thorough. From the government's own National School of Theatre on down to the smallest troupe in the smallest village every play produced in the country must pass the censor's scrutiny, though apparently the laws are not harshly applied.

In Malaysia there is censorship of radio, motion pictures, and theatre. Police are empowered to examine all play scripts (Chinese opera) and scenarios (bangsawan). Recently the tedious requirement that opera scripts be written out in complete form was rescinded, but in most other respects censorship was more rigidly administered in 1964 than in past years. In response to Indonesia's "Crush Malaysia" policy, the country was in a state of national emergency and the effect was soon felt in the theatre. During the Chinese-Malay race riots of August 1964 Chinese opera performances in Singapore's amusement parks were banned as a security measure.

By far the strongest attempts to control and channel the activities of theatre troupes are being made by the governments of Vietnam and Indonesia. Censorship under the Diem regime was designed to control all media of public communication and as part of this design there was a Censorship Board within the Ministry of Information. One of the sections of the Board was concerned with theatre. According to censorship regulations, each page of playscript had to be stamped "approved" by the Censorship Board before a play could be performed. A Central Censorship Board in Saigon handled scripts submitted from the provinces of the delta region and the central highlands; a Branch Censorship Board in Hue handled scripts submitted from the provinces of the central lowlands. In theory a script could be performed anywhere in the country without further approval once it had been stamped approved. The stamped script was to be shown the local police. The police were to follow it during performance to determine that there were no deviations from it. In practice, things worked nowhere near this simply. Often the Branch Censorship Board in Hue would not take responsibility for approving a script but would send the script all the way to Saigon for approval. Local officials—police, mayors, district officials, military commanders—often had their own ideas on what was and what was not suitable for performance in their areas. If they demanded changes in scripts already approved by the Censorship Board, there was no recourse for a troupe except to comply or pack up and leave town. When a troupe produced a play from a scenario rather than from a complete script, as most small provincial cai luong troupes and hat boi troupes did, how was a local police official to determine whether an ad-libbed performance by singers and actors was a faithful reflection of the approved scenario or not? Censorship of theatre in Vietnam has proved difficult to enforce and the system is more openly criticized by theatre people than in any other country in Southeast Asia.

The head of the Central Censorship Board in Saigon described to me how the Board operated in 1963. During that year some three hundred new cai luong playscripts and ten to twelve new kich playscripts were received for censorship. Of these less than 10 percent were passed as they were. Authors of the remaining

90 percent were called in for "conference" during which the officials of the Board discussed ways of "solving their problems." Authors were never told "do this" or "do that," but after they rewrote sections they returned the scripts for another review. Some scripts were sent back half-a-dozen times before they were approved. It is understandable that a censor with a big stick can talk softly. Following the November 1963 coup in which Diem was deposed and executed, a new group of censors replaced Diem-appointed officials, but the Board remains and censorship remains, operating under the same law as before. Presumably the censors are following the whims of each new military junta that comes to power. In the first few months after Diem's fall Board officials said they planned to liberalize the censorship system to permit greater freedom of expression, but just how much freedom of expression the military governments of Vietnam will tolerate remains to be seen.

The greatest efforts to influence and control theatre in Southeast Asia are being made in Indonesia. There is a formal, legal system of censorship. Because of the nature of Indonesian political life, however, formal censorship is less important than it is in Vietnam. According to the government of President Soekarno "liberalism"—including freedom of expression—is condemned as a vicious evil designed by imperialists and capitalists to divide and weaken the Indonesian nation. Unity of the nation must be preserved at all costs. To criticize the government or cause dissension of any kind by expressing ideas contrary to official policy is a despicable antisocial act. The entire weight of government policy denies the moral right of the individual to speak or even to hold views counter to the government. The presumption is that through constant exposure to the proper ideas—through radio, press, movies, street banners, posters, public meetings, rallys, conventions, congresses, and sporting events, and through social pressure exerted in school and at work, and through semi-government organizations like the National Front—people will either be persuaded to accept the government's views or will be socially conditioned not to express opposing ideas. In this view, official censorship is the tenth of the iceberg visible above the water; unofficial government pressures make up the invisible nine-tenths beneath the surface.

One of the basic positions of the Soekarno government is that it is not necessary to criticize the government, since, because it represents "all the people," there can be nothing to criticize. This view was echoed by many theatre managers who explained why they supported the government. A BAKOKSI troupe manager said that in 1937, when the Dutch suppressed every anti-Dutch or nationalist idea, it was patriotic for ketoprak troupes to get around the censor. After the revolution in 1945, when ketoprak became free for the first time, they could criticize anything they wished. But now in 1963, "we have established the first phase of our Revolution, we have something to defend, and we should not criticize it." A former BAKOKSI troupe manager said ketoprak was just entertainment before the war but since 1945 it had become their duty to educate the people. Under liberalism we used to criticize the government. Now we have NASAKOM—government of all factions: nationalists, Communists, and religious parties—so what is there to criticize? A nonaffiliated troupe manager put it neatly, saying, "Art is part of culture. Culture is part of the nation. At the center of the nation is the government. For me to criticize the government is to shake the foundation of our nation, our culture, and our art. I will not do this."

Formal censorship of theatre in Indonesia is two-pronged. First a troupe must obtain from local authorities a license to perform for a certain period of time in a given locality. This is usually called a "performance permit" (*idjin pertundjukan*). Troupes seldom have difficulty getting these permits, though I was told the Dutch refused performance permits to many "nationalistic" ketoprak troupes prior to the war. Second, the police must approve every play prior to performance. Ordinarily local officers of the Internal Security Police (DPKN) carry out this responsibility, often in conjunction with local officials of the Ministry of Information, the National Front, and other groups. Both censorship operations are decentralized: authority to approve both performances and plays rests solely with local officials on the village, sub-district, city, and district level. In one way this is desirable for it allows for considerable flexibility in interpreting regulations. It also makes for a perfect crazy quilt of local law enforcement throughout the country. In a district in Sunda, district (kabupaten) officials issue performance permits. In a district on Java's south coast, if a troupe performs in a village (*desa*), sub-district (ketjamatan) officials issue the permit, but if the performance lasts more than one month the permit must be obtained at the district office. In Tjirebon, west Java, a permit is issued by the Legal Division of the district government after being endorsed by district officials in Public Health, Public Works, and the Police, unless the troupe performs in a village, in which case the village head (*lurah*) can issue the permit. In a large part of east Java police do not check play scenarios at all though they often attend performances. In a district east of Bandung in Sunda, I was told that play outlines had to be submitted to the police every day. They are checked against Article 6, Paragraph 518, of the legal code which forbids antigovernment, political, or immoral activities. Furthermore, an official of the Communal Education Committee (*Pendidikan Masjarakat*) attends every Saturday performance. He suggests ways the troupe can improve the educational quality of the plays. The manager of a ludruk troupe said they never showed their scripts to the police because, "We're the President's favorite troupe and there's nothing for anyone to censor." On the first of the month, the largest sandiwara troupe in Djakarta submits to the police a list of the plays it plans to stage during that month. The police pass or reject well-known plays on the basis of the title alone but usually insist upon seeing the scenarios of new plays.

Censorship either permits a troupe to do what it wants or forbids it to do what the government doesn't want. Characteristically the Indonesian government tries to go beyond mere censorship to affect in a positive way the political content of performances. Troupes are urged to perform patriotic stories, to insert in plays government slogans like "Crush Malaysia" or "Support GANEFO," to stage pre-performance dances that carry a political message such as "Long Live USDEK," and to add between scenes songs like "Know Manipol: Be a Good Manipolist." Wayang kulit dalang and wayang golek singers are encouraged to make direct political comment in the midst of classic *Ramayana* and *Mahabharata* dramas. Most of the government's past efforts in these directions were channeled through the Ministry of Information, but there appears to be less contact between the Ministry and theatre troupes now than there once was. Local officials of the Ministry of Information used to call on troupes personally, and to give managers statements of government policy and even propaganda scripts. But, as one troupe manager said, "they stopped coming about two years ago." Apparently the government today is relying more and more upon mass organizations and upon demonstrations to keep the population, including theatre troupes, informed about government policies. Many troupes regularly insert the approved government slogans into their usual plays, but as far as I know no professional troupe in Indonesia has ever produced one of the government-written propaganda plays.

In all countries of Southeast Asia official and unofficial censorship of theatre is directed primarily at two targets: antigovernment sentiments and immorality. The case for suppressing thoughts detrimental to a government was stated by the Cultural Officer of the District of Bogor, in west Java: "As chief cultural officer of the area it is my responsibility to assure the continuation of the Indonesian Revolution by selecting those arts which conform to the spirit of the Revolution and which further the Conception of National Personality as enunciated by President/ Glorious Leader of the Revolution Soekarno. In theatre, those plays which do not conform cannot be performed." In Malaysia, where the king symbolizes the state, a play may not show a virtuous king being killed. In Cambodia a play may not show either Vietnam or Thailand in a favorable light, for Cambodia's government is at sword's point with both countries. Pan-Malayan sentiments used to be encouraged several years ago in Indonesia when Maphilindo was official government policy, but today Malaysia is an enemy and a troupe would not think of producing the same play it did a few years back. During the Diem regime Vietnamese censors banned from the hat boi and cai luong stage one of the great classic stories of China. The play was banned not because it was Chinese but because in it a tyrant king, Tsin Houng Tin, is dethroned by a heroic young warrior. The parallel with President Diem was too obvious to be allowed. One cai luong troupe manager claimed that eight out of ten classic plays he wanted to stage were rejected for the same reason. So extreme did censorship become in the latter months of the Diem regime, that, during the President's dispute with the Buddhists, the censors forbade setting any scene of a play in a Buddhist temple or monastery for fear of encouraging revolt. In Djakarta a wayang orang troupe was told it could not perform the traditional play *Bumo Moropu Kikes,* for its hero, Bumo, conquers a neighboring kingdom. That, the police said, smacked of imperialism and colonialism which the government opposes. A drama festival committee in Bandung hastily dropped plans for a production of Camus' *Caligula* when committee members discovered that the play chronicled the rise and fall of an egomaniac dictator who brought ruin to his country and his friends. The comparison was much too close to home.

Criticism of domestic problems is considered antigovernment and is also taboo. Thus, you will never see an Indonesian play in which the country's increasingly acute economic situation is a major point of discussion, for it is official government policy that no economic problems exist. The same can be said for most other countries as well. Inserted comments on social or economic problems cannot be kept out of the drama completely, however. Clowns traditionally make such remarks. Although it is forbidden, I have heard clowns make jokes about the soaring price of rice and about corrupt officials in wayang and ketoprak plays, about cruel officials who take advantage of the honest "little man" in cai luong plays, about venial monks in Cambodian lakon bassac plays, and about high officials who milk the public treasury to support vast numbers of mistresses in likay plays.

The second major taboo of the censors is immorality. What is moral and good for the stage of one country may be immoral and banned in another. Capitalism is moral in Thailand; in Indonesia it is immoral. Morality in Malaysia is Islamic morality: a play may not show divorce, gambling, or drinking, because Islamic doctrine is opposed to these evils. Gambling is perfectly all right in other countries. During the Diem regime Catholic morals, more specifically the particularly puritan Catholic morals of Madam Nhu, were the standards a Vietnamese play had to meet. An official of the Saigon Censor Board told me of a famous Chinese play that initially was disapproved for cai luong production because in the play the king marries three wives. According to the Code of the Family, a law passed by parliament in 1959 (popularly known as "Madam Nhu's Law"), multiple wives were declared illegal in Vietnam. Censors interpreted the law to apply to fictional as well as real life. Before the play could be performed two marriages had to be bowdlerized from the script. (Imagine a Western government's ordering Oedipus' incestuous marriage to his mother expurgated from *Oedipus Rex* on the grounds that incest violates Christian morality!) A Confucian view of the well-ordered society is upheld by censors in Cambodia. If a play contains a scene in which a citizen acts disrespectfully toward his ruler, or a pupil disobeys the instructions of his teacher, or a child strikes its parents, or material goods rather than knowledge are made the chief object of the hero's strivings, this scene will be cut as immoral.

Normally censorship is accomplished without the need to resort to criminal proceedings against violators of the law. The authority to forbid performance is usually sufficient to ensure compliance from the great majority of troupes. A professional troupe cannot long exist if denied the right to perform. If censor or the police give an erring troupe a warning or two this usually takes care of the matter. For those troupes which hold political, social, or moral beliefs that run counter to those of the government three courses of action are open: they can abandon their views and accept what the government says; they can disband; or they can pretend compliance while covertly attempting to present as much of their message to the audience as possible. Most troupes probably do the first. Some disband. How many continue to oppose their government surreptitiously I cannot say, but a degree of government criticism does appear on stage in every country. I remember vividly the cai luong play I saw produced in September 1963, about three weeks after a high school girl participating in an anti-Diem student demonstration had been killed by riot police in the Saigon central market. In the play an evil minister carries out a ruthless campaign to destroy his enemies. He gouges out the eyes of the good prince. He stabs to death a little girl who in childish innocence speaks out against him. The girl's father, played by the troupe clown, gathers up the crumpled, blood-stained body of his daughter in his arms. He walks down to the footlights. Tears streaming from his eyes, he holds out to the audience the body of the girl saying, "When will this cruel tyranny end?" I do not know whether the scene slipped by the censors or whether the troupe interpolated it into the play after obtaining censorship approval. But it surely was intended as a comment on and criticism of the August 25th killing of the girl, who, since that time, has become a martyr of the anti-Diem uprising. The chief clown of a large cai luong troupe spent some time in a Saigon jail for making a remark that was interpreted as being disrespectful to Madam Nhu, and in Indonesia, a wayang orang clown was sent to jail briefly for implying Soekarno was wasting the country's money on GANEFO and other prestige events. Both clowns are out of jail now and performing.

Censorship is accepted as an unpleasant but unavoidable fact of life by most people in the theatre. Some complaints are politically motivated, especially in Vietnam and Indonesia. One also hears a great deal of criticism in these two countries of censorship procedures. In Vietnam troupe managers complain that, contrary to what officials of the Central Censorship Board may say, scripts are often rejected without any grounds being given for their rejection. There is no way to correct such scripts, and it is all a very frustrating and time-consuming business. In Indonesia one hears complaint after complaint about how complex the administration of censorship is. It is ironic that most of the laws being used to censor theatre today were put on the statute books by former colonial regimes. The Indonesian censorship law is a Dutch law. Vietnamese, Cambodian, and Laotian censorship laws are French laws. The Malaysian law is British. A few decades ago national leaders were denouncing these laws as instruments of colonial oppression; now they inflict these same laws upon their own countrymen.

How effective are attempts at government control of theatre in Southeast Asia? In a general way control is effective. Plays which directly question government policy are not performed anywhere. Sniping at the authorities continues but on a limited scale. An actor in Indonesia told me, "While there are clever clowns, and brave ones, a point can be made without the police catching on." Sophisticated languages like Vietnamese and Javanese are well suited to double-entendre jokes. If challenged about the meaning of a doubtful joke, a clown can point to the innocent meaning and plead ignorance. The fact that most performances are ad-libbed also makes it difficult for a government to know exactly what is going on. Still this kind of criticism is minor. Occasionally censorship will backfire. I once heard a wayang kulit puppeteer string together a series of government slogans ("Support Manipol," "Support USDEK," "Crush Malaysia," and others) along with scathing remarks about the corruption of government officials, the high cost of living, and the appalling condition of Javanese roads. By mouthing government-approved propaganda he was buying immunity for his critical remarks. In another case, perhaps more typical, a small local ketoprak troupe became so conditioned to inserting only those political slogans that were supplied by the local Ministry of Information official that when the government cut out this program the troupe ceased to put any political content into its plays at all. It would like to. It strongly supports the government. But it is paralyzed by the fear that it will say the wrong thing and be punished.

Four over-all effects result from government control and regulation of theatre. First, government control discourages legitimate exploration of new themes and ideas via the dramatic medium to the great detriment of theatre art. Discussion of contemporary events is scarcely possible, for such discussion can be construed as criticism of the status quo.

Second, to avoid censorship problems troupes tend to rely on the old, and presumably safe, classics of the past. This is neither good nor bad in itself perhaps, but the discouragement of new plays is one of the reasons for the continued popularity of classic plays. In this case censorship is the handmaiden of conservatism in both politics and art.

Third, when governments attempt to persuade troupes to include favorable propaganda in their productions, vulgarization of theatre art is inevitable. It is a travesty of art to stick a modern political song in the middle of a traditional wayang golek performance or to shout out a government slogan at the close of a ludruk performance. The directors of BAKOKSI, who are dedicated equally to spreading Communist ideas and to improving the art of ketoprak, recognize their dilemma. They conceive as a major goal educating the village masses, but in order to do this they know they must debase their art. To a sophisticated city audience the actor can say "we wash with stones" but to the country audience the actor must spell it all out, saying "we oppressed peasants are so poor we must wash with stones because we have no money to buy soap." At least these BAKOKSI artists acknowledge the contradiction of their position, and try to find artistic justification for including their propaganda. But governments are not so concerned. When a government urges an apolitical troupe to "carry the message," the result cannot be artistically satisfactory. The troupe does not care and will not try to find an artistic rationale for including the message. Art can be propaganda, but both art and propaganda should be the products of the same commitment.

And fourth, when governments press demands on theatre troupes, it makes them more conscious of their grievances toward the government. In Vietnam a commonly expressed feeling is: "They tax us, they censor us, and what do they give us? Nothing. The French built us three national theatres. Our government turns them into meeting halls." I met three wayang orang troupe leaders who said the government unjustly had confiscated their theatre buildings (one for Radio Republic Indonesia, one for the army, and one for an unknown purpose) and forced them to move into less desirable buildings where it is harder for them to earn a living. The most bitter comment I heard in all of Southeast Asia came from a sandiwara manager. "The best time sandiwara ever had was under the Japanese. We had to do what they said but they got us lights, generators, costumes, and even built us theatres to play in. We were charged a 10 percent 'interest' fee to pay for the equipment we got. Now our government charges us 27 percent tax and we get nothing in return. I'd rather be under the Japanese." Whether these criticisms and many others like them are justified is not the point.* The point is that government interference, government control, and government regulation of the theatre, where it exists, makes theatre people conscious of government power. When troupes face problems it is natural for them to lay at least part of the blame for their troubles, justifiably or not, at the seat of this power—the government.

---

* In the Philippines, where there is no official censorship, and in Thailand and to a lesser extent in Cambodia and Laos, where governments give at least some economic support to theatre, the feeling of resentment toward government is less strong.

CHAPTER 12

Economics

A professional theatre troupe is a business organization. It is expected to make a profit for its owner (or owners), and provide a livelihood for its members. A troupe may be a family business, it may be owned and operated by one person, it may be jointly owned by troupe members, or it may be just one holding of a large capitalistic enterprise. The only troupes in Southeast Asia that I know of which are not business organizations are the Royal Cambodian Ballet and the Royal Lao Ballet, both of which are totally subsidized by royal treasuries.

To discuss the economics of theatre operation, meaningful comparisons between a half-dozen different currencies must be made. A common way of doing this is to translate local currencies into U.S. dollars, using either the official or the free-market (black market) exchange rate. Neither exchange rate helps explain the economics of Southeast Asian theatre, however, for both reflect international trading policies (the former reflects the government's view, the latter the merchant's). What is needed is a measure of the comparative domestic buying powers of local currencies. The method I have decided upon is unorthodox, perhaps, but practical. Since rice is the staple food everywhere in Southeast Asia—everyone buys it, everyone uses it—I have converted local currency figures into the equivalent number of kilograms of rice that amount of currency would buy in the local economy. In this way the relative economic condition of troupes in various countries can be compared.

Table 6. Estimated average nightly gross income of troupes.

Country and type	Type of currency	Local currency			Kilograms of rice[a]		
		Well-known	Medium-sized	Small	Well-known	Medium-sized	Small
Indonesia							
Wayang orang	rupiah	60,000	15,000	—	400	100	—
Ketoprak, ludruk, sandiwara	rupiah	35,000	10,000	2,000	230	70	13
Wayang kulit	rupiah	40,000	10,000	1,500	270	70	10
Laos							
Mohlam luong	kip	20,000	10,000	4,000	500	250	100
Malaysia							
Bangsawan	Malay dollar	150	75	25	150	75	25
Chinese opera	Malay dollar	1,000	700	300	1,000	700	300
Thailand							
Likay	bhat	3,000	1,500	700	1,500	750	350
Nang talung	bhat	1,500	1,000	500	750	500	250
Lakon jatri	bhat	1,500	1,000	700	750	500	350
Vietnam							
Cai luong	piaster	80,000	20,000	4,000	11,100	2,900	570
Hat boi	piaster	10,000	5,000	1,000	1,400	710	140

[a]The approximate retail market price of rice in late 1963 and early 1964 was: Vietnam, 7 piaster per kilogram; Indonesia, 150 rupiah per kilogram; Thailand, 2 bhat per kilogram; Laos, 40 kip per kilogram; and Malaysia, 1 Malay dollar per kilogram.

INCOME

Table 6 shows some estimated nightly gross incomes for well-known troupes, medium-sized troupes, and small troupes, first in local currencies, then in terms of the number of kilograms of rice which that amount of currency would buy. The real value of the gross income—in terms of rice-buying power—of cai luong troupes far surpasses that of any other kind of troupe. Ketoprak, sandiwara, ludruk, and bangsawan troupes have the smallest real gross incomes. On an average night the well-known cai luong troupe will gross 65 to 70 times as much as the well-known bangsawan troupe.

The real value of a commercially supported troupe's nightly gross income is determined by three factors: the number of people who buy tickets; the price of tickets; and the current purchasing power of local currency. Table 7, which examines in more detail the incomes of a few well-known troupes of differ-

Table 7. Real gross nightly income of selected well-known troupes.

| Type of troupe | Average audience | Average ticket value | | Value of gross income in kilo. of rice |
		Local currency	Kilo. of rice	
Cai luong	1,400	55 piaster	8	11,100
Wayang orang	1,200	50 rupiah	0.34	400
Ketoprak	1,000	35 rupiah	0.23	230
Likay	750	4 bhat	2	1,500
Hat boi	400	25 piaster	3.5	1,400
Bangsawan	400	40 Malay cents	0.4	150

ent genres, shows why it is that some types of troupes are well off and others are not. A well-known cai luong troupe has a large real income because it attracts a large audience willing to pay high ticket prices; a bangsawan troupe is poverty-stricken because it attracts a fairly small audience that pays little for its tickets. Although well-known cai luong, ketoprak, and wayang orang troupes play to almost equally large audiences, the real value of the cai luong troupe's gross income is from thirty to fifty times greater than that of the Indonesian troupes, for, whereas the average cai luong ticket (costing 55 piaster) will buy about eight kilograms of rice in Vietnam, the average wayang orang ticket (costing 50 rupiah) will buy only one-third of a kilogram of rice in Indonesia. The wayang orang or ketoprak troupe plays to large and devoted audiences, but to little avail. Its income just doesn't buy much in Indonesia's present inflated economy. On the other hand, a likay or hat boi troupe, which plays to a considerably smaller audience than a wayang orang or ketoprak troupe, ends up better off because each likay or hat boi ticket buys ten to fifteen times as much rice as a theatre ticket in Indonesia.

Comparing different sized troupes, regardless of genre, a large, well-known troupe commands not only absolutely greater income than a small troupe, as one would expect, but it also commands proportionally greater income as well. For purposes of comparison, Table 8 examines the typical nightly gross incomes for three ketoprak troupes located in central Java. Not only do

Table 8. Real gross nightly income of troupes of different sizes.

Troupe size	Average size audience	Average ticket price (rupiah)	Average nightly income (rupiah)	Number of troupe members
Well-known troupe	1,000	40	40,000	85
Medium-sized troupe	600	25	15,000	55
Small troupe	150	15	2,250	30

about seven times as many people come to see the well-known troupe on any given night as come to see the small troupe, but each person in the audience pays about three times as much for a ticket. As a result, the gross nightly income of the well-known troupe is roughly twenty times as great as the small troupe. Although these figures are taken from ketoprak, they could apply to most other types of troupes, and other countries as well. If a visual diagram were drawn, representing gross income of theatre troupes, it would be in the form of a triangle, with a few large, excellent, well-known, well-financed, stable and prosperous troupes of each genre at the apex, a considerable number of reasonably good, medium-sized, and fairly well-off troupes occupying the middle, and many scruffy little troupes, artistically and economically poverty-stricken, filling in the broad base of the triangle.

I have been discussing "averages" and "typical" nightly incomes, but it should be recognized that an average or typical figure is at best a rough approximation that does not reflect the very great variation of income that actually occurs. Only a few of the largest troupes have incomes that are relatively stable throughout the year. For the rest—perhaps 90 percent of the professional theatre—income fluctuates widely from season to season, and even from day to day. Most medium-sized and small troupes live, travel, and perform in country towns and villages. Southeast Asia is primarily agricultural, and, when harvest time comes and farmers have cash, they go to see plays. Harvest time usually corresponds with the dry season, so that it is by far the most prosperous time of year for theatre troupes. The worst time of the year is the rainy season, when, for months at a time, monsoon rains drench the tropical countryside. The rainy season varies from area to area (December to March in Java, June to September in Cambodia, October to January in southeastern Thailand, for example), but whenever the rains come, theatre activity outside the big cities comes to a sodden halt. In Cambodia and in Thailand daily rains make such a thunderous din on tin theatre roofs that not a sound can be heard from the stage. Javanese thatched theatre roofs are no match for the deluges that fall from the skies; water pours through roofs onto the stage and makes a quagmire of earthen floors in the auditorium. Nowhere do audiences want to dress up, venture out, and then be caught in a downpour. In most places troupes cease to perform. Puppet performances, usually held outdoors, are set aside for sunnier times. Large troupes are able to set aside reserve funds to tide themselves over this slack season, but small troupes almost never can. The rainy season is a hard, lean time. I visited a ketoprak troupe, whose theatre was flooded under a foot of water; it had not performed for six nights running. A sandiwara troupe had given only five performances in the previous three-week period.

In Indonesia, Thailand, and Cambodia a troupe usually does not have to pay theatre rent if a performance is rained out, but in Vietnam some rent is charged regardless of whether or not a troupe performs. For example, the largest legitimate theatre building in Saigon usually rents for 12,000 piaster per day, but only 1,500 piaster if a performance is rained out. Managers in Vietnam know exactly how many tickets they must sell in order to make it worthwhile to perform during the rain. If a troupe sells fewer than this minimum it cancels the performance, refunds ticket money, and gladly pays the reduced rent as the lesser of two evils. A troupe cannot prevent the monsoon rains from falling, but there are some things it can do to survive them. In Vietnam and in Thailand rainy and dry seasons alternate in different parts of the country at different times of the year. Some cai luong and likay troupes make it a regular policy to follow the dry season around the country. Or a troupe may move to a major city where audiences are more likely to venture forth, even though it rains, than are their country cousins. A troupe which performs both commercially and by contract (communal support) may try to get contract performances set up for the rainy season. If it rains the contracting person or group will suffer the loss rather than the troupe. During the dry season this troupe would try to perform on its own initiative so as to benefit from the large audiences that traditionally attend theatre at that time of year. Of course the person or group hiring a troupe will follow the same line of reasoning, but to the opposite conclusion.

The real value of a troupe's income is partly determined by the purchasing power of money within the domestic economy. Another practical matter which determines the real value of a troupe's income is the size of the troupe. Given a certain amount of gross income, the larger the troupe is, the more demands there will be for spending that income. For example, ludruk and ketoprak troupes earn similar nightly gross incomes. But the average ludruk troupe has perhaps thirty members, compared to fifty in a ketoprak troupe. Because of its size, the ordinary ludruk troupe is less expensive to operate than the ordinary ketoprak troupe; consequently, it is in a much better economic position. A small troupe, because it is small, has fewer expenses than a large troupe. However, its reduced level of expenses is almost never sufficient to offset the proportionally larger income which a large troupe is able to earn. In Table 8 the large troupe has about three times as many members as the small troupe. This reduces the previous twenty-to-one financial advantage of the large troupe to something like seven to one. The only way the large and the small troupe would be on fairly equal financial terms would be if the small troupe were one-twentieth the size of the large troupe, that is, an impossibly small four people. Puppet troupes are a special case. Because they are relatively small, they can subsist on less income than can most live theatre troupes. Thus, a nang talung troupe of four to six members is better off with its 1,500-bhat gross income than is a likay troupe of twenty members with a 3,000-bhat income, and a wayang kulit troupe in Java of twenty or twenty-five members earning 40,000 rupiah is much better off than a wayang orang troupe of one hundred members earning 80,000 rupiah. In both cases the large, live theatre troupes have double the nightly income of the puppet troupes, but they also have four to five times more troupe members to support.

EXPENSES

A troupe's major expenditures are taxes, rent, salaries, production expenses, and profit. We don't know when the first entertainment tax was levied in Southeast Asia, but the first record of one dates from 1656, when the King of Mataram in Java decreed that each time a dalang performed wayang kulit he had to pay a fixed fee to the royal treasury. Today the most common theatre tax is a ticket tax, which is levied by governments in every country except Laos. The ticket tax varies from country to country and within countries as well. In Thailand it is about 20 percent of the value of the ticket, in Cambodia about 20–25 percent, and in Vietnam 20 percent for cai luong and 10 percent for hat boi. In Singapore the tax ranges from 25 percent to 40 percent, depending on the price of a ticket—the higher the ticket price the higher the percentage of tax. Ticket tax in Indonesia differs widely from district to district inasmuch as it is assessed and collected by local governments. In the district of Tjilatjap on the south coast of Java, there is no tax at all. As a direct result eight ketoprak troupes perform in that district. The highest tax I am aware of is a levy of 40 percent in one district in eastern Java (23 percent district tax plus 17 percent city tax). In other districts of Java and Sunda taxes run between 25 and 35 percent. Wherever there is a ticket tax theatre people complain about it. A commonly expressed view is that it is hypocritical for a government to claim to support national art and culture, as all governments in Southeast Asia do, and at the same time tax theatre troupes. In fact, governments often use tax powers to help theatre. In Vietnam the usual 20 percent tax on movies and theatre has been reduced to 10 percent for hat boi. Movie tax in Kuala Lumpur, Malaysia, is 30 percent while theatre tax is 20 percent. In at least half-a-dozen districts in Java and Sunda movie tax is one-third to half again as much as theatre tax. The aim in each instance is to assist live theatre. Local officials in Cambodia often completely waive ticket taxes in order to encourage troupes to play in the provinces. When performances are for charity, taxes are waived in every country.

A second kind of tax, levied less often, is personal income tax. In Laos, where there is no ticket tax, managers are required to pay a yearly tax based on the gross income of the troupe. The amount is small—usually one percent of gross income. In theory at least a troupe manager in Vietnam is held responsible for paying the income taxes of his troupe members. In practice, however, it is difficult for the government to collect such taxes from a manager. When several years ago the government attempted to collect five years back taxes from a famous cai luong actress-manager, it created something of a *cause célèbre*. According to the tax office, she owed 17,000,000 piaster for herself and the 104 members of the troupe. She didn't have the money, so she announced she would kill herself. Radio Hanoi and Radio Peking jubilantly claimed this as another example of the Diem government's persecuting artists. Soon the tax was reduced to 100,000 piaster, the actress-manager paid, and the matter was closed. Halfhearted attempts are made in Indonesia to collect personal income taxes from performers. Actors are so often on the move it is difficult to know how much income they have received. Dalang are more apt to be assessed personal income taxes for they are permanent residents, and often landowners, and their approximate income can be estimated by local tax officials. In any case, the amount of personal income tax paid by any performer in Indonesia is low, probably no more than 5 percent of his income. Given these circumstances, the tax burden is borne almost entirely by those troupes which sell tickets directly to the general public—cai luong, hat boi, sandiwara, and most likay, lakon bassac, ketoprak, ludruk, wayang orang, and bangsawan troupes. Very little if any taxes are paid by troupes which depend upon communal support or indirect commercial support, that is, troupes which do not sell tickets—wayang kulit, wayang golek, nang talung, ardja, barong, and most lakon jatri troupes.

Theatre rent is a major item of expense for most live troupes. (For puppet troupes rent is not an item of expense for the contracting party provides a building or a stage at no charge.) Rental may be a fixed amount per night or a percentage of gross income (usually computed after taxes), and can amount to as little as 5 percent or as much as 50 percent. The average troupe probably spends 30 to 35 percent of its income on theatre rental. A troupe may pay one rental charge, which includes the building, electricity, chairs, and even some stage equipment, or it may pay separate fees for each. A few examples illustrate how widely rental practices diverge in different countries. A large cai luong troupe pays anywhere from 7,000 to 20,000 piaster theatre rental per night, depending on income; only a few top troupes can afford such high rent. A ketoprak theatre building owner told me he "hires and fires his troupes at will," keeping 45 percent of their gross income as his share. Another ketoprak troupe found an excellent spot in eastern Java two years ago and intends to stay there as long as it can: out of an average 10,000 rupiah nightly income it pays only 17 percent tax and about 5 percent (550 rupiah) nightly theatre rental. Even though the local "charity committee" takes another 15 percent, the troupe is well off. A movie house manager in Thailand said likay troupes liked to play there but seldom could afford to because they not only had to pay the normal rental for the building but they also had to pay the owner an amount equivalent to the profit he was forgoing from the usual movie. A small hat boi troupe in Saigon plays in a tiny Taoist dinh or temple because the 200-piaster nightly rental charge (out of a 900-piaster income) is the most reasonable it can find.

Its members' salaries are a troupe's largest single item of expense. Whether a troupe is large or small, rich or poor seems to make little difference: 40 to 50 percent of a live troupe's gross income goes for salaries and 75 to 80 percent of a puppet troupe's income. A member's salary ordinarily is determined by two things: the member's status in the troupe and the income of the troupe. A very few troupes apparently divide salary money into equal shares for all (at least a few troupes affiliated with BAKOK-SI and the Ludruk Association say they do), and some pay fixed salaries by the day or by the month (the Thai National Theatre and some large cai luong troupes follow this practice), but the great majority of troupes pay their members according to rank (seniority, artistic skill, or importance within the troupe), on a sliding scale that varies nightly in proportion to the troupe's gross income. As every troupe works under a slightly different arrangement, it would be impossible and unnecessary to try to describe them all. Instead let me give in Table 9 a detailed illustration of how both factors are taken into consideration in determining salary. Members of this large wayang orang troupe in

Table 9. Average nightly salaries paid members of one large wayang orang troupe.

Salary class	Type of member	Number of members	Salary rate per 1000- rupiah income	Average 50,000 rupiah nightly income	Average nightly salary (in rupiah)
I	Star actors and actresses, artistic directors, dalang, stage manager	10	$12\frac{1}{2}$	50	625
II	Supporting actors and actresses	10	7	50	350
III	Minor actors and actresses	40	$3\frac{1}{2}$	50	175
IV	Gamelan musicians and singers, supervisor stage technicians	40	$2\frac{1}{2}$	50	125
V	Apprentice actors and actresses, stagehands	40	$1\frac{1}{2}$	50	75

central Java are ranked into five classes; the few members in Class I earn about nine times as much salary as Class V members. Musicians and singers receive little more than apprentice actors and actresses and stagehands. When the troupe's nightly gross income rises, members' salaries rise proportionally and when income falls, members' salaries also fall. Each troupe member, therefore, shares to an extent the economic risks and the rewards of management.

If we compare the salaries paid by large troupes with salaries paid by small troupes, we find an extremely interesting situation: proportionally the spread of salaries in small troupes is much less than it is in large troupes. Table 10 shows average nightly salaries paid members of a large and a small ketoprak troupe. A Class I actor in the large troupe is paid three and a half times as much as a Class III actor in the same troupe, but in the small troupe he is paid only one-third more. Why is this so? I believe it is because, with a relatively large income the large troupe can reward its best people extremely well. The small troupe has such

Table 10. Average nightly salaries paid members of a large and a small ketoprak troupe.

Large troupe		Small troupe	
Salary class	Nightly salary (rupiah)	Salary class	Nightly salary (rupiah)
I	625	I	50
II	350	II	40
III	175	III	35

a small income that it cannot reward its top people with much more salary than its lower ranking members. The absolute salaries paid by the large troupe are much, much larger than the salaries paid by the small troupe (the comparison given here is typical). The Class I actor of the large troupe earns twelve times as much as the Class I actor in the small troupe; even the Class III actor in the large troupe earns three and a half times as much as the Class I actor in the small troupe. The nightly salary of 35 rupiah earned by the Class III actor in the small troupe is not even a living wage. Because of the comparatively weak economic position of a small live troupe, a good actor seldom sticks with a small troupe through his career or tries to make it famous. Instead the good actors move on to larger and larger troupes constantly seeking higher salaries. This is particularly true of actors in lakon bassac ketoprak, wayang orang, ludruk, sandiwara, and bangsawan.

How much is a troupe member's salary worth? What is the buying power of his income? Table 11 lists some typical salaries

Table 11. Typical nightly salaries paid leading actors.

Type	In local currency	In kilograms of rice
Cai luong matinee idol	3,300 piaster	470
Famous wayang kulit puppeteer	20,000 rupiah	135
Leading likay actor	30 bhat	30
Leading mohlam luong actor	1,000 kip	25
Leading wayang orang actor	625 rupiah	5

earned by top-ranking actors in several theatre forms. A leading cai luong actor-singer is one of the highest paid people in Vietnam, especially since he performs and is paid a salary almost every day of the year. The wayang kulit puppeteer (as well as the wayang golek and the nang talung puppeteer) earns a handsome salary each time he performs. However, one night's income must last several days for he does not perform every night. A puppeteer ordinarily takes around half of the troupe's income for himself—for he is owner, manager, and chief performer—and divides the other half among his assistants and musicians. Top mohlam luong, likay, lakon bassac, and Chinese opera actors earn a comfortable if not extravagant living. The star of a wayang orang troupe makes considerably less in terms of buying power than his colleagues in other countries, and leading actors in ketoprak, ludruk, and sandiwara earn even less. In addition to receiving cash salaries, actors often are given free quarters, furnished either by the troupe or by the theatre owner.

Production expenses are a fourth type of expenditure for all troupes. This includes costs of costumes, lighting equipment, and musical instruments, expenses for constructing scenery and properties, and the costs of transporting a troupe from one location to another. Perhaps 5 to 15 percent of a troupe's gross income goes to production expenses.

The fifth and final share of income, if any remains, is allotted to profit. Profits go to the financial supporter of the troupe: a high-level financier in Vietnam, Cambodia, or Indonesia; a Chinese businessman in Vietnam or Indonesia; an ex-actor-owner in Thailand, Malaysia, or Indonesia; or the actor-owner in every country. Business enterprises everywhere usually keep the amount of their profits a well-guarded secret. Presumably, some troupes earn a significant profit but it is difficult information to ferret out. Hard-luck stories, on the other hand, are a dime a dozen. One of the most complete stories of woe I heard was from the female backer of two extremely poor hat boi troupes operating in a squalid, foul-smelling Taoist dinh in the northern outskirts of Saigon. Up until a few months before the troupes had been playing in different dinh, but one was ejected and had no place to go so she invited the whole troupe to join the one she had been managing and backing for the past several years. Within the past three months she had lost 50,000 piaster, she claimed. Tickets cost only 20 or 30 piaster and so few people attended they seldom took in more than 1,000–1,500 piaster a night. She paid two or three times this amount each night to the actors, and where it will end she could not say. On the other hand, several troupe managers in Indonesia praised their backers for not taking any profit for themselves when times were bad and for allowing all income after taxes, rent, and production costs to be applied to actors' salaries.

Most large troupes—whether the Thai National Theatre, wayang orang, cai luong, ketoprak, likay or Chinese opera—undoubtedly return some profit to their owners, but the largest profits earned by anyone concerned with theatre performances accrue to the sponsoring committees that bring in troupes to perform on indirect-commercial support agreements. Temple committees in Thailand, Cambodia, and Laos keep 30 to 50 percent of the gross income earned by the likay, lakon jatri, mohlam luong, or lakon bassac troupes they engage to perform. Local sponsoring committees in Indonesia make even larger profits. When the main BAKOKSI troupe, Krido Mardi, played in Surabaya the nightly gross income was between 100,000 and 120,000 rupiah, of which Krido Mardi received 30,000 rupiah as its performance fee. Even after deducting its relatively small expenses for theatre rental and miscellaneous matters, the committee realized a profit of 60,000 to 80,000 rupiah nightly, or 60 to 65 percent of the gross income. When one of the major wayang orang troupes performed in Jogjakarta, in 1964, its local sponsoring committee paid the troupe 50,000 rupiah and kept for itself approximately 100,000 rupiah out of an average nightly gross income of 150,000 rupiah. A committee can engineer these exceptionally large gross incomes because as a charity it pays no performance tax and because it sells "invitations" at five to ten times the usual ticket price. Troupes do not object to charity committees making this much profit for they still receive their standard fees and have no financial worries. Troupes also have built-in political protection when they perform at county fairs in Thailand, at temple fairs in Thailand, Laos, and Cambodia, and for evening fairs or charity in Indonesia because local government agencies are prominently represented on the hiring committees. The committee set up by the mayor of a district town in central Java to sponsor the appearance of a ketoprak troupe is fairly typical:

Chairman	Mayor (self-appointed)
Deputy Chairman	District Military Commander
Member	City Chief of Police
Member	Chairman, National Front
Member	Principal, City High School
Member	Head, District Red Cross
Member	Wealthiest non-Chinese merchant in the district

The money collected by the Jogjakarta committee, mentioned before, was apportioned as follows: Fund for "Volunteers to Crush Malaysia," 50 percent; Radio Stars of 1964, 25 percent; Victims of Drought in Gunung Kidul (a poor area southeast of Jogjakarta), 20 percent; Public Works, City of Jogjakarta, 5 percent. Who could possibly doubt the civic propriety of these performances?

ECONOMIC PROBLEMS

Troupes often face economic problems which are not of their making but which affect their operations and their very existence. One of the most pressing is inflation, which exists to some degree in all areas of Southeast Asia. It is a serious problem in Vietnam, Laos, and Indonesia. A cai luong troupe manager in Vietnam estimated that while the cost of producing a play has increased by about 40 percent within the past five years, ticket prices and hence income have increased by only 10 to 20 percent. Inflation, spurred on by a wartime economy, is the cause of both price hikes. Accurate figures are hard to obtain in Laos, but inflation there is fairly severe; as in Vietnam it is largely due to wartime conditions. One of the results of inflation in Laos is that it encourages mohlam luong troupes to move back and forth across the Thai-Lao border, first earning money in Thailand, where they are paid in hard-currency bhat, and then spending the money in Laos, where the Thai bhat brings an advantageous rate of exchange. If hired on contract in Laos, a mohlam luong troupe may demand its pay in Thai bhat rather than in inflated Lao kip.

By far the most serious inflation is in Indonesia. During one ten-year period (1953–1963) the cost of food increased by 2000 percent, or twenty times, in Indonesia.[1] On some consumer items prices have increased one hundred times. Such runaway inflation has brought catastrophic conditions to the theatre. No troupe has been able to raise ticket prices enough to keep up with the inflationary spiral, for if any were to do so, it would price itself out of an audience. Instead, troupes are living, somehow, on constantly shrinking real incomes. According to one troupe manager, in 1947 it was possible to buy a kilogram of rice, costing three rupiah, by selling two theatre tickets, at one-and-a-half rupiah each, while in 1963 they had to sell six tickets at twenty-five rupiah each to buy a kilogram of rice costing one hundred and fifty rupiah. In other words, the purchasing power of this troupe's income sixteen years ago was three times what it is now. The individual actor is even worse off. In 1949 an average nightly salary for a wayang orang actor was fifteen rupiah; in 1963 it was one hundred rupiah. In 1949 the actor could buy five kilograms of rice with a single day's wage; now an actor's daily wage will buy only two-thirds of a kilogram of rice. Since a person eats half a kilogram of rice a day, this is scarcely more than a subsistence wage. Actors in small troupes who earn 50, 40, and even as little as 25 rupiah a day cannot live on their salary alone. They must work during the day at some other job—usually as a day laborer, fisherman, or peddler—to keep body and soul together.

War is a fact of life that cannot be ignored by troupes in Laos and Vietnam. Areas in which troupes previously performed are now occupied by Communist forces or guerillas. Between 40 and 60 percent of the land area of Laos and Vietnam is under the effective control of the Communists. It seems that mohlam luong troupes rarely venture into Communist-controlled areas in Laos. In Vietnam it is physically possible for cai luong and hat boi troupes to travel into and out of Vietcong areas and some troupes have done this fairly regularly. Apparently troupes have never been purposely molested by the Vietcong. However, as the Vietcong increases its terrorist attacks on trains, buses, and trucks, it becomes increasingly hazardous for troupes to try to travel through rebel-held territory. Economically speaking, troupes are injured because part of their potential audience is closed off to them. At the same time it seems likely that the present high level of prosperity of theatre in both countries is partly the product of a wartime boom economy and a wartime atmosphere in which escape entertainment is widely sought after.

PUBLICITY

Plays are not extensively publicized in Southeast Asia. Advertisement through the mass media is limited to a very few situations. The Thai National Theatre and half-a-dozen large wayang orang troupes advertise performances in paid daily newspaper ads. Radio Phnom Penh carries on its morning newscasts unpaid announcements of lakon bassac performances in the capital city. In Saigon large cai luong troupes use radio, newspapers, posters, handbills, and sheet music to promote their productions. A few medium-sized troupes, especially in Indonesia and Vietnam, may hang a banner across the main street of a town, giving the name of the troupe and dates of performance. Smaller troupes may hire a horse cart or even small boys to parade around town to call attention to the fact that a troupe is in town. Otherwise most troupes place a sign or two in front of the theatre on which the name of the play to be performed each evening is written. And that is about all. Theatre troupes do not employ much mass advertising because it is expensive and because managers see no point in telling people who live hundreds of miles away about a performance when only nearby residents will attend. In rural areas residents learn that a troupe is in town by actually seeing the troupe or by word of mouth. Even in large cities word of mouth appears to be one of the most effective means of advertising theatre.

Of all the printed advertisements I have seen, only those of the Thai National Theatre emphasize the classic nature of their productions as a major selling point. Even when other troupes perform classic or traditional plays, more often than not advertising is directed at popular tastes and is couched in the universal language of barkers and pitchmen. Here is the way one of the finest wayang orang troupes in Java advertised a performance of the well-known wayang play *Srikandi Ngedan:*

Here's what you've been waiting for!
Now! At last!
TONIGHT!
Tumult in Jogja's north square!!! The stuff of which horror is made: "MAD SRIKANDI"! This time more frantic than ever! Hotter than . . . fever!! The performance this time by MISS SUTIAH! Try to imagine . . . Sutiah, yes, Sutiah . . . from Surakarta . . . being this wild!! Horror . . . can you stay away from our stage tonight?!? Srikandi the source of gossip . . . her foolish caprices . . . her songs . . . yes, everything she does . . . willful . . . selfish!! More than that . . . beautiful . . . lovely . . . enchanting . . . and . . . horrifying . . . !!

Vietnamese advertisements appeal equally to lower tastes, but they do so in a sentimental style that is typically Vietnamese. The following is excerpted from a handbill publicizing a contemporary cai luong play.

In her letter she writes: "Darling, marry and find consolation and joy. Build a life of your own and don't ever think of me. Many a time I wonder why God did not make of me a mad, thoughtless girl so I might not be in such distress. Many a time I have thought to undertake the orders of God, but how could I? For your grief means the universe is dark for me. Can I change God's power? I must die to be loyal to you. And with these lines I still don't know whether or not I have recalled in my heart the true image of the man I love. Your loving and grieving sweetheart, Lu Trang Dai." Does Lu Trang Dai end her life? Does her lover marry the other woman? See the last act of "Falling Snow" and you will know.

CHAPTER 13

The Audience

No single social factor is more important to the continuing existence of theatre in Southeast Asia than the audience. To paraphrase Mao Tze Tung, the audience is the ocean and theatre troupes are the fish that swim therein. Without the ocean, the fish will die; without the audience, the troupe will die. When a troupe is functioning successfully, theatre and audience are complementary halves of the total theatre situation. The theatre reflects the audience and the audience is a kind of mirror image of the theatre. Important though the audience is, at this point we know only the most general facts about the 150,000,000 people who see plays in Southeast Asia.

AUDIENCE COMPOSITION

The size of any given audience depends upon many factors. It depends upon reputation: a good troupe is certain to draw a larger audience than a poorer one. It depends upon the weather and how far the spectator must travel to get to the theatre: if it rains, the spectator almost certainly will not go out, or if the theatre is more than two or three miles away he is not likely to. It depends upon competing entertainment: a troupe performing in the countryside almost never faces competition but in town movies or another theatre troupe may siphon off potential audience. It depends upon whether people have ready cash or not: if it is payday at the factory or harvest time in the village more people will go to the theatre than if it is between paydays or between harvest seasons. It depends upon the night of the week: like theatres everywhere in the world, Saturday night sees full houses with audiences jamming the aisles but on week-nights most troupes are happy to play to half-full houses. Psychological factors are also important, though difficult to measure accurately. In spite of falling living standards in Indonesia, audiences are larger than ever before. Several actors and managers explained that times are so bad that people want to escape and so they seek entertainment. A serious young student of theatre in Vietnam said: "Theatres have never been so full. Sons, brothers, fathers are being killed every day. It isn't easy for the common people. They need to see their ideals vindicated on stage. I'm talking about their beliefs, not how much money they have in their pockets."

Men and women of every age, occupation, and social class go see plays in Southeast Asia, but certain kinds of people tend to go to certain kinds of plays. More men than women usually see wayang kulit or wayang golek. It may be that the high philosophic tone of wayang and the many scenes of heroic combat appeal to masculine tastes. Men also go to wayang golek in Sunda to see and hear their favorite female singers (pesinden). Audiences on the mainland are predominantly female. This is true of most hat boi, lakon bassac, likay, mohlam luong, and zat pwe performances. Women completely dominate likay. At a likay performance in southern Thailand I was one of seven men in an audience of about two hundred and fifty; the rest were women. In the first-class seats six or seven elderly women held court, each surrounded by her group of younger women. At likay the women gabble, eat, drink, spit betel juice on the earthen floor, call raucously across the auditorium to each other, and in imperious voices order vendors to bring them food or soda-pop, even during the performance. I estimate the average audience for likay is 85 to 95 percent female, and for lakon bassac, hat boi, and mohlam luong 60 to 80 percent female.

Middle-aged and elderly people attend the theatre somewhat more than the young. Elderly people are strong supporters of the classic theatre forms—wayang kulit, wayang golek, wayang orang, hat boi, the Thai National Theatre—and traditional plays when performed by likay, ketoprak, lakon bassac, and cai luong troupes. Like their Western counterparts, young people seem more interested in movies than in plays. When young people do go to the theatre they prefer contemporary stories to traditional ones. It is at performances of kich, the Cambodian National Theatre (modern theatre), the Arena Theatre of the Philippines, and lud-ruk that one sees the largest numbers of students and young adults in the audience.

Young children and infants are allowed to attend plays with their parents free of charge everywhere, even in large theatres in Bangkok, Saigon, and Djakarta. They romp in the aisles and when the action gets exciting they mass by the footlights like moths drawn to a flame. In Cambodia and Vietnam children often sit on the apron of the stage as well. As one goes down the economic and educational scale, more and more children are seen in theatres. At performances of the smallest, grubbiest troupes I would estimate up to 30 percent of the audience are non-paying children and infants. Mobs of youngsters attend puppet performances in Java, Sunda, Bali, Malaysia, and Thailand, partly because children particularly enjoy puppet plays and partly because performances usually are held outdoors where it is easy for the children to come and go without restraint and to curl up and sleep when they get tired. Troupe managers everywhere welcome children. They know that every child who sees a play free of charge today is a potential paying customer in the future. In Bandung local police have advised theatre owners not to admit children under thirteen years of age, even though they might buy a ticket. In doing this the police are applying to stage plays a regulation designed to keep children out of the movies. Troupe managers have protested that plays and movies are two very different things. Children have seen plays with their parents for centuries. If children are excluded from the theatre, managers fear they will grow up in ignorance of classical drama and that a generation hence there will be no more audience for classic drama. So far no troupe has complied with the police request.

On the whole, theatre audiences reflect the fact that the majority of the population of Southeast Asia is rural and of low economic, educational, and social status. The largest number of theatre troupes perform in villages and in small country towns where the only possible audience is rural and largely lower class, and the majority of troupes are small troupes, mediocre to poor artistically, which attract, no matter where they play, audiences from the lower educational, economic, and social levels.

Granted that this is true in general, it is equally important to note the many exceptions in which audiences are not predominantly of this composition. The more artistic troupes in every country tend to draw an educated audience of the middle and upper classes. The better troupes play in large cities, where the social and educational elite live; they are larger troupes charging higher admission prices which only people in higher income brackets can afford to buy. Among the better troupes of all genres those which perform classic or traditional plays—wayang kulit, wayang golek, wayang orang, the Thai National Theatre—draw the largest number of well-educated people. Two troupes in Southeast Asia perform for audiences which are made up completely of the upper classes. They are the Royal Lao Ballet and Royal Cambodian Ballet which perform exclusively for state functions. The only people who are invited to attend are members of the Royal Family, high state officials, and foreign dignitaries.*

AUDIENCE-THEATRE RELATIONS

Theatre and troupe managers are keenly aware of the fact that their audiences are never the same twice. The audience is a highly variable factor whose composition changes with the time, the place, and the occasion of performance. In Chapter 11 I described how the main BAKOKSI troupe varies its playing style to suit either a rural or a city audience. This is rather sophisticated. It is more common to find a troupe adjusting its repertory to suit the tastes of its different audiences. Here are a few illustrations of this fascinating though complicated practice. For its regular local audience a large lakon bassac troupe in Phnom Penh mixes up its plays, so they won't get bored and will come often. During religious festivals like the Water Festival, however, country people stream into the capital for the boat races, music concerts, parades, and big-city theatre. This audience is religious and conservative. For them the troupe schedules several weeks

*From time to time members of the Royal Cambodian Ballet are also assigned to dance for tourists at Angkor Wat.

of classic plays and *Jataka* stories back to back. The manager of another lakon bassac troupe said they always perform Chinese plays during New Year's because they attract a good audience then. The manager of a large ketoprak troupe in central Java said they perform history (babad) plays for country audiences; modern plays when they play a factory town; revolutionary plays in Magelang, the site of a military academy; and, for the cultured Jogjakarta audience, they often perform *Ramayana* and *Mahabharata* stories, an unusual thing for a ketoprak troupe to do. The chief actor of a ketoprak troupe said the audience in Blambangan (the easternmost tip of the island of Java) doesn't like classic wayang stories at all, so they normally stage plays based on local history. In the cities they perform only in the Javanese language, but in some villages they speak Madurese as well, for a large proportion of the population in that part of Java are of Madurese descent. "We change two-thirds of our repertory when we play the provinces," a starring cai luong actress told me. She personally prefers playing contemporary stories, but only in Saigon and a few other large cities like Hue and Danang are audiences "ready for them." Provincial audiences insist on seeing the old Chinese, Vietnamese, and Arabic historical and mythological plays. A sandiwara actor mused that in the 1940's, during the Indonesian revolution, they performed many anti-Dutch plays; during the 1950's, when fanatical Darul Islam rebels were terrorizing much of west Java, they switched to antirebel plays; now in the 1960's both types of plays are uninteresting to audiences and they find local history plays go over the best.

Theatregoing is a relaxed, informal pastime for audiences in Southeast Asia. People drop by the theatre at night to see what is playing. If they like the play, they decide then and there to see it. First-class tickets are often bought in advance, but otherwise people do not bother. It is unnecessary, for there is no such thing as a play's being sold out in advance. Even on Saturday nights no one is turned away for lack of room. Additional chairs take care of the overflow or people shove together on the benches a little tighter. One more person can always be squeezed into the aisles to stand or, if the spectator wants to, he can go backstage and watch the play from the wings.

Another facet of the audience's easygoing attitude toward theatre is the casual way people watch a performance. The predominantly female audience at the likay performance mentioned continued to talk long after the play had begun. This is not unusual; though, as a play progresses, the audience's attention is more and more captured by the action on stage. Still, the over-all impression at most theatres is of muted chaos as food vendors, children, and adults ceaselessly move up and down the aisles. Audiences do not concentrate on each word, gesture, or nuance of meaning that comes from the stage, as Western audiences have been trained to do. If your neighbor talks, you don't try to quiet him. Plays are longer than they are in the West, and no one can be expected to sit through an eight- or nine-hour performance without talking, eating, or getting up. At wayang kulit performances perhaps a third of the audience leaves after the clowns have finished their big scenes about five hours into the play. Many who last out the night doze during less interesting scenes. Nang talung audiences bring their own straw mats on which they sit and sleep.

It is fairly common for people in the audience to form close personal relations with troupe members. I remember a likay actor's telling of a tiny village where a certain history play had been requested. After the performance several elderly villagers had come backstage to ask the troupe to repeat the play the next time they visited their village. After an interval of five or six years, the troupe was returning to the village for an engagement, and the actor was looking forward to giving the requested play again for the old people. Spectators everywhere ask troupes to perform particular plays of their preference. Regulars at a hat boi theatre in Hue send their requests to the troupe manager via messenger. Some like certain plays so much they are willing to pay the troupe a bonus (about half the cost of performance) if it will stage a favorite several nights in succession. Regular spectators also vie to play the "critic's drum" during performance. It is an ancient tradition in hat boi for a knowledgeable spectator to praise or criticize the actors as the play progresses by beating on the "critic's drum"—a single beat for encouragement, a sharp rim tap if the spectator is displeased.

Some people come night after night to see a troupe perform. The manager of a wayang orang troupe in Djakarta personally knows at least one hundred audience members because they come so frequently. According to another wayang orang manager, fifty people regularly reserve seats every night of the week. According to a likay troupe manager and leading actor fully half their audience is composed of "fanatical" theatre lovers who have come "every night for the past six months."

Spectators talk to actors while the play is in progress. A fan may whistle or shout his encouragement. At exciting moments in a play dozens of people may leap to their feet and urge the actors on. Actors may respond and a remarkably close rapport between audience and actor results. One night I took a flash picture during a sandiwara performance in Djakarta. In an instant one of the clowns knelt down reporter-style and mimicked my actions by snapping away with his cigarette lighter as if it were a camera. The audience roared its approval.[1]

Theatre fans in Indonesia, Thailand, Laos, Cambodia, and Burma may demonstrate the warmth of their feeling by giving small gifts to actors during the course of a performance. A donor will reach across the footlights to place on stage his gift of cigarettes, candy, cologne, or a small amount of money, or, if more exuberantly inclined, he may rise in his seat and throw his gift on stage. A gift is often wrapped in a note, requesting a favor of the actor in return. A clown may be asked to perform a famous comic routine or a leading lady to sing a favorite song. These are small tokens of an audience's affection and appreciation; in some cases actors receive quite valuable gifts or large sums of money. In Bandung I once saw a female singer in wayang golek receive gifts of 10,000 rupiah bills nineteen times during a single performance. Often there is a romantic attachment between the donor and the performer. Liaisons between wealthy women and handsome young likay, zat pwe, mohlam luong, or lakon bassac actors are especially common. In recent years it has been reported that well-known likay actors have received gifts ranging from expensive toilet articles and clothing to Mercedes Benz cars and a luxury apartment. According to a knowledgeable Thai aristocrat, "Most of the women in likay audiences are of the wealthy merchant class or wives of minor nobility. Some are widows; some are still married. They love to make a show of themselves in the theatre. They squander their husbands' money on actors with whom they are infatuated. They give gold, jewels, clothes, TV sets, rent apartments for them, anything to pamper them." A manager of an important lakon bassac troupe in Phnom Penh says "all" his top actors are gigolos of well-to-do female customers. "Notice how actors on stage even during a classic play wear wristwatches and four or five rings, bracelets, and necklaces? They are gifts from admirers. It's good for business too." Leading men in these popular troupes invariably are young—in their teens or early twenties—and handsome. (In contrast most actresses are singularly ugly, even given the benefit of heavy stage make-up.) The remark of an official of the mohlam society regarding mohlam actors might well apply to actors of the other theatre forms as well. "The top mohlam actor must be a certain type: handsome, tall, friendly, and with masculine sex appeal. He seldom marries the actress he performs with but usually ends up marrying an attractive village girl with a wealthy father. The girl is happy catching a man vastly more appealing than the usual village boy, and the actor is happy to settle down to a life of ease supported by his father-in-law."

Not all actors are rakes and profligates, of course. Puppeteers are generally solid, married men. In Indonesia, although actors often receive gifts, romantic attachments between actors and audience members are rare (or at least they are not talked about openly as in Burma, Thailand, Cambodia, and Laos). In Malaysia strict Moslem morality discourages such practices. In Vietnam several managers reported that, while actors received gifts from patronesses, they, the managers, made strong efforts to reduce the amount of "moral involvement" formerly associated with gift-giving.

TYPICAL AUDIENCES

Audience composition varies widely from country to country and among theatre forms, as consideration of typical audiences for some of the most important genres indicates.

ARDJA

Since ardja is ordinarily performed in small villages for temple festivals and on religious occasions and since admission is free, practically the entire population of a village attends. Large numbers of children watch. There are no chairs and the audience must stand through a performance.

BARONG

When performed as a folk dance-drama for a village celebration, the audience at a barong play represents a cross section of the local village population. When given as a commercial performance, the audience is composed of wealthy, highly educated, high-status tourists (perhaps half foreign and half from Java and the other islands), except that local residents, usually older women and children, also watch from the sidelines.

CAI LUONG

The best and largest cai luong troupes which play in Saigon and large provincial capitals draw heavily middle-class, student, and young adult audiences during weekdays, and more lower-class, middle-aged audiences on weekends. The cai luong audience in large cities is more consistently well-educated, middle-class, middle-brow than the audience of any other genre in Southeast Asia. But cai luong is not a prestige genre, and few who fancy themselves intelligentsia attend. Men and women attend in about equal numbers. Parents commonly bring young children. Gift-giving in public is rare, but star performers of both sexes are highly regarded as exciting marriage partners much as movie stars are in our society.

HAT BOI

Mainly old people, especially women, see hat boi now. They bring with them to the theatre their young grandchildren and great-grandchildren so that the audience is both very young and very old. Young adults and students say they don't like classic hat boi, don't understand it, and won't go to see it. Worn-out, pitifully inadequate troupes are the rule, and audiences are mainly rural and of low educational level.

KETOPRAK AND SANDIWARA

Audiences for both genres are similar: they are 60 to 70 percent rural or urban working class, with the remainder mostly middle-class merchants. Men tend to outnumber women in the cheaper seats; women outnumber men in the more expensive seats (where merchants usually sit). Few highly educated people see either ketoprak or sandiwara, although a scattering of intellectuals attend performances given by politically oriented ketoprak troupes. (PKI intellectuals, for example, will see Krido Mardi perform out of party loyalty even if they don't like ketoprak.) All ages and many children attend. Small gifts are often given to actors during a performance.

LIKAY

Audiences consisting of 85 to 95 percent women are usual. In past years likay appealed to a large section of the educated urban middle class and even to the aristocracy, but now audiences are composed predominantly of middle-aged wives of merchants, with an occasional upper-class wife. Male audience members are mainly laborers and farmers. Fewer children attend likay than similar genres (lakon bassac, mohlam luong, ketoprak). Gift-giving and romantic affairs are extremely common.

LAKON BASSAC

Like likay, middle-aged women make up the largest segment of the lakon bassac audience though the proportion—perhaps 60 to 70 percent—is less. Extremely large numbers of children attend. Although lower-class audiences predominate, because of lakon bassac's close connection to the art of classical dance at the Royal Court, significant numbers of educated middle- and upper-class men and, more especially, women may attend performances in Phnom Penh. Gift-giving and romantic attachments are commonplace.

LUDRUK

Performances of the modern plays of ludruk draw mainly young audiences in the cities—students and young adults—and audiences of all ages in rural areas. The ordinary troupe with its all-male cast consciously appeals to the audience's sense of the bizarre to a great extent, so that some young girls come out of morbid curiosity, some homosexual males to search for a mate, and some mature adults of both sexes to see for them-

selves what all the fuss is about. The best troupes do not consciously play upon sexual inversion but rely upon the story
appeal of their plays and the acting ability of the cast to draw
an audience.

MOHLAM LUONG

Audiences are generally similar to likay and lakon bassac
audiences except that, since almost all performances are given in
small towns and in the countryside, audiences are overwhelm-
ingly rural. The mohlam luong audience is perhaps the most
consistently low education, low economic status, and low social
status audience in Southeast Asia.

ROYAL CAMBODIAN BALLET AND ROYAL LAO BALLET

Audiences are hand-picked by officials of the Cambodian and
Lao courts from among members of the royal families, high
government officials, and the foreign diplomatic corps. The audience therefore is composed entirely of the upper-class and highly
educated. Men usually outnumber women and middle-aged and
elderly people outnumber the young since status is the determining factor in selection.

THAI NATIONAL THEATRE

Performances of the Thai National Theatre draw a high proportion of well-educated middle- and upper-class spectators, perhaps 50 percent of the total audience. Many high school and
college students attend, partly because many performers are also
students (at the Department of Fine Arts' School for Dramatic
Art). Women are more numerous than men, especially among
the student group. Girls idolize the performers (lakon is an all-
girl art form), but boys prefer action-packed American cowboy
movies to feminine lakon.

WAYANG KULIT

At performances in Java men are usually in the majority. The
classic form and religio-mystical content of the shadow drama
make it the favored entertainment of the upper-class Javanese
(*prijaji*) man. Often the host, the immediate male members of
his family, and his friends will segregate themselves from the

rest of the audience by sitting on the shadow side of the screen. Since anyone may attend free of charge, all ages are represented in the audience, and young children attend in large numbers. Middle- and lower-class men and women make up the bulk of the spectators. When the clowns are on everyone laughs uproariously. A battle scene sends children into a paroxysm of clapping, calling, and whistling.

WAYANG GOLEK

The audience for Sundanese wayang golek is about the same as for wayang kulit in Java, except that more young adult males are drawn by the attractive female singers. Wayang golek is appreciated more for its entertainment value than for its spiritual value.

WAYANG ORANG

Wayang orang draws an audience of fairly well-educated, middle-class theatregoers. Some upper-class people also attend, and perhaps 50 percent of the audience is lower-class. The sexes are about evenly divided. Many middle-aged and elderly people attend. Gifts are thrown on stage, but usually they are small ones and romantic liaisons are not the motive for gift-giving. Children attend in smaller numbers than for wayang kulit or wayang golek.

CHAPTER 1 4

Social Status of Troupes

A markedly ambivalent attitude is expressed toward theatre within Southeast Asian society. On the one hand, theatre is a deeply ingrained part of culture with honored traditions that go back a thousand years and more. Along with temple-building, the performing arts have been considered by Southeast Asians their two greatest artistic achievements. Through the medium of dramatic presentation the great literary heritages of Hindu, Buddhist, Chinese, and Islamic civilization have penetrated into and become part of local cultures. The theatre today is an inescapable part of society. Thousands of troupes perform and hundreds of millions of people attend performances. For these reasons, the status of theatre is high. At the same time, theatre is as despised as it is admired. It is improper, unsavory, even immoral. When the Vietnamese emperor Tu Duc decreed in the fifteenth century that "actors do not belong to the human kind," and excluded from government positions all "comedians and singers," he was expressing a widely held attitude.[1] This attitude did not originate in Southeast Asia. Chinese emperors voiced similar disdain for actors centuries before Tu Duc. In Indian mythology dance and drama were gifts of the gods through Brahma and Shiva, but performers later were branded as outcasts and banished to live as commoners on earth.

This ambivalence toward theatre is very much in evidence today. In Thailand a local fair committee may hire a likay troupe to perform, then tuck it away in the farthermost corner of the fairground—behind the movie, the boxing ring, the taxi-dancers, and the beauty-contest pavilion. The cultural officer of a town in Java may speak with pride of the amateur wayang, ketoprak, and seni-drama (modern drama) troupes in his district and of the many professional troupes that perform in his city every year. In the same breath he may say that "the actor is not despised, but of course no parent would want his child to become one."

Society's vitally important attitude toward a performer was determined to a large extent in the past by the tradition in which he worked. A performer in the folk tradition was a local villager first and a performer second, for he was a villager every day to his neighbors, a performer only occasionally. His status within his village depended primarily upon his usual position in the village and only secondarily upon his theatrical association, though his status usually was enhanced by his theatrical work because his skill was prized. The performer in the popular tradition has been almost universally looked down upon. Without roots in village society, his status has been that of a wandering vagabond. Especially in Confucian-influenced Vietnam, Laos, Thailand, and Cambodia, he was the lowest of the low—a landless man who, by traveling, failed in his all-important duty to honor and tend his ancestors' burial plot. The status of a court performer was relatively high. Court art had prestige, and the performer basked in its reflected glory. Royal amateurs performed alongside court professionals on many occasions. Yet the court rank of most professional court performers was not high. Typically, the wayang puppeteer, the Vietnamese harem singer, the Cambodian dancing girl, the khon performer were minor court functionaries. In the eyes of those outside the court they were held in considerable esteem, however. The status of the early performer in the Western tradition can be likened to that of a folk performer. Like the folk performer he was a bona fide member of a social group who only occasionally performed. And like the folk performer he performed not for pay but for the entertainment of others of his group. His occasional amateur performance was not a major factor in determining his social status. He was from the highly educated upper-class and therefore from a different social group than the folk performer, but within his group his function was much the same. As time went by and professional troupes came into being, the status of the performer in the Western tradition changed considerably. The actor came to be judged as a professional actor much like the actor in the popular tradition.

The social status of performers today cannot be so neatly described. One no longer can speak in a meaningful sense about the existence of "traditions of theatre." The old society of peasants and aristocrats has given way to rapidly modernizing societies in which status is not fixed by traditional rules. The status of most performers today can best be judged by considering two factors: the character of the performer himself and the value ascribed to the theatre genre in which he performs. Many of a performer's personal characteristics have nothing to do with theatre at all—inherited social position, education, financial condition, personal conduct—but they affect his social status. In ancient Rome, "troupes were gathered together by a manager, and consisted of slaves whom he could flog or put to death if he chose. Naturally, the profession of acting was as a consequence despised."[2] There are no longer slaves in Southeast Asia, but tens of thousands of performers working mainly in small commercially supported troupes are despised as a consequence of their lowly birth. At the other end of the scale is a much smaller group of well-connected performers, some of royal blood, whose high social status is inherited and undisputed. Traditionally in Southeast Asia only the wellborn have had the opportunity to become well-educated; the vast majority of theatre performers have always been illiterate, and most are illiterate today.* But the educational picture is changing. More performers are getting at least minimal education. Few precise figures are available, but Table 12, comparing the years of schooling of "young" Sundanese wayang golek puppeteers and "old" puppeteers, gives a good indication of the fact that an educational revolution is under way.† No performer yet has a university education, but a much higher percentage of the young puppeteers completed senior and junior high school than did their elders and fewer

---

*According to figures compiled by an informant in Vietnam, among cai luong actors currently playing in Saigon, some 88 percent did not complete three years of formal schooling, 10 percent finished grade school, and perhaps 2 percent finished high school.

†Based on data taken from questionnaires completed by 178 west Java wayang golek puppeteers in 1964.

Table 12. Educational level of young and old wayang golek puppeteers (in percentages).

Education	Young (20–39)	Old (40–60)
No schooling	1	6
Grade school	72	90
Junior high school	20	0
Senior high school	7	4
University	0	0
	100	100

have had no schooling at all. The manager of a small likay troupe in northern Thailand proudly told me he saved nightly from his salary in order to put his son through college in Bangkok, though he, the manager, had never gone to school.

Money talks in every country and in every profession, not excluding Southeast Asian theatre. Cai luong matinee idols and famous Sundanese wayang golek singers have high status at least partly because they earn so much money. The high status of the wayang golek singer is demonstrated by the fact that she sits on a raised dias while the puppeteer sits hidden behind his puppets and that her name appears before the puppeteer's in billing, as well as by her control over the timing of a performance, but nothing demonstrates her higher status more convincingly than the fact that she earns 100,000 to 300,000 rupiah a night compared to the puppeteer's nightly salary of 50,000 to 60,000 rupiah. In cai luong a talented commoner can rise to enormous popularity and financial success in a very short time. A few years ago Miss Tien was an attractive Vietnamese farm girl, like many others. She had a nice voice and occasionally sang in cai luong performances in her village. A large touring troupe heard her, hired her, and four years later she was famous throughout Vietnam and earned 1,000,000 piaster a year. Most commercially supported actors, however, are at the other end of the financial scale. Their income is paltry and their status is low. In the worst cases, actors who can't live on their salaries are forced to take low-status side jobs which further lowers their status in society.

A performer's moral conduct directly affects his social status. Chinese opera performers in Thailand and Malaysia and wayang kulit puppeteers in Java smoked opium in the past, as did some performers in Laos, Cambodia, and Vietnam. Few do now, but the stigma remains strong against those who do. I have already mentioned the adulterous affairs of some actors and have hinted at the perversions of others. In the eyes of most people, performers who indulge in immoral activities have very low social status.

Another important personal characteristic of a performer is artistic talent (or lack of it). Excellent performers of any genre may be accorded high social status nowadays. Recently governments in Southeast Asia have begun to give official recognition to talented theatre artists. Only once before World War II did a government honor a popular performer. That was in Burma, in 1919, when the British Government presented the great zat pwe actor Po Sein with a medal for his services to the Crown. Since World War II many rulers in Southeast Asia have actively sought higher status for performers. President Soekarno has presented his favorite ludruk troupe with a bus for touring. Each year he invites scores of actors, dancers, and musicians to perform at his various palaces on state occasions. Prince Sihanouk of Cambodia awards medals to deserving actors and actresses. In Malaysia, in 1964, the King bestowed an award on an actor for the first time; the honor went to a leading bangsawan actor. People are still talking about the King of Thailand's visit to attend a lakon jatri performance in Songkhla, southern Thailand. The building of beautiful new national theatres in Malaysia, Thailand, and Cambodia has raised the status of actors in these countries by demonstrating government interest in and approval of theatre. The inept performer in any genre is likely to have low status. Untalented performers are found in troupes of every genre, but the largest numbers of them probably will be found in small troupes that perform decadent genre (hat boi, bangsawan, wayang beber, wayang kulit Malaya, and some troupes of lakon jatri).

The second major factor which affects a performer's social status is the genre in which he performs. Some, like wayang, khon, or lakon, are considered high art, have deep religious significance, or are otherwise socially valued. Performers in such genres bask in the reflected glory of the art in which they work, at least to some extent. Other theatre forms, like bangsawan, ketoprak, ludruk, lakon bassac, and likay, are considered artistically vulgar and contain little or no religious, political, or social significance. Their performers are looked down upon for being associated with such unprestigious art forms. Generally speaking, ancient forms of theatre have higher prestige, younger forms lower. An exception may occur when one of the newer forms concerns itself with moral education. Kich troupes, which stage modern problem plays, and ludruk or ketoprak troupes, which use drama as a means of teaching nationalist or Communist ideology, have greater status than fellow troupes concerned only with entertainment. They are committed to a serious purpose, and their performers share in the troupes' higher status.

Having looked at the status of theatre in terms of both social and artistic factors, we can see at least one reason why attitudes toward theatre so often seem schizoid, why theatre is praised one moment and reviled the next. A person can admire the classic traditional art form of, say, hat boi, while despising the vagabonds who perform hat boi. Or a person can idolize a famous cai luong performer, while having little respect for the art form of cai luong. Consciously or unconsciously, people distinguish between the status of the art form and the status of the performer. The two factors may point in the same direction (they often do) or they may not. The status of a performer is not an absolute quantity; the same performer may be assigned a different status by different critics. Status tends to be strongly fixed when the status of the judger and the status of the genre are polarized at opposite ends of the social spectrum. That is, the high-status judger tends to look down on the performer of a low-status genre while the low-status judger almost always looks up to the performer of a high-status genre.

To illustrate, when a prince of royal blood in Thailand praises the excellences of khon, the peasant, who has never seen khon but only likay, will also agree to the excellences of khon. He will continue to like likay and he will accord the good likay actor some status too, but the greater status will be deferred to the performer of khon, the art form which, he has on good authority, is better than anything he knows. Conversely, most educated people look down upon cai luong, lakon bassac, mohlam luong, likay, ketoprak, and bangsawan. Unless they have some specific reason for not doing so, they assign performers of these genres low social status as well. It is harder to say how a person will judge a genre on his own level. The high-status person may not like any theatre at all, even traditional high-status theatre. The low-status person may not like low-status theatre forms either, or he may like all kinds of theatre regardless of level.

Performers with the highest social status in Southeast Asia are those in wayang kulit, khon, and lakon nai. The best performers in these genres are usually of middle or high social position by birth. They are well-educated, of high moral character. The genres have high prestige in their respective countries, and the plays contain important moral, philosophic, and social content. Years of devoted effort are required for performers to master their art, from which they earn a comfortable income. In all, then, their social status is quite high.

Most performers of wayang orang have a middle status because, though the artistic status of their court-derived theatre form is relatively high, the social, financial, and educational levels of performers are not high. The same is true of cai luong performers but for different reasons. The artistic level of cai luong is considered only mediocre, and the social origins of most performers are ordinary. But good performers earn fortunes and can gain greater personal popularity than in any other genre. Historically, Sundanese wayang golek has had as high a status as Javanese wayang kulit. Today the artistic level of performance has slipped badly, and the prestige of the puppeteer has fallen with it. The lakon jatri performer does not earn much money nor is the artistic level of performance always noteworthy but major performers have considerable social status bestowed on them because the drama is highly religious in nature.

Most performers in commercially supported, popular ketoprak, ludruk, lakon bassac, mohlam luong, likay, bangsawan, and sandiwara troupes have low status. The theatre forms have little artistic standing. Performers come from the lower social classes; most are illiterate, and many behave in a less than moral fashion. Troupes may be quite small, poor, short of equipment, and forced to subsist on the income of tiny audiences drawn from back-country villages and hamlets. I ran across one ketoprak troupe in east Java that consisted of just six members. They would arrive in a town, round up twenty to thirty aspiring villagers, train them for a few weeks, then stage plays. Their status, even among villagers with whom they worked, was about as low as it possibly could be. One village woman called them "vagrants and bums." Performers of wayang kulit Malaya and hat boi also have low social status. In abstract, both art forms have high prestige, but little of this high status accrues to professional performers, most of whom are old, not well trained, and untalented.

PART IV

Theatre as Communication

CHAPTER 15

Past and Present

In all countries of Southeast Asia and at most times theatre has been more than just entertainment. In addition to providing aesthetic pleasure, emotional release through empathic response, and even a means for accomplishing communal celebration of ritual events, theatre also functions as a channel for communication. Traditionally, three major channels were open to Southeast Asian ruling elites through which they could disseminate their ideas, beliefs, and value systems: the religious hierarchy, scholars and scribes, and theatre performances.[1] Of these, theatre has unquestionably been the most important in reaching the largely illiterate populations of the countryside and the cities. Priests, monks, and religious teachers have played their role in propagating religious ideas to large numbers of people but their work has often centered at court or in urban communities. The influence of the scholars and scribes has been limited to the very small group of elite who could read and write. The use of theatre to educate and instruct an audience is not unique to Southeast Asia. Greek citizens were educated en masse at communally sponsored tragic festivals. Horace said Roman drama should "entertain and instruct." Through Morality and Mystery plays in the Middle Ages, pagans were instructed in Christian doctrine and practicing Christians were sustained in their beliefs. In modern times playwrights from Ibsen to Shaw to Brecht, Miller, and Genet have used the stage as a pulpit. Groups of all kinds, from the Nazis and the Communists to Moral Rearmament, have used theatre as well. What is notable about the theatre in

Southeast Asia, as compared with Europe or America, is the degree to which it is involved in the educative process. It is not an exaggeration to say that, had the theatre not existed as a powerful channel for communicating to large groups of people, Southeast Asian civilization would not be what it is today. Through the medium of theatre performances, the complex religious, metaphysical, social, and intellectual values of the ruling elite were disseminated to the most unsophisticated villagers in the most remote areas.

RELIGIOUS BELIEFS

BRAHMANISM

The Khmer kings of Cambodia and the Brahmanic priestly class used theatre performances as a part of the ritual worship of the god-king. Respect for Brahmanic religious doctrine as well as belief in the divinity of the god-king were inculcated in the people through public recitations of the *Ramayana,* the *Mahabharata,* and other epics derived from India. The kings of Java, Bali, Sunda, Sumatra, and Malaya encouraged and sponsored recitations and performances of local versions of the same epics. In these performances the king is extravagantly praised. He is compared to the gods in strength and wisdom, and often called a god. His subjects offer him perfect and absolute obedience. Who can doubt the educative intent of a passage such as the following, typical of the manner in which wayang plays in Indonesia begin?

> NARRATION. And thus it happened that on a Thursday the king was sitting on his throne, which was covered with figured gold and studded with every kind of precious stone. Spread beneath his feet was a beautiful tapestry, woven in a pattern of flowers, and sprinkled with many kinds of perfume. Behind the king stood four palace bedaya dancers, each holding in her hands a symbol of his authority—a goose, a snake, a handkerchief, and an elephant—all of gold and covered with gems. Female servants to his left and right fanned the king with peacock feathers. The fragrance of the king reached out into the great square and to the highway leading from the palace gates. The king then seemed no longer human but the very appearance of the god Vishnu descending to earth accompanied by heavenly nymphs. Before him stood the prince, handsome in his

royal dress, the more so because of his virtue, thinking always of others before himself. He is wise and knows in a moment every wish of the people; he knows their actions and their behavior. He is therefore the very person in whom the king believes by day and by night.

KING. My Son, are you not surprised to be summoned before me?

PRINCE. Indeed, your Majesty, when I was to come before your Majesty I was most afraid. Outside I felt as if I were hit by lightning, yet felt safe; as if I were to be caught by a tiger, yet escaped. My heart was shattered as though crushed against a rock. Like the grass blown by the wind in the great square, my heart trembled with surprise and anxiety when I heard I was to come before the king. But when I arrived in the presence of your Majesty my heart became peaceful as if it was cooled with water in the morning and anxiety vanished from my heart. I thank you, your Majesty.

KING. My Son, how is it you were afraid to come before me?

PRINCE. I trembled that, were I guilty and to be punished, it would be your Majesty who punishes me; that, were I condemned to death, it would be your Majesty who condemns me to death. But by day and by night I am ready to offer my life with both hands, to be pierced with a sharp arrow, to be beheaded. I am ready to do what your Majesty wishes.

KING. My Son, your thoughts wander too far. You are ready to admit your guilt as if you have sinned and to place your life in my hands. We thank you beforehand for upholding the honor of our throne. But do not, my Son, forget the saying, that, however fierce a tiger may be, he will not devour his young. Though you should be judged guilty and should be sentenced to death, the king's forgiveness is always there. He who wields the power of our kingdom may cut the grass where it blocks light and give peace to the suffering where he sees fit.

It is widely agreed by scholars of Indonesia that wayang drama was the main medium through which Javanese, Sundanese, and Balinese religious and philosophic systems were taught to the people.

ISLAM

This passage reflects Hindu-Javanese concepts of kingship. You often hear in Indonesia the statement that Islam appropriated wayang kulit shadow drama, that in the sixteenth century the Nine *Wali* (famous Islamic teachers) remolded the drama to fit the requirements of Islamic doctrine, then used the drama to convert Javanese to the religion of Islam. Some Moslems go so far as to say the Nine Wali "created" present day wayang. I have mentioned that the shape of wayang kulit figures changed very greatly between the sixteenth and the nineteenth centuries, and that one of the possible reasons for this change was the Islamic proscription against portraying the human figure in any form of art. However, one must search long and hard to find even small traces of Islamic thought in the content of wayang kulit plays: Yudistira's secret weapon, the Kalimasada, is thought to be a letter containing the famous Islamic acknowledgment, "There is only one God and Mohammed is his Prophet," because the prayer's title—Kalimat Sjahadah—is so similar; prayers (*mantra*) spoken by the puppeteer before performance contain references to Allah; Arabic words are sometimes used, particularly in one story to describe the four colors of Bima's costume; and apparently Islamic partisans were responsible for changing the virtuous Brahman priest Durna (Drona in Sanskrit) into an ugly, hook-nosed, scheming archvillain. Considering the bulk of wayang kulit drama, running to several hundred plays, Islamic influence on its content is remarkable by its insignificance.

While the Nine Wali and their followers did not make over wayang kulit into a vehicle for propagating Islam among the Javanese, they did use theatre for this purpose in other ways. Apparently they often had gamelan music played and sometimes wayang performed in order to draw crowds to which they would then preach. More important, they encouraged the development of wayang golek doll-puppet theatre. In Java to this day only the Islamic *Menak* stories are performed in this genre. It is not certain how widespread Javanese wayang golek was several centuries ago when Islamic missionary activity was at its height. Certainly it never superseded Hindu-Javanese wayang kulit in popularity at any time. Today it is of miniscule importance as compared to wayang kulit though 85 percent of the population of Java nominally is Moslem.

On the Malay Peninsula, Islamic teachings penetrated wayang kulit drama more deeply. Malay versions of the *Ramayana* were written in Arabic script. Passages referring to Hindu rites, such as reincarnation, which ran counter to Islamic teaching were deleted. An Islamic copyist of the *Ramayana* in 1892 commended his version to his Sultan with these words, "All that which is not good has been excised by Your Highness's humble servant."[2] But the first task of the Islamic writers in Malaya was, as Winstedt says, "to substitute for the Hindu epics tales of the heroes of Islam, like Alexander the Great, Amir Hamza and Muhammad Hanafiah."[3] The same author goes on to say the *Panji* cycle of stories and plays may have been so widely diffused outside Java because the rulers of Majapahit were employing them as "imperial propaganda." When the *Panji* cycle began circulating throughout Southeast Asia in the fourteenth century, the Javanese kingdom of Majapahit controlled most of Malaya and aspired to rule Thailand and Cambodia, places where the *Panji* story is well known.[4]

CONFUCIANISM AND BUDDHISM

On the mainland of Southeast Asia dramatic performances facilitated the spread of Confucian and of Hinayana Buddhist thought. The plays of hat boi, all taken from famous Chinese stories, taught conservative Confucian virtues—respect for parents, devotion to the land, honesty and thrift, and, probably most important in the eyes of the emperors, veneration for the imperial person. Through performances of hat boi great numbers of Vietnamese were indoctrinated in official Confucian morality.

In Thailand, Burma, Laos, and Cambodia, Buddhist *Jataka* stories have been widely performed for several centuries, first by folk and court troupes and more recently by troupes in the popular tradition, such as likay, mohlam luong, zat pwe, and lakon bassac. *Jataka* plays contain diverse materials. Some retain elements of Brahmanic ritual; some support the authority of kingship (King Pra Law, in a Thai drama, says, as he is about to be attacked by soldiers, "There is no need to be afraid; for have we not royal blood in our veins? What common man would dare to touch the sacred person of the king?"[5]); and some are still rooted in animism. What all *Jataka* plays have in common, however, is an overlay of Buddhist thought. Unimportant Hindu gods like Indra are still popular on mainland stages, but Buddhism supplanted serious Hindu thought. Just as the Brahman priest Durna was turned into an archvillain in wayang drama by believers in Islam, Brahmans came to be reviled in Buddhist plays on the mainland. Hla Pe tells us that in Burmese popular drama of the nineteenth century "ninety-nine per cent of the brahmans presented in the plays are crooks, foisting milk mixed with water on to the people, or cunning schemers always surreptitiously hatching plots in the royal courts."[6] Previously under Brahmanism the splendors of kingship had been fused with belief in the Hindu god-king; now under Buddhism kings were pictured as Future Buddhas. The following passage from the Burmese play *Konmara* illustrates the new fusion of Buddhism with old ideas of kingly magnificence.

> PRINCE. Sire, true future Buddha, of matured and mighty attainments, incomparable, to whom the whole realm in this circle of Zambudipa island pays obeisance, the flame of whose power blazes bright, apex and crest of the hundred kings,—I, sire, your son, heir to the throne, whom you look upon with favour, the crown prince, respectfully inform you that, carrying the orders that bear your seal on my head, I present myself prostrate before you at the soaring Lion Throne.
>
> KING. Offshoot of the exalted lineage of the sun in the heavens above, most glorious crown prince, whose radiating splendour wellnigh set the whole island aflame, O pride of my eye, successor and heir apparent to the throne.[7]

During a period of several hundred years devout Hinayana Buddhist kings in Thailand supported revisions and rewritings of the *Ramayana* in which Rama was portrayed as a Future Buddha. Buddhist versions of the *Ramayana* were carried by the Thai to Burma, Laos, and Cambodia where they became standard texts for dramatic performances. In Burma on one occasion royal authority was used to compel theatre troupes to spread Buddhist doctrine. Htin Aung tells us that in the nineteenth century a new Minister of Drama, "wanted the drama to be under the direct control of the state,"[8] and decreed as one of his first official acts that all marionette troupes then being organized under the Ministry of Drama must perform only *Jataka* plays or plays of national history.

Following is a synopsis of a *Jataka* play in which Buddhism combines with other elements. The moral frame of the play is belief in Buddhism. The Black Dragon rain god is a Buddhist concept (related to ancient Chinese and Indian myths).[9] The concern the drama shows for peasant life is a modern innovation, as is the play's theme of social justice. The play, performed by a Cambodian lakon bassac troupe, is based, the troupe manager said, on a manuscript he had read in a Buddhist temple in southern Vietnam some years ago. The story, he thought, originally came from Burma. A similar story of the capture of the dragon rain god and ensuing drought is dramatized in Japan in the noh and kabuki.*

> In a happy Buddhist country the king is a just ruler. Farmers live prosperous lives for in the rivers lives the Black Dragon (Buddha in a former life), the God of Rain who brings abundant rain for the rice crop. The king is receiving the thanks of farmers for his benevolent rule, when news is brought of an attack on the country by troops of a neighboring kingdom. In the countryside starving peasants from the neighboring kingdom cross the border into the Buddhist country. They are fleeing the harsh rule of their evil king and beg for asylum. They tell how their king does not worship Buddha and how he refuses to give the proper offerings to the Black Dragon rain god. Their country is without water; the rice will not grow. Their king wishes only to steal food from his richer neighbors and to start war. The fleeing peasants are warmly received in the Buddhist country. On the river bank, the evil king uses magic powers to lure the Black Dragon from the waters. Just as the Black Dragon is about to be carried off, a brave and devout Buddhist hunter arrives on the scene. He drives off the evil king and his armies, and returns the Black Dragon to his river home. Later the good king receives the hunter at the palace, and thanks him for protecting the prosperity of their land. They all offer thanks to the Black Dragon as a Future Buddha.

CHRISTIANITY

To a certain extent Catholic missionaries utilized the appeal of theatre to gain converts to Christianity in the Philippines. Their aims were similar to those of the Moslem missionaries in Indonesia and Buddhist missionaries on the mainland of Southeast Asia, and their methods were not much different. As early as the sixteenth century Catholic missionaries established parish head-

---

*The noh play *Ikkaku Sennin* and the kabuki play *Narukami*.

quarters in outlying areas of important islands in the Philippines "to which the natives could be enticed periodically by the staging of colorful festivals. These included processions, dances, and theater performances along with religious and ritual celebrations."[10] Later, moro-moro plays, which celebrated the triumph of Christianity over Islam, were introduced as Christian propaganda vehicles.

TWENTIETH-CENTURY POLITICAL PROPAGANDA

NATIONALISM

In the late nineteenth and early twentieth centuries, when European countries and the United States had colonized most of Southeast Asia, local nationalists sometimes tried to use theatre performances as a means of arousing the people against foreign rule. Troupes performing at court (khon and lakon, wayang orang, and hat boi) were seldom involved for their repertories consisted of classic plays and their livelihood depended upon court favor. Most anticolonial, pronationalistic plays were staged by troupes in the popular tradition—cai luong, ketoprak, toneel (the forerunner of sandiwara), zarzuela, and zat pwe. Colonial authorities watched closely for any hint of opposition in theatre performances so that criticism was usually indirect or phrased as double-entendre which European officials would have a hard time unraveling. Here is one illustration. An attendant to the prince in the Burmese play *Konmara* speaks at length about the marvelous beauties of the forest through which he is passing. It was just such a Burmese forest which prompted the Buddha to utter extempore "sixty stanzas on the delightful scenery." The attendant says, "When we survey the forest, we see its complete resemblance to that garden and golden ground from which the Company (the British Government) gathers the flowers. But when it is measured closely against that garden, it is bound to be superior in its outstanding natural beauty."[11] (That is, Burmese natural beauty is bound to be superior to English beauty.)

However, theatre was not an important weapon of nationalist leaders in their campaigns of harassment and agitation against colonial rule in pre-World War II days. The small nationalist

64. Hat boi performed on television in Saigon with American technical assistance.

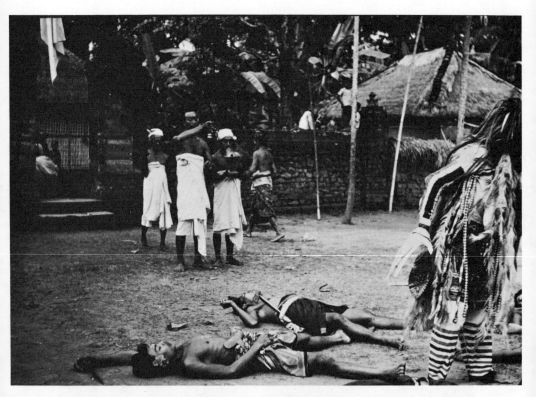

65. Barong performed by villagers of Singapadu, Bali, in 1956, as a religious ritual.

66. Eight years later, in 1964, in the same village of Singapadu, a glamorized version of barong is performed for tourists. An ornately decorated new temple with a broad stage platform has been built especially for performances; the priest's torso is covered and he is attended by pretty girls rather than village elders; and the "trance" dancers are costumed like a chorus.

67. A curvacious modern puppet with high heels, jewelry, a batik skirt, and a handbag in Malaysian wayang kulit.

68. A European soldier in Malaysian wayang kulit, whose forward arm appears to be taken from a traditional puppet.

69. The player scene from *Hamlet*, performed in Djakarta as sandiwara in costumes reflecting Arabic influence.

movements were not prepared to use theatre as a propaganda medium in any major way. It would have been difficult to mount a concerted theatrical effort in the face of stern government controls. And, in any case, the nationalist leaders had little time to think of theatre; often it was all they could do to stay alive and out of prison, to say nothing of staging plays.

JAPANESE OCCUPATION

The largest concerted effort in modern times to utilize theatre as a propaganda medium in Southeast Asia was that of the Japanese occupation forces during World War II. Between 1940 and 1945 the Japanese gained control of every government in Southeast Asia. Through both civil and military channels, Japanese authorities pressed theatre into service to help explain the aims of their Greater East Asia Co-Prosperity Sphere. Western countries were vilified through the drama, and Asian nations glorified. The Japanese recognized the communication potential of the theatre and assigned considerable sums of money and numbers of personnel to the task. Total censorship of theatre was imposed. Apparently few people in the theatre objected very much to the Japanese program of theatre control. Those who did were swiftly punished. In Indonesia, for example, one wayang golek dalang was jailed for joking about the rice shortage that got progressively worse as the war continued. I was told, whether correctly or not I do not know, that at least one Indonesian performer was executed for expressing anti-Japanese sentiments on stage.

CURRENT PROPAGANDA PROGRAMS

Few governments in Southeast Asia today attempt to use theatre as a medium of communication. In the Philippines, Malaysia, Thailand, Laos, and Cambodia, governments rarely educate, inform, or indoctrinate people through dramatic performances. Only in Indonesia and in Vietnam is government propaganda regularly disseminated via the stage.* Civil minis-

---

*The Burmese government may also be using theatre for propaganda purposes. Lack of reliable information on Burma at the moment makes it impossible to say for certain.

tries and the armed forces in both these countries organize and operate propaganda theatre troupes, and their efforts to harness the communication potential of theatre for national purposes are extremely interesting.

INDONESIA

The largest theatre-as-propaganda program within the Indonesian government is administered by the Ministry of Information through its network of offices beginning on the national and provincial level, extending through regional, district, and city levels, and reaching down as far as the sub-district and the village. Most of the government's theatre efforts are concentrated on the island of Java, where theatre traditions are strong and where more than half the population of the country lives. In its theatre program the Ministry has adopted an indirect and a direct approach. In its indirect approach the Ministry works through existing professional troupes. I have mentioned that low-level Ministry of Information officials pass along propaganda material to professional troupes, hoping they will put the material in their plays. Materials usually are prepared at the provincial level by officials of the People's Information Section. They may be merely statements of government policy or they may be play scripts and scenarios which incorporate the desired propaganda themes. Up through the 1950's a good deal of effort went into the indirect approach. Many troupes were regularly contacted by information officials. "Every week the local information man visited us," the manager of a sandiwara troupe told me. "He gave us ideas to put in our plays. He would tell us when Hero's Day was, or Cooperation Day, and we would put something in so the audience would know, too." Efforts to work through professional troupes have fallen off in recent years.

The Ministry's direct approach is to set up and run its own propaganda theatre troupes. Professional performers are hired as officials of the Ministry of Information. Their full-time job is to write, direct, or perform propaganda plays. The Ministry of Information got into the theatre business during the years of the Revolution (1945-1949), when Indonesia's struggling nationalist government sought ways of rallying the people's support. Conventional mass media—radio, motion pictures, the press—were in the hands of the Dutch. Nothing was more natural than to turn to wayang shadow drama, the traditional mode of cultural expression of the Javanese, as a means of telling the people about government policy. And so wayang suluh (*suluh* means torch or information) was born. Puppets were flat leather cutouts, as in wayang kulit. But they represented contemporary figures—Soekarno, Nehru, soldiers, Dutchmen, peasants—and they were cut and painted in realistic fashion. The puppets told stories of "national leaders and guerrilla soldiers in their struggle to obtain independence for their country."[12] Wayang suluh was ideally suited to its purpose. The Dutch controlled the cities, but it was easy for student-guerrillas to tote a dozen leather puppets, a small screen, and a lamp along back-country trails. In villages along the route of their march the soldiers performed rousing stories of the fight against the Dutch. Plays were short, for the guerrillas often had little time; they were simple, so unsophisticated peasants could understand them. It is difficult to estimate how many troupes were operating during the Revolution. The Dutch thought wayang suluh effective enough to take the trouble, during the Second Military Action of 1948, to search for, confiscate, and destroy several hundred wayang suluh puppets. When the Revolution ended in 1949 the main reason for wayang suluh's existence ended as well. People began to see and to care that the puppets were crude and the stories blatant, and no audience would pay to have wayang suluh performed. It was kept alive only through performances sponsored and paid for by the Ministry of Information.

As the deficiencies of wayang suluh became more apparent, a new form of wayang was created which, it was hoped, would retain the mystic appeal and artistic excellence of traditional wayang kulit while conveying a modern social and political message. This remarkable creation was called *wayang Pantja Sila*. It was conceived by Mr. Harsono Hadisoeseno, puppeteer and leader of a government information unit. The five heroes of the *Mahabharata* became symbols for the Pantja Sila, the five principles of the Indonesian state as proclaimed by President Soekarno. Yudistira became "Belief in God," Arjuna "Nationalism," Bima "Humanity," and the twins, Nakula and Sadewa, "Sovereignty of the People" (or "Democracy") and "Social Justice."

According to the story, there is a demon . . . the Colonizer, who, through trickery had killed . . . Miss Freedom, and had scattered the remains of her body all over the Indonesian archipelago. The scattered body of freedom becomes four princesses, who symbolize the Dutch-sponsored "member states" created by Dr. Van Mook in 1946. A hero [Arjuna] . . . comes to defend Miss Freedom. He arrives too late to prevent the scattering of her body, but succeeds in defeating the demon "Colonizer." At this point the most feared of all the figures in the Hindu epic steps in—Batara Durga, wife of Shiva, the destroyer. She brings the demon back to life again in the form of several evils facing Indonesia after it had proclaimed its independence. These are the evils of aggression, starvation, the combined evil of inflation and black-marketeering, and the evil of loss of moral standards. The hero continues the fight against these four evils . . . [but] . . . the story will not end . . . until Indonesia, in the light of its five principles, is firmly wedded to the immortal spirit of true Freedom . . . Thus a traditional method of informing and educating the public was adapted to fulfill a critical current need, at the same time enriching one of the most interesting aspects of Indonesian culture.[13]

According to Javanese mystic thought there are 144 human passions and characteristics. Puppet figures visually represent all these traits in traditional wayang kulit. It was not difficult, therefore, to select appropriate puppet figures to symbolize all the modern concepts of wayang Pantja Sila. Just as the puppets of the five Pandava brothers symbolized the five principles of the Pantja Sila, other traditionally "good" puppet figures symbolized Miss Freedom, Health Services, Education, Agriculture, and so on, while traditional demon puppet figures symbolized evils such as Plant Disease, Devaluation, Inflation, and Loss of Moral Standards, as well as the competing ideologies of Feudalism, Marxism, Individualism, Intellectualism, and others.

Wayang Pantja Sila was created by the Ministry of Information for its own performers, but it was hoped that audiences would take to the new form and that professional dalang would begin to perform it. This did not happen. Like wayang suluh and the dozen wayang forms created by Javanese princes in past centuries to glorify themselves, wayang Pantja Sila never caught on with the public. Likely its elaborate symbolism was too complex for villagers to understand (though in theory its symbolism was the strongest point in its favor). Perhaps professional dalang shied away from it because it was so closely tied to government sponsorship. Government support for wayang Pantja Sila has declined drastically in recent years. Its mild, democratically inclined message is out of date. Marxism, for example, is one of the demons in wayang Pantja Sila. But today Marxism is called by President Soekarno the most suitable economic system ("adapted to Indonesian conditions") for the country. Wayang Pantja Sila is very seldom performed any more. It disappeared as quickly as new propaganda needs pushed it aside.

Concurrent with its efforts to develop wayang suluh and wayang Pantja Sila as communication media, the Ministry of Information has hired troupes of various standard genres to tell the government's story. Wayang beber was experimented with, largely because it was simple and inexpensive to perform. A puppeteer to tell the story, some pictures painted on paper, and perhaps an assistant or two were all that was needed. Troupes of dagelan comedians were sent touring through central and east Java. Dagelan are the clown roles in ludruk and ketoprak; a dagelan troupe is made up of four or five performers, all of whom play comic roles. These troupes proved extremely successful with village audiences. In east Java, ludruk troupes were also hired or were formed by the government. Table 13 shows the number of troupes directly controlled by regional offices of the Ministry of Information in Java in 1964 and the approximate number of performers involved.

Table 13. Number of troupes and performers employed by offices of the Indonesian Ministry of Information, 1964.

Supervising office	Troupe type	Number of troupes	Number of performers
Provincial Information Office	Dagelan	11	55
Semarang, Central Java	Wayang suluh	4	12
	Wayang beber	1	2
Provincial Information Office	Dagelan	12	60
Surabaya, East Java	Wayang suluh	10	25
	Wayang beber	3	6
	Ludruk	2	20
Information Office, Special	Dagelan	1	5
District of Jogjakarta			

In 1964 the Indonesian Ministry of Information employed 44 theatre troupes made up of 185 full-time performers. This is an impressive number. When the Ministry's theatre program was in full swing in the late 1950's yearly audiences were estimated at 5,000,000 people. It is the unanimous opinion of everyone concerned that the program at that time was highly successful. But beginning around 1960, as the Indonesian economy weakened, as inflation became rampant, and as the armed forces began taking a lion's share of the national budget, the Ministry was forced to retrench on all its activities including its theatre program. Between 1960 and 1963 the number of performances given by Ministry of Information troupes in the Province of East Java decreased by almost 50 percent (see Table 14). Although the number of performances declined sharply during this three-year period the number of troupes remained about the same. Most performers stayed on the payroll as civil servants; but they did less work. Just how little performing government troupes did in the province in 1963 can be seen from Table 15's breakdown of the performances given that year. The average dagelan troupe hired by the Provincial Information Office performed less than once a month. The average ludruk troupe performed a little more than once a month and wayang beber once every two weeks. Even wayang suluh troupes, which performed more often than the others, only performed about once every ten days.

In the Province of Central Java, the Ministry's direct theatre program came to a virtual halt in 1962 because of worsening economic conditions. Sixteen troupes of performers remain on the payroll of the Provincial Information Office but they practically

Table 14. Number of performances by Ministry of Information troupes, East Java, 1960–1963.

Year	Number of performances
1960	1084
1961	811
1962	800
1963	575

Table 15. Average number of performances per Ministry of Information troupe per year, East Java, 1963.

Troupe type	Number of performances	Number of troupes	Average
Wayang suluh	338	10	34
Dagelan	123	12	10
Wayang beber	83	3	28
Ludruk	31	2	16
Total	575	27	21

never perform. There is not enough money in the Office's budget to cover transportation and production expenses which performances entail. The Provincial Office still gets its old budget, but because of inflation the money doesn't go far. In 1955 a performance reaching 10,000 people could be produced for 450 rupiah; today the same performance costs 4,000 rupiah. From time to time the Provincial Office still arranges special performances. This happens so seldom, however, they don't bother to keep records any more. Given better economic conditions within the country, the Indonesian Ministry of Information undoubtedly would be running one of the three or four largest propaganda theatre programs in the world. As it is, the Indonesian government does more than any other government in Southeast Asia to use theatre as a communication tool.

A summary of a 39-page pamphlet prepared in 1962 by the Information Office of the Province of East Java and sent to the forty District Information offices in the province follows. Its contents are typical of the kinds of information disseminated by the Ministry of Information. Although in past years guidance pamphlets of this kind were regularly prepared and distributed, they are written and sent out infrequently now.

1. Dagelan: complete script in dialogue form. Two Clowns cannot understand government policy and are mildly opposed to it until the Village Head explains to them the meaning of Sovereignty of the People, the Continuing Revolution, Socal Justice and Prosperity, the Foundation of the Indonesian Nation, and Pantja Sila.
2. Wayang suluh: brief scenario. Concerns President Soekarno's Three-fold People's Command to Bring Irian Barat (West New Guinea) Into the Nation.

3. Wayang suluh: scenario with partial dialogue. The dalang explains that, according to the command of President Soekarno of July 5, 1959, the foundation of the state must be Manipol and USDEK. Youth, Farmer, Police Cadet, and others in the village question the Village Head about government policy. The Village Head tells them the nation must become Self-Sufficient in Rice, all people must carry out the President's Three-Fold People's Command, society must utilize a Progressive System, the government firmly supports Land Reform. The District Head then enters and explains procedures for carrying out the Land Reform policy.

4. Dagelan: complete script of a play called *Pantja Sila* (in the Madurese language). The Clowns try to find out what Pantja Sila is. The local Information Officer comes on the scene and in two long speeches tells the Clowns the vital importance of: Pantja Sila (consisting of Belief in God, Nationalism, Humanism, Sovereignty of the People, and Social Justice), Land Reform, Increased Productivity, Self-Sufficiency in Rice, Social Justice and Prosperity, Cooperative Rice Harvesting, Elimination of Illiteracy, the National Front, Unity in Diversity [the Indonesian national motto], and Fighting Dutch Imperialism.

5. Wayang suluh: new lyrics for six traditional wayang melodies. Two lyrics concern USDEK and one Liberate New Guinea.

6. Wayang Pantja Sila: brief essay on performance technique (though apparently wayang Pantja Sila is not performed any more).

7. Texts of six famous poems (*tembang*) given as examples of ancient poetry containing little archaic language (*Kawi*), and hence understandable by village audiences.

8. Modern songs: topical lyrics for 19 songs about Manipol, USDEK, Land Reform, Social Revolution, the Central Rice Bank, Discipline, Eliminate Corruption, Dutch Colonial Imperialism, and so on.

Even allowing for the distortion that has resulted from summarizing the contents of the pamphlet, it is apparent that the overriding concern of the Information Office is to name current slogans as directly and as often as possible. Of the four plays in the pamphlet none demonstrates its message through the action of the play. No patriot marches off to West New Guinea to fight the Dutch. No citizen benefits from a concrete act of Social Justice. No farmers harvest their rice cooperatively nor do any receive new plots of land through the Land Reform program. No corruptor is captured and tried (or even appears on stage for that matter). No patriotic worker produces more of anything. A primary canon of playwriting is that the message or theme of a drama is most effectively communicated by the action of the play. There is scarcely any action at all in these suggested plays. In fact, they are more "staged interviews" than plays. It is no wonder that no professional troupe I visited had ever used a government written scenario as the basis for a complete performance.

If these government play scenarios are compared with the scenarios of the two plays put on by the Communist-oriented troupes mentioned before, the differences are extremely instructive. Government officials (the Village Head, the District Information Officer) are the heroes of the former; idealistic men of the people are the heroes of the latter. In the former, problems are solved through normal government channels; in the latter, the people themselves take direct action to redress their wrongs. As already mentioned, the PNI dominates the Indonesian government bureaucracy while the PKI relies mainly on mass support from outside the government structure. This is reflected in their plays. The PNI, in power and anxious to maintain its strength through its hold on the bureaucracy, emphasizes in its plays the legitimacy of policies of the government and the effectiveness of these policies as carried out by duly constituted public officials (themselves). The PKI, out of power but on the fringes of it, subtly attacks the authority of government officials (the PNI) by leaving these officials entirely out of their plays (implying that society can get along without them) and by having its "people's heroes" lead the masses—the peasants and workers—into taking direct action, quite apart from whatever the government might do.

In addition to the Ministry of Information in Indonesia, the armed services also operate a few theatre troupes. The army especially is in a powerful position within the government. Its budget is by far the largest of any branch of the government and its political support is generally considered an essential element in President Soekarno's political position. Each major command of the army has a Morale Unit (URRIL) whose assignment is to entertain troops in the command. Soldiers assigned to a URRIL unit are performers of one kind or another, and each unit maintains several more or less separate groups of performers. The URRIL unit of the West Java Military Command in Bandung contains, in addition to several dance bands and Sundanese music groups, a sandiwara troupe of thirty members, two troupes of comedians (*reog*) of eight members each, and six wayang golek puppeteers along with forty gamelan musicians and female singers (civilians on contract). The unit has excellent and ample equipment: gamelan and Western musical instruments, public address systems, costumes, scenery, and trucks and gasoline to take the troupes wherever they are needed. URRIL officers say they usually choose "patriotic or fight" plays (such as the *Baratayuda* for wayang golek, or *Diponegoro* for sandiwara) as appropriate for their military audience. The primary function of military theatre troupes is to entertain. Their secondary function is to inform. Similar morale units are found in all the armed services. Army, navy, and air force headquarters in Djakarta also sometimes send out professional troupes for one- to two-month tours of military posts on the outer islands. Actors in three troupes I visited said they had toured Celebes, Borneo, and Sumatra under military auspices.

VIETNAM

In recent years the government of south Vietnam has attempted to use theatre as a means of communicating with the masses of people, but its theatre programs have been less ambitious than those of the Indonesian government and, by and large, less successful. Prior to the coup which toppled Diem in 1963, a number of amateur and semiprofessional theatre troupes were set up within the Republican Youth, the youth arm of the Diem party apparatus. Members of the Republican Youth, mainly high school and college students, acted in the plays and worked backstage. In Saigon some twenty Republican Youth troupes were in existence in 1963. They rehearsed in a large hall set aside for them in the city office of the Department of Youth and Information and under the direction of three or four professional theatre directors on the permanent staff of the Department. Most troupes performed two or three times a year in their own neighborhoods in conjunction with government-sponsored rallies or national holidays. Performances were given on street-corners or in public squares in order to reach ordinary citizens as much as possible. In addition, the Saigon office of the Department of Youth and Information and the Department of Civic Action supported one troupe of professional actors each. The former troupe performed only in Saigon; the latter toured various parts of the country. In 1963, officials of the Department of Civic Action said the government intended to set up an amateur troupe in every ward of every city and in every fortified hamlet. This ambitious plan seems never to have been seriously attempted, however. At most a few amateur troupes were organized in larger cities such as Hue, Danang, and Can Tho, as well as in Saigon.

Plays produced by these civil ministry sponsored troupes followed three propaganda themes laid down by the central government: support the government in its policy of combating underdevelopment; support the government in its policy of combating dissension; and support the government in its policy of combating Communism. Each statement combines a positive appeal to "support the government" with a negative appeal to "combat" something being opposed. With the fall of the Diem government, the Republican Youth organization disbanded, the personnel of the Departments was changed, and all the troupes mentioned disbanded or stopped performing. It is still too early to know whether attempts will be made by succeeding governments to set up and operate propaganda troupes through any of its civil ministries.

Theatre troupes are also supported by the Vietnamese army. Each of the four Army Corps Headquarters has attached to it a Psychological Warfare Unit, containing an Art Platoon composed of military actors, dancers, musicians, stage technicians, and civilian actresses. The first Art Platoon, tried out on an experimental basis in 1963, was so favorably received that other platoons were established in the following year. The exact composition of each platoon varies somewhat from corps to corps, but their general structure and operation are similar. Typically they contain thirty to forty members. Three or four men are professional singers or actors (recruited from Saigon, often by the simple expedient of drafting them into the army). Half a dozen professional civilian actresses are hired on contract. Any soldier in the army can take a performing arts test and if accepted be assigned to an Art Platoon. These amateurs make up the rest of the platoon. A junior-grade officer, usually with some theatre experience, commands the platoon. In late 1963 the aims of military Art Platoons differed greatly from the aims of the theatre troupes managed by the departments of Civic Action, and Youth and Information. In order of importance, the aims of the Art Platoons were: to entertain, to demonstrate the cruelty of the Vietcong, and to raise money for charities. Performances were given almost entirely for military audiences rather than for audiences of civilians. In the opinion of an American army major attached as an advisor to a Psychological Warfare Unit, the Diem government in the fall of 1963 was "concentrating its propaganda on the elements in the country they fear most—their own army."[14] This assessment was made just three weeks before army leaders, with wide popular support, deposed Diem and his government.

The typical Art Platoon performs two or three times a week. This is not very often. Singers and dancers learn standard routines which they can incorporate into any performance. Pantomimes, plays, and skits are written especially for a platoon by writers in the platoon. Occasionally a script written by Psychological Warfare Headquarters in Saigon is produced by one of the platoons, but essentially the whole Art Platoon system is decentralized. Play scripts that a platoon intends to produce need not be cleared with Headquarters in Saigon, nor are they submitted to the civilian Censor Board for approval. As a result, some of the plays put on by army Art Platoons are the most freewheeling of any to be seen in Vietnam. To give just one example: In late 1963 a platoon staged an extremely appealing dance-pantomime that showed soldiers and peasants dancing together while harvesting the rice crop. They waltzed, fox-trotted, did the jitterbug and the latest twist. This was at a time when all dancing in Vietnam was banned by Madame Nhu. No one else could have staged a dance in public; but the army did. Another Art Platoon program was given in a driving rainstorm; nevertheless, about one hundred officers and noncommissioned officers filled all the chairs that had been set up and about three hundred enlisted men stood through the three-hour performance. Two plays were included in the twenty-four-act program. The first play was an anti-Communist melodrama. A foolish Vietcong recruit is forced by a leering, swaggering Vietcong cadre to send his eight-year-old daughter out to bomb a bridge. When the recruit's wife tearfully tries to intervene, the cadre laughingly shoots her through the heart. Aroused, the husband wrestles for the gun, and the cadre is slain. The little girl staggers home, battered by the bomb blast, and falls dead in her father's arms. The second play, called Honest and Cruel, had nothing to do with Communism but conveyed a nonpolitical, humanistic message. Two comic thieves break into the house of a middle-class civil servant only to find nothing to steal. The family's mortgage is about to be foreclosed by a cynical city-slicker who has designs on the householder's lovely daughter. The comic thieves expose the mortgage collector, and in the end the honesty and virtue of the "little people" triumph. Though the plays were presented in a heavy-handed manner, the actors performed with sincerity and the audience was genuinely moved.

There is a smoothly functioning propaganda troupe working in the delta country south of Saigon conceived of and organized by a United States Special Forces officer. The troupe is paid a monthly salary to perform where and when it is directed. It rehearses at its home base for several days then goes by truck into a forward area where it performs several times a day for four or five days, each time in a different location. The troupe performs for rural, civilian audiences only. Its operation is simple, self-contained, and apparently quite successful. Initially one of the biggest problems faced by the American officer in charge was to convince his young performers from Saigon that their village audiences wanted to hear traditional music (hat boi and cai luong) not modern jazz.

Considering that Vietnam is at war and has been so for the past twenty years, it is surprising to see how little effort the Vietnamese government has put into encouraging the hundred or so professional troupes in Vietnam to perform plays which support the government's war effort. Thousands of plays are produced every year by professional cai luong, hat boi, and kich troupes. Yet you will not find a single specifically anti-Communist play among them, not even one which boldly dramatizes the responsibility of patriotic citizens to support their government. But, while the Vietnamese government does little to use theatre to bring its message to the common people, the Vietcong has its own theatre troupes working quietly and continuously within south Vietnam proclaiming the Communist message. In 1963, in Ba Xuyen province in the southern delta country, the Vietnamese army captured a complete Vietcong cai luong troupe. They carried simple stage equipment hung on poles slung over their shoulders the way itinerant troupes of actors have done in Vietnam for centuries. They followed canals and rice-field footpaths far from roads and big towns. During the day they hid. At night they would enter a village, Vietcong regulars would round up an audience at gun-point, and for an hour or so the troupe would perform its propaganda plays glorifying life under Communism and contrasting it with the cruelty and corruption of the present government. Then the troupe would slip away into the darkness and move on to the next village. According to army informants there are many Communist troupes which operate as this one did. *

UNITED STATES INFORMATION SERVICE

In several countries of Southeast Asia the United States Information Service (USIS)† uses traditional theatre forms to bring its message to local populations. USIS's best-established theatre program is in Laos. Laos is the least developed country in Southeast Asia. There are few miles of road, and few newspapers and radios. Illiteracy is widespread, and the usual media USIS relies upon to reach a people—books and libraries, pamphlets, newspaper releases, radio and TV broadcasts—had little relevance to the situation in Laos. But Laos had a live popular theatre tradition, the tradition of mohlam. In 1957, when USIS entered an exhibit in the important annual fair at That Luang, it was decided to include along with the usual book exhibit, square dances, and motion pictures, a team of mohlam performers (male singer, female singer, and khen player). Traditional mohlam performers sing earthy love ballads. They often include bits of local gossip and news as well. The idea was that USIS would provide the mohlam team with a simple propaganda theme which the team would then work into its otherwise usual performance. The first theme carried by the mohlam team was "unfriendly neighbors to the north misleading the honest Lao people." The

*Another Viet Cong troupe was captured by United States forces in September 1966.
†Called the United States Information Service (USIS) abroad and the United States Information Agency (USIA) at home, both names refer to the same organization.

experiment worked so well that a mohlam program was set up on a regular basis. USIS now has four teams on contract. Each team of three members performs a minimum of fifteen nights a month. Teams are under the direction of a USIS Field Officer, who dispatches them wherever they are invited—to temple festivals, to fairs, to national and local celebrations, and, occasionally, to private celebrations. The troupes are now known in most parts of the country and USIS receives more invitations for them to perform than they can accept. Troupe members are all from the Thai side of the Mekong River. Racially they are Lao, but they are Thai citizens. The reason for this is that few Lao citizens have performed mohlam in recent years. When USIS began searching for troupes it found that the only artists available for hire lived in Thailand. An unexpected byproduct of USIS's eight-year mohlam program is that it has sparked a local revival of interest in mohlam among Laos.

The scope of the USIS mohlam program can be seen in a few figures. Over six hundred USIS-sponsored mohlam performances were given in the twelve-month period from July 1962 to July 1963 when three teams were under contract. Performances were given in every part of the country under the control of the Royal Lao Government (about 40 percent of the land area of Laos). An estimated 930,000 people saw these performances—one out of every two people living under the jurisdiction of the central government. The average mohlam performance attracted an audience three times as large as the average USIS motion picture shown during the same period.* USIS officials in both Washington and the field consider the mohlam program their single most effective means of reaching the masses of people in Laos.

A typical USIS mohlam performance is made up of half a dozen thirty-minute routines and lasts about three hours. Twenty minutes of each routine is standard mohlam fare, joyfully graphic accounts of lovemaking and courtship. Ten minutes is propaganda "freight." Propaganda items are fashioned to suit the need, but at any time around ten are in the repertory: five are basic items included in every performance and five are supple-

---

*An estimated 1,500,000 Lao attended 3500 showings of USIS films in 1962–63. The average movie attendance was approximately 430 compared to the average mohlam attendance of 1550.

mentary items used less often. The basic items in late 1963 were: Lao self-help for well-digging, school-building, and similar projects; support the Royal Lao government; pro-Buddhism; American economic aid; and Lao history. These boil down to three basic themes: encourage consciousness of a Lao national identity capable of withstanding Communist blandishments; tell the story of American economic help; and support practical, worthwhile community development projects. Anti-Communist sloganeering has never been part of the program. Abstract appeals have no meaning for the Lao farmer. Rather, appeals are couched in terms the Lao knows. Primarily positive, they are practical appeals; and they reach the Lao in the form of a traditional entertainment which he loves and understands.

Further, short movies have been made of these performances. In the usual showing three short segments are spliced together. USIS Laos has also filmed seven half-hour mohlam luong plays. The plays are built around USIS propaganda themes, but, as in mohlam, the themes are never explicitly anti-Communist. In one, an evil neighboring kingdom tries to steal rice produced in a good kingdom, but is stopped when the good kingdom combines with a third friendly country to defeat its attacker (anti-Communism is implicit here). Another dramatizes how a village can build a school with the government's help. A third is about a traitor trying to stir up trouble between brothers, who only wish to live peacefully together.

Laos is not the first country in Asia where USIS has used theatre as a medium of communication. In 1955, USIS Saigon hired two professional cai luong troupes to perform propaganda plays throughout Vietnam. For a time they performed very successfully in Saigon and on tour. Shortly after the project began, however, personal conflicts among troupe members arose and the project was set aside.* USIS in Bangkok and the Thai Ministry of Information have considered the possibility of using mohlam mu teams in northeast Thailand among the Lao-speaking population there. From time to time a mohlam team working for USIS Laos will perform in Thailand. There is no regular pro-

---

*In May 1965, USIS Saigon decided to revive the program. By July 1966, USIS was supporting between 37 and 40 *ban kich* or variety troupes in most regions of Vietnam in cooperation with the Vietnamese Ministry of Information.

gram of exchange, however. It is said that Communist infiltration from Laos is posing an increasingly serious problem for the Thai government. A Thai-based mohlam program, in which themes appropriate to the Thai situation are made the basis of performance, would be one way of reaching the isolated populations of northeast Thailand.

From the earliest times the theatre has been used as an important means of communicating ideas in Southeast Asia, particularly to the broad masses of people in the countryside. All the major religions and major political philosophies have been propagated from stages of one theatre form or another. The large-scale political propaganda programs presently being carried on through theatre performances in Vietnam, in Indonesia, and by the United States Information Service are contemporary manifestations of the centuries-old tradition of using theatre to teach and to persuade.

CHAPTER 16

Theatre and Other Mass Media

Theatre in Western societies ceased being a medium of mass communication long ago. With but few exceptions, present-day theatre audiences in Western countries represent an educated, urban minority of the population; theatre is for the elite. In Southeast Asia, however, from as far back as we know theatre has functioned as a primary medium for communicating with broad masses of the people. Today, although modern mechanical and electronic media of mass communication have entered the picture, the function of the theatre has changed but little. Theatre reaches a mass audience; it remains a part of mass culture. It must be considered one of the "mass media" in Southeast Asia, along with printing, radio, television, and motion pictures.

SCOPE OF MASS MEDIA

Printing with movable type was the first media of modern mass communication to reach Southeast Asia from the West. European colonists and missionaries brought the art of printing with them as long ago as 350 years. By the end of the nineteenth century books, magazines, and newspapers were being published in every country in the area. Printing was cheap, efficient, and versatile. It made available the whole range of world knowledge to anyone who possessed the golden key— literacy. However, since no more than perhaps 5 percent of the population was literate, printing did not actually function as a "mass" media. It reached few people (though those few were important). Between 30 percent and 50 percent of the population of Southeast Asia today still cannot read, a condition which continues to limit the effectiveness of the printed word as a means of communication.

It was not until well into the twentieth century that other mass media, similar to theatre in the use of spoken and non-verbal forms of communication, entered into competition with live theatre. These were the international mass media of the motion picture, radio, and television. Motion pictures and radio became important in Southeast Asia in the 1930's and 1940's; television is just beginning to be developed. Though they are new to Southeast Asia and none has reached maturity, the main lines of their development can be described. There are about 350 radio stations in the eight countries of Southeast Asia. There are radio stations in every country—ranging in number from 2 in Cambodia to 69 in Indonesia to 140 in the Philippines—that broadcast to the general public. There are also special stations run by the police, the army, and the navy. The King of Thailand has his own private station. Special stations beam their broadcasts to specific audiences, but anyone who wishes to can tune in. Perhaps 90 percent of the population of Southeast Asia lives within the range of some national radio signal.

Table 16, which estimates the number of radio sets in most countries of Southeast Asia, shows that about 3 percent of the

Table 16. Estimated number of radio sets and percentage of population owning radios.

Country	Estimated number of radio sets	Population	Percentage of population owning radio sets
Malaysia	700,000	11,000,000	6
Philippines	1,500,000	30,000,000	5
Thailand	1,000,000	29,000,000	3
Indonesia	2,200,000	100,000,000	2
Vietnam	200,000	15,000,000	$1\frac{1}{2}$
Laos	25,000	2,000,000	1
Total	5,725,000	187,000,000	3

people own radios.[1] If an average of five people listen to each set, something like 15 percent of the population have access to radio communication (ranging from 30 percent in the Philippines to 5 percent in Laos).

The first television station in Southeast Asia was opened in Manila in 1953. It was followed by stations in Bangkok in 1955, Djakarta in 1962, Singapore in 1963, and others. In early 1964 there were twenty stations throughout the area: eleven in the Philippines (five in Manila, six in other cities), five in Thailand (two in Bangkok, and one each in Khon Kaen in the northeast, Lampang in the north, and Hadyai in the south), two in Malaysia (Singapore and Kuala Lumpur), and two in Indonesia (Djakarta and Bandung). A station is under construction in Phnom Penh, Cambodia.* In 1963, 30,000 licensed television sets were reported in Indonesia, 31,000 in Malaysia, 70,000 in the Philippines, and 200,000 in Thailand.[2] Roughly speaking, in countries that have television, one-tenth of one percent of the people own television sets. If we imagine that as many as ten people have access to each set still, only a little more than one percent of the population of these countries now see television. Television undoubtedly has the potential of transforming the cultural scene of Southeast Asia into something far different from what it is today, and many think this potential will be realized. The remark of a Thai television official is typical: "I see [television] as a great unifying force in bringing to people in the rural areas the cultural and educational advantages of the city as no other medium can."[3] It remains to be seen whether television will in fact reach a substantial proportion of the huge rural audience in Southeast Asia in the future. At the moment, television's audience is miniscule and largely confined to major metropolitan areas.

The motion picture was introduced from Europe and America as a commercial venture in the decades before World War II. Since the war the number of commercial movie houses in Southeast Asia has very greatly increased. Table 17 gives estimates of the number of permanent movie houses, as compared with legitimate theatre buildings used for live drama, in operation in 1963. These figures show how widely the patterns of movie–theatre relation vary from country to country. In Laos there are

---

*In February 1966, the first television station in Vietnam was opened in Saigon.

Table 17. Estimated number of movie houses and legitimate theatre buildings.

Country[a]	Number of movie houses[b]	Number of legitimate theatre buildings[c]
Cambodia	25	25
Indonesia	655	230
Laos	9	15
Philippines	676	0
Thailand	264	100
Vietnam	151	143

[a] Figures lacking for Burma and Malaysia.
[b] Estimates based partly on information in *Basic Facts and Figures* for the period 1957–1962 and partly on field data.
[c] Estimates based on field data.

more legitimate theatres than movie houses. In the Philippines there are 655 movie houses and *no* theatres being used for professional live drama at all. Over-all in Southeast Asia there are about three times as many permanent movie houses as there are permanent legitimate theatres (temporary theatre buildings used by small troupes and stages for puppet plays are not included here; were they the figures might be more nearly even). On a per-capita basis, the Philippines has the most movie houses, one for every 50,000 people, and Vietnam the most legitimate theatres, one for every 100,000 people.

The great majority of movie houses are located in large cities. Although statistics are not available to demonstrate this for each country, there can be no doubt of it. Let me take as two examples sparsely populated Cambodia and heavily populated Vietnam. In Cambodia 22 of the country's 25 movie houses are in the national capital (Phnom Penh) and the five largest provincial capitals.* In Vietnam 128 of 151 movie houses are in Saigon and provincial capitals. In other words, 88 percent of the movie houses in Cambodia and 85 percent of the movie houses in Vietnam are in major cities. By way of comparison, only 52 percent of the legitimate theatre buildings in Cambodia and 51 percent

*There are 11 movie houses in Phnom Penh, 3 in Battambang, 2 in Kampong Cham, 2 in Kampok, 2 in Siem Reap, and 2 in Kratie.

of the legitimate theatre buildings in Vietnam are in the national and provincial capitals.* I think these figures underestimate the number of legitimate theatre buildings in rural areas. In the Sundanese district of Bandung, where I hunted down all the theatre troupes (and buildings used as theatres) that existed, thirteen theatres were in small towns and villages and four were in the urban Bandung area—or 77 percent in rural areas and 23 percent in the city. Taking Southeast Asia as a whole, I believe the majority of professional theatre activity takes place outside of major metropolitan areas. In terms of communication function these differences between movies and theatre are important. Movies in Southeast Asia reach an audience that is predominantly urban, while live theatre reaches an audience more largely rural. According to United Nations sources, an estimated 500,000,000 people attend movies each year in the eight countries of Southeast Asia.[4] The United Nations does not collect data on audience attendance of live drama and published data from other sources is almost totally lacking. My own estimate is that at least 150,000,000 people see plays in Southeast Asia each year.†

CHARACTERISTICS OF THE COMMUNICATION MEDIA

So much for the scope of motion picture, radio, and television as compared with theatre. Each of these four mass media has special characteristics which affect its communication function.

PUBLIC AND PRIVATE MEDIA

Theatre and motion pictures are public media while radio and television are private media. A person goes to a public building to see a play or a movie; the radio listener or television viewer stays home. Because plays and movies are both public media they often are in direct competition with each other.

---

*In Cambodia, 13 out of the country's estimated 25 legitimate theatre buildings are in Phnom Penh and provincial capitals; in Vietnam, 73 of the country's 143 legitimate theatre buildings are in Saigon and provincial capitals.

†Assuming 600 regular professional theatre troupes (assuming 70 troupes in Burma) × 300 performances per year × 700 average audience = 126,000,000, plus 600 professional puppet troupes × 50 performances per year × 1000 average audience = 30,000,000, for an estimated total yearly audience of 156,000,000.

70. In Sunda a towering figure, inspired by traditional theatrical doll figures, demonstrates how to pierce a hammer-and-sickle ballot to vote for the Indonesian Communist Party.

71. A South Vietnamese government propaganda troupe of ten members travels to remote villages by dugout.

72. Wayang Pantja Sila: traditional wayang kulit figures are modernized in Java, as Arjuna wears a shirt and clowns cavort in contemporary army uniforms.

73. A USIS crew in Laos filming the climactic battle scene of a half-hour mohlan luong propaganda play.

Both are offered to the public during the same hours (movies may be shown twice an evening) and under similar financial conditions. Movie houses and theatre buildings tend to be in the same part of town often right next to each other. They both appeal to the person "out on the town," the person who is making a special effort to seek outside entertainment. Plays and movies compete directly for the attention, even the loyalty, of the spectator. Radio and television do not compete with theatre in the same way. In theory, a person may stay home and listen to radio or watch television instead of going out to see a play. Presumably some people do. But it is not necessary that a person choose between theatre and radio or television. Both can be enjoyed at different times and under different circumstances.

Competition is keenest between theatre and motion pictures in large cities where theatre troupes and movies offer the spectator several choices of entertainment at any given time. As one moves away from large metropolitan areas the degree of competition decreases. The smaller the town the less likely it is that a play and a movie will be operating at the same time. In the smallest villages movies are never shown; here theatre troupes have no competition. In some parts of Thailand, Cambodia, and the Philippines a few traveling movie outfits tour remote rural areas from time to time, but they are of minor significance.

TECHNOLOGY AND ITS CONSEQUENCES

A second difference between the four mass media lies in the technology of the communication process employed. In simple terms, we can say theatre is a "one-step" medium, the motion picture a "two-step" medium, and radio or television a "three-step" medium. In a theatre performance the communication process occurs as a single, indivisible action: the audience receives a message directly from live actors on stage. With motion pictures the communication process is divided into two distinct and separate steps: a movie is recorded on film first and only later viewed by an audience. In radio and television the communication process consists of three steps: first, a program is produced; second, it is transmitted via electrical means through the air; and third, it is received on a radio or television set where it can be listened to or watched by an audience.

Two important consequences of these differences in the communication process are immediately apparent. First, at the theatre an audience is asked to furnish nothing but eyes and ears in order to enjoy a play. The same is true of a movie audience. It is the exhibitor, not the audience, that provides the technology—projector and screen—which makes possible the viewing of a movie. However, a completely new factor is added in the radio or television communication process: the audience itself is asked to provide an expensive piece of equipment—the radio or television receiver—necessary to watch or listen to a program. Radio and television are unique media in making such a demand. In most Western countries the fact that the audience is expected to buy its own radio or television set is of no practical consequence, as standards of living are high enough so that a majority of people can afford radios and television sets. But in Southeast Asia, where living standards are much lower, the requirement that the audience furnish part of the technology of communication presents a serious obstacle to achieving truly mass communication through these media. Millions of dollars have been invested in radio and television studios. Hundreds of millions of dollars have been invested in transmitting equipment. But there still are relatively few radio and television receivers. A radio is an expensive item for most families; a television set is a luxury only the wealthy can afford. Attempting to solve the problem, some governments have distributed community radio sets and have tried giving away individual sets free of charge. Since most villages are not electrified, even these measures have not been too successful. The ultimate answer probably lies in the relatively cheap, battery-operated transistor sets now coming on the market in Southeast Asia.

The second important consequence is that, because the production of motion pictures and television programs can be completely separated from their showing or transmission, these two media have come to have a distinctly foreign odor in Southeast Asia. Movies and television programs can be made thousands of miles away from where they are shown. They can be shown years after they have been made. The vast majority of movies and television programs seen are imported from foreign distributors. The saturation of the Southeast Asian market by foreign-made films and programs is so great now that the charge of "foreign domination" of local culture increasingly is being leveled against the two media. In contrast, theatre is an intensely "national" medium of communication. Because production and viewing cannot be separated but must occur simultaneously plays can only be produced and performed locally.

In 1962, approximately 200 feature-length movies were made in Southeast Asia (150 of them in the Philippines). In the same year some 1900 were imported from Europe, the United States, and other Asian countries. Vietnam, the Philippines, Indonesia, and Thailand each imported more than 400 films that year. Cambodia did not produce any feature films but it imported 150. China (Hong Kong/Taiwan) was the largest supplier of foreign movies (around 500), followed by the United States (around 400), Japan (150), France (125), India (125), and mainland China (30). Young people, perhaps searching for new patterns of life, flock to see these foreign films. These same young people would not dream of going to see highbrow wayang kulit, middlebrow cai luong, or lowbrow likay. The situation alarms many Asian intellectuals who wish to foster in young people a spirit of pride in their own culture. The most pessimistic see the emergence of a modern generation which is not only alienated from local society and scornful of it but also dangerously frustrated by its unrealistic attempts to fulfill foreign-inspired aspirations and ways of life which cannot be achieved under the social and economic conditions which prevail in Southeast Asia today. Nationalist feeling runs high in the Philippines, Burma, Cambodia, and Indonesia, and imported movies are a natural target. Many Filipinos resent American cultural domination, and much of the blame is placed on American movies. Most foreign movies have been banned in Burma. They are carefully screened in Cambodia. As this newspaper account shows, in 1964 American films were boycotted by extreme nationalist and Communist groups in Indonesia.

> Menado. Movie houses here have ceased to screen American films after the boycott action against United States films was announced here by the Action Committee. They also demanded the ouster of United States Peace Corps members now in Indonesia. It is the duty of the youth and the Indonesian people in general to interpret the

command issued by the Great Leader of the Revolution/President Soekarno to crush and destroy imperialist practices in all manifestations, including in the cultural field, the Action Committee maintained. Meanwhile four elite movie houses, the best four in Menado, which used to screen American films exclusively, did not open last Saturday for lack of films. In keeping with the boycott action many walls were scribbled with anti-American slogans like "To Hell With US Imperialist Films," "Screen Nefos [New Emerging Forces] Films," and "To Hell With Your Aid!"[5]

It appears that the boycott was in part, simple political retaliation, triggered by the United States Government's announcement of support for Malaysia earlier in the month. (During the boycott, German, Japanese, and Italian films went on being shown as usual; yet from a national culture point of view they are just as "foreign," just as "capitalistic," just as "imperialistic" as American films.) The point is not that politics affects films, however, but that the two-step nature of the communication process makes possible importation of vast quantities of foreign motion pictures—for good or for ill—into Southeast Asia.

Audiences in Thailand are less aware of the foreignness of imported films because local actors dub in all dialogue in Thai. They do this live at each showing of a film. An actor and an actress usually travel as a pair, accompanying a film from town to town for several months at a time. Or, a very talented dubber may work alone, playing all the roles himself. The very best dubbers are known by name throughout Thailand, and people may come to hear them act more than to see the movie. Some specialize in regional dialects and work only in those areas where that dialect is spoken. The dubbers I saw at work were consummate artists holding their audiences spellbound with their flawless timing and their creation of vivid characters.

Television programming is dominated by foreign imports almost as much as motion picture exhibition. Roughly 65 percent of the programs broadcast by Manila television stations are from the United States. Of the programs broadcast in Djakarta and Bandung, around 60 percent originate outside Indonesia (most are American). A Bangkok station broadcast twenty-one American serials each week during the 1963 season—"Range Riders," "Hawaiian Eye," "The Untouchables," "Maverick," "Combat," "M-Squad," "Harbor Command," "The Texan,"

"Dennis the Menace," "Robinhood," "The Man and The Challenge," "This is the Answer," "The Alaskans," "Mackenzie's Riders," "The Case of Dangerous Robin," "The Big Picture," "Wild Bill Hickok," "Interpol Calling," "Ripcord," "Alfred Hitchcock Presents," and, no doubt to liven up a dull week, "Mantovani." Though commercial American programs make up the largest single group of imported programs, Japanese television series are also popular and free programs of all kinds are sought. Stations often broadcast public relations films, made by large corporations for prestige purposes, merely because broadcast rights are free.

And here we reach the crux of the problem. Foreign movies and television programs do not dominate the market because of Machiavellian plots of foreign governments to subvert Southeast Asian civilizations. They are popular because they are technically superior to local productions and because they are cheap. It costs a great deal of money to produce good motion pictures and television programs anywhere, including in Southeast Asia. Foreign companies have worldwide distribution organizations which allow them to rent first-class productions at low rates. Most Southeast Asian countries possess well-equipped studios and competent production staffs, but the economic fact of life is that it is cheaper to rent from foreign distributors than it is to produce locally. Radio in Southeast Asia has escaped the fate of a foreign image. Foreign radio tapes are broadcast by local stations to be sure and Western music is often played, but by and large the great majority of programs are of local origin. One of the reasons for this is that radio programming is relatively inexpensive to produce. One or two people can produce a radio program, but it takes dozens or even hundreds of people to produce motion pictures or television programs.

Of all the mass media theatre is the most completely local. Most movies and television programs seen in Southeast Asia are products of foreign cultures. They express foreign values and mores and ways of looking at life. Radio conveys the local news, gives advice on how to grow better crops, brings to the listener speeches of government officials, provides national and popular musical entertainment, yet it is not intrinsically indigenous. Each genre of theatre, however, is completely indigenous. Each is the unique product of some particular local culture and reflects that culture. Even the twentieth-century genres, which are scarcely older than radio or motion pictures, mirror the society of their time in a way that local radio stations and local motion picture houses have never done. Theatre, because it is a totally indigenous medium, is never objected to because it is foreign.

OWNERSHIP AND CONTROL

A third way in which the four mass media differ is in patterns of ownership and control. Most radio and television stations are government owned and operated. In Burma, Cambodia, Indonesia, Laos, and Vietnam broadcasting is a government monopoly. In most cases both radio and television control is vested in the Ministry of Information. In Thailand and in Malaysia private and government stations exist side by side in about equal numbers. Private interests own and control virtually all telecommunications in the Philippines. In this the Philippines is following American example. Most local motion picture production is in private hands. The Cambodian army makes Cambodian films, and in Indonesia PFN (*Persatuan Film Negara*) is a government film unit under the direction of the Ministry of Information. Otherwise film production is carried on by numerous, usually small, independent film companies. Movie houses are mostly independently owned as well, except in Malaysia where several large chains dominate movie distribution and showing. The Thai National Theatre, the Cambodian and Lao Royal Ballets, and the wayang orang troupe Sri Wedari are government owned or controlled. BAKOKSI, the Ludruk Association, and the Society of Northeast Thailand Folksong Singers are voluntary organizations of troupes that exert influence on member troupes but exercise operational control over no more than a handful of troupes. The other 1100-plus professional theatre troupes in Southeast Asia are independently owned and operated.

It is abundantly clear that through theatre important ethical, religious, social, and political concepts have been transmitted to the broad masses of the people in Southeast Asia in the past. Today the theatre communicates no less than it did centuries ago, though newer media share its communication function to a greater or lesser extent. Certainly USIS, the PKI, and the Indonesian and Vietnamese governments believe theatre to be an effective channel for communicating their messages. Theatre, however, operates somewhat differently than the other mass media. It reaches an estimated yearly audience of 150,000,000, compared to 500,000,000 for movies and a radio and television audience of undetermined size. Theatre reaches an older and more rural audience while movies reach a younger, more urban audience. Theatre is the most "Asian" media, being a product of Asian culture. Unlike radio and television, which require the audience to provide part of the technology of the communication process, theatre asks only that the spectator bring his eyes and ears with him. Though all media are subject to a degree of government censorship and control, theatre is the most independent of direct government ownership or control.

CHAPTER 17

Theatre and the
Communication Process

In most periods of human history people have assumed that the major aim of art was communication. Whether the art was painting or music, dance or poetry, artistic creations were intended to have some meaning for the reader, the listener, the viewer. It has only been during the last fifty years or so that another school of thought regarding the function of art has come into being. According to this view, art may have as its sole aim the self-expression of the artist, and the artist may profess no interest at all in what, if anything, the art work he creates communicates to others. This most recent theory on the function of art is almost entirely a product of Western societies. It is an expression of intense interest in the individual, a reflection of a strongly egoistic view of life and the human process.

In Southeast Asia, the art of theatre has always been considered a means of communication. Theatre artists have expected audiences to understand what a play was about; audiences have expected to be able to understand what was being staged before them. Sponsors have assumed that certain ideas, beliefs, emotions, and attitudes—and not others—were being communicated through dramatic performances which they arranged or paid for. At no time, even today, has the art of theatre in Southeast Asia been used by artists primarily as a means of self-gratification. There have been no Dadaists, no Surrealists as there have been in American and European theatre.

THE PERFORMER

One of the striking differences between the process of communication in Western and Southeast Asian theatre is that in the

[314]

former the performer almost never has the opportunity to determine what will be communicated, while in the latter the performer normally does. In the West a play is written by a playwright. The performer is expected to make no contribution to the content of a play; his only function is to perform it in a suitable manner. In Southeast Asia, on the other hand, the performer has considerable latitude with regard to content. In the very broadest sense, the performer does not choose the subject matter of a play: this is fixed pretty well by tradition—the subject matter of wayang drama is *Mahabharata* and *Ramayana* stories, Chinese tales in hat boi, *Jataka* stories in lakon jatri, and so on. Plots also tend to follow standard patterns. But the puppeteer of wayang kulit or nang talung can rearrange standard scenes into "new" plays. The likay actor improvises plot as he goes along. Actors in most genres ad-lib their lines to a greater or lesser extent. In most cases performers do not consciously take advantage of these opportunities to insert their own ideas. There are many occasions, however, on which they do use the opportunity which the special nature of Southeast Asian theatre production gives them to propagate particular messages. Clowns in almost every genre invent their own topical jokes. Politically oriented performers can communicate their political beliefs to an audience in a way no Western legitimate theatre performer can do. Actual control over what is said in performances may be fragmented among several people and agencies. The owner of a troupe may dictate what plays will be given. The artistic director may choose plays and arrange plots. A government censor or the local police may object to scenes or themes within a play. Nevertheless, the performer possesses a most important communication function—that of determining at least part of what will be communicated. As a result the performer in Southeast Asia has a far more important role in communication than his Western counterpart.

CODES AND CONTENT

Another important difference between the communication process in Western and Southeast Asian theatre is that the standard patterns through which the content of a play is communicated are of relatively little importance in Western theatre, while in Southeast Asian theatre these patterns, or "codes" as they are usually called in communication terms, are quite significant. Western drama is content-centered; it focuses on "what-is-said." Audiences pay little attention to the patterns or codes through which content is communicated, and are little concerned with "how-it-is-said." Normally the only codes that are used are the ordinary codes of language, speech patterns, and vague rules about dramatic structure. In Southeast Asian theatre, however, content is conveyed through codes of music, dance, and visual production elements as well as through codes of language, speech patterns, and dramatic structure. Audiences are keenly aware of these artistic patterns or codes. A Thai spectator can enjoy the technical brillance of a khon dance scene. An Indonesian may listen primarily to gamelan melodies that accompany a wayang kulit shadow drama and watch little of the play. A likay actor may enchant his audience with the beauty of his poetic improvisation. A Cambodian watching the massed movements of the stunningly costumed corps de ballet at the royal palace in Phnom Penh can react solely to the visual beauty of the scene before him. A Vietnamese in a cai luong theatre may burst into applause when his favorite singer ends a perfect rendition of the song Vong Co for the eighth time that evening, having heard scarcely a word of the lyrics. These spectators are reacting to artistic patterns, not to content. They are enjoying beauty of form quite apart from "what it means." This kind of aesthetic pleasure is extremely important in most types of Southeast Asian theatre. Aesthetic reactions are much less pronounced in Western theatre where drama is content-centered and there are no strongly developed codes or artistic patterns undergirding an essentially realistic spoken drama. We must turn to Western ballet or opera or orchestral music to find similar performance situations within our own culture where audiences respond primarily in terms of aesthetic appreciation for beauty of form rather than in understanding of content.

Aesthetic pleasure is a learned reaction deriving from intimate knowledge of the artistic patterns which characterize a theatre form. It is essential that both performer and spectator be familiar with the same codes in order for communication to take place. In one sense this limits the communication function of theatre in Southeast Asia for not everybody knows all the patterns of a theatre genre. About one hundred figures from the

Ramayana are distinquished in khon by visual patterns—face color, mask color, mask shape, and style of headdress. In wayang kulit over one hundred and fifty puppet characters can be identified by the shape of the puppet silhouette alone. There are some one hundred and fifty gamelan melodies in Surakarta style wayang, catalogued according to mood, function, place within performance, and appropriateness to different characters. These are all fixed patterns. In theory, at least, a spectator could learn these patterns en toto. In fact few do. The task is too hard. No one but a dance teacher can identify all the khon characters. No one but a wayang expert can identify all the wayang melodies or figures. Does this mean that communication does not take place? Not at all. What it does mean is that because the codes of most traditional theatre forms are complex only devoted study will yield up all their intricacies to the spectator. Children can master a few elements of the codes, young adults more, and elderly people still more. Devotees take pride in learning all of the code they possibly can. At each level some communication takes place, more with each successive level of experience and knowledge on the part of the spectator. Also a spectator may respond to a code, after being exposed to it many times, without consciously knowing what he is responding to. Naming is not communication. The spectator may not know the name of the gamelan melody that precedes the entrance of the clown Semar, but he may recognize the implication of the melody and be able to say to you, "Here comes the clown scene." Here the spectator unconsciously knows the artistic pattern. Communication has taken place.

CONVEYING NEW CONTENT

Granted that in the initial stages of learning the various artistic patterns which distinguish a theatre genre, communication may be hampered by the spectator's lack of familiarity with these patterns, once a certain minimum level of familiarity is reached the theatre becomes an exceptionally flexible medium for communicating content of all kinds, even that not originally associated with the theatre form. A traditional play may be performed more or less as it always has been except for the addition of new content. A king may be made to heed the wishes of his subjects at the play's crisis rather than evincing no interest in their opinions, and by making this slight but crucial alteration in a standard play, convey to the audience the modern concept of equal rights of men. Or, without disturbing the over-all structure or content of a traditional play, a line of dialogue, a song, or a dance with a new message can be inserted. This is what clowns do. This is what the Sundanese wayang golek singer does. This is the technique used by the PKI in Java from at least as early as 1955.

> The PKI frequently organized village festivals, held at night in an open field and centered around a ketoprak performance; in this, popular stories were played with dialogues, which were filled with communist slogans. Large crowds were attracted from the villages, where recreational facilities are as a rule very scarce. The players, trained in propaganda, were generally skillful in inserting the slogans in their dialogue without seriously distorting the content. This technique was most effective in popularizing the slogans, which could long be remembered because of the attractive plays. So far no other political party has conducted any campaign of such a nature in Jogja, probably because of shortage of funds and shortage of organizational skills.[1]

Most intriguing to me is the way the well-known patterns of a theatre form may be retained almost intact while a totally new but analogous content is substituted for the old, traditional content of the drama. Islamic wayang golek was created from Hindu-Javanese wayang kulit in this way and in more recent years wayang suluh and wayang Pantja Sila. To illustrate this technique of "putting new wine in old bottles," here is a rough translation of the passage with which every Hindu-Javanese wayang kulit play begins, followed by the analogous opening passage for a wayang suluh play which was written in 1962 by the East Java Office of Information for use by their wayang suluh propaganda teams. The wayang suluh passage is a direct copy of the form and structure of the wayang kulit passage, though its content is modernized and quite different in many details.

Wayang kulit
(*The dalang narrates.*) Now, for the country I am going to mention first. Even though there are many countries created by the gods under the heavens, on the earth, between the oceans, even though there are

many countries, none are equal to the Kingdom of Astina. Thus do I introduce this kingdom, for if you search among a hundred countries you would not find two, or among a thousand not ten, equal to it. This country: long, powerful, oceans, mountains, fertile, cheap, trade, foreigners, peace, no evil. Long is its reputation and the telling of it. Powerful and influential is its rule. Oceans face it; mountains at the back, with rice fields on the left, and a large harbor to the front. Fertile: merchants trade day and night hindered by no disturbance of the peace. Foreigners: so many choose to live here the roofs of their houses touch, and large spaces look small so crowded is the city. Peace: the farmers are at peace and work all day long in the fields, the cattle graze untended for there are no thieves and come home at evening by themselves. No evil: no enemies are near, the ministers are experienced in their duties, honest, wise, have knowledge, know how to rule the country, and strive to keep the nation safe and honorable. The country stands firm on the world, its torch is high, it makes the world bright. Its colonies are many. Not only on Java are all countries subjugated, but kings of many foreign countries accept vassaldom willingly because they adore the perfectness of the country. Near, they bow flat to the ground before her perfectness; farther afield, they still incline to show their respect. Diplomats bring offerings as token of their countries' submission. And who rules Astina? We can say he is King Yudistira [*here follows a long list of his other names*]. Indeed, King Yudistira is like a holy ascetic who desires only perfectness. He will refuse no request; if you wish to kill him he will accept it. He is fond of religious life, fond of showing justice, strives to behave as a gentleman. A wise king, he is honored by the gods. It would take all night just to tell the many qualities of this country.

Wayang suluh

(*The dalang narrates.*) Now, for the country I am going to mention first. Even though there are many countries created by Allah under the heavens, on the earth, and between the oceans that are favored by the sun and the moon, they are far different from the country lying between Asia and Australia, between the Pacific and Indian oceans, consisting of thousands of islands, "from Sabang to Merauke," and looking like a necklace of jewels on green velvet, that is called Islands of the Indies or the Republic of Indonesia. Thus do I introduce this country, for if you search among a thousand countries you would not find ten equal to it. This country: long, powerful, oceans, mountains, fertile, cheap, trade, prosperity, peace, no evil. Long is its reputation and the telling of it. Powerful and influential is its rule. Oceans facing it. Mountains at the back. Indeed, Indonesia has many mountains, seen from every vantage, as a hermit looks down from meditation. The tops are covered with white clouds, and it seems the hermit is praying for the safety of the world. Rice fields spread to the horizon, with their dikes curved carefully. Plants are green and in harvest time all is golden-yellow like the early sun. Between are rivers winding to the shore. Fertile: the soil is rich. Cheap: all things are cheap to buy. Trade: people who trade are busy day and night hindered by no disturbance of the peace. Prosperity: the roofs of peoples' houses touch, because the country is so prosperous. Peace: the farmers are at peace and work all day long in the fields, the cattle graze untended for there are no thieves and come home at evening by themselves. No evil: no enemies are near, the ministers are experienced in their duties, honest, wise, have knowledge, know how to rule the country, and strive to keep the nation safe and honorable. They strive to make their nation self-supporting in food, clothing, and housing, like a great society with great intelligence in all things. The principle of the nation is our treasure—the Pantjasila. The compass of the state is Manipol-USDEK. Our flag is the red-and-white banner. They all show that Indonesia carries a high torch casting bright light across the world, its smoke rising high. Not only are Indonesian people united, but even foreign countries are close friends, without compulsion, because they adore the perfectness of the country. Near, they bow flat to the ground before her perfectness; farther afield, they still incline to show their respect. Diplomatic and cultural missions are exchanged. Honored guests from overseas offer gifts, and when they depart they receive as gifts our native art which increases their wonder and respect for this country. We can say the founder, both mother and father, of our country is President Ir. Hadji Mohammad Soekarno, or Brother Karno. We can see he is working hard, holding twenty important duties. In fact he is loved by the people for he knows religion, is fair in justice, guards public morality, enjoys military knowledge, and justice prevails. His Excellency is loved by the people. More and more popular is he for having held the Asian Games successfully. It would take all night just to tell the many qualities of Indonesia.

Many changes in the old content have been made. Hindu-Javanese "gods" become an Islamic "Allah," while the "Kingdom of Astina" becomes "Indonesia." Most of the ritual description of the glories of the nation are identical, but now the specific beauties of the countryside are described in detail. "Merchants" become "people who trade." The closely packed houses are not those of "foreigners" any more, but they show the prosperity of the "people." The extravagant praise of feudal Java remains in speaking about modern Indonesia—foreign countries still "bow to the ground before her perfectness." However, the "vassaldom" of foreign countries becomes "friendship," "tokens of submission" become "gifts" returned in kind, and rather than the "subjugation" of other Javanese people the Indonesian people become "united." All of this is consistent with Indonesia's official posture as an ancient, cultured, respected, and friendly nation. Major political slogans are mentioned: Manipol-USDEK, Pantja Sila, and unity of the nation. Finally, President Soekarno is described as just and religious, like Yudistira. Unlike Yudistira, however, Soekarno cannot afford the luxury of allowing himself to be killed. On the contrary, he is skilled in "military affairs." Further, Soekarno is described as being loved by the people for working hard at twenty jobs and for carrying off the Asian games so well.*

The rest of this wayang suluh script follows the standard structure of a wayang kulit play. Throughout, however, new analogous content is substituted for traditional content. A standard scene in wayang kulit has a group of brutal ogres from a foreign kingdom kidnap a royal princess; in the wayang suluh script the daughter of the Village Head is kidnapped by hooligans from across town. She is engaged to a virtuous, modest, but very attractive young graudate of the Information Academy, obviously modeled on Arjuna. He is about to set out to rescue her when he is gravely advised on the proper course of action by the village schoolteacher, the modern equivalent of wayang kulit's religious mystic. The schoolteacher warns against creating "disruptive influences within society," in an obvious reference to the standard wayang kulit scene of "turmoil in the heavens and on earth" (the *gara-gara*). There follows a scene in which the hero defeats the hooligans, paralleling the ritual scene in which Arjuna (or one of his sons) kills several ogres in the second section of a wayang kulit play (the *perang kembang*), and so on through to the end of the play. In structuring a wayang suluh play so that the Information Official hero plays a role analogous to Arjuna it is expected that the audience will transfer to this modern hero the famous attributes of the old hero. This without lifting a finger to demonstrate the new hero's good qualities. By assigning

*The wayang suluh script quoted here was written in 1962. A 1964 script would probably include references to more recent events, such as the "success of GANEFO" or the renaming of the Indian Ocean as the "Indonesian Ocean."

the schoolteacher the role of the revered religious sage the government believes the audiences will tend to transfer to schoolteachers in modern Indonesia the same respect previously accorded the sage in the old drama. And of course the reason for comparing President Soekarno to Yudistira is to suggest to the audience that in modern Indonesia President Soekarno should command the people's total allegiance in the same way Yudistira did in mythological times. In every way the government hopes the audience will be more prone to accept the new content of the wayang suluh play by retaining the old and beloved wayang kulit form. It is possible in an extreme instance, for example, that some people in the audience would be only vaguely aware of the new content while enjoying the familiar music, songs, and patterns of action of wayang kulit that have been retained. As a hypothesis, I suggest there is less likelihood that an audience will reject new content when it is presented via old and familiar artistic patterns. Even if a spectator disagrees with some part of the new message, he may return to see other performances because he likes the theatre form. If both content and theatrical form are new, however, unfamiliarity with the new form may interfer with the spectator's ability to absorb the new content.

Traditional plays may also be used consciously as allegories of contemporary situations. The bad kingdom "to the north" in the USIS mohlam luong play mentioned earlier is of course China. Although this is not stated it is expected that the audience will understand the allegory. It was through association of two seemingly unrelated events—the murder of a high school student and the showing on stage of a dead child—that the cai luong audience understood the meaning of the traditional Chinese play to be a criticism of the Diem government. The following advertisement for a wayang orang performance appeared in a Jogjakarta newspaper on June 6, 1964:

Kresna the Ambassador

Peace or War? Dependent on the outcome of the summit conference between the heads of state of the Pandawas and the imperialistic Kurawas—the play "Kresna The Ambassador." This play illustrates the attempt to restore the Kingdom of Astina to its rightful rulers— through peace, diplomacy, and consultations—but this is harshly challenged by the imperialist Kurawas.

Kresna the Ambassador is a standard play in the wayang orang repertory. It relates how Kresna attempts to persuade the Kurawas to return the Kingdom of Astina to its rightful owners the Pandawas. He fails and the Great War, the *Baratayuda,* commences. Except for the modern epithet "imperialist" there is nothing in the ad to suggest that the play has any special meaning. But, if we look at some Indonesian news items of the same time it is cast in a completely new light.

> Maphilindo summit peace talks [concerning Malaysia] still hang in the balance today with the Kuala Lumpur regime threatening to defer negotiations unless conditions were met. (June 3, 1964)

> President Soekarno re-emphasized Indonesia's stand with regard to the Malaysia issue was that solution through "consultations" was preferable [but now] was the time to crush imperialists . . . outside the country. (May 21, 1964)

> Malaysia [the government said] is within the wider scope of imperialism. (June 3, 1964)[2]

Now we can see the play as the Indonesian audience saw it. The play was brilliantly selected as an allegory to Indonesia's confrontation policy with Malaysia. Astina represented the territory of Malaysia, which was in dispute. The Malaysian government (and by extension Great Britain) was symbolized by the "imperialist" Kurawas. Kresna's talks with the Kurawas were Soekarno's talks with the Tunku at the Maphilindo summit conference. The outcome of the Maphilindo conference was very much in doubt at the time the play was staged. To the best of my knowledge the play was performed exactly as it is done traditionally. No new "messages" were added. No topical slogans were inserted. The troupe manager told me they often select plays to make an allegorical comment upon current events. The wayang repertory of several hundred plays encompasses "so many incidents and episodes we can always find one that fits," he said.

I have taken these last two extended examples from wayang drama because wayang is the most highly structured drama form in Southeast Asia and the examples vividly illustrate the way strong artistic patterns, or codes, make of Southeast Asian drama a rather special communication medium. Throughout Southeast

Asia plays are used to communicate new ideas in similar ways. Of course playwrights in the West sometimes compose allegorical plays in the vein of Kresna the Ambassador. Nevertheless, in Western theatre we lack the great traditions of artistic form in music, in dance, in dramatic structure, and in visual production elements which are essential to this form of communication. It seems unlikely that we shall ever in our own theatre match the subtle communication possibilities which inherently exist in Southeast Asian theatre as a result of its long artistic traditions.

APPENDIX

Major Theatre Genres as Performed in 1964

This book is primarily about plays in Southeast Asia as they are performed today. Details of performance have changed, often radically, since Western travelers and scholars first began recording theatre performances several hundred years ago. Even recent descriptions have not always been complete or accurate. Partial descriptions of theatre forms have appeared in various chapters of this book; this appendix will summarize in one location the major artistic characteristics of each major genre, listed alphabetically. (Those rarely performed are not described.) Typical performances are described insofar as possible. Most information has come from firsthand observation of performances and from conversations with performers and theatre troupe managers to assure its accuracy. However, no two performances are exactly alike, and the knowledgeable reader will undoubtedly know of exceptions and variations to the descriptions given here.

Ardja (Bali). An operetta performed by professional troupes of actors and actresses. Sung passages alternate with lively action and danced sections. The style of performance is romantic comedy. Most plays are *Panji* stories; *Ramayana* and *Mahabharata* stories, Javanese romances, and Chinese love tales are also performed. A three- or four-piece gamelan ensemble provides musical accompaniment. Usually performed on a marked-out square of earth in a temple courtyard rather than on a raised stage. A jerry-rigged draw curtain conceals performers prior to entrance. A performance lasts for three or four hours and is given either in the afternoon or evening.

Bangsawan (Malaysia). A spoken play interspersed with songs and dances performed by actors and actresses. Arabic and Malay history plays as well as plays about contemporary life are performed in swashbuckling, romantic style. Songs are accompanied by piano, drums, guitar, violin, saxophone, or some combination of these instruments, or by simple gamelan instruments. There is no offstage chorus. Dance is seldom used during the action of the play and is of little importance. Costumes are theatricalized versions of historical dress. Make-up is fairly natural. Performances are given on raised stages, usually temporary structures, using drop-and-wing scenery. Performances are in the evening and last three to four hours.

Barong (Bali). A folk dance-drama depicting the ritual confrontation between the "good" Barong lion figure and Rangda the witch. Includes scenes of preadolescent legong dancing, comedy, and dramatic action and culminates in the so-called "trance dance" in which village actors, presumably in trance, thrust daggers against their own bare chests without drawing blood. Full gamelan ensemble accompanies the action. Normally performed as a religious rite, it is now also performed on demand for tourists. Always staged in the open air in a temple courtyard using temple walls and gates as a natural backdrop. Given in the morning as a rule, a barong performance lasts about two hours. (In a strict sense barong is not a genre of drama but a single play.)

Cai luong (Vietnam). Usually serious drama sung and spoken by a mixed cast. Song is the most important form of expression; the average play contains forty to fifty separate vocal numbers. Solos and duets are most common. There is no choral singing, on- or offstage. Chinese-style instruments, usually fiddle, zither, lute, and wood-block, accompany songs and action. Song melodies are traditional; new lyrics are composed for each play. Plays are adapted from hat boi or based on Chinese novels, Vietnamese history, or contemporary events. Scripts are written in dialogue form and memorized by the cast in large troupes; performers in small troupes ad-lib from scenarios. Movement and gesture patterns are simplified versions of Chinese opera dance movements. Costumes reflect Cantonese opera influences (vivid colored silks, bold designs, spangles) and only vaguely resemble Chinese or Vietnamese historical dress. Make-up is slightly stylized. Performances are given on platform stages (in excellent, air-conditioned theatres in Saigon). If a production is important, scenery will be especially built; if not, stock drop-and-wing scenery will be used. Evening performances run from nine until midnight. Sunday matinees are common in Saigon.

Hat boi (Vietnam). A serious form of drama sung and acted in highly stylized fashion by actors and actresses to the accompaniment of Chinese-style cymbals, gong, fiddles, and wood-block (and sometimes West-ern instruments as well). Some parts of the play may be spoken, but song is the predominant artistic element. Solos are usual; there is no choral singing and no offstage chorus. Movement is closely patterned after Chinese opera dance movements. Other than battle scenes, dis-tinct dance episodes do not occur. Traditional stories are taken directly from Chinese opera. Lyrics and dialogue are written in classical Viet-namese and contain a high proportion of Sino-Vietnamese words diffi-cult to understand. Some troupes perform plays based on Vietnamese history and insert non-Chinese story elements into classic plays in order to appeal to modern audiences. A performance may consist of a single two- or three-hour play or excerpts from several plays. Standardized cos-tumes identify basic character types, such as scholar, evil warrior, man-darin, and so on. Make-up is highly stylized for clowns and evil char-acters, less so for other characters. Scenery consists of a single standard backdrop in front of which a table and two chairs are used as stage properties. Hand properties are often used symbolically as in Chinese opera (a whip stands for a horse, for example).

Ketoprak (Java). A spoken play in which important action is accom-panied by gamelan music. Actors and actresses neither sing nor dance during the action of the play, though they may before the play as a curtain-raiser. Javanese history plays and Arabic plays are most com-monly staged. All characters speak modern Javanese. Actors improvise dialogue. Acting is relatively realistic in style. Costumes generally fol-low historic precedent. A clown, or dagelan, appears in every play. Oc-casionally actresses play the roles of refined heroes (a custom taken from wayang orang). Scenery is drop-and-wing. Performances, given in the evening, last three or four hours.

Khon (Thailand). Traditionally referred to as "masked-pantomime," nowadays only monkey and ogre roles are masked. Men and women perform. Actors in clown roles improvise dialogue. Other actors and actresses do not speak; an offstage chorus speaks their lines in a rhyth-mic manner, or chants poetic passages of narration describing the ac-tion of the play being danced and pantomimed by the actors. A large pi phat orchestra accompanies dance sequences. Only classic episodes from the *Ramayana* are staged. Language is largely archaic and difficult to understand. Major characters are identifiable by design and color of costume, mask (or make-up), and headdress, all of which are fixed by tradition. Scenery is usually especially built for each production.

[3 2 7]

Appendix

Kich (Vietnam). Spoken drama, usually in extended one-act form with neither song nor dance as elements. A mixed cast memorizes a written script and performs in realistic acting style. Contemporary costumes are worn; make-up is completely realistic. Plays utilize contemporary subject matter. Dramatic structure is essentially the same as that of Western drama. In performance a kich play is preceded by a long program of jazz music, popular songs, solo and group dance numbers, and comedy acts.

Lakon bassac (Cambodia). Spoken drama with elements of dance and music. Chinese-style wood-block, cymbals, and fiddles (sometimes with zither) punctuate the action of the play. When actors and actresses occasionally sing, they are accompanied by Chinese fiddles. Scenes of Cambodian classic dance, drawn from the repertory of the Royal Cambodian Ballet, are accompanied by pi phat instruments. Noble women dress in Cambodian court costume; male villains dress in Chinese-Vietnamese costume and wear highly stylized make-up. There is no offstage chorus. Most commonly staged are *Jataka* stories, and other plays tend to be presented as so-called *Jataka* stories. Contemporary subject matter is not used. Plays often consist of forty to fifty scenes. One or more clowns appear in every play. The style of performance is romantic comedy mixed with farce. Like likay, plays are staged with drop-and-wing scenery and a bench placed center stage. Performances are in the evening, lasting from around 8:30 until midnight.

Lakon jatri (Thailand). In its original form, a simple type of dance-drama based on the *Jataka* story *Manora* and performed by males to the accompaniment of drum, double gong, and small bell-cymbal. Songs chanted by an onstage actor are repeated in alternating verses by an offstage chorus (usually female). Performances in the original style are sometimes seen. Other so-called lakon jatri performances are greatly modernized, incorporating pi phat or Chinese-style instruments or both, lakon nai style of dance, stories other than *Manora* (including purely contemporary stories), and mixed casts of actors and actresses. Plays are staged simply with a single bench set in front of a standard drop. Performances are usually in the evening and last for about three hours.

Lakon nai (Thailand). Dance-drama performed only by actresses except that a few minor roles are played by men. Lakon nai exhibits Thai female dance in its classic form. Dance is the major artistic element of performance, though actresses also speak dialogue and sometimes sing. An offstage, all-female chorus sings and chants narration explaining the action of danced and pantomimed scenes. Scenes of pure dance are common. A standard pi phat orchestra accompanies performance. Episodes from *Inao* (the *Panji* story) are traditionally the only subject matter, but other stories now are performed in similar style. Songs are in verse, dialogue is in prose. Plays are written in modern Thai and completely memorized by the cast. Neither masks nor stylized make-up are used. Costumes, modeled after Thai court dress, seldom identify specific characters but usually only character types. Scenery is built especially for each production. Performances, given during the daytime and at night, last for two and a half to three hours.

Likay (Thailand). Spoken drama set in a loose framework of songs and dance. Refined characters move in lakon nai dance style throughout a performance accompanied by a pi phat ensemble minus, usually, the set of tuned brass bowls. Dance set-pieces rarely occur. Actors and actresses sing songs of self-introduction and love songs accompanied by bell-cymbals and drum. There is no offstage chorus. Dialogue, song lyrics, and the plot of a play are improvised by the cast during performance. *Jataka* stories, local history, Arabic stories, and adaptations of movies and contemporary subjects are all treated in a light, romantic-comedy vein. Modern Thai is spoken throughout. Costumes follow no historical period; they are totally stage creations: pantaloons, flowing blouses, sashes, and bandannas round the head, along with calf-length nylon stretch-socks decorated with silk garters. Drop-and-wing scenery, with a single bench center stage, is usual. Performances are staged in the evening, usually from nine until midnight.

Ludruk (Java). Improvised spoken drama based on contemporary subject matter only. Songs and dances are never part of a play but are often performed as between-scenes entertainment. A ngremo dance precedes each performance. An all-male cast performs male and female roles in realistic style. An actor speaks whatever language is appropriate to the character being portrayed—usually Javanese, but also Indonesian and Madurese. Modern situation comedies and melodramas are popular. Costumes and make-up are the same as would be used for ordinary street wear. Scenery is drop-and-wing. Performances last three to four hours in the evening.

Mohlam luong (Laos and Thailand). A sung and spoken play coupling mohlam music with likay drama. Subject matter, character types, costumes, make-up, scenery, and acting style are almost identical with likay. Actors and actresses improvise dialogue and, often, song lyrics. There is no offstage chorus. Singing by actors and actresses to khen accompaniment is the most important element in a performance, and as much as three-fourths of a play is sung. Occasionally pi phat instruments accompany the action. Plays contain much earthy, physical humor. Scenery usually consists of a standard drop with a bench in front of it. Performances are in Lao and staged in the evening hours.

Nang talung (Thailand). A shadow-puppet play performed by one puppeteer who speaks the lines of the puppet characters, chants narration, sings, and manipulates the puppets before a white screen so as to cast shadows on the screen. Southern Thai is the dialect spoken. A performance is accompanied by a double pear-drum, bell-cymbals, and double gong (Chinese fiddles or an oboe may be added). Puppets are leather cutouts, one to one and a half feet high; most have a single movable arm and are patterned after khon and lakon dance figures. Clown figures may have a movable jaw; cowboy, gangster, and other modern puppets are also used, usually all mixed up together. A set consists of one hundred to one hundred and fifty pieces. *Ramayana* episodes comprise the traditional repertory; *Jataka* and other stories (including contemporary ones) also are performed. Plays are performed on special stages raised on stilts about six feet off the ground with walls on both sides and the back; the front is covered with a cloth screen for performance. The audience sits or stands only in front of the stage. The puppeteer and musicians inside the stage building cannot be seen by the audience. Playing time varies from two to six hours, depending upon the occasion; a performance may occur almost anytime during the night hours.

Royal Cambodian Ballet (Cambodia). In most essential respects—dance style, music, dramatic repertory, costumes, masks, and make-up—the same as lakon nai and khon in Thailand. Excerpts from dance-dramas are usually performed. Cambodian is the language spoken. Performances are given either in the open before the temple of Angkor Wat (mainly for tourists) or in the Royal Palace at Phnom Penh; hence no scenery is used. Performances may be by day or night.

Royal Lao Ballet (Laos). Dance and music are almost identical with Thai lakon nai. Performances are by female dancers only. Dance excerpts, rather than full-length dance-dramas, are staged. Performances are usually given in the Royal Palace where scenery is not used. Performances may be during the day or night.

Major Theatre Genres

Sandiwara (Sunda). Drama performed by actresses and actors in the Sundanese language. Strictly speaking, this is not a genre, for sandiwara troupes perform *Ramayana* and *Mahabharata* plays in wayang orang style, Javanese history and Arabic plays in ketoprak style, and, occasionally, plays about contemporary life. Gamelan and vocal music are Sundanese style. Drop-and-wing scenery is standard. Performances last from nine until midnight.

Wayang golek (Java). A doll-puppet play given in the Javanese language and patterned in many ways on wayang kulit shadow-drama. There is no screen, no lamp to cast shadows, and the technique of moving the puppets is rather different from wayang kulit, but the over-all conception of the drama is the same: a single puppeteer manipulates the puppets, speaks dialogue, sings mood songs, and chants narrative passages to the accompaniment of a gamelan orchestra which includes one or more female singers. The basic three-part dramatic structure and many details of dramatic construction are identical with wayang kulit drama. Subject matter, however, is solely Islamic, usually stories about Amir Hamzah (called *Menak* stories in Java). Puppet heads and costumes identify characters by type: as Arabic or Javanese, as god, hero, clown, and so forth. Around one hundred and fifty puppets compose a set. Performances are staged in an open-sided pavilion or on a temporary stage with the audience watching from the front side only. Puppets are stuck into the soft pulp of a banana log serving as the stage "floor" to hold them in position; head, and shoulder and elbow joints of both arms are movable. No scenery or backdrop is used, so the puppets are seen by the audience as moving in open space. A performance begins at nine in the evening and ends just before dawn.

Wayang golek (Sunda). A puppet play, in which *Mahabharata* and *Ramayana* stories are performed by wayang golek doll-puppets. The puppeteer speaks modern Sundanese except in mood songs where Old Javanese or Kawi may be used. The gamelan ensemble is smaller than in Javanese wayang golek, and the female singers sing a great deal more (up to thirty minutes at a time). Facial characteristics of the puppets and their costumes are similar to wayang kulit puppets, but less stylized. Puppets are slightly smaller than corresponding wayang kulit puppets; one hundred to two hundred puppets make a set. Performances last from nine in the evening until just before dawn. *Wayang golek moderne* is a new form of wayang golek occasionally seen in Sunda: four or five puppeteers simultaneously manipulate up to six or seven puppets within a miniature stage setting complete with tiny drop-and-wing scenery.

Appendix

Wayang kulit (Java). A shadow-drama, performed by a single puppeteer (almost always male) who speaks the dialogue of all characters, narrates between scenes, sings mood songs to establish the proper atmosphere, and manipulates flat puppets of stiff leather before a large white screen. A lamp overhead casts shadows of the puppets against the screen. Action of the play and songs are accompanied by a full gamelan ensemble. One or more female singers may be part of the ensemble. *Mahabharata* stories are most commonly performed; *Ramayana* and Javanese animistic stories are performed occasionally. Song lyrics and much narration are in archaic Kawi and are very difficult to understand. The puppeteer improvises much of the dialogue while narration and certain standard scenes consist of set speeches. Puppets represent figures in profile position. Their design is highly stylized in a manner unique to wayang kulit. They are intricately cut so as to cast delicate patterns of light and shadow on the screen. A puppet is mounted on a buffalo-horn stick; ogres have one arm movable at the shoulder and the elbow, other characters have two arms movable at the shoulder and the elbow. Puppets range in size from six inches to over three feet in height. Through body shape, size, coloring, head style, and costuming of the puppets individual major characters are clearly distinguishable; minor characters are identifiable by type (refined character, ogre, god, clown, and so forth). A complete set of puppets consists of three hundred to four hundred pieces. Performances are given in open-sided pavilions or on porches of homes as a rule. The audience sits on both sides of the screen: those on the screen side see a shadow-play, those on the puppeteer's side see a puppet play. A performance begins with the puppeteer (or his assistant) sticking upward of a hundred puppets in banana logs on either side of the screen. An open space is left in the middle of the screen. This is where the action of the play takes place, where puppets are manipulated, either in the air or after being fixed in one spot by sticking them in the banana log. Tradition requires that a performance begin at 8:30 P.M. and that it continue without pause until the sky turns grey just before dawn (that is, for about nine hours). Daylight performances are sometimes given on animistic occasions.

Wayang kulit (Bali). A shadow-puppet play derived from Javanese wayang kulit and sharing its essential characteristics: a single puppeteer manipulates cutout leather figures before a screen and at the same time sings and speaks dialogue and narration, to the accompaniment of gamelan instruments. The puppets are smaller and more crudely designed than Javanese wayang kulit puppets. The gamelan ensemble consists of four gender (xylophones). There is no female singer as in Javanese wayang kulit. *Mahabharata* and *Ramayana* stories are about equally popular; local Balinese legends such as *Tjalonarang* are sometimes performed. Song lyrics and narration are mainly in archaic Kawi; clowns speak in modern colloquial Balinese. A play ordinarily lasts three or four hours, and is performed at night on a small, temporary stage. The audience watches mainly from the shadow side of the screen.

Wayang kulit (Malaysia). A shadow-play derived from and similar to Javanese wayang kulit. *Ramayana* stories are most popular; *Mahabharata* and Islamic stories are also staged. Language is a mixture of Malay and archaic Javanese. Puppet figures are leather cutouts: some are cut in the style of Javanese wayang kulit; others in the style of Thai classic dance figures. Musical accompaniment may be a small gamelan ensemble or just double-bowl, drums, and a few gongs. Performances are given in the evening in small stage houses, like those used for nang talung, and usually last three to six hours.

Wayang orang (Java). A play in which actors and actresses perform stories from the wayang kulit repertory (*Mahabharata* and *Ramayana* stories) accompanied by a gamelan ensemble and female singers. Performers dance, sing, and improvise dialogue on stage; dance is the most important element of performance. The "puppeteer" of wayang kulit sits with the gamelan; he sings mood songs and chants narrative passages between scenes. Actresses commonly play roles of refined (alus) heroes such as Arjuna. Plays follow wayang kulit dramatic structure, but scenes are shortened to reduce performance time to three or four hours. Major characters can be identified by traditional costume and make-up. Plays are staged on large permanent or temporary stages using drop-and-wing scenery. Evening performances are usual.

Zat pwe (Burma). A classical dance-play based on Burmese history or *Jataka* stories, sung, acted, and danced in classical Burmese dance style by actors and actresses. Musical accompaniment is by a pi phat ensemble with added Burmese tuned drum set, cymbals, and flute. There is no offstage chorus. A contemporary play (pya zat), a spirit-invocation dance (nat pwe), and a courting dance (*thissahta*) are often performed on the same program with a zat pwe, in which case zat pwe is the final number beginning usually not before one or two in the morning.

BIBLIOGRAPHY

GENERAL

Basic Facts and Figures,1961: International Statistics Relating to Education, Culture, and Mass Communication. Paris: UNESCO, 1962.

Bowers, Faubion. *Theatre in the East: A Survey of Asian Dance and Drama.* New York: Thomas Nelson and Sons, 1956.

Cady, John F. *Southeast Asia: Its Historical Development.* New York: McGraw-Hill, 1964.

Geertz, Clifford. *The Religion of Java.* Glencoe, Ill.: Free Press, 1960.

Ghosh, Manomohan. *Contributions to the History of the Hindu Drama: Its Origin, Development and Diffusion.* Calcutta: K. L. Mukhopadhyay, 1958.

———— *The Natyasastra: A Treatise on Hindu Dramaturgy and Histrionics Ascribed to Bharata-Muni,* vol. I. Calcutta: The Royal Asiatic Society of Bengal, 1950.

Groslier, Bernard Philippe. *The Art of Indochina: Including Thailand, Vietnam, Laos and Cambodia,* trans. George Lawrence. New York: Crown Publishers, 1962.

Hall, D. G. E. *A History of South-East Asia,* 1st ed. New York: St. Martin's Press, 1955 (2nd ed., 1964).

Harrison, Brian, *South-east Asia: A Short History.* London: Macmillan, 1954.

Hatto, A. T. "The Swan Maiden: A Folk-tale of North Eurasian Origin?," *Bulletin of the School of Oriental and African Studies,* 24:326–352 (1961).

Laufer, Berthold. *Oriental Theatricals.* Chicago: Field Museum of Natural History, 1923.

Majumdar, R. C. *Hindu Colonies in the Far East.* Calcutta: K. L. Mukhopadhyay, 1963.

le May, Reginald. *The Culture of South-East Asia: The Heritage of India.* London: George Allen and Unwin, 1954.

Nicoll, Allardyce. *The Development of the Theatre: A Study of Theatrical Art from the Beginnings to the Present Day,* 4th ed. rev. London: George G. Harrap, 1958.

Redfield, Robert. *Peasant Society and Culture: An Anthropological Approach to Civilization.* Chicago: The University of Chicago Press, 1956.

Scott, A. C. *The Classical Theatre of China.* London: George Allen and Unwin, 1957.

Bibliography

Statistical Yearbook, 1964. New York: Department of Economic and Social Affairs, United Nations, 1965.

"Television Booms in Asia," *Free World* (Manila), 12:4-11 (August 1963).

Werner, E. T. C. *Myths and Legends of China.* London: George G. Harrap, 1922.

BURMA

Hla Pe, ed. and trans. *Konmara Pya Zat: An Example of Popular Burmese Drama in the XIX Century by U Pok Ni,* vol. I. London: Luzac, 1952.

Htin Aung, Maung. *Burmese Drama: A Study, with Translations, of Burmese Plays.* Calcutta: Oxford University Press, 1937.

Sein, Kenneth (Maung Khe) and J. A. Withey. *The Great Po Sein: A Chronicle of the Burmese Theater.* Bloomington, Ind.: Indiana University Press, 1965.

CAMBODIA

Briggs, Lawrence Palmer. "A Sketch of Cambodian History," *Far Eastern Quarterly,* 6:345–363 (August 1947).

Daniélou, Alain. *La Musique du Cambodge et du Laos.* Publications de L'Institut Francais d'Indologie, No. 9. Pondichéry: Institut Francais d'Indologie, 1957.

Thiounn, Samdach Chaufea. *Danses Cambodgiennes.* [Phnom Penh:] Institut Bouddhique, 1956.

INDONESIA

Anderson, Benedict R. O'G. *Mythology and the Tolerance of the Javanese.* Monograph Series, Modern Indonesia Project. Ithaca, N.Y.: Southeast Asia Program, Department of Asian Studies, Cornell University, 1965.

The Arts of Indonesia. Washington, D.C.: Indonesian Embassy, n.d. Mimeograph.

Batchelder, Marjorie. *Rod Puppets and the Human Theatre.* Columbus, Ohio: Ohio State University Press, 1947.

Belo, Jane. *Bali: Rangda and Barong.* Monographs of the American Ethnological Society, No. 16. New York: J. J. Augustin, 1949.

Brandon, James R. "Types of Indonesian Professional Theatre," *Quarterly Journal of Speech,* 45:51–58 (February 1959).

Chandra, Lokesh. "A New Indonesian Episode of the Mahabharata Cyclus," *Archiv Orientalni,* 27:564–571 (1959).

Covarrubias, Miguel. *Island of Bali.* New York: Knopf, 1950.

Hazeu, G. A. J. *Bijdrage tot de Kennis van het Javaansche Toneel.* Leiden: E. J. Brill, 1897.

Holt, Claire. "The Dance in Java," *Asia,* 36:843–46 (December 1937).

Hood, Mantle. "The Enduring Tradition: Music and Theater in Java and Bali," in *Indonesia,* ed. Ruth T. McVey. New Haven, Conn.: Human Relations Area Files Press, 1963.

Hooykaas, C. *The Old-Javanese Ramayana Kakawin: With Special Reference to the Problem of Interpolation in Kakawins.* The Hague: Martinus Nijhoff, 1955.

Kats, J. *Het Javaansche Toneel,* I: *Wajang Poerwa.* Weltvereden (Batavia): Volkslectuur, 1923.

van der Kroef, Justus M. "The Hinduization of Indonesia Reconsidered," *Far Eastern Quarterly,* 11:17–30 (November 1951).

van Lelyveld, Theodore. *La danse dans le théâtre javanais.* Paris: Floury, 1931.

Lentz, Donald A. *The Gamelan Music of Java and Bali.* Lincoln, Neb.: University of Nebraska Press, 1965.

McPhee, Colin. *A House in Bali.* New York: John Day, 1944.

Bibliography

Nojowirongko, M. Ng. *Serat Tuntunan Padalangan,* vol. I and II. Jogjakarta: Djawatan Kebudajaan, Departemen P. P. dan K., 1960.

Paauw, Douglas S. "From Colonial to Guided Economy," in *Indonesia,* ed. Ruth T. McVey. New Haven, Conn.: Human Relations Area Files Press, 1963.

Peacock, James. "Class, Clown, and Cosmology in Javanese Drama: An Analysis of Symbolic and Social Action," unpub. ms., Princeton, N.J.

Pigeaud, Theodore G. Th. *Java in the 14th Century: A Study in Cultural History: The Nagara-Kertagama by Rawaki Prapanca of Majapahit, 1365 A.D.,* 3rd ed., vol. III. The Hague: Martinus Nijhoff, 1960–1962.

Pigeaud, Th(eodore G. Th.). "Wayang Wong," *Djawa,* 9:8–9 (January 1929).

Raffles, Thomas Stamford. *The History of Java,* 2nd ed., vol. I. London: John Murray, 1830.

Rassers, W. H. *Panji, The Culture Hero: A Structural Study of Religion in Java.* Koninklijk Instituut voor Taal-, Land- en Volkenkunde Translation Series 3. The Hague: Martinus Nijhoff, 1959.

Sajid, R. M. *Bauwarna Wajang.* Jogjakarta: Pertjetakan Republik Indonesia, 1958.

Schrieke, B. "Wayang Wong," *Djawa,* 9:5–7 (January 1929).

Selosoemardjan. *Social Changes in Jogjakarta.* Ithaca, N.Y.: Cornell University Press, 1962.

Serrurier, L. *De Wajang Poerwa, Eene Ethnologische Studie.* Leiden: E. J. Brill, 1896.

Siswoharsojo, Ki. *Pakem Pedhalangan Lampahan Makutharama.* Jogjakarta, 1963.

Wagner, Frits A. *Indonesia: The Art of an Island Group,* trans. Ann E. Keep. New York: McGraw-Hill, 1959.

Wayang Kulit. Washington, D.C.: Indonesian Embassy, n.d. Mimeograph.

"R. M. T. Wreksodiningrat," *Ketoprak,* March 1960, p. 3.

de Zoete, Beryl and Walter Spies. *Dance and Drama in Bali.* London: Faber and Faber, 1938.

LAOS

Phouvong Phimmasone. "Literature," in *Kingdom of Laos: The Land of the Million Elephants and of the White Parasol,* ed. René de Berval. Saigon: France-Asie, 1959.

MALAYSIA

Barrett, E. C. G. "Further Light on Sir Richard Winstedt's 'Undescribed Malay Version of the Ramayana,' " *Bulletin of the School of Oriental and African Studies,* 26:531–543 (1963).

Cuisinier, Jeanne. *Le Théatre d'Ombres a Kelantan,* 2nd ed. Paris: Gallimard, 1957.

Rentse, Anker. "The Kelantan Shadow-play," *Journal of the Royal Asiatic Society Malayan Branch,* 14:284–301 (December 1936).

Winstedt, Richard. *The Malays: A Cultural History,* 6th ed. London: Routledge and Kegan Paul, 1961.

THE PHILIPPINES

Phelan, John Leddy. *The Hispanization of the Philippines.* Madison, Wis.: The University of Wisconsin Press, 1959.

Bibliography

Ravenholt, Albert. *The Philippines: A Young Republic on the Move.* Princeton, N.J.: D. Van Nostrand, 1962.

Zaide, Gregorio F. *Philippine Political and Cultural History,* rev. ed., vol. I, *The Philippines Since Pre-Spanish Times.* Manila: Philippine Education Co., 1957.

THAILAND

Anuman Rajadhon, Phya. *Five Papers on Thai Custom.* Southeast Asia Program Data Paper, No. 28. Ithaca, N.Y.: Department of Far Eastern Studies, Cornell University, 1958.

—— *Thai Literature and Swasdi Raksa.* Bangkok: National Culture Institute, 1950.

Bridhyakorn, H. H. Prince Dhaninivat Kromamun Bidyalabh. *The Nang.* Thailand Culture Series, No. 12. Bangkok: The National Culture Institute, 1956.

—— and Dhanit Yupho. *The Khon.* Bangkok: The Department of Fine Arts, 1954.

Coedès, George. "Origine et evolution des diverses formes du théâtre traditionnel en Thailande," *Bulletin de la Société des Études Indochinoises,* 38:489–506 (1963).

Dhanit Yupho. *The Khon and Lakon: Dance Dramas Presented by the Department of Fine Arts.* Bangkok: The Department of Fine Arts, 1963.

—— *The Preliminary Course of Training in Thai Theatrical Art.* Thailand Culture Series, No. 15. Bangkok: The National Culture Institute, 1956.

—— *Thai Musical Instruments,* trans. David Morton. Bangkok: The Department of Fine Arts(?), 1960.

Nicholas, René. "Le Lakhon Nora ou Lakhon Chatri et les Origines du Théâtre Classique Siamois," *The Journal of the Siam Society,* 18:85–110 (August 1924).

—— "Le théâtre d'ombres au Siam," *The Journal of the Siam Society,* 21:37–52 (July 1927).

Prem Chaya. *Magic Lotus: A Romantic Fantasy: An Adaptation for the English Stage of the Fifteenth-Century Siamese Classic Pra Law,* 3rd ed. Bangkok: Chatra Books, 1949.

VIETNAM

Dao Si Chu. "The Vietnamese Classical Opera," Saigon *Times of Viet-Nam,* n.d. Part 1, pp. 12–14. Part 2, pp. 14, 15, 20.

Nguyen-Dinh Lai. "Étude sur la musique sino-viêtnamienne et les chants popularies du Viêt-Nam," *Bulletin de la Société des Études Indochinoises,* 31:11–86 (1956).

Nguyen Phouc Thien. "The Vietnamese Stage," unpub. ms., Saigon.

Réalités Vietnamiennes: Les Réalités Permanentes. Saigon: Ministèrs des Affaires Étrangères du Vietnam, 1966.

Song Ban. *The Vietnamese Theatre.* Hanoi: Foreign Languages Publishing House, 1960.

Tran Van Khe. *La Musique Viêtnamienne Traditionnelle.* Paris: Presses Universitaires de France, 1962.

—— "Problems of Far-Eastern Musical Tradition Today," *France-Asie/Asia,* 17:2261–66 (July–August 1961).

—— "Le théâtre vietnamien," in *Les théâtres d'Asie,* ed. Jean Jacquot. Paris: Centre National de la Recherche Scientifique, 1961.

The Vietnamese Theatre. Saigon: Review Horizons, n.d.

NOTES

NOTES TO CHAPTER 1. INTRODUCTION

1. Reginald le May, *The Culture of South-East Asia* (London, 1954), p. 28.

NOTES TO CHAPTER 2. THE CULTURAL SETTING

1. Frits A. Wagner, *Indonesia: The Art of an Island Group* (New York, 1959), p. 19.

2. W. H. Rassers, *Panji, The Culture Hero* (The Hague, 1959), pp. 95-215.

3. D. G. E. Hall, *A History of South-East Asia,* 1st ed. (New York, 1955), pp. 9-10.

4. Dhanit Yupho, *Thai Musical Instruments* (Bangkok, 1960), p. 61.

5. L. P. Briggs, "A Sketch of Cambodian History," *Far Eastern Quarterly,* 6:346 (August 1947).

6. Hall, 2nd ed., pp. 35–36.

7. Bernard Philippe Groslier, *The Art of Indochina* (New York, 1962), p. 49.

8. Hall, 2nd ed., pp. 19–21; Justus M. van der Kroef, "The Hinduization of Indonesia Reconsidered," *Far Eastern Quarterly,* 11:25 (November 1951).

9. Hall, 2nd ed., p. 73, drawing upon the theories of C. C. Berg.

10. Robert Redfield, *Peasant Society and Culture* (Chicago, 1956), p. 82, quoting Raghavan.

11. Manomohan Ghosh, *Contributions to the History of the Hindu Drama: Its Origin, Development and Diffusion* (Calcutta, 1958), p. 3.

12. Hall, 2nd ed., p. 116.

13. Hall, 2nd ed., p. 68.

14. Ghosh, *Contributions,* pp. 17–18.

15. Maung Htin Aung, *Burmese Drama* (Calcutta, 1937), p. 21.

16. Dhanit Yupho, *The Khon and Lakon* (Bangkok, 1963), p. 42.

17. Phouvong Phimmasone, "Literature," *Kingdom of Laos,* ed. René de Berval (Saigon, 1959), p. 341.

18. The popular name for stories based on *Candakinnara, Jataka* number 458.

19. There are many versions of the story. This is a Thai version, condensed from Dhanit Yupho, *Khon and Lakon,* pp. 79–83.

20. Kenneth Sein and J. A. Withey, *The Great Po Sein: A Chronicle of the Burmese Theater* (Bloomington, 1965), p. 15.

21. Hall, 2nd ed., p. 27.

22. Hall, 2nd ed., p. 99.

23. Samdach Chaufea Thiounn, *Danses Cambodgiennes* (Phnom Penh, 1956), p. 89.

24. Htin Aung, p. 35.

25. Hall, 1st ed., p. 15.

26. Brian Harrison, *South-east Asia: A Short History* (London, 1954), p. 43.

27. Richard Winstedt, *The Malays: A Cultural History* (London, 1961), p. 34.

28. Winstedt, pp. 144–146.

29. Hla Pe, in introduction to *Konmara Pya Zat,* by U Pok Ni (London, 1952), p. 4.

NOTES TO CHAPTER 3.
THE DEVELOPMENT OF THEATRE GENRES

1. G. A. J. Hazeu, *Bijdrage tot de Kennis van het Javaansche Toneel* (Leiden, 1897), p. 3.

2. Berthold Laufer, *Oriental Theatricals* (Chicago, 1923), p. 36.

3. Rassers, *Panji,* pp. 96–215. Rassers discusses in great detail the various theories of the origin of wayang kulit and adds his own construct.

4. J. Kats, *Het Javaansche Toneel* (Weltevreden, 1923), p. 35.

5. L. Serrurier, *De Wajang Poerwa, Eene Ethnologische Studie* (Leiden, 1896), pp. 48–70.

6. R. M. Sajid, *Bauwarna Wajang* (Jogjakarta, 1958), p. 53.

7. Serrurier, pp. 48–70.

8. From a conversation with Mrs. K. R. T. Kusumubroto concerning a rare wayang beber performance she saw near Patjitan, Java, in 1962.

9. Theodore van Lelyveld, *La danse dans le théâtre javanais* (Paris, 1931), p. 53.

10. Theodore G. Th. Pigeaud, *Java in the 14th Century,* 3rd ed. (The Hague, 1960), III, 107–109.

11. B. Schrieke, "Wayang Wong," *Djawa,* 9:5 (January 1929).

12. Wayang wong is the Javanese and wayang orang the Indonesian term for the same dance-drama.

13. Th. Pigeaud, "Wayang Wong," *Djawa,* 9:8–9 (January 1929).

14. "R. M. T. Wreksodiningrat," *Ketoprak* (March 1960), p. 3.

15. From a conversation with Ki Soemadji Adji, a former ludruk troupe manager.

16. Marjorie Batchelder, *Rod Puppets and the Human Theatre* (Columbus, 1947), p. 40.

17. From a conversation with M. A. Salmun, scholar of Sundanese wayang, Bandung, 1964.

18. Beryl de Zoete and Walter Spies, *Dance and Drama in Bali* (London, 1938), pp. 116–117.

19. De Zoete and Spies, p. 162.

20. De Zoete and Spies, p. 155.

21. De Zoete and Spies, p. 179.

22. Hall, *History,* 2nd ed., p. 199.

23. Quoted by Winstedt, *The Malays,* pp. 35–36.

24. Jeanne Cuisinier, *Le Théâtre d'Ombres a Kelantan* (Paris, 1957), pp. 45–50.

25. Anker Rentse, "The Kelantan Shadow-play," *Journal of the Royal Asiatic Society Malayan Branch,* 14:287 (December 1936).

26. R. C. Majumdar, *Hindu Colonies in the Far East* (Calcutta, 1963), p. 208.

27. From a conversation with Prince M. R. Kukrit Pramoj, Bangkok, 1963; George Coedès, "Origine et evolution des diverses formes du théâtre traditionnel en Thailande," *Bulletin de la Société des Études Indochinoises,* 38:493 (1963).

28. René Nicolas, "Le Lakhon Nora ou Lakhon Chatri et les Origines du Théâtre Classique Siamois," *The Journal of the Siam Society,* 18:94 (August 1924).

29. Nicholas, "Lakhon Nora," p. 86.

30. Dhanit Yupho, *Khon and Lakon,* p. 145.

31. H. H. Prince Dhaninivat Kromamum Bidyalabh Bridhyakorn, *The Nang* (Bangkok, 1956), p. 5.

32. Bridhyakorn, p. 6; René Nicolas, "Le théâtre d'ombres au Siam," *The Journal of the Siam Society,* 21:40 (July 1927).

33. Dhanit Yupho, *Khon and Lakon,* p. 52.

34. H. H. Prince Dhaninivat Kromamun Bidyalabh Bridhyakorn and Dhanit Yupho, *The Khon* (Bangkok, 1954), pp. 13–15.

35. Faubion Bowers, *Theatre in the East* (New York, 1956), p. 156.

36. Cuisinier, pp. 45–49.

37. Dhanit Yupho, *Thai Instruments,* p. 77; Wagner, *Indonesia,* p. 174.

38. Tran Van Khe, "Problems of Far-Eastern Musical Tradition Today," *France-Asie,* 17:2262 (July–August 1961).

39. Htin Aung, *Burmese Drama,* p. 1.

40. Htin Aung, p. 27.

41. Htin Aung, p. 148.

42. Sein and Withey, *Po Sein,* pp. 19–20.

43. Hla Pe, *Konmara,* pp. 6–7.

44. Sein and Withey, pp. 70–71.

45. Dao Si Chu, "The Vietnamese Classical Opera," part 1, Saigon *Times of Viet-Nam,* n.d., p. 13.

46. Tran Van Khe, "Le théatre vietnamien," in *Les théatres d'Asie,* ed. Jean Jacquot (Paris, 1961), pp. 203–204; Song Ban, *The Vietnamese Theatre* (Hanoi, 1960), pp. 18–19; Dao Si Chu, part 1, p. 13.

47. *The Vietnamese Theatre* (Saigon, n.d.), p. 7.

48. Nguyen Phouc Thien, "The Vietnamese Stage," unpub. ms., Saigon, p. 3.

49. Nguyen Phouc Thien, p. 4; Song Ban, p. 28.

50. Sometimes *thoai kich* or *kich noi.*

51. Albert Ravenholt, *The Philippines* (Princeton, 1962), p. 154.

52. Gregorio R. Zaide, *Philippine Political and Cultural History* (Manila, 1957), I, 74–75.

53. John Leddy Phelan, *The Hispanization of the Philippines* (Madison, 1959), pp. 140–142.

54. Bowers, p. 265.

NOTES TO CHAPTER 4. TRADITIONS OF THEATRE

1. De Zoete and Spies, *Dance and Drama*, p. 7.

2. Redfield, *Peasant Society*, p. 70.

3. Clifford Geertz, *The Religion of Java* (Glencoe, 1960), p. 228.

4. From a conversation with Prince Bhanupan Yugala, Bangkok, 1963.

NOTES TO CHAPTER 5. DRAMA

1. C. Hooykaas, *The Old-Javanese Ramayana Kakawin* (The Hague, 1955), p. 34.

2. From Dhanit Yupho, *Khon and Lakon*, pp. 44–47.

3. Condensed from Ki Siswoharsojo, *Pakem Pedhalangan Lampahan Makutharama* (Jogjakarta, 1963), pp. 8–122.

4. Htin Aung, *Drama*, p. 26.

5. Phya Anuman Rajadhon, *Thai Literature and Swasdi Raksa* (Bangkok, 1950), p. 20.

6. From Dhanit Yupho, *Khon and Lakon*, pp. 145–161.

7. Winstedt, *The Malays*, p. 142.

8. Dhanit Yupho, *Khon and Lakon*, p. 123.

9. Thomas Stamford Raffles, *The History of Java*, 2nd ed. (London, 1830), I, 460.

10. Jane Belo, *Bali: Rangda and Barong* (New York, 1959), pp. 32–33.

11. Hla Pe, *Konmara*, p. 157.

12. Sein and Withey, *Po Sein*, p. 11.

13. Colin McPhee, *A House in Bali* (New York, 1944), p. 33.

14. Geertz, *Religion*, p. 275.

15. Condensed from Lokesh Chandra, "A New Indonesian Episode of the Mahabharata Cyclus," *Archiv Orientalni*, 27:570–571 (1959).

NOTES TO CHAPTER 6. MUSIC AND DANCE

1. Donald A. Lentz, *The Gamelan Music of Java and Bali* (Lincoln, 1965), p. 33.

2. Alain Daniélou, *La Musique du Cambodge et du Laos* (Pondichéry, 1957), p. 26.

3. Anker Rentse, "The Kelantan Shadow-play," p. 287.

4. Dhanit Yupho, *Thai Instruments*, pp. 33, 100.

5. Tran Van Khe, *La Musique Viêtnamienne Traditionnelle* (Paris, 1962), pp. 60–61.

6. Hla Pe, *Konmara*, p. 16.

7. Nojowirongko, *Serat Tuntunan Padalangan*, I, 30–44.

8. Htin Aung, *Drama,* p. 144.

9. A. C. Scott, *The Classical Theatre of China* (London, 1957), pp. 54–57.

10. Tran Van Khe, *Musique Viêtnamienne,* pp. 87–88; Nguyen-Dinh Lai, "Étude sur la musique sino-viêtnamienne et les chants populaires du Viêt-Nam," *Bulletin de la Société des Études Indochinoises,* 31:72–77 (1956); Dao Si Chu, "The Vietnamese Classical Opera," part 2, pp. 14–15.

11. Scott, pp. 92–137.

12. Manomohan Ghosh, *The Natyasastra,* vol. I (Calcutta, 1950). See especially chapters 8, 9, and 10.

13. Dhanit Yupho, *The Preliminary Course in Training in Thai Theatrical Art* (Bangkok, 1956), p. 24.

14. Dhanit Yupho, *Preliminary Course,* p. 23.

15. De Zoete and Spies, *Dance and Drama,* pp. 20–21.

16. Claire Holt, "The Dance in Java," *Asia,* 36:846 (December 1937).

17. Scott, pp. 96–137.

18. Sein and Withey, *Po Sein,* p. 23.

NOTES TO CHAPTER 7. PRODUCTION

1. Rassers, *Panji,* p. 139.

NOTES TO CHAPTER 8.
TRANSMISSION OF THEATRE ART

1. Rassers, *Panji,* p. 61.

2. Sein and Withey, *Po Sein,* p. 5.

3. Lentz, *Gamelan Music,* p. 62.

4. Hla Pe, *Konmara,* p. 6.

5. *Verhandelingen van het Bataviaasch Genootschap van Kunsten en Wetenschappen* (Proceedings of the Batavia Society for Arts and Sciences).

6. Office of Culture registrations included both professional and amateur troupes. I estimated the percentage of amateur troupes in order to arrive at an estimate of the number of amateur troupes of each genre. The percentage estimates are purely arbitrary, but I have tried to make a conservative estimate in each case.

Theatre genre	Number of groups registered	Estimated percentage amateur	Estimated number of amateur groups
Wayang kulit	2096	60	1258
Ludruk	849	70	594
Wayang orang	357	80	286
Ketoprak	172	70	120
Seni-drama (modern drama)	112	100	112

NOTES TO CHAPTER 9. EXTENT AND DISTRIBUTION

1. I am indebted to James Peacock, Princeton University, for this suggestion.

2. I do not have statistics to substantiate this statement, but Javanese and Sundanese dalang unanimously remark on the increase.

NOTES TO CHAPTER 10.
THEATRE AND THE SOCIAL CONTRACT

1. Thiounn, *Danses,* p. 36.
2. Lamlung in Lao.
3. Sein and Withey, *Po Sein,* p. 95.

NOTES TO CHAPTER 11. THE TROUPE

1. Sein and Withey, *Po Sein,* p. 103.
2. From a mimeographed release issued by the Congress, August 1964.
3. Winstedt, *The Malays,* p. 29.
4. Winstedt, p. 30.
5. Winstedt, p. 30.
6. *Réalités Vietnamiennes* (Saigon, 1966), p. 87.
7. De Zoete and Spies, *Dance and Drama,* p. 118.
8. Mantle Hood, "The Enduring Tradition: Music and Theatre in Java and Bali," in *Indonesia,* ed. Ruth T. McVey (New Haven, 1963), pp. 444–445.
9. Sein and Withey, p. 34.
10. Geertz, *Religion,* p. 27.

NOTES TO CHAPTER 12. ECONOMICS

1. Douglas S. Paauw, "From Colonial to Guided Economy," in *Indonesia,* ed. Ruth T. McVey (New Haven, 1963), p. 204.

NOTES TO CHAPTER 13. THE AUDIENCE

1. James R. Brandon, "Types of Indonesian Professional Theatre," *Quarterly Journal of Speech,* 45:57 (February 1959).

NOTES TO CHAPTER 14. SOCIAL STATUS OF TROUPES

1. *The Vietnamese Theatre,* p. 7.
2. Allardyce Nicoll, *The Development of the Theatre,* 4th ed. rev. (London, 1958), p. 57.

NOTES TO CHAPTER 15. PAST AND PRESENT

1. Redfield, *Peasant Society,* p. 98, quoting Milton Singer on India. The same can be said of Southeast Asia.

2. E. C. G. Barrett, "Further Light on Sir Richard Winstedt's 'Unde-scribed Malay Version of the Ramayana,'" *Bulletin of the School of Oriental and African Studies*, 26:543 (1963).

3. Winstedt, *The Malays*, p. 145.

4. Winstedt, p. 142.

5. Prem Chaya, *Magic Lotus* (Bangkok, 1949), p. 103.

6. Hla Pe, *Konmara*, p. 29.

7. Hla Pe, p. 132.

8. Htin Aung, *Drama*, p. 148.

9. E. T. C. Werner, *Myths and Legends of China* (London, 1922), pp. 208–209.

10. John F. Cady, *Southeast Asia: Its Historical Development* (New York, 1964), p. 251.

11. Hla Pe, p. 139.

12. Indonesian Embassy, Washington, D.C., *The Arts of Indonesia*, mimeo-graph, n.d., p. 12.

13. Indonesian Embassy, Washington, D.C., *Wayang Kulit*, mimeograph, n.d., pp. 3–4.

14. Personal conversation with author in Saigon, October 1963.

NOTES TO CHAPTER 16.
THEATRE AND OTHER MASS MEDIA

1. The estimates are my own, based on information in the UNESCO pub-lication, *Basic Facts and Figures* (Paris, 1962) for the years 1958–1963 and in-formation obtained through the courtesy of USIS Radio Officers and person-nel of local radio stations. Data is lacking for Cambodia and Burma.

2. Reported in United Nations *Statistical Yearbook, 1964* (New York, 1965).

3. Quoted in "Television Booms in Asia," *Free World* (Manila), 12:7 (August 1963).

4. From *Statistical Yearbook, 1964* and *Basic Facts and Figures*.

5. Djakarta *Daily Mail*, July 14, 1964, p. 3.

NOTES TO CHAPTER 17.
THEATRE AND THE COMMUNICATION PROCESS

1. Selosoemardjan, *Social Changes in Jogjakarta* (Ithaca, 1962), p. 182.

2. News items are taken from the Djakarta *Daily Mail*.

GLOSSARY

(The place name following the word meaning indicates where it is used.)

Ajak-ajak: Name of a gamelan melody played in wayang kulit. Java.

alus: Refined; a refined type of character in a wayang play. Java.

anito: Animistic spirits. Philippines.

anjali: Gesture of respect made by placing palms together and lifting hands before face; derived from Indian dance.

anyein: Type of variety show of singing and dancing. Burma.

apsaras: Heavenly dancing nymphs. Cambodia.

apyodaw: Votaress of animistic spirits. Burma.

ardja: Type of operetta. Bali. (see Appendix)

babad: History; a history play in ketoprak or sandiwara. Java, Sunda.

Bai Dien: Name of hat boi song; sung by fool. Vietnam.

Bai Phuong: Name of a hat boi song; sung by a poor character. Vietnam.

Bai Thuy Thuoc: Name of a hat boi song; sung by a doctor. Vietnam.

Bai Tuong Tran Ai: Name of a hat boi song; a lament sung by a barrier guard. Vietnam.

BAKOKSI: Badan Kontak Ketoprak Seluruh Indonesia or All-Indonesian Ketoprak Organization; Communist-oriented association of ketoprak troupes. Java.

bandjar: Men's association. Bali.

bangsawan: Type of popular theatre. Malaysia. (see Appendix)

ban kich: Another name for kich.

Baratayuda: Final section of the *Mahabharata* epic in which the five Pandava brothers destroy their enemies, the ninety-nine Kaurava brothers; dramatized in wayang kulit. Java, Sunda, Bali.

baris: Type of war dance. Bali.

barong: Type of dance-drama. Bali. (see Appendix)

bedaya: Type of female court dance. Java.

besut: Chief performer of early folk ludruk. Java.

bhat: Thai currency.

bonang: Inverted set of tuned bronze bowls. Java.

boun: Celebration or festival. Thailand, Laos, Cambodia.

bugaku: Ancient form of Japanese court dance adopted from China and Korea.

buta: Foreign ogre or giant character in wayang play. Java, Bali, Sunda.

cai luong: Type of popular operetta. Vietnam. (see Appendix)

chap choa: Cymbals. Vietnam.

ching: Small bell-cymbals. Thailand.

ching hsi: Type of classic Chinese opera.

chud: Set of nang yai puppets; a play performed by nang yai puppets or khon dancers. Thailand.

dagelan: Clown in ludruk or ketoprak; type of improvised comedy performed by several clowns. Java.

[3 4 7]

dalang: Chief puppeteer and performer of wayang kulit and wayang golek. Java, Bali, Sunda, Malaysia.

dan co: Two-stringed fiddle with cylindrical sounding box. Vietnam.

dan gao: Two-stringed fiddle with coconut-shell sounding box. Vietnam.

dan kim: Moon-shaped lute. Vietnam.

dan nguyet: Another name for dan kim.

dan nhi: Another name for dan co.

dan tranh: Zither with sixteen strings. Vietnam.

daswati II: Another name for kabupatan.

desa: Village. Java, Bali, Sunda.

digar: Religious chant of Shiite sect of Islam.

dinh: Taoist temple. Vietnam.

djanger: Type of adolescents' dance popular from 1920's until 1950's. Bali.

djedjer: Major scene; the first scene in a wayang play. Java.

djedjer sabrangan: Foreign scene: introduces second kingdom in wayang play. Java.

Dwemenaw: Another name for *Manora.* Burma.

gagah: Strong or muscular; muscular type of character in wayang play. Java.

gambang: Wooden xylophone. Java.

gambuh: Old type of dance-drama based on *Panji* stories; seldom performed. Bali.

gamelan: Musical ensemble which accompanies theatre performances in Java, Sunda, Bali, Malaysia.

gara-gara: Turmoil of nature; name of first scene in second part of wayang play. Java.

gender: Bronze xylophone with resonance chambers. Java.

gending karasmen: Type of opera; seldom performed. Sunda.

glong: Large tripod drum struck with padded stick. Thailand.

gong: Large hanging gong of bronze. Java, Bali, Sunda, Malaysia.

gong ageng: Great gong gamelan ensemble; largest of Balinese gamelan groupings. Bali.

grap: Length of bamboo beat to mark time. Thailand.

graw: Length of bamboo beat to mark time. Thailand.

gru: Another name for guru. Thailand.

guru: Teacher. Java, Bali, Sunda, Malaysia.

hasta: Another name for mudra.

Hasta Brata: The Eight Precepts by which a ruler should govern. Java.

hat boi: Type of opera. Vietnam. (see Appendix)

hat cheo: Type of satirical folk play in north Vietnam.

hat khach: Chinese-derived songs sung in hat boi. Vietnam.

hat nam: Local Vietnamese songs sung in hat boi. Vietnam.

hne: Double-reed oboe; same as Thai pi. Burma.

hu chin: Several varieties of two-stringed Chinese fiddle.

hu hu: Two-stringed Chinese fiddle with coconut-shell sounding box.

idjin pertundjukan: Performance permit issued to a troupe. Java, Sunda.

Inao: Another name for *Panji* stories or plays. Thailand, Cambodia, Laos.

Jataka: Buddhist Birth Stories; performed as plays in Burma, Cambodia, Laos, Thailand.

Jajasan Padalangan: Foundation for the Art of the Dalang, an association of wayang golek dalang. Sunda.

Kabor: Name of a gamelan melody; played in first part of a wayang play. Java.

kabuki: Traditional popular theatre form in Japan.

kabupaten: District; a political unit smaller than a province. Java, Sunda, Bali.

kasar: Coarse or rough; rough type of character in a wayang play, usually an ogre. Java, Bali, Sunda.

Kawi: Archaic form of Javanese language containing many Sanskrit words. Java.

Kawit: Name of a gamelan melody; played in first part of a wayang play. Java.

kayon: Puppet figure of "tree of life" in wayang kulit. Java, Bali, Malaysia.

kempul: Medium-sized hanging gong of bronze. Java.

kendang: Horizontal drum beat with fingers on both ends. Java.

kenong: Single inverted bronze bowl. Java.

Glossary

ken tau: Reed horn which produces an ear-splitting sound; accompanies hat boi. Vietnam.

ketchak: Monkey dance; performed for tourists only. Bali.

ketjamatan: Sub-district; there are several ketjamatan in each kabupatan. Java, Sunda, Bali.

ketok: Knocking sound; first part of the word ketoprak. Java.

ketoprak: Type of popular theatre. Java. (see Appendix)

ketoprak Mataram: Jogjakarta-style ketoprak. Java.

Ketoprak Mataram: Name of an important ketoprak troupe affiliated with the Nationalist Party. Java.

ketuk: Single inverted bronze bowl. Java.

Khach Tu: Name of a Chinese-derived hat boi song; sung as a funeral dirge or lament. Vietnam.

khamphak: Narration during a khon performance. Thailand.

khen: Reed organ used to accompany mohlam singing. Laos, Thailand.

khon: Type of classic dance-drama. Thailand. (see Appendix)

khong vong: Set of tuned bronze bowls arranged in semi-circle; same as Thai kong wong. Laos.

kich: Western-style theatre form. Vietnam. (see Appendix)

kich noi: Another name for kich.

kin: Ancient seven-stringed zither of China.

kinnara: Mythological race of bird people who appear in *Manora* plays. Burma, Thailand, Laos, Cambodia, Malaysia.

kinnari: Feminine form of kinnara.

kip: Lao currency.

kledi: Reed organ played by Dayak tribes of Borneo; related to Lao khen.

komedie: Type of amateur play performed in Western manner in early twentieth century; forerunner of sandiwara. Sunda.

kong thom: Set of tuned bronze bowls arranged in semi-circle; same as Thai kong wong. Cambodia.

kong wong: Set of tuned bronze bowls arranged in semi-circle. Thailand.

Krawitan: Name of a gamelan melody; played in first part of a wayang play. Java.

kris: Type of dagger. Java, Bali, Sunda, Malaysia.

ksatriya: Ruling warrior class; term borrowed from India and used in *Ramayana*- and *Mahabharata*-derived plays.

kyi waing: Set of tuned bronze bowls; same as Thai kong wong. Burma.

lakon: Generic term for drama or play. Java, Bali, Sunda, Malaysia, Thailand, Cambodia, Laos.

lakon bassac: Type of popular theatre. Cambodia. (see Appendix)

lakon dukdamban: A variation of court dance-drama utilizing scenery and in which old stories are dramatized. Thailand.

lakon jatri: Type of folk and popular theatre. Thailand. (see Appendix)

lakon kawl: Type of male masked dance-drama; similar to khon. Cambodia.

lakon nai: Type of female court dance-drama. Thailand (see Appendix)

lakon nang nai: Original term for lakon nai.

lakon nok: Type of popular dance play acted by men; forerunner of lakon nai; rarely performed. Thailand.

lakon phantang: A variation of court dance-drama, similar to lakon nok; seldom performed. Thailand.

lakon pud: A variation of court dance-drama, incorporating much dialogue; seldom performed. Thailand.

lamlung: Type of taxi dance; same as rambong. Laos.

lam mu: Another name for mohlam luong.

langendrian: Type of court opera; rarely performed. Java.

langenmandra: Type of court opera; rarely performed. Java.

legong: Type of classic dance performed by preadolescent girls. Bali.

LEKRA: Lembaga Kebudajaan Rakjat or People's Art Association, the official cultural organization within the Indonesian Communist Party.

Lembaga Ludruk: Ludruk Association; Communist-oriented organization of ludruk troupes. Java.

Lere-lere: Name of a gamelan melody; used in first part of a wayang play. Java.

lesung: Hollow log used for stamping rice. Java.

likay: Type of popular theatre. Thailand. (see Appendix)

likay Lao: Another name for mohlam luong.

LKN: Lembaga Ketoprak Nasional or Association of Nationalist Ketoprak, an organization of ketoprak troupes affiliated with Nationalist Party. Also, Lembaga Kebudajaan Nasional or Nationalist Cultural Association, the cultural arm of the Nationalist Party. Java.

lontar: Type of palm leaf on which ancient Javanese and Balinese literature was written.

ludruk: Type of popular theatre. Java. (see Appendix)

ludruk bendang: Type of dance which grew out of ludruk lerog. Java.

ludruk besutan: Type of folk play in which the life cycle of man was enacted. Java.

ludruk lerog: Type of folk dance of invulnerability; origin of present-day ludruk. Java.

lurah: Village head. Java, Sunda, Bali.

Mahabharata: Indian epic in which the five Pandava brothers are chief figures; most wayang kulit plays in Java and wayang golek plays in Sunda dramatize episodes in the lives of the Pandavas. Java, Sunda, Bali.

mana: Magic power; according to animistic belief it can be possessed or created by a person and used for his own purposes.

mandarin: A civil servant of the highest rank. Vietnam.

Mangu: Name of a gamelan melody; played in first part of a wayang play. Java.

Manora: Play based on *Jataka* story recounting adventures of the kinnari princess Manora. Burma, Cambodia, Laos, Malaysia, Thailand.

Menak: Stories about the Islamic hero Amir Hamzah; plays based on these stories. Java, Sunda, Malaysia.

mohlam: Type of singing accompanied by khen music. Laos, Thailand.

mohlam luong: Type of popular theatre. Laos, Thailand. (see Appendix)

mohlam mu: Another name for mohlam luong.

Moncher: Name of a gamelan melody; played in first part of a wayang play. Java.

moro-moro: Type of folk play; glorifies triumph of Christian army over Moslems. Philippines.

mudra: Hand position or hand gesture; derived from Indian dance.

naga: Huge dragonlike serpents. Burma, Thailand, Laos, Cambodia.

Nam Di: Name of a hat boi song; expresses melancholy. Vietnam.

Nam Xuan: Name of a hat boi song; expresses gay mood. Vietnam.

nang talung: Type of popular shadow theatre. Thailand. (see Appendix)

nang yai: Type of classic shadow theatre utilizing large nonarticulated puppets to perform *Ramayana* episodes; rarely performed. Thailand.

nao bat: Small bell-cymbals; same as Thai ching. Vietnam.

nat: Animistic spirits. Burma.

natkadaw: Dancer who performs as a medium through which a nat may foretell the future. Burma.

nat pwe: Current type of theatre in which plays are presented as offerings to animistic spirits. Burma.

Natya Sastra: Well-known Indian treatise on Sanskrit dramaturgy and performance techniques.

ngremo: Name of dance which traditionally precedes a ludruk performance. Java.

nibhatkhin: Type of ancient popular play ostensibly presented as an offering to animistic spirits. Burma.

noh: Type of classic Japanese dance-drama in which masks are worn.

ong dich: Flute. Vietnam.

pak dalang: Literally "grandfather dalang"; used as term of respect. Java, Bali, Sunda, Malaysia.

Panji: A group of stories about the Javanese prince Panji; plays based on these stories. Java, Sunda, Bali, Malaysia.

Pannasa Jataka: Fifty Buddhist Birth Stories; often dramatized. Thailand, Cambodia, Laos.

pannen: Harvest season. Java.

parwa: Type of dance-drama; similar to Balinese wayang wong. Bali.

pasar malam: Evening fair; the occasion for many theatre performances. Java.

paseban djawi: Outer audience hall scene; occurs in all wayang plays. Java.

pataka: Name of one mudra in which the palm of the hand is held flat.

patma: Large tripod drum; same as Thai glong. Burma.

pattala: Wooden xylophone; same as Thai ranat. Burma.

pedjah: To fall unconscious or to fall dead in a play. Java.

pendapa: Type of open pavilion in which court dance and dance-drama were performed. Java.

Pendidikan Masjarakat: Communal Education Committee; a semi-government organization. Sunda.

perang ampjak: Battle scene in Part I of a wayang play in which an army forces its way through a forest. Java.

perang gagal: Battle scene which usually concludes Part I of a wayang play. Java.

perang kembang: Battle scene in which the refined Pandava prince kills several ogre antagonists; in Part II of a wayang play. Java.

pesinden: Female singer in gamelan ensemble. Java, Sunda.

pi: Animistic spirits. Thailand, Laos, Cambodia. Also, double reed oboe. Thailand.

piaster: Vietnamese currency.

pi phat: Musical ensemble; accompanies theatre performances of many kinds. Thailand, Laos, Cambodia.

PKI: Partai Kommunis Indonesia, or Indonesian Communist Party.

PNI: Partai Nasional Indonesia, or Indonesian Nationalist Party.

po the hi: Type of hand puppet theatre based on Chinese stories and performed by Chinese descendents in the Indonesian language. Java.

prada: Gold or gold leaf. Java, Bali.

prijaji: Former Javanese aristocracy; member of the upper-class. Java.

pura desa: Chief temple of a desa or village. Bali.

pu-tai-hi: Type of Chinese hand puppet theatre from which po the hi in Java is derived.

pya zat: Type of contemporary play. Burma.

raga: Melodic system used in Indian music.

rai: Type of chanting in lakon jatri and other Thai dramatic forms; verses are chanted alternately by an actor on stage and the offstage chorus. Thailand.

raket: Old form of dance-drama; no longer performed. Java, Sunda.

rakshasa: Ogre; same as buta.

Ramayana: Indian epic which recounts the story of Rama's life and adventures; episodes are often dramatized in court theatre forms. Thailand, Cambodia, Laos, Burma, Malaysia, Bali, Java, Sunda.

rambong: Type of taxi dance. Thailand.

ram tawai: Gift dance; performed as an offering of thanksgiving for receipt of a favor from the gods. Thailand.

ranat: Wooden xylophone. Thailand.

raneat: Wooden xylophone; same as Thai ranat. Cambodia.

rangnat: Wooden xylophone; same as Thai ranat. Laos.

rasaksa: Ogre; same as buta.

rebab: Two-stringed fiddle with large sounding box. Java, Malaysia.

reog: Type of comedian or folk comedy. Sunda.

roman: Exotic European stories dramatized in popular theatre. Java, Sunda.

rupiah: Indonesian currency.

ruwatan: Animistic ceremony in which magically vulnerable child is blessed to protect it from being eaten by the god Kala. Java.

Sabah: Name of a gamelan melody; played in first part of a wayang play. Java.

sabrangan: Foreign; ogres are all from foreign kingdoms in wayang plays. Java, Sunda.

saing: Main musical ensemble used to accompany theatre performances; same as Thai pi phat ensemble. Burma.

saing wong: Set of twenty-one tuned drums. Burma.

sakti: Magic power; same as mana. Indonesia.

Sampak: Name of a gamelan melody; accompanies battle scenes in wayang plays. Java.

sampho: Horizontal drum beat at both ends with the fingers; same as Thai saphon. Cambodia.

sandiwara: Type of popular theatre. Sunda. (see Appendix)

Sang Thong: The Golden Prince of the Sea Conch; name of a *Jataka* story often dramatized. Thailand, Laos, Cambodia.

sao: Flute; another name for ong dich. Vietnam.

saphon: Horizontal drum beat at both ends with the fingers. Thailand.

saron: Xylophone made of heavy bronze bars. Java.

saw duang: Two-stringed fiddle with cylindrical sounding box; similar to Vietnamese dan co. Thailand.

saw u: Two-stringed fiddle with coconut shell sounding box; similar to Vietnamese dan gao. Thailand.

semangat: Magic power; same as mana. Java.

serunai: Reed oboe; related to Thai pi. Malaysia.

sheng: Chinese reed organ; related to Lao khen.

sho: Japanese reed organ; derived from Chinese sheng.

Sin Xai: Name of a *Jataka* story; often dramatized. Thailand, Laos, Cambodia.

Sin Xay: Another name for *Sin Xai*.

skor thom: Large tripod drum; same as Thai glong. Laos, Cambodia.

slametan: Feast celebrating a religious occasion. Java, Sunda.

so i: Two-stringed fiddle; same as Thai saw daung. Laos.

song lang: Wooden clackers. Vietnam.

so u: Two-stringed fiddle: same as Thai saw u. Laos.

sralay: Double reed oboe; same as Thai pi. Cambodia.

Srikaton: Name of a gamelan melody; played in first part of a wayang play. Java.

srimpi: Type of female court dance. Java.

stambul: Term for Malaysian bangsawan used in Indonesia.

suling: Flute. Java.

suluk: Type of mood song sung by dalang during wayang performance. Java, Sunda.

sutra: Buddhist prayer. Burma, Cambodia, Laos, Thailand.

taphon: Another name for saphon.

Tau Ma: Name of a hat boi melody; accompanies running horse. Vietnam.

tembang: Form of classical poem; can be spoken or sung. Java.

than lwin: Small bell-cymbals; same as Thai ching. Burma.

thoai kich: Another name for kich.

Tjalongarang: Name of Balinese legend; sometimes performed in wayang kulit. Bali.

tjelempung: Zither of thirteen double strings. Java.

ton: Episode; identifies a dramatized episode from an epic. Thailand.

toneel: Dutch for drama or play; type of popular theatre which developed into sandiwara. Sunda.

topeng: Another name for wayang topeng.

trong: Small stick drum. Vietnam.

trott: Type of animistic deer-hunting dance. Cambodia.

tro u: Two-stringed fiddle with coconut shell sounding box; same as Thai saw u. Cambodia.

tuong tau: Type of popular opera; simplified and popularized from hat boi; rarely performed. Vietnam.

vidusaka: Type of clown-servant in Indian Sanskrit drama.

Vong Co: Name of most popular cai luong song, a love lament. Vietnam.

wat: Buddhist temple. Burma, Cambodia, Laos, Thailand.

wat boun: Temple fair; the occasion for many theatre performances. Burma, Cambodia, Laos, Thailand.

wayang beber: Type of paper scroll play; rarely performed. Java.

wayang Djawa: Type of shadow play; leather puppets for stories about Prince Diponegoro of the nineteenth century; never performed. Java.

wayang djawa: Type of shadow play using Javanese style leather puppet figures. Malaysia.

wayang gedog: Type of shadow play; leather puppets tell *Panji* stories; almost never performed. Java.

wayang golek: Type of play performed by doll puppets. Sunda, Java. (see wayang golek Sunda and wayang golek Java in Appendix)

wayang golek moderne: Puppet play in which several dalang manipulate simultaneously many doll puppets; seldom performed. Sunda.

wayang klitik: Type of puppet play in which flat wooden puppets enact stories about Damar Wulan of Majapahit; never performed. Java.

wayang krutjil: Another name for wayang klitik.

wayang kulit: Major type of shadow drama in Southeast Asia. (see wayang kulit Java, wayang kulit Bali, and wayang kulit Malaysia in Appendix)

wayang lemah: Wayang kulit performed in daytime without a screen. Bali.

wayang madya: Type of shadow play; stories about east Javanese kingdoms enacted by leather puppets; never performed. Java.

wayang melayu: Early form of Javanese wayang kulit adopted in Malaysia; puppets have one movable arm. Malaysia.

wayang orang: Type of classic dance-drama performed by popular troupes. Java. (see Appendix)

wayang Pantja Sila: Type of modern wayang kulit adaptation; traditional figures are given new symbolic interpretation; seldom performed. Java.

wayang siam: Type of shadow play; Thai style dance figures cut out as leather puppets enact *Ramayana* episodes. Malaysia, Thailand.

wayang suluh: Type of modern wayang kulit adaptation; realistic puppet figures enact contemporary stories; rarely performed. Java.

wayang tengul: Type of shadow play; leather puppet figures enact Islamic *Menak* stories; never performed. Java.

wayang topeng: Type of masked dance-drama. Java, Bali, Sunda.

wayang wong: Type of masked dance-drama. Bali. Also, another name for wayang orang. Java.

Xuan Xe: Name of a cai luong song. Vietnam.

yi i: Two-stringed fiddle with cylindrical sounding box; same as Thai saw daung. Cambodia.

zarzuela: Type of light operetta imported from Spain; previously performed as popular theatre, now occasionally performed as folk theatre. Philippines.

zat pwe: Type of classical dance-drama. Burma. (see Appendix)

INDEX

Actors: key troupe members, 147; illiteracy of, 157–158; side jobs, 182, 252, 270; as managers, 207; movement among troupes, 208, 248; contracts and indebtedness, 211–212; as religious mediums, 221–223; income tax, 245; as gigolos, 261–262; role in communication, 315. *See also* Performers; Salaries; Status; Troupes

Ad-libbing, 147, 149, 150, 235–236, 315. *See also* Production, system of

Aesthetics, 314, 315–316

Airlangga, Javanese king, 52, 53

Ajak-ajak, 134

Alexander the Great, 108

Alim, epic, 77

Allah, 67, 92, 280, 320

All-Indonesian Ketoprak Association. *See* BAKOKSI

Alus, 54, 140

Amateur theatre: in Philippines, 38–39, 79; number of troupes, 165–166; defined, 172; compared to professional in Bali, 204–205; politically affiliated, 215, 216, 294

Amir Hamzah, 44, 57, 108, 109, 121. See also *Menak*

Ancestor worship, 10, 44, 45, 46

Angkor, Cambodia, 8, 26, 27, 58, 59, 65

Angkor Wat, 16, 126, 258n

Animism, 7, 50, 52; and magic power, 10; as source of theatre, 10, 42, 44, 45, 48n, 84; and prehistoric epics, 11, 77; and kingship belief, 14–15; and shadow theatre, 42–43; ceremonies in Thailand, 61; performances connected with worship, 195. *See also* Folk theatre

Anito, 10

Anjali, 137, 139

Annam, 13, 28, 29

Anyein, 200

Apsaras, 59

Apyodaw, 72, 223

Ardja: professional troupes, 34; description of, 54; plays of, 54, 106; music of, 128; troupe support, 202, 205; amateur troupes, 203–204; audience, 262–263. *See also* Balinese theatre; Troupes

Arena Theatre of the Philippines, 79, 163, 257

Arjuna, 21, 77, 287, 321; traits of, 117; wives of, 119; and magic power, 121; entrance music for, 134

Armed forces: soldier performers, 216; propaganda troupes, 293–294, 295–297; radio stations, 303; motion picture production, 312

Artistic director, 147–148, 207, 315

Artistic standards, 45, 153, 214; of the different traditions, 43, 82, 84–86, 196; and tourist performances, 204–205; and propaganda, 236–237, 287; and audiences, 257–258

Ascetics, 122, 123, 124, 321

Assam, 18

Association of Nationalist Ketoprak. *See* LKN

Astina, kingdom of, 21, 22, 114, 161, 320, 323

Audience, theatre: size, 1, 240–241, 242, 252–253, 255–256, 306; city and rural, 79, 179–180, 181, 184–185; response, 117, 120, 258, 259–260; seating of, 150, 151, 152–153, 193, 196; and mass media, 166–

Index

Duryodhana (Duryodana), 21, 22, 134
Dutch, in Indonesia, 34, 35, 36, 37, 44, 51, 235, 287
Dwarfs, 15
Dwemenaw. See *Manora*

Economic support, 35, 36, 86; government, 188–191, 198, 200, 205; direct commercial, 191–192, 198, 199, 200, 201, 202, 205, 245; indirect commercial, 192–194, 202, 205, 245; communal, 195–198, 199, 200, 201–202, 203–204, 205, 242–243. *See also* Income; Performance occasions
End of Love's Raging War, play, 101–102

Facial expression, 138
Fa Ngoun, Prince of Laos, 26, 69
Falling Petals in the Garden, play, 105–106, 117
Farce, 116, 120, 148
Female impersonation: in *ludruk,* 49, 264–265; in *ardja,* 54; in *lakon jatri,* 62; in *wayang golek,* 194
Fiddles, 126, 127–128, 129. See also *Rebab*
Fifty Jataka. See *Pannasa Jataka*
Flute, 11, 48, 126, 127, 128, 129
Folk theatre, 1, 23; and animism, 11–12; in Bali, 34, 53; in Java, 48; in Cambodia, 58, 60; in Thailand, 62, 66, 68; in Vietnam, 73; in the Philippines, 77, 78; "tradition of," 80–81, 84; artistic level, 84–85, 204–205; staging of, 150; teaching of, 156–157; in Sunda; 157–158; performers' status, 268. *See also* Economic support; Performance occasions; Troupes
Foreigners, as dramatic antagonist, 103–106, 113. *See also* Ogres
Foundation for the Art of the Dalang, 165n, 214. See also *Dalang*
Francis Xavier, 35
French, 35; touring troupes, 38; influence on theatre, 60–61, 76; motion picture exports, 309
Funan, kingdom of, 12, 25
Future Buddha, carving of, 24. See also *Jataka*

Gadja Mada, Prime Minister, 54
Gagah, 140
Galunggan, festival, 203
Gambang, 127
Gambuh, 54n
Gamelan music, 11, 48, 57, 113; myth of origin, 44; instrumentation, 127; thea-

tre orchestras, 128; theatre usage, 132; standard melodies, 134; number of melodies, 316, 317
Games for the New Emerging Forces (GANEFO), 215, 231, 235
Gan Kam, troupe manager, 47
Gara-gara, 321
Gareng, 167
Gender, 128, 210
Gending karasmen, 132
Genres of theatre: variety of, 1–2; in Java, 42–49; in Sunda, 50–52; in Bali, 52–55; in Malaysia, 55–58; in Cambodia, 58–61; in Thailand, 61–68; in Laos, 68–70; in Burma, 70–73; in Vietnam, 73–77; in the Philippines, 77–79; and play production, 146–147; preservation of, 155–159; cross-genre influences, 158; defined, 171; artistic standards in, 271–274. *See also* Troupes
Gia Long, Emperor of Vietnam, 74
Gianjar, Bali, 203
Giri, Sunan of, 44
Glong, 127
Gobut, 121
God-king, 18, 278, 282
Gods, as dramatic characters, 122, 123
Golden Prince of the Sea Conch, play, 100, 122, 196
Gong ageng, 128
Gongs, 11, 48, 126, 127, 128, 129
Government control of theatre: colonial, 37, 76, 78, 230, 232–233, 284–285; precolonial, 72, 282; during Japanese occupation, 237, 285; current, 214, 229, 236–237. *See also* Censorship
Grap, 11
Graw, 11
"Great Tradition" of culture, 83–84
Gru, 155
Guru, 155

Habirando, *dalang* school, 164
Hagoromo, play, 62n
Handbooks, 159–160. *See also* Play scripts
Hanoman the Volunteer, play, 91–92, 121
Hanuman, 20
Happy Wedding, A, play, 110–111
Harp, 126
Harsono Hadisoeseno, puppeteer, 287
Harvest season performances, 9, 10, 241
Hasta. See *Mudra*
Hat boi: development of, 37, 73–74; make-up, 84; Chinese plays in, 101, 315; music in, 129, 132, 133, 135; singing in, 132; dance in, 136, 142–143; support of,

[359]

Index

Index

Index

Index

Index

Index

Index